INCIDENT AT SAKHALIN

THE TRUE MISSION OF KAL FLIGHT 007

BY MICHEL BRUN

Translated by Robert Bononno

Four Walls Eight Windows, New York/London

Incident at Sakhalin

Incident at Sakhalin

The True Mission of KAL Flight 007 by Michel Brun

Four Walls Eight Windows, New York/London

© 1995 Michel Brun

Published in the United States by
Four Walls Eight Windows
39 West 14th Street, Room 503
New York, NY 10011

U.K. offices:
Four Walls Eight Windows/Turnaround
27 Horsell Road London, N5 1XL, England

P. 19 The map of the Japanese Radar Track, courtesy Japanese Defense Agency
P. 31 The Kirkpatrick map, courtesy Foreign Service Journal
P. 36 The Tsushima Shio, courtesy French Hydrographic Office
P. 43 The ejection seat and other debris, courtesy Kimura
P. 45 The bulkhead, courtesy Kyodo
P. 46 Debris N3, the JMSA sketch, courtesy Japanese Maritime Safety Agency
P. 58 The debris found at Tsugaru, courtesy Hokkaido Shimbun
P. 65 The author and fragment of titanium wing, courtesy Yoshida
P. 164 The little girl of Pereputye, courtesy Misha Lobko
P. 222 Osipovich voice spectrogram, courtesy Dr. K. Tsuboi, Iwatsu Laboratory, Tokyo
P. 241 The KADPO waypoint and Soviet planes, courtesy UPI
P. 245 The debris N3, color photograph, courtesy Japanese Maritime Safety Agency

All other illustrations and/or photographs are the author's.

Library of Congress Cataloging-in-Publication Data:
Brun, Michel.
Incident at Sakhalin : the true mission of KAL Flight 007 / by Michel Brun.
p. cm.
Includes index.
ISBN 1-56858-054-1 (hc)
1. Korean Air Lines Incident, 1983. I. Title.
E183.8.S65B78 1995   95-21661
909'.096454--dc20   CIP

10 9 8 7 6 5 4 3 2 1

Printed in the United States

To my daughters, Dolorès, Michiko, and Yuko,
in the hope that they will know a better world.

CONTENTS

LIST OF ILLUSTRATIONS

ACKNOWLEDGEMENTS

Many persons, all over the world, have helped or encouraged me in my undertaking. I lack the space to cite them all. As representatives of all of them, I wish particularly to thank:

Mr. Edward T. Chase, former senior editor at Scribner's, although I have not yet decided whether he should be thanked or blamed for having contributed to my starting this seemingly endless task.

Prof. Shôzo Takemoto, of the Japanese Association of KAL Accident Victims and cofounder of the Research Group, who lost his beloved wife and eldest son in the tragedy.

Mr. Kawano, president, Mrs. Haba Yumiko, and the members of the Japanese Association of KAL Incident Victims.

Mr. Shigeki Sugimoto, engineer at Japan Air Lines, member of the Research Group.

Mr. Miyano, Mr. Kashima, the mayor, and the people of the village of Sai, on the Shimo Kita peninsula.

Mr. Iwao Koyama, of NHK, Wakkanai, at the time of the tragedy.

The mayor and the municipal staff at Wakkanai.

Admiral Kato, Adm. Kessoku Konomu, and the officers of the JMSA at Wakkanai, Otaru, Yokohama, and Tokyo headquarters.

Captain M. of the Japanese Air Self-Defense Forces.

Mr. Takeda, bureau chief of the *Too Nippo,* at Aomori.

Mr. Makio Yazaki, former vice president, Mr. Michio Nakano, former assistant vice president for engineering, and Mr. Takashi Kondo, assistant vice president for engineering development, Japan Air Lines.

Mr. K. Sawano, general manager, Dr. K. Tsuboi, director of the research laboratory and colleagues at the Iwatsu Electric Company, Kaguyama, Tokyo.

Mr. Ryuji Osaki and the staff at Ortus Japan.

Mr. Hajime Noguchi, plant manager, Mr. Kunihiko Hirosaki, chief of engineering, and Mr. Tetsuo Harada, manager of quality control, Honeycomb Section, Showa Aircraft Co.

Mr. Ishizaki and colleagues from HBC Television at Sapporo, and Mr. Yoshida from HBC Wakkanai.

Mr. Kenji Matsumoto, reporter, *Asahi Shimbun*.

Mr. Philippe Robert de Massy, from Montreal, who lost a dear younger brother in the tragedy, and who gave me much encouragement and invaluable advice.

Mr. Pierre Sparaco, former editor in chief, *Aviation Magazine International*.

Capt. (ret.) Henri Avril, colleague, airline pilot, and former fighter pilot with the French Air Force, for his invaluable advice on military matters.

Mr. Pierre Marion, former head of the French Intelligence Service.

Mr. Yves Lambert, former secretary general of the ICAO.

Prof. Cees Wiebes, Amsterdam University.

Mr. Misha Lobko, director of Dathanna International, a French investigative TV reporter of Russian origin who interviewed Admiral Sidorov and Lieutenant Colonel Osipovich and others in Russia and on Sakhalin and, before he learned of my investigation, came to many of the same conclusions as I have.

Mrs. Katharine M. Bullitt, Mr. Patrick R. McGraner, and Mr. Eric Swenson, who organized a symposium on KAL 007 at the University of Washington at Seattle, which gave me a chance to debate the principal supporters of the U.S. government's position on the case.

My friend and colleague John Keppel, principal investigator in the KAL 007 project of the Fund for Constitutional Government in Washington, D.C. He has devoted more time and effort to the case than anybody else and deserves much more credit here than he is prepared to agree to. His reviewing, rewriting, and careful polishing of the manuscript of this book has been so diligent, thorough, and extensive that, although he will protest the idea, he deserves to be named a coauthor.

The small and distinguished group of donors to the KAL 007 inquiry project of the Fund for Constitutional Government, which supported my beach-walking trips in Japan in search of debris. I should, in particular, mention the Evenor Armington Fund, which also financed the translation of the book and has unwaveringly given the idea of this book moral support and encouragement.

Finally I wish to mention my dear Nariko. More than anyone, she suffered from my stubborn determination to go through the challenge of this endeavor in spite of the hardship, the suffering, and the dangers it entailed. I only wish I could have taken all the suffering on myself and protected her from being hurt by any of it—which, of course, was just an empty dream. I feel I need to be bestowed another full life in order to make her forget all that she has silently suffered.

Among the crises of the Cold War, the Korean Air Lines Flight 007 incident has been the most widely misunderstood. The story of how the truth has been kept from the public is as astonishing, and unjustifiable, as the events of the disaster itself. The black boxes that have been produced and are supposed to tell us what happened to the airliner are from other planes. What did happen at the time of the disaster and has happened since involves injustice to individuals, the distortion of democracy, and the threat of nuclear war. Many of the factors that gave rise to both the disaster and the cover-up remain dangerously in place. Their lessons concern the future as much as the past. We cannot learn them unless we know what happened. That is why Michel Brun's book is important.

Perhaps the best way I can show you the extent to which he has transformed our knowledge of the case is to tell you what it looked like to me before and after I began to work with him.

KAL 007 first came to my attention on the morning after the disaster in a two-line item in the local newspaper on Nantucket Island, where my wife and I had been spending a couple of days with friends. The item merely said that the Korean airliner, en route from New York, was overdue at Seoul. That struck me as disturbing, but left me wondering why in itself it should be national news. Driving home that morning, we turned on the radio and heard an account of Secretary of State Shultz's announcement to the world—that the Korean airliner had been, brutally and inexcusably, shot down by the Soviets. When we understood from the broadcast that the airliner was 350 miles off course, had overflown sensitive parts of two strategic Soviet areas, the Kamchatka Peninsula and Sakhalin Island, in a row, and had done so in the small hours of the morning, we were far from sure we were being told the truth about the flight.

As a Foreign Service officer at our Moscow embassy, I had analyzed Soviet statements during the Stalin and Khrushchev periods. Both Grace and I had learned to look at statements with a skeptical eye in the effort to separate information from disinformation. As a member of an interagency working group in Washington after Francis Gary Powers's U-2 went down over Sverdlovsk on May 1, 1960, I had taken part myself in official lying. Not realizing that the Soviets had the U-2's cameras virtually intact and Powers himself alive, we (the members of the working group) very stupidly recommended that President Eisenhower stick to the cover story that the U-2 was a weather plane that had inadvertently strayed off course. It is hard to realize today that when Eisenhower got caught in the lie we thrust upon him, it was the first time many Americans realized that a U.S. president would lie to them on an important subject. We had made our contribution to the erosion of truth-telling, on which democracy in large measure depends.

For the next few days after getting back from Nantucket, I followed the KAL 007 news with interest. On the evening of September 5 my son and I listened to President Reagan's TV address. He played a bit of the tape of the intercepted voices of the Soviet pilots over Sakhalin. We heard a Soviet interceptor pilot, who the president told us was pursuing the Korean airliner, say, "I have accomplished the launch," and then, two seconds later, "The target is destroyed." At first it sounded convincing to us. Then, in view of the case's importance to U.S.-U.S.S.R. relations and the danger of war, we decided to review everything we knew about the case to see how probable or improbable the story of the disaster really was. After a review of the facts that had been in the newspapers, we concluded that it wasn't probable at all.

I had already been worried that the Reagan administration was pushing the Soviet Union too hard and that the situation might go wholly off the rails. We had overflown a Soviet island in the Kuriles with carrier aircraft and had stopped a Soviet ship on the high seas in the Caribbean. The Soviet minister of defense had spoken of the dangers of "appeasement" in terms reminiscent of 1939. I had written of my concerns to George Ball, former undersecretary of state, one of the saner elder statesmen I knew, who shared them. Against this background, it seemed to me that the KAL 007 case was worth an objective look by some competent body.

I went down to Washington, with supporting memoranda, twice that September to say so to members of Congress on relevant committees. On my first visit I met with considerable interest. On my second, ten days later, I might as well have had leprosy. Reagan had escalated the rhetoric so much that he had made it seem virtually disloyal to the United States to say, "Wait a minute, let's look at the evidence more carefully."

I realized it would take more than considerations of probability to convince anybody to touch the case, however cautiously. Over the next six months I wrote a draft memorandum reviewing the evidence. I also talked over the case with other people working on it: Robert W. Allardyce, a thoughtful ex-TWA captain; James Gollin, a writer and Allardyce's collaborator; and Seymour M. Hersh, who had been running into my material one place or another around Washington. Anne Zill, the president of the Fund for Constitutional Government, knew what I was doing and told me that if my expenses started getting too big for the family budget, to come to the FCG and say what I needed and why.

In March 1984 I told her I wanted to go to Japan in search of better evidence. I flew over on Korean Air Lines Flight 007, a flight that had not yet changed its infamous name. In Tokyo I got to know Shozo Takemoto and the other leaders of the Japanese next-of-kin's investigation group. I talked to knowledgeable members of the Japanese and foreign press and got a better idea of what had been carried in the Japanese press but had not been printed in the United States.

Before I left the United States, Victor Navasky, the editor of the *Nation,* had sent me a promising draft analysis of the KAL 007 case by a graduate student, whose name Navasky withheld. He asked me what I thought of it. I replied favorably. When I got back from Japan, I met the author of the study, David E. Pearson, then a Ph.D. candidate in sociology at Yale, with whom I started to collaborate. The book he wrote, expanding on the insights of his initial study, he did with characteristic objectivity and attention to detail. Published by Summit Books in 1987 as *KAL 007: The Cover-Up,* it is a cogent and highly useful compilation of data showing why one should not believe the official U.S. account of events.

By the time he closed the text, David Pearson and I had identified reasons why many of the things the government said had happened could not have happened. But neither he nor I had any idea of what had actually taken place toward the end of the Korean airliner's flight. In so far as I, at least, thought I knew, I was substantially wrong. What had happened was more startling than anyone outside several intelligence services, with the exception of Michel Brun, had any inkling. And what Michel had at that stage was "merely" the key that would unlock the door to the rest. One day in the spring of 1987 I was talking on the telephone with Richard Witkin, the aviation editor of the *New York Times,* another person who has followed the case with care. He told me that a French pilot named Michel Brun said that a number of U.S. military aircraft had been shot down over Sakhalin that night and asked me what I thought of the theory. I said it sounded pretty far-out to me, and we went on to other matters.

After I hung up, I sat at my desk for a while staring into space. It came to me that in following my hypothesis of what had happened over Sakhalin, I had discarded a number of contradictory pieces of evidence, dismissing them as disinformation or simple garbles. I saw that the pieces I had thrown away fitted nicely into what Brun was saying. I decided to go back to Japan to check out his evidence and to collect as many relevant documents as I could.

Before I left New York, Ned Chase, a senior editor at Scribner's with whom Brun had been corresponding, introduced me to Brun over the telephone. He was in Tahiti at the time. He has two daughters in Paris, one in Tahiti, and a wife in Tokyo. He lives pretty much all over the world and works wherever he is. He was in Tokyo the first few days after my arrival. I telephoned and he came over to the hotel where I was staying, and we talked. Later on we went to a helicopter show, which he wanted to see for professional reasons, and went on talking. Although we signed no treaty of alliance, since then we have worked together.

I was already impressed by what he was saying. As we worked, my respect for him only grew. I saw that he brought to the case an unparalleled range of relevant knowledge and experience. He knows aviation and aircraft. He has been the pilot of multiengine aircraft, the CEO of an overwater airline based on Tahiti, an aircraft-accident investigator, and an aircraft broker. He knows navigation on the sea as well as in the air. He still holds a master's ticket in the Merchant Marine, having started on the sea before he took to the air. He was decorated for the radio work he did during a raft voyage he undertook with his brother and three others from Tahiti to Chile. This experience and these skills were very much to the point in understanding the evidence in the Korean Air Lines case. Equally important was that he could read and speak Japanese—which he does along with English, Spanish, and Polynesian. There is real knowledge of the case in the Japanese government and among some others in Japan. Japan was geographically close to the disaster and had first-class radar and signals-intelligence capabilities.

But most important of all has been Michel's intellectual curiosity and his unusual, almost fierce, intellectual independence—he is not only French, he has Basque blood on his father's side and Corsican on his mother's. He is aware of, but is not dominated by, what other people are thinking and saying. He thinks for himself. When he has a piece of evidence he does not understand, he does not discard it. He keeps chewing at it until it yields something intelligible. When he has understood a new piece of data, he reviews the case carefully to see what the implications of the new piece are for his interpretation of the rest of the evidence.

Before I discuss the successive stages of his achievement in the KAL 007 case, it may be worth mentioning some of the larger bodies of source material he analyzed. They have included the tape of the intercepted voices of the Soviet pilots over Sakhalin, the FAA and Japanese Ministry of Transportation tapes of air-traffic-control communications between Anchorage and Tokyo on the one hand and KAL 007 and its sister ship KAL 015 on the other, the archives of the Japanese press in the Diet Library in Tokyo, as well as the relevant proceedings of the Diet, Japanese Maritime Safety Agency situation maps showing the successive positions of the U.S., Soviet, and Japanese ships during the naval search off Sakhalin, the after-action report of the U.S. Navy task force taking part in the search, the sixty or so articles *Izvestiya* printed on the KAL 007 case, the documents Boris Yeltsin turned over in November 1992 to the U.S. next of kin and the Republic of Korea, and the two reports the International Civil Aviation Organization issued in 1983 and 1993 concerning its investigations of the KAL 007 case, misleading but accompanied by useful documentation.

Some of the many interviews Michel conducted in Japan included officers of the Japanese Maritime Safety Agency, the Japanese media, both national and on Hokkaido, fishermen and local officials on the Shimokita Peninsula on the Tsugaru Strait, target-drone and aviation-honeycomb manufacturers in Tokyo, and electronic and frequency measurement experts in Tokyo. He searched many miles of beach on both sides of the Tsugaru Strait, the western coast of Honshu south from the strait to Niigata, and on Okushiri and Sado Islands.

The thing that let Michel understand what no other writer or investigator had understood, and to see evidence they had passed by, was his realization that the early statements of Japanese Air Self-Defense and intelligence officers simply could not be fitted into the single-intrusion, single-interception, single-shootdown story insisted on by the United States. Understanding that several intruding aircraft had overflown Sakhalin and had been shot down nearby, he understood the meaning of the fact that, while floating aircraft debris had been seen on the surface off Sakhalin on the morning of the disaster, no floating debris from KAL 007 itself had reached the search area off Sakhalin for more than a week. Given the nature of the currents, that pointed to a crash site for the Korean airliner far to the south.

This realization in turn prompted Michel to confirm the southern crash site in the two ways available to him. First, he talked to people who had found KAL 007 debris in the south in September 1983 and searched the relevant beaches himself for debris from the airliner still on them. Second, he examined the air-traffic-control tapes covering the period *after* KAL 007 was supposed to have been shot down. He did this first by ear, then with a personal oscilloscope, and finally with the aid of a world-class expert working with state-of-the-art equipment. I mention all this not to scoop what Michel tells you in his book, which goes far beyond any hints I have given you, but to make it clear that his investigation proceeded by logical stages and was accomplished by a staggering amount of work.

Before I sign off, I will answer two questions often asked. First, how does Michel Brun's book differ from that written by Seymour Hersh, *The Target Is Destroyed,* generally held by the media to be the last word on the subject? Second, what is the importance of the KAL 007 case now that twelve years have passed since the disaster?

As to Hersh, some of whose other work I admire, in *The Target Is Destroyed* he dismissed the obvious possibility that KAL 007's diversion from course had been intentional in a footnote saying that he found no evidence that it was. I will deal with his book almost as briefly but more factually. He missed the two most important things about the case: that there had been a battle over Sakhalin between U.S. and Soviet military aircraft; and that KAL 007 itself was not shot down there but was destroyed four hundred miles to the south, off Honshu.

As to the continued importance of the KAL 007 case: The lives of ordinary airline passengers were put at risk without their knowledge or consent. Two hundred and sixty-nine civilians, of whom sixty were American citizens, were killed, as were some thirty or more U.S. Air Force and Navy officers and enlisted men. All this was the result of a wholly unjustified and badly planned intelligence and provocation mission. The government lied to the next of kin of both these groups and has failed to show them the consideration it owes them. A substantial risk of World War III was run for inadequate reason—if, indeed, there could have been an adequate one for risking a nuclear holocaust.

Through the manipulation of evidence, lying, and the subornation of witnesses, the Reagan administration turned its own ghastly blunder into a renewed political attack on the Soviet Union. In doing so it further committed itself to its mistaken quest for a decisive victory rather than striving for a gradual way of bringing U.S.-Soviet relations into a viable accommodation. The disastrous results are only now beginning to dawn on us—Chechnya, economic disintegration, the spread of disease, the illicit sale of nuclear materials. In turning the truth of its own blunder in the KAL 007 operation into an aggressive fiction tailored to its purposes, the administration committed itself (and, sad to say, its successors) to years of lying to the very people from whom in a democracy it derives its powers.

How could such a badly conceived and dangerous initiative have been undertaken? By no means least among the contributing causes were the dangers inherent in covert-action programs. In operations shielded by secrecy and conducted with the compartmentalization of information, true controls shrink virtually to zero. The senior officials who approve the plans have no real understanding of their dangers. The great majority of those carrying them out have little idea of what is being done beyond their own specific tasks. Effective congressional oversight is impossible—at least, it has never existed in the United States. At the root of clandestine operations is the mind-set that separates out simple objectives and considers anything justified in the drive to achieve them.

If the KAL case were no longer important, why would the U.S. government devote such considerable resources to keep what happened from the public? It is not only trying to cover up a past blunder. It is also trying to protect a present and future "capability," the license to conduct clandestine operations that may differ from the KAL case in their specifics and their targets, but are similar in their disregard for democratic restraints and in the risk that they, too, will end in disaster.

There is every reason to think that covert operations continue to be a major element in U.S. policy—indeed, one that enjoys broad bipartisan support. Republican and Democratic directors of Central Intelligence, Robert M.

Gates and James R. Woolsey, have both stressed that the end of the Cold War only increases the number of our potential enemies and the need for clandestine operations. In December 1992, Mr. Woolsey told the World Affairs Council, we may have slain the dragon (the U.S.S.R.), but there remain a vast number of snakes (from Islamic fundamentalists to Mexican peasants) who can fit the blanket label of "terrorist" and justify intervention abroad and curbs on civil liberties at home.

I hear people say, "Michel Brun may be right about what happened in the KAL case, but couldn't we correct the mistakes quietly with less cost to the U.S.'s reputation" (and to the interests of those who took part in the cover-up)? I am reminded of the eminent Victorian lady who, on being told that Darwin said we were descended from the apes, remarked, "I hope it is not true. But if it is, I trust it will not become widely known."

To the contrary. An open discussion is essential to build the political will to prevent such abuses in the future. There will be both institutional pressures against disclosure (from the intelligence agencies and others who fear their interests might be damaged) and specific temptations to engage in new clandestine operations (for it is true we live in a chaotic world). In the 1970s the Church Committee in the U.S. Senate began the process of airing. For a time it may have had a restraining effect. That is why it was abandoned—first in the heightened Cold War of the 1980s and now in the "chaos" of the 1990s.

But must we abandon democracy to defend "democracy"? The KAL tragedy shows the cost of such a policy: the cost to the passengers who boarded the airliner in good faith, the risk the operation ran of nuclear war, and the damage to responsible government involved in the cover-up. Future risks will be different in their specifics but equally real.

At the CIA headquarters in Langley, Virginia, are inscribed the words from the Gospel according to St. John: "Ye shall know the truth and the truth shall make you free." Only if we meet the challenge, will we have freedom. The KAL case is not only one of the most remarkable events of recent history. It is a present opportunity we dare not miss.

John Keppel
Essex, Connecticut
August 15, 1995

Korean Air Lines Flight 007 disappeared somewhere over the Sea of Japan in the early morning hours of September 1, 1983. On the flight from New York to Seoul via Anchorage were 269 passengers and crew. None of them were ever found—dead or alive. Even the sunken wreckage of the giant plane could not be located. Yet other passenger planes had been found in much deeper waters. Why did no one ever find KAL 007 in waters whose depth is barely twice the length of a Boeing 747? It is one of the mysteries surrounding this tragic affair. But it is not the only one.

Another mystery is the true purpose of flight KAL 007. Canadian general Richard Rohmer, himself a pilot and former commander of the Air Force Reserve, writes in *Massacre 747* that the overflight of Russian territory by the Korean airliner was a deliberate act. General Rhomer suggests it was done to save fuel. But that seems improbable given the dangers that the overflight of strategically important and heavily defended Soviet territory involved in those Cold War days. Other suggestions have been made by other writers. KAL 007 was on a spy mission. It was acting as a decoy to turn on the Soviet defense system so that American listening devices would capture the flow of data. It was another *Lusitania* case, to boost the *U.S.* military effort.

What is the primary role of a commercial airliner? There are probably as many answers to this question as there are individuals. To the public its primary role is, naturally, to transport passengers to their destination. To the airline's financial managers, it is to earn a profit. To the crew, it is to arrive safely. To military chiefs of staff it is to provide support services during wartime, as was the case during the Gulf War. These objectives are not necessarily compatible and are occasionally in direct conflict with one another. Decisions that put the passengers at risk may be made without their knowledge. Choices can be forced upon crew members against their will. The crash of a Pan American 707 shortly after takeoff from Papeete on Tahiti in October 1973 is an example. The pilot judged a crack in a cockpit window too dangerous to risk flying the plane. He was ordered by corporate headquarters to take off immediately or face dismissal. Only two persons, both passengers, were alive when they were recovered from the water.[1]

A civil court in Washington, D.C. has found that Korean Air Lines was guilty of willful misconduct in KAL 007's off-course flight in that the cockpit crew must have known that the airliner was dangerously off course. The court's decision implies that the pilot had purposes other than his airline duties of delivering his passengers to their destination as safely and expeditiously as possible. But what were his motives? We may never know. What is certain is that the destruction of KAL 007 gave rise to one of the greatest propaganda campaigns that either side of the Iron Curtain had known. The truth about the events that occurred in the sky over Sakhalin on the night of August 31–September 1 has been carefully concealed beneath a barrage of contradictory accounts. It has taken ten years to sort it out.

This book recounts a long and difficult investigation, whose conclusions call into question not only the circumstances of the Korean airliner's destruction, but also the time and place it happened. As the reader will learn, KAL 007 was not shot down over Sakhalin. It continued to fly undisturbed for nearly an hour after other intruding aircraft were shot down there by Soviet fighters. It sent several messages in Korean to other KAL planes. The last message was sent while the airliner was within radar range of Tokyo Control, somewhere over the Sea of Japan and approximately 435 miles from where it was claimed to have crashed.

Figure 1. *The author holding a piece of honeycomb from the Korean airliner that he found in 1990 on a southern Hokkaido beach on the Tsugaru Strait.*

Along with doubts about the time and place of the airliner's destruction, there are questions as to the identity of the Soviet pilot who shot down over Sakhalin the airplane said to have been KAL 007. The Japanese and Americans, whose monitoring stations captured the communications of the Soviet interceptors, have identified fighter 805 as the plane that shot it down. In 1990 the Soviets disclosed the name of the pilot who is supposed to have attacked "the intruding plane." He is Lt. Col. Gennadi Osipovich. If we simply connect the two statements without further question, we conclude that it was Colonel Osipovich, the pilot of fighter 805, who shot down

KAL 007. But Osipovich himself stated that on the day in question, he was flying fighter 804. This has been confirmed by analysis of the voice print and transmitter profile, which shows that Osipovich and the pilot of fighter 805 were different people, flying two different planes. Each of them shot down at least one airplane. These planes were not, however, the Korean Boeing 747. What actually happened to Flight 007, and what occurred that night in the sky above Sakhalin? The question intrigued me. I thought it would make a good book.

I had written two earlier books, one on a raft voyage I had made from Tahiti to Chile and the other on navigation in the Sea of Japan. There was ample material here to make an interesting story. But before committing myself to the project—I was unaware at the time that it would nearly bankrupt me—I thought it would be a good idea to contact several editors and determine my chances of success.

I received a favorable response from Ned Chase, senior editor at Scribner's/Macmillan in New York. Chase told me he would gladly look at the manuscript when it was completed. He didn't promise to publish the book. But I knew how difficult it is to get an editor's attention, and this meant that someone would at least read the manuscript. It was certainly a step in the right direction.

I wrote my first manuscript in English and entitled it *Mission 007*. The framework for the story was real and followed what had been published in the Japanese papers. But the events I used to flesh out the framework—within the CIA, inside the cockpit of the 747 or the different interceptors—were imagined. The story reflected what had actually transpired and my rendition of events was plausible, but still imaginary. I envisioned a mission organized by the CIA for the purpose of triggering the Soviet defenses, allowing American electronic intelligence services to harvest a maximum of information.

But the idea that an American intelligence agency, even the CIA, could have jeopardized the lives of 269 people was an affront to the moral values of American society and, at the time, appeared untenable (and anti-American) to the New York editor. When Chase received the manuscript, he read it carefully as promised but reacted strongly. He wrote me a curt letter telling me that I had wasted my time and his, that I was an agent provocateur, maybe even a KGB agent.

I wrote a long reply offering to rewrite the manuscript along new lines. I flew to New York, where we met in person for the first time. Chase saw I was serious and neither a provocateur nor a KGB agent. He invited me to lunch in the private dining rooms at Macmillan's headquarters on Third Avenue. To help him in his assessment of the hypothesis that Flight 007 was accompanied by several other planes, he had invited David Pearson, the author of *KAL 007: The Cover-Up,* and Dick Witkin, the aviation editor of the *New York Times,* to join us. They listened attentively to my arguments. They agreed that my findings were disturbing and could throw light on many of the questions surrounding the disappearance of Flight 007.

Ned Chase introduced me to John Keppel, who had helped David Pearson when he was preparing his book about the 007 affair. Keppel, a retired diplomat, had twice been assigned to the American embassy in Moscow and read and spoke Russian. He was working with the Fund for Constitutional Government, a public-interest group in Washington, trying to get to the bottom of the KAL 007 disaster. Convinced that the American government was not an innocent bystander in the affair, he knew that unless confronted with incontrovertible evidence proving its involvement, the government would not admit it had organized an intelligence mission over Soviet territory. What I had to say interested him a great deal.

Ned Chase and his colleagues were particularly intrigued by one part of my story: the sources of my information in Japan. They were surprised to learn of the interception and firing sequences of the Soviet fighters against not one but several intruding planes. I told them there was nothing mysterious about my sources. I had found the information about the firing sequences and other details of what had occurred over Sakhalin in the Japanese archives. Anyone could do what I had done. You simply had to go to Japan and be able to read Japanese.

We agreed that I would rewrite the manuscript, this time taking into consideration only facts for which I had proof that would be accepted in a court of law. We had to be prepared for any legal attacks and be ready to respond to them. John Keppel offered me his assistance, and I promised— this was March 1987—to finish the new manuscript by December. On December 15 the manuscript was ready, and I sent it to Chase with the title *The Battle of Sakhalin.* Nothing about the new manuscript was fictional. Everything was based on published material and other available sources. As Chase reported to his editorial board:

> *I am writing this to you at the culmination of some three years of developmental work on one of the most bizarre and sensational book projects in my years of publishing, with the outcome a potential best-seller.*

The facts revealed by the book were so extraordinary that Chase requested more tangible evidence. Publication of the book was put on hold while I went in search of additional proof. With the support of the Fund for Constitutional Government, John Keppel acted as the liaison with Congress and Senators Nunn, Kennedy, and Levin, in particular. The discovery of additional evidence and new material required daily corrections to the original manuscript.

Then one day, encouraged by the development of glasnost, *Izvestiya* began publishing a long series of articles on the disappearance of Flight 007. On the surface the authors appeared to defend the American thesis according to which the Korean plane had unwittingly strayed from its route and been shot down by a Soviet interceptor over Sakhalin. But the *Izvestiya* journalists provided testimony from pilots, divers, and others who had participated in the operation. And their testimony, analyzed with reference to documents that John Keppel and I had obtained, together with the results of my investigation, said something quite different. They confirmed my findings. To take account of the new information, I had to begin again and rewrote the manuscript one more time, this time in French. Meanwhile, Scribner's was sold, and Chase, though continuing his interest in the project, had to bow out. I found a new publisher in Four Walls Eight Windows, a translator in Robert Bononno, and a new editor in Dan Simon.

Michel Brun
Montreal
September 3, 1995

PART ONE

FLIGHT 007 HAS DISAPPEARED

The Flight from New York

Seoul, September 1, 6:00 A.M. It was the end of summer, 1983, and the "Land of Morning Calm" was still waking up. The sun had risen nearly an hour earlier and was already high in a cloudless sky. The night chill quickly began to dissipate. Kimpo International Airport in Seoul, which closed after midnight so as not to disturb the adjoining neighborhoods, awoke to the hustle and bustle of the new day. A dense crowd was forming in the airport's arrivals building to greet relatives and friends. One of the first scheduled arrivals was Korean Air Lines Flight 007 from New York via Anchorage. The arrivals board indicated that the plane was scheduled to land at 6:05 but would be delayed. In the immense hall, with its cathedral-like ceiling, the crowd milled about, uncertain and impatient. From time to time they glanced at the board. At 6:05 the numbers on the screen began to turn with their characteristic rattling, and the attentive crowd watched for a new arrival time for Flight 007. The board indicated that the delay was now "indefinite." What had happened? Where was the plane from New York? Had some kind of equipment failure forced the plane to land elsewhere? Korean Air Lines employees at the information desk were besieged by the nervous crowd, whose anxiety was visible on their strained faces. But the employees were unable to provide any information that would have reassured them.

In Japan, the Search and Rescue Coordination Center, alerted by Air Traffic Control at Narita, which had heard nothing from the plane since 3:27 A.M., had already begun a search operation for Flight 007 starting from its last known position along route Romeo-20 above the North Pacific. No one in the expectant crowd at Kimpo Airport was aware of this, however.

6:20 A.M. Another Korean Air Lines plane, Flight 015, which had also made a stopover at Anchorage and was flying along the same route as 007, landed at the scheduled time. Was there any possibility that they had information about 007? They had made the same trip, at the same time, over the same route, with only a few minutes difference between the two flights. They must know something. The crowd would soon be reassured. But as time passed and there was no news, anxiety mounted.

Finally, at 7:20, after more than an hour of official silence, executives of Korean Air Lines announced to the waiting crowd that the plane had encountered unexpected difficulties, but there was nothing to worry about. The plane had enough fuel on takeoff to remain in the air for twelve hours, meaning it had another three hours of fuel left. They provided no further details. Why was the plane late? Was there a problem with one of the engines? Had there been a hijacking? Questions began to circulate, but there were no answers. The only thing that seemed certain was that the plane was still in flight and could remain in the air for another three hours. It was the only reassurance the crowd was given.

Also at 7:20 A.M., KBC, the Korean television station, announced that Korean Air Lines Flight 007 was missing. For some reason an identical story had been broadcast a half hour earlier by ABC in America. America was on the other side of the world, and the airplane was Korean, not American. Why would an American television station be interested in a Korean airliner that was late in arriving? And was the news important enough in itself for the American station to scoop the Koreans? The waiting continued. There was still no new information. The plane had enough fuel to remain in the air until at least ten in the morning. What would happen if they still hadn't landed by then? As the hour approached, the crowd's anxiety mounted, and the official silence continued. The crowd of relatives and friends, now joined by the idle and the curious, continued to swell.

10:00 A.M. Still no news. The Boeing jumbo jet, its tanks nearly dry, would be exhausting its last drops of fuel somewhere in the sky. Like an enormous wounded bird it would be allowing itself to be carried by the wind. In minutes, its engines would stop and the giant plane would begin the inexorable descent toward its destruction. The waiting crowd was aware of this, and emotions were strained to the breaking point. Korean Air Lines staff were besieged with questions but remained silent. Then, something broke the tension.

At precisely ten o'clock, the South Korean minister of foreign affairs announced that he had received confirmation from the CIA that "the plane had landed at Sakhalin. The crew and passengers are safe." The nervous crowd went wild upon hearing the news, which dissipated fears and restored hope. It had come at the right moment to defuse the crowd's despair. Many saw this as the work of divine providence. Coming from the minister of foreign affairs, who quoted the CIA as his source, the news carried enough weight to sweep away lingering doubts. The same information was made public in Tokyo by the Japanese government, which also quoted the CIA source. In a different part of Seoul, an aide handed Sen. Jesse Helms, who had just arrived on Flight KAL 015 to attend an international conference, a message stating that the Korean airplane "was on the ground at Sakhalin and all the passengers are safe."

Seoul airport, 10:47 A.M. Charley Cho, vice president of Korean Air Lines, appeared in person to reassure the families and meet with journalists. He stated that he had been informed that Flight 007 had landed at Sakhalin.

"I can't tell you how it happened, but that's unimportant as long as the passengers are all right." Vice President Cho continued, "In my opinion the plane was forced from its route." Just then a subordinate handed him a message and Cho joyously announced, "It has now been confirmed. The minister of foreign affairs has been informed by the United States CIA that the plane is down on Sakhalin and the passengers are safe."

A few minutes after making this statement, at eleven in the morning, Vice President Cho took off for Tokyo and Sapporo on board one of his company's DC-10s to organize the repatriation of the passengers and crew of Flight 007. "In less than twenty-four hours the problem will be straightened out, and I promise to bring them back to you," he told the crowd. Assured that they would shortly see their loved ones, the anxious relatives who had spent an agonizing morning in the airport returned home. Calm returned to Seoul airport, and the long, long wait began.

Let us examine the CIA announcement about which so much has been written:

The aircraft did not explode in flight and did not crash, but is known to have landed on Sakhalin. The passengers and crew are safe, and the aircraft is undamaged.

This information was simultaneously made public by the minister of foreign affairs of the Republic of Korea and by the Japanese government. It was issued at the very moment the waiting crowd in Seoul airport, knowing that the plane would soon run out of fuel, was near panic. The coincidence, significant in itself, has been noted by other authors, including R. W. Johnson in his book *Shootdown: Flight 007 and the American Connection.* Johnson believes that while there is no question the announcement was made, it relates to no tangible reality and could have been made simply to avoid panicking the crowd in Seoul airport. It is clear the statement had that effect, for the crowd dispersed calmly in expectation of the plane's return. Charley Cho, vice president of Korean Air Lines, left for Japan in his special DC-10 in order to arrange for the passengers' repatriation. That would imply that Korean Air Lines considered the statement legitimate. As Charley Cho was flying from Seoul to Tokyo, the head of Korean Air Lines in Tokyo announced that Flight 007 had been forced to land at Sakhalin "at approximately four o'clock in the morning." This would lead us to believe that he had accurate information about the landing.

Commentators and experts have been divided into two camps in their opinions about the CIA announcement. The first claims that the story is false and the announcement never took place. The second believes that the announcement is real enough, but that the contents were fabricated to stop the flow of news long enough to allow the various intelligence agencies time to create a plausible story that would exonerate the U. S. government. But in the case of Japan, at least, the CIA announcement did not have the effect of stopping the flow of news. It was published as one episode among many surrounding the affair and, interestingly enough, was supported by information from Japanese sources.

The September 1 afternoon edition of the *Mainichi Shimbun* contained both the CIA account of the forced landing at Sakhalin and details of the observations of the military radar facilities at Wakkanai.

The Korean plane suddenly veered from its route and overflew the Chishima archipelago in the Kuril Islands;[1] crossing the Sea of Okhotsk, it violated the airspace over Sakhalin, where fighters intercepted it. Radar facilities at Wakkanai in northern Japan observed a group of three interceptors flying parallel to the Korean plane in the vicinity of Yuzhno-Sakhalinsk[2] on three occasions. The first occurred at 03:20, the second at 03:32, and the third at 03:53. These observations confirmed that the fighters pursued the plane for more than a half hour above Sakhalin and forced the Korean plane to land.

The CIA announcement of the landing at Sakhalin apparently reflects observations by the Wakkanai radar facilities. The radar operator concluded that the plane had been forced to land. On the basis of reciprocity agreements, Japanese intelligence agencies passed this information to their American counterparts, and the CIA decided to make the information public. Leaving aside the CIA's motivations in releasing the information, examination of the circumstances surrounding the announcement leads to the conclusion that it corresponds to some tangible reality.

Sitting in front of his console, the Japanese radar operator saw what he thought was the interception, or escort, of a transportlike aircraft at different times by three different Soviet fighters. The trace of the interception seemed to form a spiral centered on Yuzhno-Sakhalinsk, the Soviet commercial airfield (also a military field) on the southern part of the island. The spiral seemed to close on the field and appeared to terminate there. Observing these events as they happened, the radar operator had neither the time nor the means to make the time and distance calculations that would have told him that what he had seen was the interception of three, not one, intruding aircraft. His observations, however, formed the basis for the September 1 *Mainichi Shimbun* story that KAL 007 had been forced to land at Yuzhno-Sakhalinsk.

These events in East Asia had their reflection in the United States. The simultaneous announcement in Korea and Japan that, according to CIA, KAL 007 had landed on Sakhalin and the passengers were safe had come at 10:00 A.M. Tokyo time, and the similar announcement by the office of Korean Air Lines in Tokyo at 11:00 A.M. Also at 11:00 A.M. Tokyo time, which was 10:00 P.M. Eastern Daylight Time, Orville Brockman, the duty officer at FAA headquarters in Washington, reached Tommy Toles, by telephone at his home in Georgia. Toles was the press secretary of Rep. Larry McDonald. McDonald, the head of the John Birch Society and of Western Goals, organizations of the extreme right in U.S. politics, was a passenger on KAL 007. Brockman told Toles that he had learned from Mr. Takano of the Japanese Ministry of Transport that Japanese radar had followed the Korean airliner to a landing on Sakhalin. At 10:50 P.M. EDT this information was "confirmed" to Toles by Reed Clark of the State Department, who added that KAL 007 had landed safely.

The United States had no radar facilities of its own in Japan. The three reports that KAL 007 had landed on Sakhalin—CIA's, that of the Japanese Ministry of Transport, and that of the KAL office in Tokyo—appear to be independent of each other except in their ultimate source, the Japanese radar observations at Wakkanai. As we have seen, the conclusions the Wakkanai radar operator initially reached, that he had observed a single intruder, were incorrect. Obviously, the Korean airliner did not land at Yuzhno-Sakhalinsk. It is, however, less clear whether some other intruder may have landed there or crashed nearby.

But the identification dilemma was, of course, not known to the members of the crowd at the Seoul airport. They returned home convinced that the airliner had landed safely on Sakhalin. The next step, they had been led to believe, would be the repatriation of the plane's passengers and crew.

The Landing at Sakhalin

Confident of his ability to accomplish his mission, Vice President Cho left Kimpo International Airport promising that he would quickly reunite the passengers with their families. In the first-class compartment of his specially equipped DC-10, Vice President Cho laid out his strategy for obtaining Soviet authorization to land at Yuzhno-Sakhalinsk and bring back the passengers. His confidence in being able to settle the matter quickly was reinforced by the fact that this was not the first time a Korean Air Lines plane had been intercepted by Soviet fighters while overflying restricted territory. The first incident had occurred five years earlier, on April 20, 1978.

Korean Air Lines Flight 902 took off from Paris en route to Seoul, westbound over subpolar regions. It made a virtual U-turn near Greenland in broad daylight, obvious even to the passengers, who saw the sun shift from one side of the airplane to the other. KAL 902 then flew through Soviet defenses to the Kola Peninsula (site of new Soviet ICBM activities). Near Murmansk (headquarters of the Soviet Northern Fleet) it was forced down on a frozen lake by a Soviet fighter. A Soviet source claimed that its flight had been coordinated with that of a U.S. satellite able to monitor some of the Soviet radar and communications it had stirred up.[1]

Even so, the passengers on that occasion were turned over to Korean Air Lines within twenty-four hours. The crew was freed a few days later, after the captain had signed a confession stating that he had knowingly gone off course on a spying mission. After being repatriated he claimed he had signed the statement under duress and that his instruments had malfunctioned. The Boeing 707's captain's career was unharmed. Once home he was greeted as a hero and received a promotion. Vice President Cho assumed that things would go as well the second time around.

Cho landed in Tokyo at approximately 13:00 hours. But he went no farther. A piece of bad news was waiting for him upon his arrival, which cut short his attempts to return the plane's passengers. Around noon the Soviet Ministry of Foreign Affairs had informed the Japanese embassy in Moscow that Flight 007 had not landed on Sakhalin Island and that they had no knowledge of the plane's whereabouts. There was nothing else to do but wait. But wait for what? Vice President Cho was certain that the plane was out of fuel and no longer in the air. Aside from the false information about the plane's landing on Sakhalin, he had received no further news as to its position and began to fear that it had crashed. Disturbing rumors began to circulate.

Japanese defense radar had observed activity over Sakhalin, which they had initially interpreted as an interception attempt followed by a landing. Later analysis of the radar data showed, however, that this did not involve a lone plane circling Yuzhno-Sakhalinsk, but several planes, one of which disappeared at 03:29. Accordingly, the Japanese Defense Agency (JDA) signaled the disappearance of an unknown aircraft west of Sakhalin, near the small island of Moneron. The Japanese Maritime Safety Agency (JMSA) sent planes and two patrol vessels, the *Rebun* and the *Sarubetsu*, to look for that plane.

When it received the order to head for a point at 46°30′ N, 141°30′ E, where the unknown plane had disappeared from the radar screens, the *Rebun* was already at sea. An hour later it was 14 NM north-northeast of Moneron, when it spotted three Soviet warships accompanying a cargo vessel and a fishing boat, all of which were collecting debris on the ocean surface. The cargo vessel had two boats in the water and looked as if it was trying to haul up large, heavy objects. Several years later it was learned that the fishing vessel was the *Uvarovsk*, under the command of Captain Bilyuk, returning from a seven-month fishing expedition in the Indian Ocean. When it caught sight of the *Rebun*, the Soviet fishing vessel ran up signal flags indicating, "Stand clear. Do not approach." To make certain the *Rebun* understood it was in earnest, the ship began zigzagging back and forth across the *Rebun*'s bow. At the same time one of the Soviet warships approached and removed the covers from its guns. The *Rebun*'s commander continued his patrol without further disturbing the movements of the Soviet ships. Later on he acknowledged he had been very much afraid.

Back on the mainland, Narita air traffic control had received no news of the Korean plane since 03:27 hours. Following standard procedures, they had issued an alert to try to locate the plane. A distress procedure was then implemented. A rescue fleet and two groups of planes were directed toward Flight 007's last stated position, the NOKKA waypoint along Romeo-20, over the North Pacific. It included a military contingent made up of the escort ships *Ooi*, *Ishikari*, and *Yubari*, the minesweeper *Oumi* and another minesweeper from the Forty-seventh Escort Group, accompanied by several P2J airplanes, used for maritime rescue operations, and a group from the JMSA of eight ships and four planes. There was a possibility the Boeing 747 had been forced to make an emergency sea landing, in which case there would be survivors. The fleet made for the open sea at full speed in the hope of reaching them in time.

Chapel Hill, North Carolina, August 31, 1983. Prof. Shôzo Takemoto was a happy man. He was a visiting professor at the University of North Carolina where his elder daughter, Yukari, was an exchange student. His wife, Tomiko, and his son, Kiyonori, had come to the States to spend their summer with them. This was the first time in a long while that the entire family had been together. Tomiko and Kiyonori had left the evening before for Japan. They had flown on a Korean Air Lines plane, Flight 007.

Enjoying the mild summer evening, Professor Takemoto and his daughter were sitting comfortably in their living room, talking about the holidays that had just drawn to a close. The warm presence of Tomiko and Kiyonori still seemed to fill the room. Around seven in the evening they were about to sit down to dinner when a grave voice from the television caught their attention. Korean Air Lines had been mentioned. Glued to the set, they listened with horror as the newscaster announced that Flight 007 had not arrived in Seoul and was missing. Stunned by the news and somewhat incredulous, they remained motionless. The words coming from the TV speaker reached them through a wall of cotton wool. Deeply shocked, Professor Takemoto and Yukari were unable to sleep that night. Early the next morning they decided to return to Japan that same day. While packing her bags, Yukari remembered a note her mother had left her just before leaving. Written on the paper was a poem by Tanigawa Shintarô:

Picnic on Earth
The joy of living.
It's this very moment.
A miniskirt.
A planetarium.
It's Johann Strauss,
Picasso, and
The view from the Alps.
It's a kiss for all that's beautiful.
But we remain vigilant in our resistance
To evil well concealed.

Yukari was unable to stop her hands from trembling. In tears, she fell to the sofa and hid her face in her hands.

At approximately the same moment Secretary of State George Shultz officially announced that Korean Air Lines Flight 007 had been brutally shot down by a Soviet interceptor after it had deviated from its route. The accusation of "an act of premeditated barbarism" and "the cold-blooded murder of 269 innocent people" seemed strangely remote. His violent words seemed unconnected with the human meaning of the injury. Moreover, they conveyed little information.

Once in Tokyo, Professor Takemoto fell into a state of lethargy, a mixture of confusion and profound grief, which he was unable to shake off. The terrible pain combined with the emotional and mental shock had drained him of his strength. Sleep, with its ability to shield him from the terrible reality, was his only respite. Exhausted, he slept, not knowing whether it was day or night. It took him several months before he could confront his grief. He then made a resolution. He would not rest until he had gotten to the facts behind the tragedy.

Wakkanai, Hokkaido, in the extreme north of Japan, September 3, 1983. The search for Flight 007 in the vicinity of the NOKKA waypoint along route R-20 between Anchorage and Seoul had turned up nothing and was canceled the night of September 2. No one knew what had happened to the plane. Had it been intercepted above Sakhalin? Had it been shot down near the island of Moneron? Having called off the search in the Pacific, the JMSA had considerably increased its efforts in the zone around Moneron, where there were now more than twenty ships, planes, and helicopters. Rear Adm. Isamu Imamura, who was directing the operations from Wakkanai, was baffled. In spite of three days of intensive search, no trace of the Korean plane or its passengers had been found. It was simply incredible. Normally, whenever a large plane—and the Boeing 747 is one of the largest—goes down at sea, large quantities of airplane debris and human bodies are found floating on the surface. Often there are survivors. But this time there was nothing. Not the smallest piece of debris, not the slightest trace. Rear Admiral Imamura did not hide his frustration.

In fact, more than a week would pass before the first signs of debris from the airliner appeared on the beaches. This suggested that the debris appearing then did not originate in the area of the search; it had taken nine days for it to drift there. The plane hadn't crashed near Moneron, but much farther south, a distance great enough to account for nine days of drifting at sea. Seeing the debris of the Korean Boeing arrive on the shores of Hokkaido, another Japanese officer, Rear Adm. Kessoku Konomu, also of the JMSA, noted that it would have been impossible for the plane to have fallen near Moneron. Debris does not drift against the current and the wind. The current flowed from south to north, and the wind had been from the southeast.

Near Moneron the JMSA's ships had been joined by American and Soviet fleets. With such an impressive armada of ships of all sizes crisscrossing the area, it was a miracle no accidents occurred. The largest search effort ever undertaken for a civilian airplane, using the most modern methods, would last more than two months. On November 10, 1983, as if by common agreement, the search was simultaneously halted by the Soviets, Americans, and Japanese, without any sign of the wreckage. Yet the average depth in the area was barely 160 meters (525 feet), and the ocean floor was flat. How could they have missed a plane that was nearly 262 feet long with 269 persons on board? The Korean Air Lines Boeing 747 had in fact disappeared.

The mystery of the disappearance of Flight 007 remained unsolved.

Tokyo, December 1983. Along with fifty individuals belonging to twenty families of the Japanese victims and a Korean victim living in Japan, Professor Takemoto founded the Japanese Association of the Families of the KAL 007 Incident Victims, of which he was the vice president. The association included highly visible political figures, including Sen. Hideyuki Seya, vice president of the Higher House National Assembly, Mrs. Takako Doi, president of the Japanese Socialist Party, Shun Oide, a deputy in the Lower House of the Diet, and many others. Along with Senators Den Hideo and Yukata Hata, Deputy Oide greatly assisted the association by asking the government numerous questions. A number of labor leaders were involved as well, including Tadanobu Usami, president of the General Labor Confederation, and Takeshi Kurokawa, president of the General Council of Japanese Labor Unions. There were also attorneys, university professors, and others from a wide variety of backgrounds. On September 1, 1984, the first anniversary of the tragedy, a Technical Research Committee was formed to throw as much light as possible on the affair. I later participated on the Research Committee, working with Professor Takemoto, Mr. Sugimoto, an engineer from Japan Air Lines, and the journalist Masuo, to help resolve a mysterious aspect of the affair: Flight 007's radio communications. As if from beyond the grave, the pilot's voice could be heard on the tape of communications with Narita Airport forty-six minutes after the plane was supposed to have been shot down.

Tokyo, June 1985. At the time of the disaster in September 1983 I had been in Montreal. By June 1985 I was back in Japan, working as an aeronautical consultant. As a pilot I was interested in the disappearance of Flight 007. Intrigued by the fact that the wreck of the giant plane had never been found in such shallow water, I decided to find out more about the incident. I used my free time to check the archives of the Japanese Diet Library looking for any clue that would put me on the right track. I found what I was looking for and a great deal more. What I discovered was beyond belief, and I looked for any information that would prove me wrong. I did not want to confront the implications of my discovery.

But the documents were all there. They indicated that the Korean plane was not alone at Sakhalin Island. Other aircraft had overflown the Soviet island at the time, some of which had been shot down. They could only have been military. There was enough evidence here to show that the KAL 007 disaster was by no means the simple story we had been told. I set about analyzing the available materials.

PART TWO

THE INVESTIGATION

The Investigation Begins

The world, except Japan, believes that the news of Korean Air Lines Flight 007's destruction was broken by U.S. Secretary of State George Shultz in his press conference on the morning of September 1, 1983, in Washington. In point of fact, Shultz was not the first to break the news. KAL 007's shootdown had been announced more than two hours earlier in Japan. Shultz spoke at 10:45 A.M. Eastern Daylight Time. At 9:10 P.M. in Tokyo (8:10 A.M. EDT in Washington) the chief of the Japanese Defense Agency had publicly discussed the shootdown. In itself it is of little importance who first broke the news. What is important is that the two men, although both ostensibly describing the shootdown of KAL 007 by a Soviet interceptor, were clearly talking about two different incidents.

Geography played a role in the discrepancy in the timing of the announcement in the two countries, and indeed, in the difference between the two versions of the shootdown. It was 11:45 P.M. in Japan when George Shultz made his televised announcement, far too late for it to have made an impact on the Japanese public. The Japanese Defense Agency held its press conference at 9:10 P.M., as late as television in Japan and the realities of effective communication between the government and the public would allow. However, along the shores of the Potomac it was only 8:10 A.M., too early for a major U.S. government announcement.

The JDA's statement—claiming that Flight 007 might have been shot down by a Soviet interceptor—had reached newsrooms throughout the United States. But the news was supplanted before it went to press by Shultz's statement two hours later on the same subject. Shultz's bluntness, in contrast to the JDA's carefully chosen words, and the fact that the story had now become an American issue, orchestrated from Washington, quickly overshadowed the statements by the Japanese government. The press, after having been momentarily stunned by the news coming from Tokyo, simply ignored the Japanese information once the disaster had been announced by the secretary of state. For an American journalist, as for the majority of the Western press, the news is made in Washington not Tokyo. Because the thrust of the two stories was similar, the details that accompanied the Japanese Defense Agency's statement were simply ignored. As a result the American public, and most of the world, learned only one side of the story of the destruction of Flight 007, George Shultz's side.

In Japan, events took a different turn. The morning papers had carried the JDA's press conference in its entirety, and the Japanese public was soon familiar with the incident. Shultz's version was mentioned in the evening papers simply as a foreign interpretation of what was felt to be a domestic issue. The Japanese version of the story read as follows:

According to the Japanese Defense Agency, what may have been the Korean airliner appeared on the radar screens at 03:12, flying at a speed of 430 knots. A Soviet MiG-23 appeared at a distance of 25 NM [29 miles], behind the airliner. It cut across the airliner's path, flying from left to right, and 2,000 meters below it, at 03:25 Japan time [18:25 GMT]. The two planes disappeared from the radar screens a few minutes later, at 03:29. The track of the Soviet fighter reappeared as it began to make a climbing turn, but it looked as if what was assumed to be the Korean airliner exploded in flight at an altitude of 32,000 feet at the moment when the plane's transponder, emitting code 1300 in mode A, stopped working. If the interceptor did attack the Korean airliner, it could only have done so before cutting across its flight path at 03:25.

The head of the Japanese Air Self-Defense Force used a map showing the radar tracks observed by the Wakkanai facility, copies of which he handed out to the journalists. (See Figure 2.)

According to the American version of events, as summarized by George Shultz, the Korean Boeing had gone off course and had unwittingly over-flown Kamchatka, where it was unsuccessfully pursued by Soviet fighters. It then crossed the Sea of Okhotsk and headed for Sakhalin. Over Sakhalin a MiG-23 interceptor tailed the airliner for about twenty minutes before firing a missile at 18:26:20 GMT. By 18:30 GMT the Korean airliner had descended to 16,000 feet. At 18:38 GMT it disappeared from the radar screens and crashed into the sea.

Shultz didn't use a map during his press conference. Several days later at the United Nations, however, Ambassador Kirkpatrick displayed a map of the radar tracks of the Korean plane during its overflight of Kamchatka and Sakhalin. According to Ambassador Kirkpatrick, these were Soviet radar tracks that the Americans had intercepted. Ambassador Kirkpatrick's map is reproduced on page 31.

The Japanese and American versions clearly refer to two separate events:

- The "Korean" plane mentioned by Shultz was closely pursued by the Soviet fighter for twenty minutes, while the aircraft in the Japanese version was near the fighter for only an instant, when the latter cut across the jetliner's flight path from left to right.

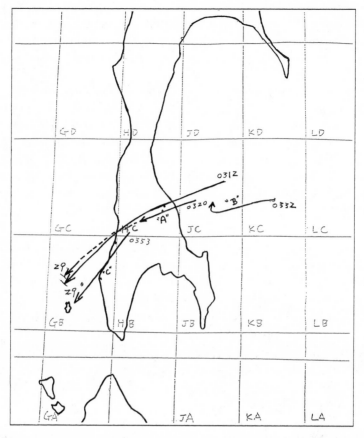

Figure 2. *The Japanese Defense Agency map. Distributed at 9:10 P.M. in Tokyo on September 1, 1983, as explaining the shootdown of KAL 007. It actually shows the course of three (U.S. military) intruders and three Soviet interceptors, all of which must in fact have been pursuing their own, different targets.*

- The fighter pursuing Shultz's plane fired a missile at 03:26:20 (Tokyo time). The fighter pursuing the plane sighted by the Japanese fires before 03:25, before crossing its path.
- The Japanese plane exploded at 32,000 feet at 03:29. Shultz's plane lost altitude. By 03:30 it had descended to 16,000 feet.
- The plane mentioned by Shultz crashed into the sea at 03:38.

The difference between the two versions was not lost on the Japanese press. It emphasized the "mysterious" difference of nine minutes between the two times given for the destruction of the airliner—03:29 in the Japanese version, 03:38 in the American. When on September 2 the Pentagon claimed that the Soviet fighter that had shot down the Korean airliner was not a MiG-23, as Secretary Shultz had said, but an SU-15, the

Japanese press was quick to point out the discrepancy between the two versions of the story coming from Washington. For the Japanese, moreover, loyal to their own version of the incident, it had to have been a Mig-23 that shot down the airliner. The Mig-23 versus SU-15 question become a major point of agitation in the Japanese media.

The difference between the two original announcements, Japanese and U.S., is worth a word of explanation. There seems little doubt that the two governments had agreed they would assert that the airliner had been shot down over Sakhalin by a Soviet fighter. But owing to the shortness of time for coordination, and other factors that I will discuss later in the book, the two governments seized on two different incidents, the details of which they presented as those surrounding the shootdown of Flight 007.

As I read my way in the spring and summer of 1985 through the newspaper files in the Diet Library, what struck me was that the difference between the two versions of the story meant that more than one interception and more than one shootdown had occurred over Sakhalin. This changed the picture entirely. I was impelled to go further in my study.

To my surprise, I discovered that the Western press mentioned almost no technical information of any value. The Japanese papers, however, especially the Hokkaido papers, provided a wealth of technical detail. This was because the radars that had observed the event were located in Hokkaido. The local journalists were able to interview the radar technicians and facilities managers, with whom they had developed personal contacts over the years. In the hours immediately following the event, they gathered an extraordinary amount of detailed information before the government found out and imposed a standard version of the event. Because of their consistency and accuracy, their reports constitute an important historical document and help us to understand the multiple events that took place over Sakhalin that night.

Mainichi Shimbun, September 1, 1983

The afternoon edition of the *Mainichi Shimbun,* which appeared on the stands around 2:00 P.M., reported that the Korean airliner with its 269 persons on board had been forced to land on Sakhalin. All the passengers, including 27 Japanese nationals, were safe. The paper went on to describe in detail the observations made by the radar facilities at Wakkanai. Two maps accompanied the articles. One showed the tracks of the Korean plane deviating from its route, crossing the Kuril Islands and heading for Sakhalin. The other showed the track of the aircraft crossing Sakhalin from east to west. Both maps bore a legend indicating that the observations were made from Wakkanai.

Hokkaido Shimbun, September 1, 1983

> *At 03:23 an unknown aircraft was observed crossing Sakhalin from east to west on a heading of 270 degrees; the aircraft was 112 miles [97 NM] north of Wakkanai, at an altitude of 31,500 feet.*

Both the *Hokkaido Shimbun* and the *Mainichi Shimbun* articles refer to an intruder aircraft on a westerly course (270° heading). They are the only such accounts. All the other sources have the plane crossing Sakhalin northeast to southwest. The *Hokkaido Shimbun* article also mentions that another plane crossed Sakhalin heading southwest, flying directly over the towns of Dolinsk and Gornozavodsk. The latter information is accompanied by a map. Comparison with the map made public by the Japanese Defense Agency shows that they relate to two different events. Whereas the route traced on the JDA's map shows a distinct curve, the map in the *Hokkaido Shimbun* is absolutely straight. Moreover, the two routes are quite far from one another, the JDA's passing over the town of Kholmsk and the *Hokkaido Shimbun's* passing directly over Gornozavodsk, thirty-four miles to the south. This couldn't have resulted from an observational error because the Japanese radars were accurate to within 1,600 feet at that distance. In fact the latter track exactly corresponds to the path of the plane pursued and destroyed by interceptor 805, which the U.S. claimed was an SU-15 and the interceptor that shot down the Korean airliner.[1]

Asahi Shimbun, September 2, 1983

> *At approximately 03:20 hours the intelligence services of the Japanese Self-Defense Forces intercepted radio communications between Soviet interceptors and their ground controllers, suggesting that an attack was conducted shortly before the echo of the Korean airliner disappeared from the radar screens. The communications were as follows:*
> *"Prepare your missiles."*
> *"Ready!"*
> *"Fire!"*
> *"Missiles fired!"*
> *This same communication was heard three times, suggesting that the Korean airliner might have been shot down by three missiles launched by three different interceptors. This information has been confirmed by other sources, including American satellites and monitoring stations in Japan.[2]*

The mention of three firing sequences by three different interceptors suggests that not one but three different planes were shot down at this time.

Asahi Shimbun, September 2, 1983

> *Government Secretary Masaharu Gotoda stated that, according to reports issued by the Self-Defense Forces and other official Japanese sources, there is a possibility that the Korean airliner crashed at 03:38 hours.*

Statements by the Japanese military continued to cite 03:29 as the time of the airliner's destruction. Gotoda was a member of the government, and his mention of 03:38 was the first reflection of the government's desire to play down the contradiction with the United States.

Yomiuri Shimbun, September 2, 1983

> *During a meeting of senior government officials held Friday morning, Minister of Foreign Affairs Shintaro Abe stated that, in his opinion, the plane was shot down at 03:38 hours.*

Asahi Shimbun, September 3, 1983 (from Washington)

> *American secretary of state George Shultz announced Tuesday that the South Korean Boeing 747 was destroyed by a missile fired by a MiG-23. American intelligence services, however, subsequently claimed that the missile was fired by an SU-15.*

Hokkaido Shimbun, September 3, 1983

> *The destruction of the aircraft was monitored from Japan. Based on observations made by the Japanese Air Self-Defense Force (JASDF) on Wakkanai, the Korean plane was shot down by an air-to-air missile fired by a Soviet MiG-23 interceptor. This is based upon radar tracks of the Korean airliner and the Soviet interceptors, as well as an analysis of the radio communications among the Soviet planes and their ground-station controllers, which were intercepted by JASDF intelligence services. "The American version of events is completely at odds with our own observations," commented General Hayashi, head of the JASDF's Department of Air Defense, during a press conference. "There is a difference of nine minutes between their statement and our observations. The*

Americans also claim that the Soviet interceptor was an SU-15, whereas our observations indicate that it was a MiG-23."

General Hayashi went on to say that the JASDF radar facilities indicated that the plane's echo disappeared from their screens at 03:29, while Secretary of State George Shultz claimed that the plane disappeared at 03:38, a difference of nine minutes.

Despite moves toward American positions by members of the government, General Hayashi insisted on the correctness of the Japanese version of events and specifically took issue with the Americans' SU-15 interceptor and their 03:38 destruction time.

Mainichi Shimbun, September 4

Television station NHK, quoting sources within the Japanese government, announced that intercepted radio communications establish that the plane was shot down after being pursued by three Soviet MiG-23 interceptors. This contradicts earlier American statements according to which the Korean plane was shot down by an SU-15.

Although the points being disputed seem minor, the dispute itself reflected serious differences between the United States and Japan concerning the case, the nature of which did not come to light for some years.

Mainichi Shimbun, September 4, 1983 (from UPI Washington)

According to information from NATO, the SU-15 was armed with two missiles but did not have any guns. As a result it could not have fired any warning shots to draw the pilot's attention.

A September 3 news release from Tass in Moscow claimed that an intruder plane had disappeared from the Soviet Defense Force's radar screens and left Sakhalin airspace ten minutes after warning shots were fired by a Soviet fighter. The American government initially denied that any warning had been given. Changing the type of interceptor involved may have been intended to lend credence to the American version of events. On September 11 the American government reversed itself on this point, however, because the pilot's remark about firing cannon bursts could clearly be heard on the tape it had released to the United Nations on September 7.

None of this helped to allay the controversy within the Japanese press.

The Japanese military stuck to their initial statement of 03:29 hours. Those who had claimed 03:38 was the correct time were high-placed political leaders. There were, however, several efforts to reconcile the two figures. Foreign Minister Abe did not refer to the plane "disappearing from the radar screens," but stated that "the plane was shot down at 03:38." While appearing to support the American version of the story, Abe maintained a certain distance from it by indicating 03:38 as the time of the attack (and not 03:26:20). He may also have been trying to fuzz up the conflict between the Foreign Ministry and the military. The 03:38 he cited as the time of the shootdown was, in fact, the time another intruder was shot down, possibly on the other side of Sakhalin by Fighter B of the JDA map.

The Japan Times, September 5, 1983

> *A member of the Air Self-Defense Force Chiefs of Staff stated that what appeared to be a Soviet fighter flying at 450 knots appeared on the radar screens at 03:20 in pursuit of the airplane that crossed Sakhalin from the east. The two planes came in contact at 03:25 hours at an altitude of 24,000 feet, and the track of what may have been the Korean plane disappeared from the screens at 03:29. The pursuing aircraft reappeared on the screen at the moment it was making a climbing turn. It is believed that the 747 exploded in flight.*

The military continued to maintain the figure of 03:29 hours and to restate the Japanese version of the shootdown. Other sources, however, mentioned an attack occurring at 03:38, with the aircraft disappearing from the screen at 03:39.

Hokkaido Shimbun, September 6, 1983

> *According to a highly placed official in the Ministry of Foreign Affairs, the Korean airliner had its navigation lights on at the time it was shot down. He added that the United Nations would be informed of the fact. The official also provided the following chronology for the sequence of events observed by the JASDF.*
>
> *September 1, 03:20 hours. The Korean airliner informed Narita control that it was passing the NOKKA waypoint. Because the point at which the radars observed the Korean airliner did not agree with the position given by the plane, Narita control requested the Korean plane to confirm its position. The Korean plane did not respond to the request.[3]*
>
> *03:25. One of the three Soviet MiG-23 fighters informed Sakhalin Air Defense control that it was in visual contact and 2 km behind the*

intruder plane. The fighter then informed ground control that he was climbing to a higher altitude to follow the intruder from behind and above.[4] He also stated that the plane's navigation lights were blinking. According to radar observations at this time (03:25), when the navigation lights had been seen blinking, the Korean airliner[5] was still in international waters and had not yet penetrated Sakhalin airspace. The Korean plane then began to zigzag. Sakhalin Air Defense Control Center did not respond to the news about the blinking lights and ordered the interceptor to prepare its missiles and then open fire.

03:38. At 03:38 hours the Soviet MiG-23 belatedly radioed, "I fired my missiles at 03:29." Although the pilot of the MiG-23 stated he had fired at 03:29, radar observations show that the event took place at 03:38.

03:39. At 03:39 the echo of the Korean plane disappeared from the radar screens.

Commenting on the above observations, the Japanese government declared that they prove the Soviet MiG-23 fighter did not follow the normal interception procedures with the Korean airliner. By blinking its navigation lights the airliner signalled its intention to follow the Soviet fighter.

The intent of this Foreign Ministry statement was (a) to give the impression that there was no real contradiction between the Japanese and American versions of the alleged shootdown of KAL 007, (b) to take account of some facts being mentioned by the military, and (c) to accuse the Soviets of improper interception procedure. In detail the statement is composed of one error (03:20 was when KAL 007 told Narita it was leaving 33,000 feet for higher altitude),[6] one wholly new statement (the alleged 03:38 report by the MiG-23 of having fired its missiles at 03:29), and details from at least three different shootdowns of intruding aircraft other than the Korean airliner. The report of an intruder zigzagging as it entered Sakhalin airspace was to show up again years later in a Soviet pilot's statement.

Asahi Shimbun, September 6, 1983

According to information supplied by the Defense Agency on September 5, one of the MiG-23s that took off from the airbase on Sakhalin caught up with the Korean airliner at 03:25. He radioed to ground control, "The target is in sight." One or two minutes later the following exchange could be heard, "Prepare to fire." "I am ready to fire." "Fire." "I have fired." At 03:29 the pilot radioed back, "Confirm plane destroyed."

The Japanese military continued to insist on 03:29 as the time of the intruder's destruction. The next day's newspapers, however, gave a different version of events, one that was disseminated by government sources. It is of interest that here, as in other early Japanese statements, ground-to-air as well as air-to-ground transmissions are quoted. By contrast, the United States denied that ground-control transmissions had been intercepted.

Asahi Shimbun, September 7, 1983

> *To prove that the Korean Boeing was shot down by a Soviet fighter, the Japanese government published an excerpt from radio communications between the Soviet pilots and ground control. These communications were intercepted by Japanese listening posts and made public by Cabinet Secretary Masahura Gotoda during a press conference that took place at the prime minister's official residence. The time indicated is Japan time.*
> *03:26:20. "Fire!"*
> *03:26:21. "Target destroyed."*

The press conference was held at 08:30 in the morning of September 6 in Tokyo, thirty minutes before President Reagan's 8:00 P.M. (EDT) September 5 speech on the destruction of the Korean plane. Masaharu Gotoda's statement, which used American data, was clearly made to show that Japan was acting in solidarity with the United States. The effort backfired, however, for there were now three separate Japanese statements giving three separate times for the destruction of the target. The first by the Japanese military at 03:29 hours, the second at 03:39 as indicated earlier, and the current announcement of 03:26:21.

If any high-placed government official made the above comparisons, he must have feared the public would begin to understand that several aircraft had been destroyed that night. The Japanese government did all it could to shrink the nine-minute difference between the American and Japanese versions, trying to combine distinct and unrelated events into a single shootdown.

Yomiuri Shimbun, September 12, 1983

> *The Japanese Defense Agency has just revealed that a detailed study of the recordings of another radar facility on Wakkanai shows that the Korean airliner made a series of wide spirals for ten minutes, beginning at 9,100 meters [29,800 feet].*

Asahi Shimbun, September 13, 1983

> *It has been revealed that the Korean airliner was closely observed by radar facilities at Wakkanai as it descended in a series of wide spirals. The plane was tracked as it began its descent from 9,000 meters [29,500 feet] above Moneron Island until its disappearance from the radar screens at an altitude of 600 meters [2,000 feet], at which point it fell vertically into the sea. The Soviet pilot stated that he shot down the airplane at 03:26,[7] but the plane did not disappear from the radar screens until 03:38, twelve minutes later.*

This from the *Asahi Shimbun* attempts to blend the Japanese and the American versions of the KAL 007 shootdown over Sakhalin into a single event. But is it plausible that it took the Japanese intelligence services twelve days to realize that one of their radars had recorded the crash without the operators knowing about it? What are we to make of the fact that an airplane that the Japan Defense Agency had said exploded at 33,000 feet at 03:29 was suddenly flightworthy again and glided through the air for nine more minutes?

But military specialists were not the only ones who observed the events that took place that night. A group of fishermen saw the explosion of an aircraft, and their testimony was printed in detail by all the Japanese and several Western papers. The following is from the *Hokkaido Shimbun* of September 2, 1983:

> *The Japanese fishing vessel* Chidori Maru *No. 58, operating out of Sakaiminato in Tottori Prefecture, was fishing for squid near the island of Moneron in the company of approximately 150 other Japanese ships based at Wakkanai. The ship was located at 46°34' N, 141°16' E, 36 km north of Moneron when, at 03:30 on the morning of September 1, the eight-man crew under the command of Capt. Shizuka Hayashi observed the destruction of an airplane. The men first heard the sound of its engines as the plane suddenly approached, but they were unable to determine the direction. The noise was immediately followed by a muffled explosion. For two or three seconds they observed an orange flame low on the horizon in an east-southeasterly direction. When the first flame disappeared from sight, they noticed a succession of orange flames, lasting five or six seconds, and at the same moment, they heard a second explosion, which was not as loud as the first. Five minutes later there was a smell of burned kerosene. The wind was blowing at five or six meters per second [10 to 12 knots], and despite the overcast sky, visibility extended for 10 to 20 km.*

The fishermen heard the first detonation *before* they saw the flame. According to the laws of physics, light travels faster than sound. We can use these laws to calculate where a bolt of lightning has struck. All we need to determine is the time in seconds that elapsed between the initial flash of lightning and the moment we hear the sound of the thunderclap. We then simply multiply the difference by 1,200, the speed of sound in feet per second, to arrive at the answer.

The first detonation heard by the fishermen cannot be the one associated with the explosion they *subsequently* saw. This explosion must be associated with the second detonation. And it places the explosion at two to three times 1,200 feet, or between 2,400 and 3,600 feet east-southeast of the ship. This is supported by the time it took for the odor of kerosene to reach the fishermen. There are three hundred seconds in five minutes, which, at five meters (16 feet) per second, the wind speed, gives 1,500 meters (4,921 feet). This gives us the approximate distance of the explosion ESE (east-southeast) of the ship. But it does not correspond, however, to the explosion of an airplane at an altitude of 33,000 feet, for the explosion took place just above the surface of the water and at a distance of roughly 1,500 meters from the fishing vessel. From an altitude of 33,000 feet, it would have taken much longer for the sound of the explosion to reach the ship; and the smell of kerosene would never have reached sea level. The airplane that the *Chidori Maru* saw explode thus cannot have been the one that disappeared from JDA radar at 03:29.

How can we explain the sound of the muffled explosion heard by the fishermen that followed the sound of the engines from an approaching plane? We'll start with the engine noise. The airplane exploded 1,500 meters from the fishermen; and they heard the sound of an engine suddenly approaching just prior to the muffled explosion. The *Chidori Maru* No. 58, is a 99-ton fishing vessel. It was fishing for squid when the explosion occurred. The noise of the ship's diesel, the winches, and the general fishing activity, together with the sound of the wind and sea, created a background noise on the ship's bridge of approximately 85 to 90 decibels. This is roughly equivalent to the noise of a subway train. Under these conditions and at a distance of 1,500 meters, the crew would not have been able to hear a Boeing 747's engines against the background noise. What's more, at that distance the fishermen would have been unable to detect "the sudden approach" of the sound source. To detect the rapid approach as they claim, the Doppler effect would have had to be fairly significant to overcome the background noise. This implies that the sound source passed relatively close to the fishermen, practically above their heads. That, in turn, excludes the possibility that the aircraft whose engines they heard suddenly approaching was the same one that exploded 1,500 meters farther away, for the explosion occurred barely a few seconds later.

Two aircraft were involved. And this may provide the answer to the mystery of the initial detonation.

The fishermen first heard a muffled detonation followed by an orange light that lasted two to three seconds in an east-southeasterly direction. When the initial flame went out, they saw a succession of orange flames, which lasted five to six seconds, and at the same moment, they heard a second explosion, less powerful than the first. The first explosion could easily correspond to the firing of a missile from a plane flying directly overhead. The firing of a missile creates a slightly muffled sound, just as the fishermen described. The first orange flame, which lasted two to three seconds, would correspond to the combustion of the missile's engine, which the fishermen saw from directly behind the missile, which would have taken two to three seconds to reach its target. That gives it a relative speed (relative to the target) approximately equal to the speed of sound, which seems reasonable. The succession of orange flames appeared when the first flame went out, which is normal since the missile's engine stopped working when it exploded. The second flame lasted five or six seconds. This accurately characterizes the explosion of a plane whose fuel tanks have been hit. And it corresponds perfectly to the explosion that was heard by the fishermen two to three seconds after the missile's impact, when the flame from the explosion was still visible. This explains the fishermen's claim that they occurred simultaneously. The odor of kerosene detected by the fishermen indicates that the plane's fuel tanks were hit.

This is a reasonable explanation but does not tell us which airplane was hit. All that can be said is that it was not the same aircraft that exploded at 03:29 at an altitude of 33,000 feet. Nor was it the plane that disappeared from the radar screen at 03:38 or the one hit by a missile at 03:38, which disappeared from the radar screen at 03:39.

Reviewing the material from the Japanese press as we have done, we find three different times given at which the one Korean airliner was supposed to have been intercepted, four different times at which missiles were fired and struck their target, four different times at which the airliner is supposed to have disappeared from radar, and four different times given for its destruction. The data given indicate a total of four interceptions and at least four, perhaps five, aircraft shot down. The fifth would be the airplane that may have been forced to land shortly after 04:00 or that, alternatively, may have crashed or crash-landed. The question is no longer were they all KAL 007. It is what aircraft were they, and which, if any, was the Korean airliner?

The Japanese Map

The map of the radar tracks observed above Sakhalin Island by the radar facilities at Wakkanai was submitted to the press by the Japanese Defense Agency, during the press conference on September 1 at 9:10 P.M. It shows the tracks of "what appeared to be the Korean airliner" and three Soviet fighter planes. Fighter A, as shown by the map, is the one that cut across the Korean airliner's flight path at 03:25. The two other fighters, B and C, are simply indicated on the map by their tracks and the time at which the tracks begin, 03:32 for B and 03:53 for C. During the press conference the explanations were limited to the track of fighter A and the plane it pursued. The tracks for planes B and C are clearly marked, however. If the "Korean plane" was shot down at 03:29, the only conclusion is that fighters B and C were not pursuing the "Korean plane" but two other aircraft, one of which they may have forced to land at Yuzhno-Sakhalinsk.

The Japanese Defense Agency had been aware as early as 02:30 Tokyo time that alarming events were taking place to the north of Japan. The commanders of the Air Self-Defense Force were roused out of their beds and met at JASDF headquarters in Tokyo about 04:00. As we shall see later, encounters over Sakhalin were still taking place. At 05:10, after hearing reports of events as they were happening, the commanders decided, as they slowed down and stopped, to review the data from all the radar sites on Hokkaido and northern Honshu. It may have been at this time that the analysts realized that the distance between the end of the 03:29 track and the beginning of the 03:32 track was too great for them to have been made by the same aircraft. The plane whose track disappeared at 03:29 and the plane whose track appeared at 03:32 must have been two different planes. This meant that the plane whose track had disappeared at 03:29 might have been shot down. This fear was reinforced by the fact that the plane was emitting transponder code 1300 on Mode A, and the transmission suddenly stopped as soon as the track disappeared.

Its track seemed to have originated in the Kuril Islands and the Pacific, near Romeo-20. That was the route assigned to Flight 007, which stopped responding to attempts at radio contact shortly after 03:27. It could be assumed that the plane coming in from the Kurils was Flight 007, an assumption that was made after the search and rescue operations at NOKKA were cancelled. The track ending at 03:29 was identified (by the Japanese, at least) as the one probably from the Korean airliner. We need to identify the 03:32 track, which ended at 03:38, and the 03:53 track, which ended at 04:01.

The American government indicated that the Korean plane disappeared from radar at 03:38. This time corresponds to the termination of the track for fighter B, which begins at 03:32. However, the map submitted by Ambassador Kirkpatrick to the United Nations, which purports to show the track of the Korean airliner leading up to its 03:38 disappearance, requires a close look, in the process of which its plausibility dissolves.

Figure 3. *The map submitted by Ambassador Kirkpatrick to the United Nations on September 7, 1983, ostensibly showing the route of KAL 007. Although it is stated to have been drawn on the basis of intercepted Russian radar tracking data of the Korean airliner, analysis shows it to be a composite of the tracks of at least three different aircraft, which must have been U.S. military planes.*

The American Map

The map is supposed to represent the track of the airliner as it was observed by Soviet radar. There is a continuous track, which begins at 1551Z[8] in the Bering Sea, crosses Kamchatka, where it is sighted at 1654Z near Petropavlovsk, continues across the Sea of Okhotsk to Sakhalin, where it is sighted at 1821Z, and finally ends in the Tatar Strait at 1838Z. As it stands, the map does not faithfully represent the Soviet observations. It does not indicate that the Soviets lost sight of the intruding plane several times, and consequently, its track should not be represented by a continuous line.

The Soviets first lost sight of the airplane over Kamchatka, just prior to the plane's entry into Soviet airspace. To be accurate, the track should show a break above Kamchatka. The same applies to the plane's path above Sakhalin. Here, too, Soviet radar lost sight of the plane all the time it was above the island. Consequently, the track should also show a break above Sakhalin. The continuous line indicated in Ambassador Kirkpatrick's map should be shown as three separate segments, the first from the Bering Sea to the coast of Kamchatka, the second from Kamchatka to the coast of Sakhalin, and the last from Sakhalin until its disappearance in the Tatar Strait. Further study shows, moreover, that the three segments do not belong to a single aircraft.

The map of the Korean airplane's route presented by Ambassador Kirkpatrick shows tracking points identified by the time of observation. Based on this information, it is easy to measure the distance between the points and calculate the plane's speed. Calculated speeds between points are 510 knots for the first leg, 500 knots for the second, and 280 knots for the third. The first two speeds are plausible for a Boeing 747 on an intercontinental flight; the third is not.

KAL 007's computerized flight plan gives M .84 as the airliner's speed, which works out at 455 knots for the leg up to Kamchatka. The speed of 510 knots for the first leg indicated on the Kirkpatrick map thus does not correspond to KAL 007's speed during this segment of its flight.[9] The second leg starts at 1654Z above Kamchatka, and the calculated speed of 500 knots corresponds to Flight 007's speed of 496 knots during this part of its flight. The Soviets claim to have observed the plane flying over Kamchatka at a speed of 800 km per hour, or 432 knots. The plane indicated by Mrs. Kirkpatrick, whose speed is different, thus seems not to be the plane that the Soviets observed over Kamchatka. The third segment of the track shown of Mrs. Kirkpatrick's map also has problems. The pilot who the United States says shot down the Korean airliner has stated that Soviet ground control lost radar contact with both his own interceptor and his target over Sakhalin, hence the map is again incorrect in showing a continuous track. Moreover, owing to time and distance factors, and the very slow speed of 280 knots, the latter part of the track shown in the map west of Sakhalin seems not to belong to the aircraft whose course is plotted across the Sea of Okhotsk.[10]

The Soviets, the Japanese, and the Americans refer to all intruder radar tracks as that of "the Korean plane." What we are being shown by them are in fact the radar tracks of several different airplanes. The "Korean plane" tracked by the Soviets over Kamchatka had a speed of 432 knots, a speed it maintained all the way to Sakhalin. Japanese radar (according to their official story) first observed the "Korean plane" at 03:12 Japan time off Sakhalin, flying at a speed of 430 knots. But this cannot have been the plane tracked by the Soviets from Kamchatka. Flying at a speed of 432 knots, it could not have arrived at the spot Japanese radar saw the "Korean plane" at 03:12; it would not have got there until 03:35 at the earliest.

The plane Japanese radar observed off Sakhalin at 03:12 seems to have been the one that *Mainichi Shimbun* said came in from the Pacific, crossing the Kurils—thus never having crossed Kamchatka. As for the plane Soviet radar saw crossing Kamchatka and then the Sea of Okhotsk, it could very well have been the target of fighter B shown on the Japan Defense Agency map. That map starts its track at 03:32 off Sakhalin, shows a turn to the north still over international waters, and then ends the track at 03:38, a time associated by the Japanese with the shootdown of a plane that crashed at 03:39.

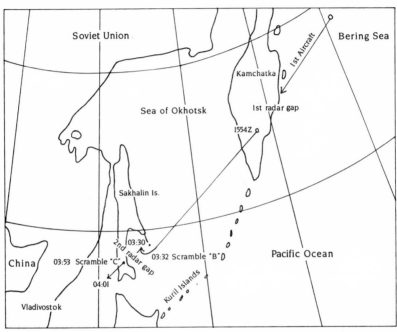

Figure 4. *A corrected version of the Kirkpatrick map, illustrating the different segments of which it is composed.*

According to the Japanese, the plane looking like the Korean airliner that was shot down at 03:29 was intercepted by fighter A.[11] Its tracking line begins at 03:20 and leads to the destruction of the plane at 03:29. This "Korean plane" does not appear on the Kirkpatrick map. It cannot, for time and distance reasons, have been the one the Soviets tracked from Kamchatka. As we can piece together from other evidence, it came in from the North Pacific, crossed the Kurils, and arrived at Sakhalin before any of the events shown on the Kirkpatrick map.

That map strings together data from the flight of three different aircraft that serve its purpose. And it ignores the aircraft whose shootdown was featured in the Japanese story, which the United States wanted to consign to oblivion. Starting over the Bering Sea and ending at 03:38 west of Sakhalin and north of Moneron, the track Mrs. Kirkpatrick's map shows is a fabrication, largely made out of real data referring to aircraft other than KAL 007, chosen to support the U.S. version of events. Figure 4 corrects the errors on the Kirkpatrick map.

The Admiral's Frustration

S oon after the disaster, Adm. Isamu Imamura, in command of the Japanese Maritime Safety Agency's search, was frustrated by JMSA's inability to locate any debris from the Korean plane in the area where it was said to have crashed. On September 3 the admiral told the press, which had been assembled at JMSA headquarters in Wakkanai, that "if no debris from the Korean airliner is found in the next few hours, we must accept the evidence and conclude that the plane did not crash in this area."

A brief look at the geography and ocean currents in the region will help explain the admiral's insight. Most important is the massive current of warm water, the Tsushima Shio, that flows from south to north on the eastern side of the Sea of Japan. It flows all year round, warming southern Sakhalin—and determining the direction in which floating debris drifts. Debris from a crash in the south drifts north. Debris from a crash in the north drifts north. It will not drift south against the dominant current.

Sakhalin Island

Sakhalin Island is an isolated region in the North Pacific, little known to Westerners. The island was a penal colony under the tsars. Its southern half was a Japanese territory known as Karafuto, but was reclaimed by Russia after the Second World War. Often referred to as hell on earth, the island is heavily militarized, and most of it has been off-limits to foreigners. Separated in the north from Siberia by a narrow channel of water, which is iced over during the winter months, Sakhalin is a tongue-shaped strip of land that measures no more than fifteen miles at the narrowest point. Its terrain is mountainous and heavily wooded, with a mixture of steep cliffs and sloping hills. There is frequent fog during June, July, and August because of the warm Tsushima Shio flowing from the south. As it travels through the Tatar Gulf (which is the northern end of the Sea of Japan), the current flows at speeds of one to two knots. Near the shore, because of tidal action, an intermittent current sometimes flows weakly south, at speeds of less than one knot. Ports in the north are closed in winter because of ice. Nevelsk and other ports in the south remain open under the influence of the warm water from the south.

It was in Nevelsk that the Soviet authorities later turned over to the Japanese floating debris from the Korean airliner. There is a ferry service from Nevelsk to the island of Moneron to the southwest. The ferry operates all year long because Moneron, bathed in the warm waters of the Tsushima Shio, is never icebound. Kholmsk, another port on southern Sakhalin, is the administrative center of western Sakhalin. The Murmansk divers who worked on the sea bottom searching for aircraft wreckage were based here. There is little information about the town of Pravda, the small fishing village over which, according to the Soviets, one of their fighters "stopped the flight of an intruder plane" at 06:24 Sakhalin time, on September 1.

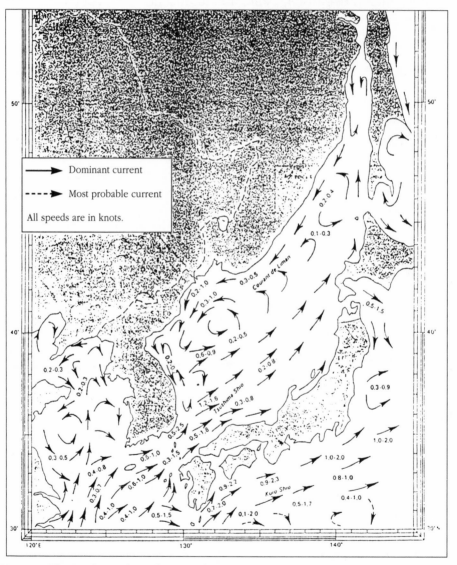

Figure 5. *The Tsushima Shio. The powerful north-flowing current that dominates the eastern side of the Sea of Japan. It carried floating debris from KAL 007 north from its true crash site off Honshu to the beaches of Sakhalin and Hokkaido, where it was found nine days later.*

West of southern Sakhalin is the small island of Moneron, still known to the Japanese as Kaiba. Moneron has a mild climate and provides an abundance of fish. The Tsushima Shio plays very much the same role here as the Gulf Stream does in Cornwall and Brittany. It can reach a speed of two knots in the vicinity of the island. This powerful current, originating in the Tsushima Strait between Korea and Japan, sends branches to the east through the Tsugaru Strait, which separates Honshu, the main Japanese island, from Hokkaido, and again, farther north, through La Pérouse (Soya) Strait, which separates Hokkaido from Sakhalin. In these two narrow straits the current can reach a speed of up to seven knots. Because of the year-round current, any object that falls into the water in the vicinity of Moneron drifts north, never south. It is impossible for any object to drift from Moneron down to the Japanese coast.

Iwao Koyama and the Phantom Current

Iwao Koyama was the head of the local office of the Japan Broadcasting Company NHK, in Wakkanai, a fishing village in the extreme north of Hokkaido. The KAL 007 affair brought Wakkanai to the center of world attention. As station head and reporter, Iwao Koyama was at the heart of events as they unfolded before his eyes. When the flurry of interest died down, he wrote a book called *Kieta Itai (The Bodies That Disappeared)* based on the voluminous notes he took at the time. The title refers to the 269 persons who perished on Flight 007, not one of whose bodies was ever found.

On page 36 of his book Koyama reproduces a map he got from government sources showing the way in which debris from the airliner supposedly drifted from Moneron to the Hokkaido coast. Being neither a navigator nor a sailor, he published the map untouched, using it as the basis for his observations. It shows the island of Moneron and the search area. The latter was laid out to deal with a crash north of Moneron or near it to the east or west and extended far to the north to take into account ocean drift. It excluded the Japanese coastline. The map shows three separate search areas. The first is the American, northwest of Moneron and completely separated from the other two. The second, north of Moneron, corresponds to the sighting by a Japanese fishing vessel, the *Chidori Maru*. It is indicated as the Soviet search area. The third is located near the coast of Sakhalin, close to Nevelsk.

Although floating debris was recovered north of Moneron on the day of the crash by the Soviets and, no doubt, also by Admiral Imamura's own vessels, debris identifiable as coming from the Korean airliner did not arrive in the search area for nine days. At that time it was found by the Soviets in Sakhalin territorial waters near Nevelsk and, simultaneously, by the Japanese police along the northern Hokkaido coast near Wakkanai. To explain the presence of debris that was found simultaneously in the vicinity of Nevelsk and along the Japanese coast, Koyama's map shows a series of small arrows between the supposed location of the crash (the position of the *Chidori Maru*) and Nevelsk on the Sakhalin coast. These arrows point *across* the direction of current flow and *contrary* to the direction of the wind, which was east-southeast at the time. The debris, once it managed to overcome the opposing current and wind, was then picked up by a second series of arrows, descending from north to south, along the coast of Sakhalin. These arrows are supposed to represent a countercurrent that enabled debris from the airplane, which had supposedly crashed to the north of Moneron, to drift all the way down to the Japanese coast after a brief stopover along the Sakhalin coastline.

When I met Koyama following the publication of his book, I mentioned to him that his "countercurrent" did not exist. Current reversals do occur from time to time along the coast due to strong tides and opposing winds, but these are always local and temporary, lasting at most a few hours until the tide changes. To prove to him that the countercurrent did not exist, I had brought with me the Japanese version of the *Nautical Instructions* used by ships to determine current movement. I explained to him that the first debris (from the tail of the Boeing 747) had turned up at *exactly the same time* at Nevelsk and Wakkanai. How was this possible if debris from Wakkanai had first to pass by Nevelsk to take advantage of his countercurrent? Not only would it have had to move against the current and the wind, but against time as well.

Moreover, if Koyama's countercurrent really did exist, Nevelsk would not be a temperate port, one that is *never* icebound. For his supposed countercurrent flowing from the north would have had to be a cold current, just as the Kogarashi, the north wind, is always cold. There does exist a cold current from the north, the Liman current. But it does not reach Sakhalin. It is located on the other side of the Tatar Strait and washes up against the shores of Siberia, which partially accounts for the severity of the winters along that coast. If there had existed a regular countercurrent flowing south along the coast of Sakhalin, it would have imprisoned everything in its path in a cage of ice at the first sign of the north wind. This was obviously not the case. Koyama was embarrassed at having been taken in so easily.

I had met Koyama on Hokkaido in a small bar where we took shelter from a storm. Although the wind blew fiercely, we were protected by the double-pane glass windows that are characteristic of the island known for its cold. Somewhat numb from the sudden warmth, we drank to our resolve to get to the truth of the KAL 007 mystery with several lilliputian cups of warm sake. The conversation soon took a philosophical turn, and we decided that whatever the apparent good faith and authority of our sources of information, we would always exercise an independent sense of critical judgment.

The Search Area

Whenever maritime search efforts are undertaken, an examination of the currents is essential for defining the search area. In the case of Flight 007, the search area went around the island of Moneron and extended far to the north to take current flow into account. But the search area delimited by Admiral Imamura around Moneron did not include the Japanese coast. That was because it was impossible for debris to drift from Moneron to the coast of Japan.

The first step, after studying the current map, was to determine the point of impact as precisely as possible. The admiral had at his disposal radar information that placed the disappearance of the airliner at 46°30′ N, 141°30′ E, northeast of Moneron, over a small area of international water between the territorial waters of Sakhalin and those of Moneron. The airplane that disappeared at this spot was believed to have exploded in flight at an altitude of 33,000 feet.

From the explosions of the Pan Am jetliner near Lockerbie and of the UTA plane in the Ténéré desert, which occurred at similar altitudes, it is known that airplane debris can fall over an area three to six miles long and a half mile to a mile wide. This limits the dispersion of the debris, at the moment of impact, to a circle several nautical miles in diameter. Any debris that fell within this circle and was light would have remained on the surface, drifting slowly north under the influence of the current. The wind, which blew from the east-southeast, would have helped push this material away from the Japanese coast.

In the first few hours of the search, the admiral was given a second position, one based on the sighting of the fishermen on the *Chidori Maru*. The ship's crew had observed a plane at the moment it crashed into the sea, noting its position about 1,500 meters east-southeast of a point 46°35′ N, 141°16′ E. Because the plane had exploded just above the surface of the water, the dispersal area was much smaller, no greater than several hundred feet. This was equivalent to a circle of about half a nautical mile in diameter (approximately 3,000 feet) at the moment of impact. But according to the admiral's findings, not only did the two areas—the one indicated by radar tracking and the one of the *Chidori Maru*'s sighting—not overlap, they were more than twelve miles apart.

Admiral Imamura was also given official information about a third impact point, situated far from the other two. On September 2 the Soviet ambassador to Japan, Vladimir Pavlov, told the Japanese government that the Soviet Union had tracked an airplane that had crashed in the water west of Moneron Island. West of Moneron! The Japanese radar track had placed the point of impact northeast of that island, and the *Chidori Maru* sighting had placed it north of it. A distance of more than thirty miles separated the first and third points of impact.

The Debris

The admiral was also baffled for another reason. During the first week after the disaster, no floating debris from the Korean airliner was found in any of the three impact areas indicated to him. If the airliner had really crashed here, some debris would have been found in at least one of the three areas by JMSA patrol boats. I am specifically referring to debris from the Korean airliner. For, although they found no debris from Flight 007, Admiral Imamura's patrol boats, which kept a close watch on the Soviet ships in the area, saw them hauling in large amounts of material from the surface but were unable to approach close enough to determine exactly what it was. Even at night the Soviet ships continued to work, with the aid of searchlights.

The Soviet ships collected debris from three principal areas, only one of which, that of the *Chidori Maru* sighting, corresponded to one of the points of impact the admiral had been given. The *Chidori Maru* sighting was north of Moneron. Another area the Soviets were searching was approximately twelve miles east, near the territorial waters around Sakhalin. Any debris floating on the surface in these two areas was collected. The Soviets then concentrated their efforts on a third area, which was well within Sakhalin's territorial waters.

Here, approximately 5 NM from the shore and following a depth line of 100 meters (55 fathoms) along the ocean bottom, an impressive number of ships had gathered in a narrow oval space 2 NM wide and 9 NM long. The majority were fishing vessels and minesweepers. They combed every square inch of the ocean floor with steel cables and trawl nets. On September 8 more than eighty vessels, including a large number of trawlers, were in the area.[1] All of this intense activity took place approximately six miles within Soviet territorial waters, an area where the JMSA's patrol boats had no right to enter. They could observe the Soviets on radar and through their binoculars, but were unable to determine what the Soviets were hauling up from the seafloor. The Soviets said nothing. Officially, they had still not found anything. Admiral Imamura became increasingly frustrated. There was no doubt in his mind that the Boeing 747 hadn't fallen in the area where he was looking for it and that the plane he was ordered to look for was not the Boeing airliner.

In Wakkanai, without realizing that wrecks other than that of KAL 007 were involved, Iwao Koyama had the wit to realize that Soviet trawlers collecting surface debris had no means of sending or receiving coded information and would have to communicate with their base in the clear. He took a radio and a recorder up the hill at Wakkanai and, sure enough, could receive VHF Russian-language messages in the clear between the fishing boats and Nevelsk. He recorded them and got the gist of their contents. Nevelsk was instructing the fishermen what to do with the debris and bodies they collected. Koyama was aware of the importance and the sensitive nature of the information that the Soviets were recovering bodies. He did not report the news but instead sent the tape to his head office in Tokyo, thus depriving himself of the chance to make a well-deserved scoop. Sometime later he decided he would like to review it carefully. But no. He was no longer granted access to his own tape. It was in a safe somewhere. Probably not NHK's.

Out at sea it appeared as if the Soviets were the only ones collecting debris. Up above, the sky was crisscrossed by Soviet, Japanese, and American planes and helicopters, which flew at low altitude. To help locate the wreckage, several Orion P-3C antisubmarine planes patrolled the surface in close formation. There was great confusion throughout the search area and a very real risk of open conflict. The Americans had brought in an AWAC accompanied by six F-15 fighters from Okinawa. These served as reinforcements for the fifty-odd American F-16s already stationed at Misawa. That amount of force was more appropriate to a small war than to what was supposed to be the humanitarian search-and-rescue effort on behalf of the victims of the crash of a civilian airliner.

On September 2, a P-3C belonging to the American Navy discovered, south of Moneron, a small inflatable life raft, which was immediately picked up by a helicopter. It was never learned where the raft came from or, indeed, whether anybody had been on board.[2] There are, however, no life rafts, large or small, on a Boeing 747. The inflatable chutes are used instead. Having learned of the discovery, Admiral Imamura immediately ordered the patrol ship *Chokai,* which was in the area, to move in as close as possible to the spot where it was picked up. The *Chokai* went but found only an orange marker flag. Did it come from the inflatable raft? Or from an aircraft searching for survivors? No information was forthcoming. The raft was, however, the first hint I had that there might have been a crash south of Moneron (as well as northeast, north, and west).

I knew, of course, that most, if not all, of the crashes near Moneron had to have been those of military aircraft. But at first we had no documentary evidence of that, or what kinds of aircraft were involved. Soon, however, we found evidence of the kinds of aircraft in newspaper photographs of debris in the hands of the JMSA and Hokkaido police officers. But we also needed a way of proving where and when the floating debris had been found. In the case of debris washed up along the northern coast of Hokkaido, we had press reports that told us the date and place of the find. We still needed the same data for the debris found north of Moneron. We got it some years later when the headquarters of the Japanese Maritime Safety Agency in Tokyo made available to John Keppel and me a log of events during the search off Sakhalin that the JMSA had prepared for publication but had released only to a few people.

The log includes a special JMSA report, dated September 5, 1983, that mentions that fifty-four pieces of debris were collected north of Moneron by JMSA patrol vessels, but stated that none of them had any relation to the Korean airliner. Indeed they did not. From a news source we had the photograph reproduced in Figure 6, which shows pieces of debris from this series bearing tags numbered from 29 to 33.

Debris number 31 is a piece of a flap from a small to midsized airplane. The flap is unusual in that its leading edge (the front edge) is square. Most leading edges are streamlined. The only plane to have flaps with a square leading edge is the high-tech, two-seat fighter the F-lll or its electronic-warfare twin the EF-111. Debris number 31 reveals a sandwichlike structure made of aluminum sheet and honeycomb material. A two-inch-wide mark parallel to the leading edge appears to have been made by a flap brake when it was retracted. The brake holds the flap in position and acts as a vibration damper. Number 31 also shows another mark, at an angle of sixty degrees with the leading edge. This line is characteristic of variable-geometry supersonic aircraft. It represents the maximum sweep angle of the wing when it is withdrawn into the fuselage. Its position corresponds to the shape of the swing wings of the F-111/EF-111, which are the only planes on which the edges of the wing cavity are parallel to the fuselage and make an angle of sixty degrees with the wing in their swept-back position. On other variable-geometry aircraft (the F-111 was a precursor), the fairing that protects the pivot makes an angle of ninety degrees with the wing axis and the mark it leaves is perpendicular to the leading edge.

The photograph in Figure 6 shows another piece of debris that can only have come from a high-performance military aircraft and again appears to have been of U.S. manufacture. It bears the tag number 34 and is part of a pilot's ejection seat, of which the propulsive charges appear to have been fired. It is the shell for a McDonnell Douglas ACES II Zero Zero ejection seat, or one similar to it (see Figure 6).[3] A Pentagon specialist to whom I showed the photograph recognized it immediately, before I even had a chance to tell him where it came from. The implication here is not only that we are dealing with the crash, north of Moneron, of a U.S. military aircraft; it is also that the pilot, his plane having been hit by Soviet fire, sought to eject and parachute.

We have no evidence that any U.S. pilot parachuted successfully, still less that one was recovered alive by the Soviets. Later in the text, however, I will review the factors involved in such possibilities.

Before discussing floating debris coming from the Korean airliner itself, I should mention other Japanese press photographs of military debris we obtained—sometimes with and, unfortunately, sometimes without their accompanying news stories. With one possible exception, these pieces of debris were picked up on or just off the northern beaches of Hokkaido on La Pérouse Strait and the Sea of Okhotsk. That means, as we have seen in our study of ocean currents, that they cannot have come from crashes north of Moneron.

Figure 6. *Floating debris from military aircraft recovered north of Moneron Island in the first three days by the Japanese Maritime Safety Agency. The item in the left of the photograph appears to be part of the wing flap from an EF-111. The item in the top of the photograph is a pilot's ejection seat, whose propulsive charges appear to have been fired—that is to say, the ejection seat was used.*

The recovery of one piece of debris, in particular, is of interest in that, as well as providing information as to the kind of aircraft involved, it gives us a more specific indication of where the crash took place. The piece of debris was found on or just off the beach on September 10 at Mombetsu, which is near the middle of the long curve that forms the Hokkaido coastline bordering the Sea of Okhotsk. The photograph we have shows a large fragment of an engine cowling that bears a Pratt and Whitney logo. So did KAL 007's engines. But the point here is that the Pratt and Whitney logo on the Mombetsu fragment and those on KAL 007's engines are not the same. We are dealing with another airplane, also of American manufacture. A photograph of a similar fragment was given—along with other photographs of debris ostensibly from KAL 007—by the Russian government to the U.S. next of kin in 1993. The edges of the two fragments indicate that the two were torn, presumably on impact with the water, from the same engine cowling. Before we can see the implications of this for the location of the crash point—in the Sea of Japan or the Sea of Okhotsk—we would need to know where the Soviets recovered their fragment. The crash may have been in the Sea of Okhotsk; the Soviets did not turn the fragment over to the Japanese together with the debris given them in September 1983.

Among other photographs of military debris printed by the Japanese press is one of the throttle quadrant from a two-engine jet in the hands of a Japanese policeman. It was among the debris, ostensibly from KAL 007, given to the Japanese by the Soviets in September 1983 and probably came from a crash north of Moneron.

Probably from a crash in the Sea of Okhotsk is what appears to be a bulkhead, made of carbon fiber, possibly from the nose, or from an external wing tank, of an airplane the size of a fighter.[4] (See Figure 7.) In any event, it is not from a Boeing 747. It was found on September 14 at Abashiri, farther east along the Hokkaido coast, about halfway from Mombetsu to the peninsula on the eastern end of the beach. Abashiri is south of the point where, six years later, a Japanese boat fishing for sole on the sandy bottom accidentally got a titanium wing fragment caught in its net. It appears to have come from an SR-71 (Blackbird), a U.S. high-speed, high-altitude reconnaissance aircraft. The bulkhead could have been from the same crash as the wing fragment, but we have no way of proving when the wing fragment went into the water.

It is worth saying a word here about the difference between sunken debris and floating debris as evidence. Floating debris comes complete with its own clock and calendar. That is to say, if you know where and when it arrived along the beach or in the water, and know the direction and speed of the current, you have a good way of knowing whether or not it was associated with a given crash of which you know the time and place. If you know the time but not the place of the crash, the piece of floating debris will give you the basis for a good estimate of the location of the crash. Sunken debris tells you precisely where the crash took place—but it tells you nothing about the time. Sunken debris could have entered the water at any time prior to its recovery.

For another piece of debris that was mentioned in the JMSA log, the meaning is not yet fully established, though I have spent a great deal of time on it. It was found twenty-nine miles north of Moneron on September 10 by a JMSA patrol boat. Along with the report on its recovery, the JMSA log that I have mentioned contains a sketch of what I will call the N3 piece, because it carries the mark N3. (See Figure 8, page 46.) The sketch presents it as the aileron from a light twin-engine propeller plane approximately the size of a Beechcraft 18. It was not that, but something more interesting.[5]

Figure 7. *The bulkhead. Floating debris found on September 14 at Abashiri toward the eastern end of the Hokkaido beach on the Sea of Okhotsk. The wheellike object appears to be a bulkhead from a military aircraft, of which at least one crashed in the Sea of Okhotsk.*

Starting on September 10, along the northern coast of Hokkaido on the Sea of Okhotsk, airplane debris, some of it from KAL 007 and some, as we have seen, from military aircraft was found farther to the south and east with every passing day. That was entirely normal, for the current flows down the coast toward the east.

However, toward the eastern end of the northern Hokkaido coast at this time, we see a strange phenomenon. The headless torso of a child was found on September 8 by a fisherman off the Shiretoko peninsula opposite the Kuril Islands. Other fragmentary human remains were subsequently found, but always farther and farther to the west—in a direction opposite to that in which other KAL 007 and military debris moved on the western part of the coast. That appears to point to a crash in the Sea of Okhotsk from which floating debris was blown onto the Hokkaido beach by a north, or northeast, wind. The easternmost fragments arrived on the beach first presumably because they were the nearest to it.

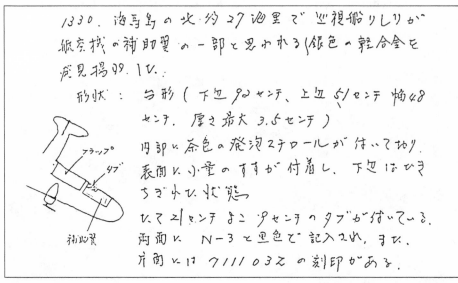

Figure 8. *The original JMSA presentation of the N3 piece. This is the page from the JMSA report, which presents the N3 piece of debris as part of the aileron from a light aircraft. The debris was recovered north of Moneron Island by the JMSA on September 10, 1983. I later saw JMSA photographs that indicated that the piece was in fact part of the tail fin of a missile.*

Were it not for the body of the child, we could think that the human remains came from a military crash in the Sea of Okhotsk. The media in Japan and elsewhere interpreted them as coming from KAL 007. But the time at which the child's body was found, and the fact that it does not fit what is known about KAL 007 passengers, appear to rule that out. Fragments of glass were embedded in the body. There is, however, no glass in an airliner cabin other than an occasional pair of spectacles. The phenomenon deserves further investigation.

As I have indicated, for the first eight days after the disaster no debris from the Korean airliner was found. On September 9 the Soviet ambassador in Tokyo told the Japanese government that the Soviets had found four fragments near Moneron, for each of which he gave the coordinates.[6] On the tenth, a JMSA patrol boat found two pieces of debris from the Korean airliner south of Moneron off the mouth of La Pérouse Strait in locations that implied that they would have been carried north by the current between Moneron and the Sakhalin coast rather than east through the strait into the Sea of Okhotsk. Three fragments from the vertical fin of the tail of the airliner, each bearing part of the aircraft's registration number HL-7442 on it, were found on September 10 at Sarafutsu on the Hokkaido shore 10 miles east and south off Wakkanai. A fourth fragment of the airliner's vertical fin, also bearing a part of the registration number, appeared at the same time ninety-three miles to the north along the west coast of Sakhalin near Nevelsk.

That this debris could not have come from a crash site for KAL 007 north of Moneron was recognized by the senior JMSA officers concerned. Adm. Kessoku Konomu, who was supervising the search effort from JMSA headquarters at Otaru on the west coast of Hokkaido, later cited to me both the current (north of Moneron flowing only north) and the wind (blowing from the ESE at the time) as reasons why a KAL 007 crash north of Moneron was impossible. He told me he concluded that it was impossible for the debris collected on the beaches of the Sea of Okhotsk to have come from the Tatar Gulf.

As if to corroborate the admiral's statements, debris from the Korean airliner, primarily pieces of honeycomb panels identified as coming from the 747's cabin, were found far to the south, in the Sea of Japan, and in the Tsugaru Strait between Hokkaido and Honshu. The story of these fragments and their discovery adds another bizarre twist to the circumstances surrounding the disappearance of Flight 007. The following account is based on articles published in the Japanese press at the time of the disaster.

Tatewaki Toshio is a Japanese kelp gatherer, age fifty-nine, from the village of Sai, on the Shimo Kita peninsula. The peninsula juts out in the shape of a fist into the Tsugaru Strait, which separates the main island of Japan from Hokkaido to the north. On September 13, 1983, at around five in the morning, he went, as he usually does, to his favorite spot near Nakaisoya, two miles from his home. Tatewaki Toshio collects seaweed, and a few days earlier he had found a spot where a large quantity of fresh, tender seaweed stretched along rock that just broke the surface of the water. The best time for harvesting is early in the morning, when the seaweed is still cool and wet from the night before. Toshio rose early and followed the road along the shore. The sun had just risen and was still hidden behind the hills that dotted the peninsula. A soft light bathed the shore, and sharp glimmers of silver were reflected off the calm mirror of the sea, which was occasionally disturbed by the lapping waves.

Low tide had left the rocks exposed. It was ideal weather for gathering seaweed. Preparing his tools, nothing more than a knife blade on a long handle and a sack, he waded into the water, his attention then caught by a brilliant object lying flat on a dry rock, as if it had been thrown up by the wind or an unusually powerful wave. Curious, he approached the object and picked it up. Approximately nine by twelve inches long and about half an inch thick, it was made of shiny metal, "as if it were new," and was extremely light. It was made of a brownish honeycomb core covered with aluminum. There were marks along the edges as if it had been broken or torn. Tatewaki Toshio felt that it was the sort of material that could be used to build planes. In fact, hadn't there been an accident twelve days earlier? Could this be . . .? No, it's not possible, he thought. The crash had been more than four hundred miles north of here, and this debris couldn't have drifted here against the current. Intrigued just the same, Tatewaki Toshio took the fragment with him.

That evening, over a cup of sake with his friends, he decided to surprise them and, pulling out the piece of metal, said laughing, "Look. I found a piece of the Korean plane!" Naturally, no one believed a word of what he said, but Tatewaki Toshio was still proud of his catch, which he displayed on top of the television set in his living room. Three days later, on September 16, the evening news from the Hokkaido TV station, HBC, broadcast an update from Wakkanai on the search for the remains of Flight 007. As Toshio sat in front of the set with his family, something suddenly caught his attention. There on-screen he watched a policeman from "the north" (Wakkanai is at the extreme northern end of the island of Hokkaido) hold up a fragment of the Korean plane exactly like the one he had found and which was now sitting on top of his television. He couldn't take his eyes from the screen. His intuition had been right after all. It really was a piece of the Korean plane. But what about the current?

That evening the fragment was the center of conversation. Tatewaki Toshio hardly slept and the following day went to see Mr. Ishizawa, the mayor of the village, to tell him about his discovery. Mr. Ishizawa informed the police and the JMSA at once and called a meeting of the town council. Other debris might have drifted to shore, and it was decided to organize a search along the beaches of the community. The entire village took part in the expedition. Members of the press, journalists, photographers, and even a television crew joined in. A neighbor of Tatewaki Toshio's, Mr. Miyano, a businessman and owner of a small hotel, led a group of six men, who explored a beach near Nagahama that was extremely difficult to reach. On the very first day, Mr. Miyano's team found nearly a dozen fragments, including one that was more than six feet square. In all, they found more than twenty pieces of wreckage.

The news was soon published in the papers. Other debris had been found in the Tsugaru Strait and the Bay of Uchiura, along the southern coast of Hokkaido. The JMSA decided to mount a search operation with whatever means were available in Aomori, the regional capital. This included the patrol ship *Oirase,* helicopters, and land-based search teams organized by the townships and local fishing associations. But one thing bothered the authorities. How did debris from the Korean airliner, which was supposed to have crashed in the Tatar Gulf near Moneron, drift so far south against the current? The papers constructed elaborate hypotheses that had the debris crossing the Sea of Okhotsk and the Kuril Islands, and descending the Pacific coast. Finally on September 19, the JMSA Hydrographic Service published a report. According to it, the debris would not have been able to drift from Moneron to the places where it had been found in the Tsugaru Strait. Because of the Tsushima Shio it would not have been able to drift south in the Sea of Japan. From the Pacific it could not have gone against the east-flowing current in the Tsugaru Strait.

Consequently, though JMSA's report did not say so, the debris found in the Tsugaru Strait could only have come from a spot in the Sea of Japan south of the entrance to the strait. This explained why no debris from the Korean airliner had been found near Moneron for nine days. As Admiral Imamura suspected, the Korean Boeing had not fallen in the area, but much farther south. It had simply taken time for the debris to drift north to Moneron. The mystery of the disappearance of Flight 007 began to resolve itself. If it were admitted that the plane hadn't fallen near Moneron but much farther south, the mystery would have been partly solved. The absence of debris during the first few days, the time it took for pieces to appear, their dispersion throughout the area, and their presence so far south—it all began to make sense.

But now another problem came into focus. If the Korean Air Lines jetliner didn't fall near Moneron, what would account for the radar data, the debris there on the day of the disaster, and the plane explosions sighted by the *Chidori Maru?* If it wasn't KAL 007 that had crashed near Moneron, what had? As long as it was possible to claim that Flight 007 had crashed there, it was also possible to obscure the meaning of the data, which would otherwise imply that several planes had been shot down, and to camouflage the whole affair under the guise of a single accident—thus anesthetizing public suspicion with facile explanations. If, however, it became clear that 007 had not crashed near Moneron but four hundred miles to the south, the explosion sighted by the *Chidori Maru* could not have been the Korean Air Lines Boeing 747. This was a possibility that no one in authority was prepared to accept. To avoid reversing themselves in public, exposing the United States, and throwing doubt on the good faith of their own role, a decision had to be made and quickly.

The dilemma was elegantly resolved, at least from the Japanese government's point of view, on September 20. A spokesman for the Japanese Air Self-Defense Forces (JASDF) announced that the debris found in the south was from target drones used by the JASDF to train their pilots. *Se non è vero, è ben trovato* (a good explanation, even if not true). In Japan, official statements carry a great deal of authority and are rarely questioned. If the JASDF claimed that the debris found south of the crash area came from target drones, the problems arising from their appearance there were resolved. The search efforts in the south were called off. From that day on there was no further mention of the debris in the Tsugaru Strait. When I began my own search along the Japanese beaches, the debris for which I was looking had officially long since ceased to exist.

The JASDF announcement prevented further speculation about the origin of the debris, but did not necessarily make the problem go away. Debris had been found south of Hokkaido in the Tsugaru Strait and had been registered at the time of discovery by the local police administration, who kept a record in their archives. The debris was sent to the airbase at Chitose, where an expert commission examined it. They identified the pieces as coming from a Boeing 747. Their report is kept in an archive somewhere. The JASDF later rejected the commission's findings, declaring that the debris had not come from the Korean jetliner but from target drones. This debris was, however, returned to Korean Air Lines, a fact that was confirmed to me by Adm. Masayoshi Kato. Was all of the debris returned? I have no idea. But if the debris did not come from a Korean Air Lines plane, why was it returned to the airline?

The Wing Section

During this time, there was increased activity around Moneron. On September 16 the Soviet Navy salvage vessel *Georgi Kozmin,* working with a manned submersible, hauled up from the bottom at a depth of only 160 meters what appeared to be an airplane wing section approximately ten meters long. None of the Japanese papers, with the exception of the September 17 issue of *Too Nippo,* the local Aomori paper on northern Honshu, reported the news. No English-language or foreign newspaper reported the incident. If the Boeing 747 had in fact crashed there, the wing would have had to come from the plane, and this would have been a sensational discovery. Why the conspiracy of silence? The Soviets said nothing about it, even though Ambassador Pavlov had announced the discovery of four fragments on September 9. Evidently the Soviets didn't think the wing section came from the Korean plane.

The American Navy must have known about the discovery, however, for the news came from the JMSA from Otaru, where units of the Seventh

Fleet were stationed. What was the reason for the Navy's silence? If the Soviets had dredged up a ten-meter wing section from the Korean airliner, it meant they had located the wreck and were in a good position to find the black boxes as well. Is it likely that the Navy would simply have sat around and allowed the Soviets to recover the black boxes right under their nose without saying a word? When, ten days later, on September 26, the Soviets turned over to the Japanese patrol ship *Tsugaru,* in the presence of ICAO (International Civil Aviation Organization) officials, the first debris found in their territorial waters, the wing section was not among them. If it did not come from the Korean airliner, where did it come from?

A few days after the wing section was found, the American Navy announced that one of its ships, the *Narragansett,* had heard the localizer for the airliner's black boxes. But whereas the *Georgi Kozmin* had recovered the wing section north of Moneron, near where the *Chidori Maru* had watched an aircraft explode, the *Narragansett* said it had heard the localizer in a different location, northwest of the island. Observers from the ICAO and Mr. Subrenat, representing France, which was responsible for decoding the boxes in the event they were found, were officially invited to be present during salvage operations. It was only a false alarm—or a red herring. The black boxes were not found and the observers were returned to the mainland.

At about this time Adm. Masayoshi Kato of JMSA announced that an American warship working on its own had discovered a large piece of the fuselage of the Korean airliner in a spot that was far from the other search areas. This news was never confirmed by the Pentagon.[7] Years later, when I met Admiral Kato, I asked him for details about that piece of fuselage, especially about its location far from the other search areas. Unfortunately the admiral was by then as laconic as the Pentagon. The Navy's find sounds like a sunken piece, perhaps at its intensive search area NW of Moneron. If so, it too must have come from an aircraft other than KAL 007.

As Iwao Koyama demonstrated in his book, the Soviets and Americans each mounted their own search efforts in different locations, as if each was looking for its own planes, while keeping an eye on its adversary to see what he was finding.

Within their territorial waters the Soviets searched two distinct areas, one near Nevelsk on the Sakhalin coast, the other just north of Moneron. Out in international waters they concentrated their search activities north of Moneron, while the Americans operated nineteen miles away, 16 NM northwest of the island. The JMSA patrolled a square area 100 by 150 km. Despite all their efforts, the wreckage of the Boeing was not found. And yet the average depth where the giant plane—whose fuselage is over 230 feet long—was supposed to have crashed was no more than 160 meters (525 feet). Under these conditions, if the plane had really crashed in this vicinity, it would certainly have been found. Once more Admiral Imamura's words come to mind: If they didn't find the plane, it's because it simply wasn't there.

After more than two months of intensive effort, the search to locate the wreckage of Flight 007 ended on November 10, 1983, when American and Soviet ships left the area. The Soviets made no statement. The American Navy stated that it was virtually certain the Korean airliner had not fallen in the international waters around Moneron. The mystery of Flight 007, which, for a brief moment, looked as though it might be solved, became more impenetrable than ever. Planes had crashed in other parts of the world in thousands of feet of water and had been located, and the bodies recovered, sometimes within days by a single ship. How was it possible that a massive search effort, involving hundreds of ships, was unable, after two months of intense effort, to turn up any sign of the Boeing 747 or its passengers, in a basin of water whose average depth was barely twice the length of the plane's fuselage?

Flight 007 did not crash near Moneron. The delay in the appearance of the debris in the Tatar Gulf and its dispersion, as well as the south-north ocean current, lead to the conclusion that the plane fell well to the south, in the Sea of Japan. The debris that was found in that area supports this hypothesis. But by declaring the debris in the south to be from target drones and not from the 747, the JASDF brought an end to the search there. Could the debris there really have come from target drones? The commission that initially examined the material had identified it as coming from a Boeing 747. It was eventually turned over to Korean Air Lines. To prove its origin, I needed to conduct an independent study of the debris found south of Hokkaido.

Let us return now from the chronology of the events themselves to the chronology of my investigation.

The Cemetery of Tsugaru

When I began my investigation in Japan, I found it impossible to get my hands on any debris at all, regardless of where it had been found along the coast. Even the debris from the "target drones" couldn't be located. The first fragments had been found by Tatewaki Toshio, the kelp gatherer, who lived in the village of Sai, on the Shimo Kita peninsula. His discovery had alerted public opinion and soon led to the discovery of other debris in the region and the beginning of a search operation based on Aomori. I decided to question Tatewaki in the hope of gaining additional information. On November 14, 1989, I left Tokyo on the night train to Aomori, capital of the Aomori Prefecture.

Aomori was an excellent place from which to prepare the trip to Sai, which is in the extreme north of Honshu. On the train I had a berth in a spacious sleeper that came equipped with a bathrobe and slippers. I arrived in Aomori the following morning at 10:28. By 11:00 I was at the hotel. At 11:05 I telephoned the local newspaper, the *Too Nippo,* to set up an appointment. At 11:25 my taxi dropped me off at the paper's offices, and at 11:35 I had the information I had come for, including clippings and photographs. By 12:05 I had a complete file on the debris located in the region, and I left the office quite satisfied. I was now ready to begin my search.

Sai is a very small village tucked away at the extreme end of the Shimo Kita peninsula. You need a boat to get there. In the port I stopped at a stationery store to buy some maps of the area, a guide, and a book on the local Japanese dialect. This book turned out to be very useful.

After three hours on the bay's calm waters, I landed at Sai, which extends over a quarter of the peninsula. There are four thousand residents, divided among several small hamlets, including Old Sai, New Sai, Nakaisoya, and Koshiya. There were two small bed-and-breakfasts, where you could rent a room from the owner. I decided to stay in Nakaisoya, near the home of the kelp gatherer Tatewaki Toshio. By pure coincidence I found a room with the Miyano family, not far from Tatewaki's house. My host Mr. Miyano had himself led a search group along the beaches and had been given a place of honor in the municipal archives. He and his team had made several forays in the area of Nagahama, which is only accessible by boat. They had found there six fragments of honeycomb sandwich and a large number of fruit-juice cans with Korean markings. He was later told that the fragments he and his team had found did not belong to the Korean jetliner but to the target drones used by the JASDF. He had been disappointed when he heard this, for it was his initial impression that he had helped write an important page of contemporary history. For that reason he was very interested in my own investigation.

Mr. Miyano was a member of the town council. He telephoned the police station at Ooma, the capital of the canton, where they were storing the debris and the files, to ask permission for me to view the material. The police did not give an answer right away. They called me several times directly, however. Once at the Miyano home and then at town hall, where I had gone to consult the archives. They wanted to know who I was, who had authorized my visit, what I was doing, why I wanted to see the debris from the Korean plane, what was the purpose of my investigation, what was I going to do with the information, etc. With each new call there was a new series of questions. Finally at the end of the afternoon, a last call came to tell me that there was no information, and no archive containing information about the debris from the Korean plane. "No debris from the plane was ever found in this area," the police told me. "That's why there's no archive. There's no point in coming over."

About a half hour after the phone call from the police, there was a call from the JMSA in Aomori, whom Mr. Miyano had also telephoned, to tell me that they had no information, and no archive on the debris or the search effort. If I still wanted to visit them, however, I was entirely welcome.

The people in Sai were surprised at this turn of events and even more surprised that the police and the JMSA claimed to have no archive on the debris found in the region. They themselves had participated in the search, turned over the debris they had found to the police, and helped establish archives, both for the police department in Ooma and the JMSA in Aomori.

News travels fast in small communities, and the village of Sai was no exception. The village had been bubbling with excitement when news of our unexpected rebuff by the authorities got around. Then fortune smiled on us in the form of a rather ordinary bit of information that was broadcast on the evening news. It concerned an accident that had taken place in 1988 in Tokyo Bay involving a tourist boat and the submarine *Nadashio,* which resulted in many casualties. The broadcaster stated that it had been discovered that the submarine commander had changed the time of his maneuvers in the ship's log in order to absolve the submarine of any responsibility for the accident.

Everyone in Sai was disturbed by what the government had done. Within a day their faith in an impartial and reliable authority had been shaken three times in rapid succession. They were now ready to admit that the debris found in their village might have come from the Korean plane as they had initially believed. It was indeed possible that KAL 007 had not crashed at Moneron but at Tsugaru, their home. Why else would the police try to hide the fact by pretending that no debris had been found when they themselves had found it?

I showed Mr. Miyano a small piece of a Boeing 747 cabin floor that I had brought with me. He was impressed by its resemblance to the debris he had found. He held it respectfully and examined it a long time, then passed it around. I explained to him the other aspects of my investigation and the reasons why I felt that KAL 007 had not crashed at Moneron but much farther south, not far in fact from the village of Sai.

Mr. Miyano was not alone with me as I spoke. He had assembled a group of the village's senior members, together with some younger men. My speech clearly had an effect on them. Not only because I was a foreigner who spoke Japanese, which is unusual in itself, but also because I had taken the precaution of larding my speech with several expressions from the local dialect. Many of those assembled that evening were fishermen. I had been a professional fisherman for several years. Thanks to the cold beer and warm sake, they began to consider me as one of their own. I explained to them how I used to fish for tuna (the king of fish in Japan, where it is highly regarded for its use in sashimi) with a helicopter.

I took advantage of the situation to draw closer to the older members of the village and spoke to them about the history of Japan and ancient Japanese, which I had studied for years. Slowly they let down their guard and allowed themselves to introduce more of the local dialect into the formal Japanese that is spoken with foreigners. I gradually began to make friends with the villagers, who are so often ridiculed by people from the large cities for their local dialect. By association, my popularity spread to my host Mr. Miyano. He had taken the refusal by the police in Ooma and the JMSA as a personal offense. The villagers could hardly believe their ears. In that heightened situation there was a nearly perfect symbiosis between their frustration and the hot sake we were drinking. Soon they began to talk.

The village of Sai was well-known in the region as the "cemetery of the Tsugaru suicides." It hadn't sought its macabre reputation. It resulted from the location of the village at the extreme point of the Shimo Kita peninsula, which advanced sharply into the middle of the Tsugaru Strait. The strait was crisscrossed by a number of ferry services, which traveled from Aomori on Honshu to Hakodate on the other side of the strait. Perhaps more than any other nation, Japan abounds in tales of suicide. For some obscure reason, it seems that the Tsugaru Strait holds a special attraction for those in despair, somewhat like the Eiffel Tower in Paris. Every year, especially in the spring, several hapless individuals decide to end their days—preferably at nightfall— by throwing themselves into the water as the ferry leaves the entrance of the bay. Their bodies wash up on the beaches of Sai. Mr. Kashima, the secretary at the town hall, had helped find the bodies of many suicides on the canton's beaches. He lamented the injustice that had turned his village into the "cemetery of the Tsugaru suicides" and at the same time robbed it of the glory of becoming the village "closest to the real point of impact of KAL 007."

I assured Mr. Kashima that I would personally see to it that Sai's role in the case would go down in history, and then I realized it wasn't merely coincidence if debris from the Korean airliner had landed here in Sai, the cemetery of Tsugaru. The common denominator was the current. I learned that the bodies generally turned up three or four days after the news of their disappearance was announced in the papers. Since the news generally appeared the following day, this meant it took four or five days for the current to carry a drifting object from the entrance of the bay to the beaches of Sai. This was helpful in calculating the time it took for an object to drift with the current, for even if the current reached seven knots at Ooma point, its speed in the bay opposite Sai's beaches was much slower.

The village was now on my side, and my host got the township's approval to help me in my investigation, offsetting the cavalier attitude of the police and the JMSA. The villagers kept their word, and the next day a car provided by the town and driven by Mr. Kashima, my guide and driver for the day, came to pick me up early in the morning. If they couldn't show me any debris, they could at least show me the places where they had been found.

Our journey started with an interview with Tatewaki Toshio, who had found the first fragment, on a flat rock about a foot above the water and ten or twelve feet from the beach. I asked Tatewaki Toshio if the debris could have been there long before he found it. He told me he didn't think so because he went there every day to collect seaweed and it hadn't been there the night before. It must have arrived during the night, pushed by the waves. Mr. Kashima then drove us to Nakaisoya. I inspected and took photographs of the spot where the first debris from KAL 007 had been found, four hundred miles south of the area where the American, Soviet, and Japanese navies were ostensibly looking for it. We continued along the coast, stopping in the different places where other debris from the airliner had been found. I learned that almost thirty fragments had been found within a twelve-mile area, all of them honeycomb sandwich covered in aluminum, one of which was more than six feet long.

The road followed the coast for a while and then turned inland, for the hills here drop directly into the sea and the beach is no longer accessible from the road. The area is called Nagahama, and here, within an area of several miles, Mr. Miyano and his team had found their debris. Continuing along the road, which snaked through the surrounding hills, Mr. Kashima drove us to a place known as Hotoke-Ga-Ura (The Land of the Gods), from which spot we could reach the beach by means of a wooden footbridge nearly a mile long, anchored to the side of the cliff.

This was the point farthest along the peninsula from Sai at which debris had been found and, consequently, the southernmost point in Japan where debris from the Korean airliner was found in 1983. The path down was long and steep. We had just set foot on the beach when I noticed a piece of aluminum a few feet from me, apparently a piece of honeycomb material that had been worn by the weather. The same type of honeycomb and aluminum panel had been found by the villagers on this same beach six years earlier. It was identical to fragments picked up in the north, at Wakkanai. Mr. Kashima and I could hardly believe our luck. This fragment must have arrived shortly after the others and remained here, forgotten by the world in this isolated spot. We discovered the fragment at eleven-thirty on November 17, 1989. It measured twenty-two by twelve by one inches. When I was able to weigh it three hours later, still full of water and sand, it weighed 3.4 pounds. Dry it couldn't have weighed more than an ounce or two.

A few minutes later I noticed what appeared to be a piece of the interior paneling of the Boeing 747 cabin, as I remember having seen it during another trip on that same Flight 007, which had not yet changed its name. Mr. Kashima picked up a "bottle" floating in the ocean. This turned out to be a folded message inside a transparent film spool. It had been thrown into the sea by students at a school on the island of Sado, near Niigata, on the Sea of Japan, on October 1, 1989. For those who were still incredulous, this would serve as proof that the current did indeed flow from south to north—and that part of it could carry a floating object from Sado Island, north of which the Korean airliner must have crashed, to a beach on which KAL 007 debris was found. On our return to the village, we registered our discovery with the municipal archives. I then cut the fragment of honeycomb into several pieces: one for the village, one for John Keppel in the United States, one for the Technical Research Committee in Tokyo, and one that I kept with me.

The following day, November 18, on my return to Aomori, I stopped off at the offices of the *Too Nippo* to inform them of the discovery and give them time to take photographs. It was Saturday and I met the staff reporter. I told him what had happened, thinking he would jump at the opportunity to publish something new about the KAL 007 affair. Instead, he listened to me politely and, seeing that I was perplexed by his lack of enthusiasm, told me, "It's impossible to find any debris from the Korean plane here, south of Moneron. The JASDF has already announced that the debris aren't from KAL 007 but from the target drones. We can't contradict the government." Given his outlook on the world, I wondered how sensational a story had to be before the papers would agree to publish anything about it.

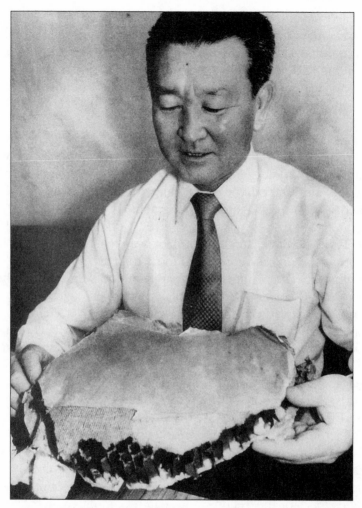

Figure 9. *Honeycomb debris from KAL 007 found in the Tsugaru Strait in September 1983, more than three hundred miles south of where the airliner was said to have crashed. The Japanese Defense Agency realized that if it were known that the Korean airliner had crashed in the south, the public would understand that the debris in the north was military. It got the search in the Tsugaru Strait called off by claiming that the debris was from drones used for target practice.*

I took the JMSA up on their invitation and went to their offices. The first thing I saw on the desk of the officer who met me was a two-page message from the police in Ooma concerning my stay in the village of Sai. The report did not mention the fragment I had found. I showed the fragment to the officer together with the copy of the registration certificate stamped by the township. The JMSA made a copy. If there hadn't been an archive for the debris found in the south, there was now.

As my discovery in Sai demonstrated, many more pieces of debris might be waiting to be found on beaches where no one had thought of looking for them. Before leaving Tokyo I had planned to visit the villages of Haboro and Minato Machi, along with the island of Teuri To in the Sea of Japan, where debris had been found in 1983. But after my experience in Sai, I realized that I would have the same difficulty in gaining access to the local archives and would end up looking for debris on my own. The beaches in the areas most likely to contain debris were not in those villages, however, but on the island of Okushiri, at the entrance to the Tsugaru Strait. Its position just north of the entrance to the strait, in the very center of the Tsushima Shio current, meant there was a good chance that debris from the plane had washed up on its shores.

November 21, Sapporo. I was invited to stop by the studios of the Hokkaido Broadcasting Company (HBC), the local television station. There I met the reporter Ishizaki, who would become my mentor and work with me when I was in the area. We recorded some footage about my discovery in Sai, which was broadcast that same evening. I spent several days making contacts and examining the archives before taking off for Okushiri, a forty-minute flight on a small plane. During the flight I had time to talk to the pilot, who told me he had never heard of debris from the Korean airliner being found on Okushiri. At eleven I was in the Okamoto hotel, and by noon I was on the beach. I began my search on the west side of the island. A half hour later I found the first fragment, a piece of honeycomb identical to that found on Sai. Next to the fragment was a miniature plastic fan on which a Korean dancer was embossed. I remembered that during my flight from Seoul to Tokyo with Korean Air Lines, a hostess had offered me an identical fan. That afternoon I found two more honeycomb fragments. But night was falling and it began to grow cold. I returned to the hotel for a warm bath, a hearty meal, and a good night's sleep on the tatami.

The next day I was back on the beach early, having first arranged for the hotel manager to pick me up at the end of the afternoon. I found four other fragments that morning, one of which was nearly a yard long. Shortly after that I met a group of workers who were repairing a small jetty. Taking advantage of the situation to rest awhile, I began speaking to them and showed them the fragments I had found. I asked them if anyone on the island had spoken about the debris at the time of the crash. To authenticate my discoveries, I took several pictures of the workers holding in their hands the fragments I had found. Around noon I located another fragment. This one was completely different, however. It was a piece of honeycomb sandwich, but it contained three layers of some plastic material, not aluminum. It was curved in two planes and was covered with gray paint, the same color paint used on the enormous fairings on the flap actuators of a KAL Boeing 747.

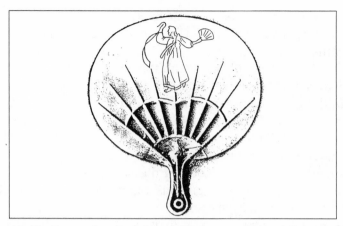

Figure 10. *The Korean fan. Found by the author together with honeycomb debris from KAL 007 on Okushiri Island, just north of the entrance to the Tsugaru Strait, in 1989.*

I found another piece of aluminum-sheathed honeycomb, this time painted red. Then another one, also red, which looked as though it had received a severe impact. I then noticed a police car drive along the road, slow down, and stop. A policeman got out and shouted something in my direction. I looked around. There was no one. I realized the policeman was speaking to me and I went toward him. As soon as I was within speaking distance, he asked me if it was true that I was looking for debris from the Korean plane on the beach. Since that was exactly what I was doing, I told him that it was true. He then asked me why I had come to Okushiri, why I was looking for debris from the Korean airliner, and a number of similar questions. After he had checked my papers, I asked him how he had known that I was on the beach looking for debris. He told me that the workers on the jetty had told him. News travels fast in small towns! I gave him one of the fragments I had found and he became a bit less severe. He even offered to drive me to the next village where I could get some hot coffee to warm up, and we parted amicably. Faithful to his promise, the hotel manager came to get me at the end of the afternoon. I had found ten fragments that day.

That evening after a hot bath and an excellent meal, I laid down on the tatami in my room, protected from the cold wind by the paper shoji, and had begun to put my notes in order when the telephone rang. It was local police headquarters. They had been contacted by the policeman who had questioned me that morning, and they wanted additional information about my investigation. Did I have authorization to search for debris from the Korean plane on the beaches of Okushiri? (I needed none.) Who was I working for? (Myself.) Why? (I was writing a book.) Along with a number of personal questions including my reason for being in Japan, my visa number, and so on. I began to get nervous. They asked for my wife's name—she happens to be Japanese—and the address and phone number of her employer. Fortunately she was an executive secretary at a large company that was doing a lot of work at the time for the American embassy. The next day when local police headquarters telephoned her office, the policeman on duty became wary when the receptionist answered, "American embassy. Whom would you like to speak to?" Slightly embarrassed, the policeman asked to speak to my wife, then apologized for having disturbed her about such an insignificant matter. That evening the police commissioner himself called my hotel to apologize for the inconvenience.

This story has a curious epilogue. Early the next morning I had just finished breakfast when the sliding door to my room opened and the same policeman who had questioned me on the beach entered. I was preparing for another round of tedious questions when something about his expression caused me to hesitate. His features showed none of the characteristic disdain he had previously displayed, but the much more humble expression of someone who has come to ask a favor. He called me *sensei* and launched into a litany of other polite formulas, apologizing for having disturbed me so early in the morning. He wanted to know if I would be willing to assist the local police in my capacity as an expert! During the night a storm had washed up a partially inflated life raft on the beach with no one on board.

I went with the policeman to the spot, where a group of people had already assembled, and examined the wreckage. The life raft was similar to those used on board merchant ships and fishing vessels. The ship's name and the date of the most recent inspection were clearly visible in Japanese. Traces of talc were still visible from when it had been placed in its protective container, which is used to launch the life raft. The raft, which was inflated automatically with CO_2 cylinders, appeared to have been put in the water very recently. I thought it might have been a life raft from a ship that had been caught in the storm not too far from the island. Now that we knew the name of the ship, we simply had to inform the JMSA. The policeman thanked me profusely for my advice.

The storm was still blowing the following day, and the local plane couldn't land. I continued my search amid the wind, rain, and cold and during the day managed to locate four other fragments. Air traffic was still suspended because of the storm, so I left Okushiri by boat with a total of fifteen new fragments from the Boeing 747 in my bags. The concentration of fragments found in such short time, which more than equaled that found on Sai in 1983, and their distribution along the coast, meant many more fragments were still to be discovered. KAL 007 must have crashed somewhere south of this island

and near enough so that a large amount of the debris remained together.

When I returned to Sapporo, I informed Ishizaki of my findings on Okushiri. The studio was so impressed with my discoveries that they decided to prepare a two-hour broadcast on my investigation. The following day they went with me to film my interview with the governor of Hokkaido. During the interview the governor showed me an album of photographs of the complete collection of personal objects found on the Japanese beaches. I tried to find the STAR*FLIGHT sneaker that matched one that had been found on the beach at Rebun Island in September 1983, but it wasn't there. To my great astonishment the governor had no photographs of structural debris from the plane. When the governor asked me why I was so interested in them, I told him about fragment N3, which I briefly described (see page 45 and footnote there). I added that I had hoped to visit JMSA headquarters in Otaru to consult their archives.

It is worth saying a word here about people on Hokkaido, official or otherwise. While sharing some of the caution of other citizens of Japan in matters in which the government of Japan had used its authority to discourage curiosity, in the KAL 007 case Hokkaido residents do not share all of their countrymen's reticence. The Korean Air Line disaster had taken place, they felt, on their doorstep, and thus to some extent it was their disaster—one about which, if possible, they should do something. The same is true of JMSA officers, although as part of a government service its officers are cautious.

Otaru was located within the governor's district. He telephoned the JMSA and spoke to the admiral in charge, who agreed to see me. The meeting was set up for the following morning. Before the governor hung up the phone, Ishizaki, who was in charge of the television crew, asked the governor if he could say a few words to the admiral before he hung up. The governor handed the phone to Ishizaki. Ishizaki told the admiral that he was filming a story with me in the governor's office and asked his authorization to accompany me the following day. Somewhat taken aback, the admiral remained silent a moment. He was aware that the scene at the other end of the line was being filmed and our conversation recorded. Moreover the call had come from the governor himself. The admiral couldn't refuse and agreed to let an HBC news crew accompany me.

The next day a caravan of taxis and HBC cars arrived to bring Ishizaki, our camera crew, and me to JMSA headquarters in Otaru. They were expecting us. Although run like a branch of the military, the JMSA is a civilian organization. The Japanese are very insistent on this point, even though the JMSA has an officer hierarchy and uses armed ships. Because I had been a sea captain before becoming a pilot, I was warmly received by the people at headquarters. They showed me the archives, which I examined as the cameras rolled. And I was able to make photocopies of the material. Unfortunately there were no photographs of airplane debris, which was what I was looking for, and the N3 piece in particular. They promised to forward a copy to me if they could locate the picture. My trip to Otaru was not in vain, though. I found a number of references to floating debris recovered in the Sea of Okhotsk or on its beaches that could only have come from U.S. military aircraft.[1]

After Otaru I went to Wakkanai, which had been temporary headquarters for the search around Moneron. I had heard that the town council had done a great deal to welcome the families of the victims and had set up a permanent exhibit of personal objects belonging to the passengers. When I arrived, however, all the objects had been packed into crates. I then went to the local JMSA headquarters. After some hesitation, I was shown—in the greatest secrecy and for a few seconds only—a photograph of N3. This gave me a better idea of what it was. I saw that there were finger marks on the fresh soot covering it. The mark N3 was visible in the lower right corner, indicating that the plane was obviously not Soviet, since the letter N doesn't exist in the Cyrillic alphabet. I did not see the serial number 7111032, which had been shown on the sketch in the log. Maybe it was on the other side. Its overall shape, however, convinced me the fragment was more likely a rudder than an aileron. The officer who had showed it to me swore me to secrecy. I returned to Sapporo, intrigued by the deepening mystery of N3.

By a curious coincidence, on the day of my return to Sapporo, six years after the destruction of KAL 007, the local edition of the *Asahi Shimbun* announced that the crew of the Japanese fishing vessel *Jukyu Maru* had hauled up a triangular piece of metal in their nets. The piece, which the article said was made of stainless steel or titanium, and measuring sixty-three by sixteen by four inches, was found in the sea at a depth of 360 meters (200 fathoms) on November 12, 1989, at 22:25 hours at a point 45°08' N, 144°00' E. The point of the triangle was so hard and sharp that one of the sailors cut himself on it and had to be rushed to the hospital at Wakkanai.

I decided to return to Wakkanai at once. I spoke to Ishizaki, who put me in contact with an HBC cameraman located there. I arrived the next day and met the cameraman Yoshida. Before going to the fishing company's office where the debris was being stored, Yoshida telephoned to tell them we were coming. To his surprise an employee informed him that the fragment had been sent the previous evening to JMSA headquarters. Yoshida then telephoned the JMSA to set up an interview. The fragment had been packed and was about to be placed on a noon flight to Chitose, where a group of experts would examine it. Fortunately, the officer in charge was the same one who had secretly shown me the N3 fragment. He authorized our arrival and opened the carefully sealed crate containing the fragment.

After inspecting the piece, I thanked my friends at the JMSA.

Before leaving, however, I took the opportunity to ask the officer if he wouldn't mind showing me the photograph of N3 once again, so I could examine it more thoroughly. With a worried look on his face, the officer quickly took me aside and, speaking softly, said, "It's not a good idea to talk about the photograph in front of strangers." Generally, in Japan, the word *stranger* is used to refer to any non-Japanese. Looking around me, I realized that aside from myself, there were no foreigners. Suddenly I understood. The concept of the clan is strong in Japan. Every Japanese belongs to a clan, and the idea of belonging to a group is one of the strongest forms of social bonding in Japan. When he told me to be careful around strangers, the officer was telling me that my companion, Yoshida, who did not belong to the JMSA and was unaware of the N3 photograph, was not a member of the group. This implied that I did belong. I apologized profusely for my blunder. I promised to be more careful in the future. Once these essential formalities were out of the way, and as a newly minted member of the clan, I again asked to see the photograph of N3.

Although Japanese social relationships are elaborate and appear unnecessarily complicated to a Western observer, if the proper protocol is followed, it initiates a process whose final outcome often depends not on the will of the parties involved but on the complex network of mutual obligations associated with questions and answers. Those who understand the protocol can manipulate a social situation to their benefit. Presented in this way, the officer was unable to refuse my request and showed me not one but three photographs of N3, one of which was of the opposite side of the piece, which I hadn't seen before. The other side clearly showed the trim tab's drive mechanism, consisting of a circular actuator held by six bolts and a small rod attached to the tab. The mechanism extended about an inch from the surface and must have been covered by a streamlined fairing. I still couldn't locate the serial number 7111032, either because it was too small or, as I had begun to suspect, because there was another, identical N3 fragment that bore the serial number. The latter was confirmed by Adm. Kessoku Konomu when I met him at JMSA headquarters in Yokohama. By now, however, I had enough information about the N3 piece to turn my mind toward the idea it might have been part of a missile fin.

Yoshida and I then returned to the fishing company's office, where I was able to get a document authenticating the *Jukyu Maru*'s recent discovery. I telephoned Sapporo to tell Ishizaki the results of our expedition. I told him that the fragment was not stainless steel but titanium. It appeared to be from the wing of an American SR-71 reconnaissance plane, the only airplane known (other than experimental) whose wings are made entirely of titanium. I returned to Sapporo, where I arrived early that same evening.

After dinner, we went to the studio to prepare the next day's footage. Ishizaki left us to answer the phone. I saw him grow pale and he began to look worried. It was a bomb threat. The caller, who spoke English, American English with a Southern accent, had threatened to blow up the studio in twenty minutes. This was the first time HBC in Sapporo had ever had a bomb threat. Should we take it seriously? Was it somehow connected to my investigation? After talking with his supervisor, Ishizaki decided to ignore the threat. We still had a quarter of an hour. From a nearby bar Izhizaki ordered enough sake to get us through our last fifteen minutes of existence with dignity or to toast our survival if the bomb turned out to be a hoax. We went back to work as if nothing had happened.

Figure 11. *The author and the fragment of titanium wing recovered by chance from the seabed of the Sea of Okhotsk in 1990 by a Japanese sole-fishing boat. It is from a high-tech aircraft, which may have been one of the casualties during the air battle of Sakhalin.*

During the night a hastily assembled group of engineers from JMSA, the JASDF, and All Nippon Airways, all based at Chitose (a half-civilian, half-military airfield serving Sapporo), wrote a report, a copy of which was immediately faxed to us at the Hokkaido Broadcasting Company. It said that the technology used in the triangular fragment was not advanced enough for it to have been made in the West, and because it was made of stainless steel, the fragment was too heavy to have come from an airplane.

Handing me a copy of the report, Ishizaki told me that an American TV station had already broadcast the substance of the report and its conclusions. Considering the fact that Chitose is a little off the beaten track, this was a truly remarkable example of modern Western reporting and communications. Ishizaki and I couldn't help thinking that the report had hastily been prepared in the hope of dissociating the fragment from any Western aircraft. I had examined the piece myself, and my findings were diametrically opposite to those stated by the experts group.

In fact the piece of debris was too light to be stainless steel and its workmanship was very advanced. It looked like part of the leading edge of a sharply swept-back wing and appeared to be made of titanium. I had been able to obtain a fragment in Wakkanai; and a little later in Tokyo I had it analyzed. The metal was an alloy, 89 percent titanium.[2] This triangular piece of high-tech aviation debris could, indeed, have been the forward point of a wing from an SR-71.

Not wanting to appear behind their peers in the audiovisual world, the local newspaper, the *Hokkaido Shimbun,* sent a team of reporters and photographers to my hotel for an interview the next day. In spite of the bomb alert and the evening's sake, I managed the interview well enough. I accompanied the reporters to their office in order to consult the paper's archives, hoping to discover additional information about the debris found south of Moneron.

I had now fulfilled the goals I had set for myself when I left Tokyo. I had collected enough debris to analyze and could try to determine whether or not it came from the target drones, as the JASDF had stated, or the Korean airliner. I could return to Tokyo with a clear conscience and prepare my report for the Technical Research Committee of the Association of the Families of KAL 007 Accident Victims.

The Meeting in Tokyo

During my first trip walking on the beaches in northern Japan in November 1989, I had kept the Fact Finding Committee of the Association of the Japanese Families of KAL 007 Accident Victims in Tokyo, as well as John Keppel and, through him, the Fund for Constitutional Government in Washington, informed of my progress. The Japanese Association was preparing to hold its twenty-fourth regular assembly on December 17, 1989, fifteen days after my return from Hokkaido, and planned to devote the entire meeting to reviewing the results of my research.

I did not want to present the Association with a full-blown theory of what had happened in the KAL 007 case. I am suspicious of theories. In theories, hypotheses tend to get piled on top of other hypotheses. The temptation is then to make observations selectively and to use both fact and logic in support of preconceived ideas. The results are even worse when strong political or institutional interests drive the process.

From the start, the problem with the KAL 007 case has been that several governments, dominated by the United States, have presented the world not so much with a theory as with an orthodoxy. Namely, that KAL 007 had gone off course accidentally, unwittingly, and alone, violating Soviet airspace at Kamchatka and Sakhalin, until it was shot down by a Soviet interceptor and crashed into the sea off Sakhalin.

Much of the initially voluminous press discussion of the disaster at the time, and what little there has been since, have been variations on this theme. The airliner had gone off course unwittingly because coordinates had been entered incorrectly into the aircraft's inertial navigation system. Alternatively, it had gone off course because the pilot had unwittingly left the autopilot coupled to the magnetic compass. And so on and on. The public was offered a whole smorgasbord of theories about minutiae within the same false framework. Even the supposedly revolutionary theory that the Soviets had mistaken KAL 007 for an RC-135 and shot it down over Sakhalin in error was in line with the fundamental orthodoxy.

My idea was to look for facts. When you found one that contradicted the orthodox version of events, that was, of course, important. But more important was to see what its implications were, so you could then look for other evidence to disprove or confirm them. By the time of the meeting of the Association, the facts already said a good deal. Many questions remained. But two broad points emerged from study of the evidence. First,

KAL 007 had not been shot down over Sakhalin but had crashed in the Sea of Japan some four hundred miles south of the official search area. The facts that the current flowed north and that debris from the airliner did not show up in the official search area for more than a week indicated this. Second, the debris found on the day of the disaster in several distinctly different areas near Moneron showed that several military aircraft, at least some of them American, had been shot down.

The Association sent a press release in advance to all the Tokyo newspapers, television stations, and many papers outside the city. Early on the morning after my return from northern Japan, I received a call from Kenji Matsumoto, a reporter for the *Asahi Shimbun,* one of the largest dailies in the world with a circulation of more than 6 million. He had received the press release and asked to see me as soon as possible. We agreed to meet at 8:00 A.M. in the lobby of the JAL hotel, in Kawasaki, where I lived. Matsumoto arrived on time. He was shorter than me and rather stocky. With his round, inquisitive face he reminded me of the fictional French detective Rouletabille—a Japanese Rouletabille, that is. He spoke rapidly, often swallowing his words, and I had difficulty following him. The meeting was still a week away, but Matsumoto wanted as many details as possible for the article he was preparing. He was most impressed by the fact that much of what I told him was already publicly available in newspaper archives and at the Japanese National Assembly Library.

Because he had been convinced, like so many others, that a single airplane had been shot down, he had never attributed importance to the contradictions and inconsistencies in the official story. As for the differences between the Japanese and American versions of events, he had attributed them to political posturing by the two governments. But now I provided coherence to the mass of facts and drew his attention to the evidence indicating a number of shootdowns.

He realized that I might be right. I invited him to my home to examine the documents I had assembled and the fragments of debris I had found on the beaches of Sai and the island of Okushiri. Matsumoto became extremely disturbed. He was young, a cub reporter, and still under the influence of the harsh discipline of the Japanese school system, where respect for authority and obedience to one's elders are paramount. That is why he was, at first, unable to admit that the government or the JASDF could deliberately have claimed that these fragments came from target drones if they were really from the Korean airliner. His natural tendency was to accept unquestioningly that the debris came from the drones because the JASDF had claimed this was so. The notion of questioning their authority was virtually sacrilegious to him. And the idea of conducting an investigation to prove them wrong was, for Matsumoto, tantamount to a crime against the state.

But I had created an element of doubt in his mind; and as a reporter, Matsumoto had a job to do. His editor in chief had assigned him to me so that he could get as much information as possible for the paper, and he couldn't get out of it. He would be a witness to my efforts to determine whether or not the JASDF was telling the truth in saying the debris had come from the target drones. I could sense the conflict between his respect for authority and his duty as a reporter. The latter finally won out. The following day he went with me to Air Force headquarters, where he had contacted a staff officer.

Captain M. was expecting us. He was a pilot, temporarily assigned to staff headquarters. Matsumoto had told him over the phone the purpose of our visit, but unfortunately, he had no documents about the much discussed target drones. "Well, we don't really use them that much," he told us. I showed him one of the fragments of honeycomb I had brought with me and asked him what he thought.

"Could this be from one of your drones?"

Captain M. looked closely at the fragment.

"I'm not an engineer. I'm a pilot and have only seen the target drones from a distance. One thing I can tell you is that the drones are never painted, but I see traces of paint on your fragment. Also, our drones use a metal armature, and I see traces of wood on your debris. And given the dimensions of your fragment, I doubt that it came from one of our drones. We use them for machine-gun practice, which leaves lots of holes. We never use drones for missile practice because it would be too dangerous for the plane towing it. So our targets don't disintegrate in the air; they maintain their original shape, even if they end up looking like strainers. I can't be absolutely sure, but I don't think this fragment came from one of our drones. To be completely sure, you'd have to have it analyzed by the manufacturer."

Taking a piece of paper, the captain then drew a sketch of the target drone and handed it to me. We thanked him and left.

Matsumoto looked uncomfortable. We still had no proof that the debris came from the Korean plane, but we were pretty sure it hadn't come from a drone. Why lie and say it came from target drones unless to cover an important fact? The logic of the situation pointed to the Korean airliner.

Initially, Matsumoto had come to me with the intention of writing one or two columns about my investigation. Suddenly he saw things differently. Given the increasing importance of the subject, he was now considering an in-depth article of one or two double-page spreads, or even a series. Within two days he had become so involved with the story that in addition to his original article, he now wanted to conduct an investigation of his own.

Alerted by the Association's announcement, other journalists began asking for preconference interviews. Among them were two Soviet reporters, Sergei Agafonov, *Izvestiya's* Tokyo correspondent, and Sergei Vykhukhulev from the *Novosti* Agency. I decided to organize a press conference for December 15, two days before the Assembly, to which I invited several journalists, including the two Soviet reporters, Agence France Presse, the Kyodo Agency, the *Yomiuri Shimbun,* and Matsumoto on behalf of the *Asahi Shimbun.*

At the press conference on the fifteenth, Agafonov and Vykhukhulev behaved well and were quite friendly. Both spoke perfect Japanese, which facilitated matters a great deal since all the other participants were Japanese. They asked a number of questions and seemed to have difficulty in admitting that the Soviet interceptors had shot down several planes over Sakhalin. I showed them the ICAO report in which Soviet representatives claimed that the taped conversations of their pilots was a CIA forgery.

"If the Soviet representatives rejected the American version, it's because the original Soviet version is different, and I would very much like to see it," I told them. "Could you pass my request along to your government?" They laughed and promised they would try. I gave them and the other journalists a press kit. Agafonov forwarded it to his paper in Moscow. Two years later this press kit contributed to *Izvestiya's* decision to publish its series of articles on KAL 007.

On December 17, again accompanied by Matsumoto, I arrived early at the Assembly, where there was already considerable activity. Television crews were setting up their equipment and testing their spots. Journalists opened their pads and checked their cameras. The room was large, with a row of low trestle tables that had been set up on the tatami mats.

The rear wall was almost entirely covered by a large blackboard, on which someone had chalked the meeting's program down to the minute, with the time allotted to each speaker. I had been given forty-five minutes at the opening of the meeting to discuss my investigation. There would be twenty minutes of questions, followed by thirty minutes for journalist Masuo, a director of the Inquiry Group, and twenty-five minutes for Shigeki Sugimoto, the JAL engineer, to comment on my findings and conclusions. Plenty of time was allotted for questions and answers.

The room slowly began to fill. Sen. Hideyuki Seya, vice president of the Higher House of the National Assembly was there, as were Senators Den Hideo, Yukata Hata, Representative Shun Oide, and many others. They took their places around the low tables along with the representatives of the Association. The president of the Association, Masakazu Kawano, flanked by Professor Takemoto and the members of the Fact Finding Committee, sat at the place of honor, their backs to the chalkboard. According to Japanese etiquette, guests of honor are seated facing away from the most interesting or most pleasing view, which they can't see without turning around. In contrast they have the honor of being an integral part of that view. In all, with late-arriving members of the press squeezing into remaining free spots wherever they could find them, the room was filled to capacity.

The Association had intentionally chosen to use a Japanese room with tatami mats for the meeting. A Western room of the same size encumbered with tables and chairs could not have accommodated the number of people present. Here everyone was seated on the floor around the low tables. Squeezed shoulder to shoulder, they took up the minimum amount of space. As was customary, everyone left their shoes in the entrance hall. There was the soft crunching sound of their feet in socks on the tatamis. The ceiling was so low I could touch it with my fingertips when I stood, but once I was seated, the room spread up and out before me like a cathedral. When everyone was finally seated, President Kawano spoke briefly, introduced me to the audience, and gave me the floor.

I had a great deal to say but only forty-five minutes to speak. Not much time to convince an audience, especially since my presentation contradicted the government's position. I had been preparing my talk for several days, mentally rehearsing the way I would present my findings.

I knew that most people had difficulty accepting that KAL 007 could have crashed anywhere other than Moneron. The destruction of KAL 007 had been so closely associated with Sakhalin and Moneron in headlines around the globe that it was ingrained in the collective unconscious. At every stage of my presentation I had to start again from the beginning, pointing out every inconsistency, every improbability, every impossibility, before my listeners began to open their eyes.

Aware that the greatest obstacle to my credibility was the audience's respect for authority, I extolled that sense of respect by saying that every good citizen is required to accept statements from on high, and that to question those statements would be a sign of civic irresponsibility. I had set and baited my trap.

I mentioned that since it had issued its statement two hours before the Americans, the Japanese government should be credited for announcing the disappearance of KAL 007 to the world. I stressed the apparent contradictions between the Japanese government's announcement (MiG-23, launch before 03:25, and disappearance at 03:29) and Washington's (SU-15, launch at 03:26:20, disappearance at 03:38). I implied that proper respect for government required that we could not claim that either statement was incorrect. Let's assume both statements are correct. In that case there must be two different sequences of interception, launch, and destruction, both of which were real. The time of 03:38 put forward by Washington had even been confirmed by information from the Japanese government, indicating there had been a missile launch at that time, followed by the disappearance of an airplane at 03:39. Moreover, the whole American sequence of events was on the Kirkpatrick tape, which the United States had obtained from the government of Japan.

There were three official firing sequences: one prior to 03:25 from the JDA statement, the second at 03:26:20 from the Kirkpatrick tape, and the third at 03:38 from both U.S. and Japanese sources. Times for disappearance from the radar screens were given as: 03:29 (Japanese), 03:38 (U.S.), and 03:39 (Japanese). The three firing sequences had been confirmed independently by the Japanese government when Masaharu Gotoda said that three different MiG-23 interceptors had fired missiles. I never questioned the government's good faith. In fact, I took them at their word. But I also held them to their word.

I then reported the statement by the *Chidori Maru,* confirmed by the JMSA, another official body. I demonstrated that the airplane sighted by the fishermen could not have been any one of the three planes destroyed above. It could not have been the plane that disappeared from the radar screens at 03:29 because that plane had exploded at 33,000 feet, whereas the plane sighted by the fishermen had exploded at sea level. It could not have been the plane that disappeared at 03:38 or 03:39 because of the difference of eight and nine minutes respectively from the 03:30 explosion.

I discussed a number of technical factors about the plane's disappearance. The radar at Wakkanai had indicated that the plane whose radar tracks seemed to belong to KAL 007 was transmitting transponder code 1300 on Mode A. A transponder is a device that enables ground radars to distinguish aircraft individually in a radar-controlled area. Each plane is assigned a unique code, which it alone is authorized to use. By calling up this code on the radar, the ground controller knows which airplane he is tracking.

But the Korean airliner, flying the civilian route R-20 (Romeo-20) over the Bering Sea had no use for an active transponder and would normally have had it turned off. Approaching Japan and preparing to enter the Japan airways system, its transponder should have been tuned to code 2000 in Mode C to let the Japanese know what it was doing. Code 1300, Mode A, something entirely different, referred then to a different airplane. My argument was cogent, it was based on the official version of events. I took advantage of the moment to advance my argument one step further.

The JDA, the Japanese Defense Agency, had released a map of the radar tracks that were supposedly from the Korean airliner accompanied by three Soviet interceptors, fighters A, B, and C. According to the Japanese version of events, it was fighter A, a MiG-23, that had shot down the "Korean airliner." According to American statements it was fighter 805, an SU-15, that had shot it down. Fighter 805 and fighter A should thus have been one and the same plane, because both had shot down the "Korean airliner." As a result, the actions of the interceptor observed by the Japanese (fighter A) should correspond in all respects to those of the plane (fighter 805) observed by the Americans.

But they didn't. At 03:20 hours, fighter 805 fired warning shots at the "Korean airliner" from a distance of less than 1,000 meters (3,000 feet), the maximum range of its guns. At that moment fighter A appeared on the Japanese radars at a distance of 25 NM (29 miles) from the "Korean airliner." It is impossible to fire warning cannon shots at that distance. Therefore, fighter A of the Japanese and fighter 805 of the Americans were two different airplanes. We already had an indication of this: one was a MiG-23, the other an SU-15. Now, we had proof: at 03:20, one was less than a mile from the airliner and fired cannon bursts at it. At the same time, the other was twenty-nine miles away. Both the MiG-23, fighter A of the Japanese, and the SU-15 fighter 805 of the Americans shot down an airplane—one at 03:25, the other at 03:26:20.

I noted that fighter 805 followed the route described on the map published by the *Hokkaido Shimbun* on September 1, 1983, clearly overflying the towns of Dolinsk and Gornozavodsk. This route was clearly different from the route on the JDA's radar map. They each represented a different event. The JDA's map showed the pursuit of an intruder plane by fighter A.[1] The map from the *Hokkaido Shimbun* represented the pursuit of another intruder aircraft by another interceptor, fighter 805. We had reliable information indicating that neither of the two intruder planes was the Korean airliner, KAL 007.

The aircraft pursued by fighter 805 had been observed flying at a speed of 430 knots between 03:12 and 03:19 hours. It then accelerated to 450 knots, possibly its maximum speed. On the leg of its flight corresponding to that time, however, Flight 007 had maintained a speed of 496 knots, considerably faster. The target of 805 could not have been Flight 007. As for the intruder pursued by fighter A, the JDA radar map indicates that from 03:25 to 03:29, it had been recorded flying the 48 NM of the final section of the radar track in four minutes. That meant it was flying at a speed of 720 knots, or Mach 1.25, and no Boeing 747 can achieve supersonic speeds. Two aircraft, one of which was capable of supersonic speeds, were thus shot down over Sakhalin and apparently neither was the Korean Boeing. What, then, had happened to Flight 007?

The news about its disappearance had been contradictory from the start. Initially it was believed that it had had problems along route R-20, on its assigned route over the Pacific. The Japanese Navy and JMSA rescue fleets and aircraft had first looked for the plane near NOKKA, a waypoint where KAL 007 was due at 03:26, Japan time. They had found nothing. Then it was announced it had landed on Sakhalin and the passengers were safe. It was then learned that the airliner hadn't landed on Sakhalin and might have been shot down. Which of the stories was true? The first, which claimed it had crashed near NOKKA in the North Pacific? The second, which claimed it had landed safely on Sakhalin? Or the third, according to which it had been shot down?

Two airplanes had been shot down over Sakhalin but neither of them appears to have been the Korean jumbo jet. A third, over the Pacific, had not been found. This tended to confirm the fact that none of the three versions was correct, as far as KAL 007 was concerned. There was one way to see the truth: by realizing the implications of the direction in which the debris from the airliner had drifted and the length of time it had taken to reach Moneron. This showed that Flight 007 had not crashed near Moneron.

I now had a very attentive audience. I had the impression that I had convinced them so far, but the most difficult part of my talk was ahead of me. For now, based on analysis of the debris, I had to contradict the official versions of the events. I would need to present my arguments with the utmost diplomacy. Unfortunately I had been so wrapped up in speaking that I had lost track of the time. I had ten minutes left. Not much time for what I had to do.

I began by remarking that no debris from the Korean airliner had been found north of Moneron. If I drop a bottle of milk or sake, I'm likely to find milk or sake mixed with broken glass on the ground near the spot where I dropped the bottle. This is what led Adm. Isamu Imamura to remark, "If we don't find any debris from the Korean airliner in the next few hours, we will have to assume that it did not crash in the area." *No KAL 007 debris reached the supposed crash site for more than a week after the crash*. If debris drifted to the official crash site, the airliner must have crashed elsewhere.

The Korean airliner hadn't crashed near Moneron. So where did it crash? Because the debris had drifted with the Tsushima Shio, which flows from south to north, the airliner must have crashed south of Moneron. But where exactly? Debris from the plane, identified as having come from the cabin of the Boeing 747, had been found as far away as the Tsugaru Strait. The airliner must have crashed at sea near the Tsugaru Strait, sufficiently west and south for some of the debris to enter the strait, while the remainder continued drifting northward in the Sea of Japan before reaching Wakkanai and Sakhalin.

For those last minutes, I had spoken nonstop, my eyes glued to the clock, which showed that my time was up. I ended by telling my audience that I would be happy to answer any questions and took my seat to a burst of applause. Passing through the crowd, I felt the audience's encouragement in their expressions and smiles of agreement and watched as they nodded their approval. The next fifteen minutes were given over to a kind of free-form discussion, which served as an intermission between my talk and the next speaker's. Masuo and Sugimoto spoke next, adding comments and analyzing my conclusions.

During the animated discussion period that followed, I found that the government's statements were still able to influence these people, even in the face of the evidence I had presented. The audience's respect for authority still outweighed both reason and logic. This impression was reinforced by the next morning's papers. They covered the meeting and my talk, but their commentaries were used to cast doubt on my credibility. There was nothing to do but to continue my investigation.

KAL 007 Does Not Answer

After my lecture at the Victim's Association Assembly, I went to the offices of Showa Aircraft Co., near Tokyo. Because I had contacts in the field of Japanese aviation, I was able to obtain a recommendation from a vice president of Japan Air Lines, head of the Research Division, to see one of his friends, the head of the engineering department at Showa and a specialist in the division that manufactured honeycomb. I brought along several pieces of the honeycomb I had found on the beaches at Sai and Okushiri. They were immediately sent to the laboratory. The analysis concluded that they were not from target drones as the Japanese Air Self-Defense Forces had claimed. They were not of Showa manufacture nor of Japanese manufacture. I later found that some debris bore Korean markings. KAL 007's airframe (HL7442) had been refitted in Korea.

To be thorough, after my visit to Showa Aircraft, I went to Nippon Freuhauf, a Japanese container manufacturer. I had been given an introduction by another Japan Air Lines vice president, Mr. Kondo, to the general manager, Mr. Makio Yazaki, who had been with Japan Air Lines for thirty years, the last fifteen as head of the honeycomb panel and container-research division. If anyone could identify the debris I had found, Mr. Yazaki could.

After analyzing the debris, Mr. Yazaki concluded that some of the honeycomb debris could be from an inside bulkhead panel for a passenger compartment.[1] Other debris showed all the characteristics of a panel used for transport containers for valuable goods shipped by air, such as electronic instruments, computers, etc. Several years later, on March 11, 1993, the Russian government in Moscow handed representatives of the families of victims of the KAL 007 disaster[2] a set of ninety-three photographs of various debris. Among them was a photograph of a piece of honeycomb material identical to the pieces of debris found in the Tsugaru Strait and on Okushiri Island. And stuck on its surface was an airway bill from Korean Air Lines. Mr. Yazaki had been right in his evaluation.[3]

So the debris found far south of Moneron in the Tsugaru Strait had not come from target drones as the Japanese Air Self-Defense Forces claimed. There was every reason to believe it had come from KAL 007. The debris included pieces identical to those found in the north that had been identified as coming from KAL 007. Some found in the south were clearly of

Korean origin. It was aircraft material of a type used in large transport aircraft, including Boeing 747s; and no other large transport aircraft had crashed in an area from which it could have come.

That the JASDF claimed the debris in the south had come from target drones, when they had not, was the first concrete evidence I had come across in my investigation indicating that someone, somewhere, wanted to hide the fact that the Korean airliner hadn't crashed near Moneron, but four hundred miles to the south, not far from the city of Niigata. Niigata was the next waypoint on KAL 007's assigned route to Seoul. Thus the airliner had continued flying almost all the way to the waypoint, where it could again have communicated openly and freely as though nothing unusual had happened along its route. Sadly, it never reached Niigata. Even so, there seemed to me a good chance that it had communicated by radio in one way or another after the time it was said to have been shot down.

Tokyo Control had declared that the Korean airliner had talked to ground control for the last time at 03:27 hours. Many uninformed observers assumed it was trying to send a distress signal. The text of the message as published soon after the disaster by the *Asahi Shimbun* is as follows:

> *03:27:00 (KE 007): TOKYO RADIO, KOREAN AIR ZERO ZERO*
> *SEVEN.*
> *03:27:05 (Tokyo): KOREAN AIR ZERO ZERO SEVEN, TOKYO.*
> *03:27:10 (KE 007): KOREAN AIR ZERO ZERO SEVEN . . .*
> *(weak and unintelligible)*

Radio communication is the primary means of air-traffic control. The procedures and language have been standardized to improve understanding between controllers and pilots. One of the most serious aviation accidents, the one at Tenerife involving two Boeing 747s, was a direct result of failure to follow proper radio procedure. To avoid confusion and burdening the radio waves with needless chatter, radio communications follow strict protocols.

The calling party first announces the call sign of the station he is calling, followed by the words *this is* (often omitted to speed up things) and his own call sign. The caller must wait to allow the other party to respond. He then calls again, repeating the initial procedure, followed this time by the message he wants to transmit. Following the correct procedure is critical to the smooth flow of radio traffic. Pilots and ground control personnel are forbidden to transmit routine messages without following the above call procedure.

In emergency situations, however, a different protocol is followed. There is no time to call, wait for a response, and repeat the same words again until communication has been established. In an emergency, a pilot may transmit a message directly provided his message is preceded by the word *pan* (from the French word *panne*, meaning "breakdown") or *Mayday* (from the French *m'aider*, "help me")—depending on the degree of urgency. These are repeated three times. This alerts anyone listening that an urgent message is about to be transmitted. Most important, it acts as a signal to other aircraft and radio stations using that frequency to stop transmitting and free the channel.

There is no doubt that KAL 007's "final communication" was a routine message. The conventional format of the transmission excludes the possibility that it was a distress signal. This is extremely significant. The transmission took place at 03:27:00 Tokyo time. But KAL 007 is said to have been hit by a missile at 03:26:21. One second before, the pilot of Soviet interceptor 805, who is supposed to have shot down the airliner, said he had fired his missiles; and one second later he said his target was destroyed. How could the Korean airliner have calmly called Tokyo with a routine message thirty-nine seconds *after* it had been declared destroyed? But send a routine message is what it did or, rather, start to do—even if the transmission, for whatever reason, was then cut short.

There was a good reason for KAL 007 to send a routine message at 03:27. The airliner had previously given its estimated time of arrival at waypoint NOKKA, over the northern Pacific, as 03:26. Even if, as we know, it was not actually there, there is every reason to expect that, as it had been doing all the way from Alaska, it would have sent a report saying that it had passed the waypoint.

But how could it have sent a routine message thirty-nine seconds after it had been declared destroyed? That is a question to which we already know the answer. KAL 007 was not the target that Soviet interceptor 805 said he destroyed with one or both of his missiles at 03:26:21. It cannot have been, because it crashed not nearby but four hundred miles to the south. The real question is why, after a brief wait and Tokyo's reply to KAL 007 to go ahead with its message, the Korean airliner's transmission quickly became "weak and unintelligible."

The International Civil Aviation Organization (ICAO), the U.N. affiliate in the field of civil aviation, which had undertaken to investigate the disaster, interpreted the difficult part of the transmission as "rapid compression . . . descending to one zero thousand." That supported the U.S. claim that the airliner had not crashed until 03:38. A Japanese expert interpreted it as, "All engines . . . rapid compression . . . one zero one zero delta." Larry Porter, an independent American aviation expert, had a chance to study the tape of this communication. John Keppel provided him with a copy of the tape from Narita Airport and asked him to analyze it for the Fund for Constitutional Government's KAL 007 inquiry. Porter is a former air controller who worked for the FAA for a number of years. He now operates his own well-equipped electronic research laboratory. He found no sign of either the Japanese "All engines . . . rapid compression . . . one zero one zero delta" or the ICAO's "rapid compression . . . descending to one zero thousand." What he heard was

KE 007:   THAT WAS KOREAN AIR ZERO ZERO SEVEN . . .
           REPEAT CONDITIONS.
           GONNA BE A BLOODBATH . . . REAL BAD.

Porter later told Keppel that the "gonna be" might have been in the past tense—"must have been." Some years later a more detailed analysis of the transmission was made by the laboratory of the Iwatsu Electric Company in Tokyo. It became clear that, although the communication definitely came from KAL 007, it was not all spoken by the airliner's copilot, who was handling the communications. Part of the communication taped at Narita came from another aircraft on a frequency to which one of the aircraft's receivers, for whatever reason, was tuned at the moment. The other aircraft's words, which were made audible in the KAL 007 cockpit by the cockpit loudspeaker, were picked up by copilot's microphone, together with his own words, and transmitted to Narita on the airliner's assigned frequency. Surprised by the gravity of what he heard during his transmission to Tokyo, the copilot had absentmindedly forgotten to take his finger off the mike-open button. As I have reconstructed it, the sequence goes as follows:

KE 007:   TOKYO RADIO, KOREAN AIR ZERO ZERO SEVEN.
Tokyo: KOREAN AIR ZERO ZERO SEVEN, TOKYO.
Unknown: That was . . .
KE 007:   KOREAN AIR ZERO ZERO SEVEN
           (speaking to Tokyo control).
Unknown: . . . repeating
KE 007:   REPEAT CONDITIONS. (To whom was this addressed?)
Unknown: Gonna be [or must have been] a bloodbath . . .
           real bad . . .

This would explain why KAL 007's transmission to Tokyo suddenly seemed to weaken and become incomprehensible: the voice heard by ground control was no longer that of the copilot but the much weaker sounds of the transmission of the other aircraft. The copilot must have realized that his microphone was still open to Tokyo control for he switched it off, and thus the balance of what sounds like a clandestine transmission was not recorded at Tokyo.

KAL 007's routine call-up of Tokyo, the time that passed after 805's missile exploded, and the rest of KAL 007's transmission, all indicate that KAL 007 was still flying normally at 03:27:10, the time at which it intentionally stopped transmitting, simulating a problem with its radio. An examination of the tape for the period after 03:27:10 was the next logical step in determining whether KAL 007 had again tried to communicate with anyone on its assigned frequency before its destruction. Because my own experience in the field of radio communications is directly related to the discovery of KAL 007's last radio messages, a brief digression is appropriate.

An airplane that was part of the fleet of planes I was operating several years ago had disappeared during a flight over the Pacific, between Hawaii and Tahiti. Our airplane had taken off from Hawaii at dusk and was supposed to land in Tahiti sometime in the morning. During the night, the oil pressure in the left engine had fallen, and the pilot, Ron Autrand, had been forced to cut the engine. He was flying over the equator, roughly midway between Hawaii and Tahiti. Legally he was still within the Honolulu Flight Information Region (FIR) but, because of the difficulty of HF (high-frequency or shortwave) radio communication, had been in contact with Tahiti for over an hour. Tahiti was relaying his messages back to Honolulu. Realizing that Honolulu couldn't hear him, it was natural for him to call Tahiti and let them know about the problem.

I was able to determine, when I later listened to a copy of the tape, that his call had come in loud and clear to Tahiti; it was perfectly understandable on the tape. But the controller on duty apparently hadn't heard him. A Quantas plane flying in the region heard his message and relayed it to Honolulu for him. Ron maintained radio contact with the Quantas plane, and for twenty long minutes the Quantas pilot gave him encouragement and advice. Ron told him he was slowly losing altitude and was unable to hold his plane level with only one engine. The other pilot offered Ron his friendship and support the way we would extend our hand to a drowning man: "Try to reach the ground effect region,[4] you'll increase your lift and endurance."

But Ron answered, "I'm already at a thousand feet and don't want to go down any lower. I don't have a radio altimeter and I can't see anything. It's pitch-black outside. I don't want to hit the waves unless I have to."

The Quantas plane continued on its flight and soon the frail thread that connected Ron to the outside world broke. When he lost contact, the Quantas pilot made an emergency call to Honolulu—using the standard formula, Pan, Pan, Pan, on behalf of Ron, whom Honolulu ground control was unable to pick up. Ron himself had not sent out any Mayday or SOS message.

For all but Mayday and SOS messages, the official procedure is for the ATC to issue an ALERFA, or alert phase, until the plane runs out of fuel. At this point the plane cannot continue flying and has either landed somewhere or crashed. A DETRESFA, or distress phase, is then called, which initiates search and rescue (SAR) operations.

In Ron's case SAR operations were jointly conducted by the American Navy from Honolulu and the French Navy from Tahiti. The Americans sent a C-130 SAR plane and the French a P2V SAR plane toward the probable point of impact, somewhere in the middle of the ocean, 1300 NM (1,500 miles) and five hours by plane from both Honolulu and Tahiti.

The most important factor in any SAR operation is the probable point of impact. If a mistake is made in determining its coordinates, even the most sophisticated detection devices in the world won't find the downed plane. This is exactly what happened with KAL 007 over Sakhalin Island. The most massive SAR operation ever mounted was incapable of locating the wreckage of the giant plane in extremely shallow waters because, in fact, the plane wasn't where they were looking.

The probable point of impact for Ron's plane had arbitrarily been placed near Christmas Island because one of the controllers on Tahiti thought he had "heard an airplane say Christmas" and so informed Honolulu. Honolulu was directing the SAR operations because Ron was still in the Honolulu FIR. When I arrived at the control center, the SAR planes hadn't yet left and I could do nothing. I felt something was wrong. I thought this was simply because the rescue operations involved one of the planes for which I was responsible. And Ron was my friend. But this wasn't the real reason for my uneasiness.

I had often flown with Ron Autrand. Of the two of us he was the more experienced pilot and had been my instrument flying instructor when I was still a young pilot. We had made several flights together across the Pacific under similar conditions. Whatever the nature of the flight and whoever the pilot flying with him, Ron always remained something of a teacher. Ferry flights, especially those over the sea, require a great deal of skill, experience, and composure from a pilot. Something rubbed me the wrong way about the Christmas Island report. Instinctively I felt that the decision to locate the probable point of impact near Christmas Island and use it as the center of the search operation was wrong. It was only a vague feeling, but I couldn't shake it off.

Christmas Island is located slightly north of the equator, halfway between Hawaii and Tahiti, and approximately 400 NM west of the direct route Ron was flying. When Ron detected the problem with his engine at 1:34, he was abeam of Christmas Island. When he called Tahiti to inform them of his trouble, it was 1:54 and he had already passed the island. When the Quantas plane radioed Honolulu twenty minutes later, calling "Pan, Pan, Pan," he was even farther away. The island was equipped with a runway that Ron could have used to make an emergency landing, but there was no radio assistance and it was pitch-black outside. Ron's plane had a weather radar with a mapping function. But at an altitude of one thousand feet, it carried only 25 or 30 NM, which was better than nothing but insufficient to compensate for the uncertainty he had accumulated after eight hours of flight above the ocean, with neither landmarks nor radio beacons to help him navigate. I remembered what Ron had drilled into my head on our long flights together under conditions like these.

"If anything ever happens over the water, keep heading straight on the route laid out in your flight plan. Never get off it. If someone comes to get you, they'll know you're somewhere along your route. Even if you're tempted to fly to an island, don't do it unless it's in front of you and relatively close and you're absolutely certain you'll make it. Whatever you do, don't turn around. Given the problems with ocean navigation, and without a radio to guide you, you'd be losing the security of ditching the plane in the only spot where they'd be able to find you—along your route—for the illusion of a landing strip you'll never be able to reach."

Years had passed since then, but Ron's words had remained engraved in my unconscious. And this was the real reason for my uneasiness. I feared that they might be searching for Ron where he wasn't, where he couldn't possibly be. I asked about the transmission where he indicated going off course near Christmas Island. I questioned the controller who had issued the statement. It turned out he was no longer at all sure of what he had heard. I got hold of copies of the tapes from Tahiti Control. After listening to the tapes between Ron and the Quantas pilot for hours on end, from the first call all the way to the "Pan, Pan, Pan" message, I became even more certain that Ron's intention had never been to make a detour to Christmas Island. Twice the Quantas pilot gave Ron information about the Christmas Island landing strip, but each time, Ron answered that he had no intention of making a detour and would continue along his flight path. I was also certain that Ron didn't hit the water at the moment he lost radio contact with the Quantas plane but had continued flying, though the Quantas pilot believed the opposite.

Along with one of my pilots, I decided to examine all the tracks at every frequency from the moment of last contact with Quantas until the time Ron would have run out of fuel, ten hours later. That meant ten hours of tape for each of the four HF tracks, or a total of forty hours of listening. Finally I found what I was looking for at 07:05 A.M. Roughly five hours after Ron had been given up for lost, he was still flying. The proof was a call that could barely be heard on one of the HF tracks and that had escaped the controller's attention. After listening to this track again and again, my pilots and I were convinced that it was Ron calling an American SAR plane. The French director of SAR operations in Tahiti was shaken by the news, but not entirely convinced. I had the tape processed by the local radio station, FR-3, to improve the quality of the sound. It wasn't great, but it was enough to strengthen my position. I grabbed the tape, jumped into an Air New Zealand plane, and took off for Los Angeles, where our agent drove me to the Acoustic Laboratory at Stanford Research Institute, the same lab that had analyzed the famous Watergate tapes. The results of their analysis helped me convince the SAR people in Honolulu and Tahiti to resume the search they had abandoned, using an impact point calculated from the new data.

But ten days had passed and Ron was never found.

I never forgot that the information that might have saved Ron's life had always been there on the tape from Tahiti Control. If only it had been made available to the SAR people. If only they had listened . . . In the case of KAL 007 and the Narita tape where all KAL 007's communications with Tokyo are recorded, no amount of analysis will bring back the lives of the 269 people on board. But it might help unravel the mystery of their disappearance. I studied the Narita tape and found oddities that my experience in listening for Ron's last message on the Tahiti tape helped me put into perspective. Although I had no direct experience of the way the tape had been recorded, I could at least base my understanding on what I knew from Tahiti. Aviation technology is pretty much the same all over the world.

The Tahiti Control recording device was brand-new and, at the time, still being tested. It was a magnetic tape recorder that could record simultaneously twelve different tracks, each allocated to a different channel. There were four VHF (short-range) channels, including the 121.5 MHz international distress frequency, four HF (long-range) channels, three telephone channels, and one channel for a time signal. Each of the tracks could be listened to individually, and the time signal could be superimposed on any of the tracks. The time signal consisted of Morse code, which provided the hours and minutes, and an oscillator, which marked the seconds. That gave an accurate signal for all the tracks without interfering with the sound quality or intelligibility.

The recorder represented the cutting edge of technology in 1974, and we were on a small island in the middle of the ocean. In contrast, on the copy of the 1983 tape from Narita released to the Diet, the time track was spoken aloud by a female voice. It not only gave the time but also repeated all the protocols used in polite Japanese conversation. Although the voice was pleasant enough, it masked the transmissions and interfered with the listener's understanding of the tape. It simply didn't make sense. Japanese technology in 1983 couldn't have been less advanced than what was found on an isolated island in the Pacific in 1974. In spite of this obfuscating factor, I discovered that KAL 007 had sent several messages after its "final" communication at 03:27:10, once at 03:52 to KAL 015, a fellow Korean airliner, and once again at 04:10 to KAL 050, another Korean airliner.

After its 03:27:10 transmission was cut short by the alarming transmission heard on another channel, the Korean airliner simply stopped transmitting to Tokyo—although the copilot did not switch off his microphone as quickly as he might have. Tokyo, quite naturally failing to understand the strange and incomprehensible transmission that went out on the air, remarked, "Unreadable, unreadable," and asked the Korean airliner to repeat. But KAL 007 did not do this, nor did it answer any of Tokyo's subsequent calls attempting to reestablish contact. Nor did it again openly identify itself. Why?

To answer the question we must take account of the fact that in departing from its authorized course without admitting it in its position reports, KAL 007 was doing something that had nothing to do with its duties as a civilian airliner. As we shall see when I examine the events of its flight across the Bering Sea, to keep air traffic control from realizing what it was doing, KAL 007 twice simulated VHF (short-range) radio failure and had KAL 015, flying the same route, relay position reports for it, the incorrect contents of which misled air traffic control as to its position.

I will not try to read the minds of the pilot or the copilot of KAL 007, but will let the evidence suggest what their motives must have been in failing to reply to Tokyo's calls. The evidence shows that while they did again use the radio briefly on three occasions, they did not identify the airliner by the normal use of its call sign. We know from a study of the ocean currents and the debris evidence that shortly after 03:27 KAL 007 turned south. Had it flown in any other direction its debris would not have turned up where it did.

An hour's flying time south was Niigata on the west coast of Honshu, the last waypoint in Japan on KAL 007's assigned course to Seoul. Unlike NOKKA, which was merely a stated geographical position in the Pacific, NIIGATA was a radar-controlled waypoint. If KAL 007, after its long, unauthorized diversion from course, wished to reintegrate itself into the system of air traffic control along its assigned route, NIIGATA was the obvious place to do it. Over Niigata all it would have had to do was to identify itself to Tokyo and report passage of the waypoint.

The fact that on its way south KAL 007 did not mention its call sign suggests this was in fact its intention. Flying down the west coast of Hokkaido, it was in radar range of Japanese Defense Agency radar. And from the Tsugaru Strait on, flying at its assigned altitude of 35,000 feet (which it would have wanted to do for safety reasons), it was in radar range of Tokyo (Narita). That is also to say that its VHF (short-range radio) transmissions, which like radar follow a line-of-sight path, would be heard by Tokyo. Had it clearly identified itself, Tokyo, which had been looking for the airliner ever since its strange transmission and subsequent failure to respond to calls, would have spotted its position, some four hundred miles off course, by radio direction finding and by radar. All sorts of questions would have been asked.

When I came to understand both the implications of the debris evidence and what was wrong with the official interpretation of KAL 007's "last transmission" at 03:27, I realized that I would have to study the part of the Narita tape after the 03:27 transmission in the same way I had studied the Tahiti tapes. I did this first by ear, then on a personal oscilloscope, and then with the help of Dr. K. Tsuboi, the director of Iwatsu Laboratory in Kaguyama near Tokyo. Dr. Tsuboi is a world-class acoustic and frequency expert and has state-of-the-art equipment at his disposal.

It was he who caught the first transmission after 03:27:10 that came from KAL 007. It consisted on one word:

03:30:05 (KE 007): ROGER.

Dr. Tsuboi's computer had automatically analyzed the transmission along with the others and produced a voice print recognizable as that of the KAL 007 copilot. Short as the transmission was, it was evidence that the Korean airliner was flying, apparently normally, at that time. It appears that KAL 007 was responding to a call, transmitting only what was necessary to be understood by the caller but not enough to be detected by Tokyo. It is not clear why the "Roger" was spoken on the airliner's official frequency rather than that of the station to which KAL 007 was responding. It seems clear that the airliner was not responding to Tokyo since it did not then do what Tokyo had asked it to do, which was to repeat its last transmission.

Meanwhile Tokyo, unable to contact KAL 007, asked any aircraft flying in the vicinity to try to contact it. The first aircraft Tokyo asked was, of course, KAL 015, which (according to the position reports of the two airliners) was only a few minutes behind it on R-20 and thus, Tokyo thought and in fact, was able to call it on their VHF, a much more reliable channel than the HF radio. On Tokyo's request, KAL 015 called KAL 007, but over the HF radio:

03:43:07 (KE 015): ZERO ZERO SEVEN, ZERO ONE FIVE.

KAL 015 called KAL 007 *once* only on the HF radio and received no response. It told Tokyo, "KAL 007 is not responding." Somewhat surprised at KAL 015's lack of interest in contacting its sister plane, Tokyo radio asked it to try again, but on VHF this time, using the 121.5 MHz international calling frequency. KAL 015 called and, this time, *made contact.*

03:52:09 (KE 015): ZERO ZERO SEVEN, ZERO ONE FIVE.
03:52:15 (KE 015): ZERO ZERO SEVEN, ZERO ONE FIVE.

03:52:40 (KE 007): ZERO ONE FIVE.
03:52:45 (KE 015): ZERO ZERO SEVEN, ZERO ONE FIVE.
03:54:35 (KE 015): ZERO ZERO SEVEN, ZERO ONE FIVE.
03:54:45 (KE 015): ZERO ZERO SEVEN, ZERO ONE FIVE.
03:54:45 (KE 007): (transmission in Korean)
03:54:47 (KE 015): ROGER.

In the above exchange KAL 015 called KAL 007 twice. A few moments after the second call, KAL 007 responded, somewhat ambiguously and not according to protocol, but in a way often used between aircraft when pilots know one another and have been in continuous communication throughout a flight. KAL 015 appears not to have heard and continued to call KAL 007 three more times. KAL 007 then transmitted a short sentence in Korean that KAL 015 received and must have understood, because it responded "Roger" and stopped making any further calls.

It is likely that KAL 015 was aware of what KAL 007 was doing. There is evidence earlier in the flight that KAL 015 was covering for KAL 007's unauthorized divergence from its assigned course. As the reader will see when I discuss KAL 007's flight from Anchorage across the Bering Sea, KAL 015 twice transmitted position reports for its sister ship that cannot have been bona fide relays. In the present instance their conversation remained short and cryptic. KAL 015 cooperated with KAL 007's scheme of simulating a radio failure by reporting to Tokyo radio that they had been unable to contact KAL 007, although the fact is, recorded on the Narita tape, that they did contact it.

A few minutes later another Korean plane, KAL 050, arrived in the Tokyo control zone. With the very first call, Tokyo Control announced, "Radar contact," and requested that it attempt to contact KAL 007.

04:08:14 (Tokyo):   KOREAN AIR ZERO FIVE ZERO, STAND BY
YOUR REQUEST. ALSO, WE HAVE REQUEST.
WOULD YOU ATTEMPT CONTACT WITH AH,
CALL SIGN KOREAN AIR ZERO ZERO SEVEN,
AND IF YOU HAVE CONTACT WITH HIM,
ADVISE HIM TO CONTACT AH, TOKYO
CONTROL ONE ONE EIGHT DECIMAL NINER.

KAL 050 followed through on this request and obtained contact with KAL 007.

04:08:30 (KE 050): AH TOKYO, AH KOREAN AIR ZERO ZERO
SEVEN, THIS IS KOREAN AIR ZERO FIVE ZERO.

04:09:15 (KE 050): AH, KOREAN AIR ZERO ZERO SEVEN,
KOREAN AIR ZERO FIVE ZERO, ON ONE ONE
EIGHT NINER [VHF 118.9].
04:09:34 (KE 050): KOREAN AIR ZERO ZERO SEVEN, THIS IS
KOREAN AIR ZERO FIVE ZERO ON ONE TWO
ONE DECIMAL FIVE, HOW DO YOU READ?
04:09:51 (KE 007): ZERO FIVE . . . SEVEN.
04:09:54 (KE 050): AH, ROGER, AH, TOKYO CENTER ADVISES
YOU TO CONTACT AH, ONE ONE EIGHT
DECIMAL NINER, OVER.
04:10:04 (KE 007): (transmission in Korean)
04:10:10 (KE 050): (transmission in Korean)

In the above transmissions in Korean, KAL 007 explains to KAL 050 in a cryptic way that Tokyo Control was unable to identify its echo on radar, confusing it with that of KAL 015. Hearing this, KAL 050 says, "In that case, you better keep radio contact with KAL 015." To this KAL 007 answers, "We are in permanent contact with KAL 015."

Right after the transmissions in Korean, KAL 015, which was listening in on the frequency, broke into their Korean conversation with a standard call-up in English.

04:10:47 (KE 015): AH, KOREAN AIR ZERO FIVE ZERO, THIS IS
KOREAN AIR ZERO ONE FIVE, KOREAN AIR
ZERO ZERO SEVEN
(rest of the message in Korean).
04:10:58 (KE 050): (answers in Korean)
04:11:01 (KE 015): (first part of message in Korean)
ONE TWO THREE FOUR . . .

The Korean parts are very suggestive. KAL 015 asks KAL 050 if he had been communicating with KAL 007. KAL 050, guessing that for some reason KAL 007 wanted to simulate a radio failure but not knowing for sure whether KAL 015 was in on the secret, answered a prudent no. KAL 015 then said, "You can contact KAL 007 at any time with our special apparatus. Just come in on one two three four." One two three four is a chatter frequency on 123.4 MHz that is not monitored by air traffic control. Pilots often use it for private conversations. KAL 015 had thus invited KAL 050 to come in on the chatter frequency 123.4 and promised it would hook him up on its special radio apparatus to contact KAL 007.

Some observers have attributed the KAL 007 transmissions above to KAL 015. But the logic of the situation says this is wrong. If KAL 050 had been communicating with KAL 015, he would not have asked him to "stay in contact with KAL 015," and KAL 015 would not have answered that he was "in contact with 015." If KAL 015 had been referred to by both participants, it is obvious that he was not one of the participants!

Dr. Tsuboi at the Iwatsu Laboratory has confirmed the voice in the transmissions above ascribed to KAL 007 is indeed that of the copilot of KAL 007. If we review the whole sequence, we see that KAL 050 received a response from KAL 007 at 04:09:51, immediately following its first call on 121.5 MHz. The response consisted of a shortened call sign for KAL 050 followed, after a pause, by an abbreviated call sign for KAL 007, using a clipped style of communication often used by pilots who know one another. The full message would have been "ZERO FIVE (zero), (zero zero) SEVEN."

This isn't the officially approved method of communication, but it's very useful whenever there is no possible ambiguity about the caller's identity, and when brevity—and secrecy in this case—are desired. KAL 050's pilot clearly understood who was answering. His response proves it. To the message "Zero Five . . . Seven" issued by KAL 007, he immediately answered, "Ah! Roger. Tokyo Center advises *you* to contact it on 118.9 . . ."

Clearly the pilot of KAL 050 had no doubt as to the identity of the aircraft that had answered him. He then transmitted Tokyo's message to KAL 007: "Tokyo is asking *you* to contact . . ."

The remainder of the conversation took place in Korean. These Korean communications show that KAL 050 had not been in on the secret from the start but agreed to go along with KAL 007's game of simulating radio failure. As for KAL 015, he seems to have been an active part of whatever game KAL 007 was playing.

The radio communications are not the only sign that KAL 007 was still flying normally over the Sea of Japan, as late as forty-four minutes after the alleged attack at Sakhalin. There are indications that the Tokyo controller saw KAL 007's echo on his radar. At the very moment KAL 007 was communicating with KAL 050, Tokyo Control was having trouble identifying KAL 015. The controller was unable to distinguish which of two echoes on his screen belonged to KAL 015. At that time of night there was little air traffic above Tokyo. Aside from KAL 015 the only aircraft that showed up on the controller's radar were KAL 050 coming from the Pacific Ocean on its way to Seoul and a U.S. military plane Navy Foxtrot Bravo 650 (FB650), out of Atsugi Airbase. These aircraft had been correctly identified and presented no problem to the controller. The only aircraft he had trouble identifying was KAL 015, aside from KAL 007, which hadn't yet been identified and continued to simulate radio failure at least as far as Tokyo was concerned. Hence, the only aircraft whose radar echo could have been confused with KAL 015 was the still unidentified KAL 007.

In his effort to identify which of the two echoes was KAL 015, Tokyo Control had asked KAL 015 to change its transponder code *three times* in a short period. Finally, in despair, he requested that KAL 015 change its heading by 35 degrees, for confirmation of its identity, from its heading of 245 degrees to a new heading of 280 degrees, an identification procedure that is virtually unheard of. The implication here is that the other echo on the controller's screen was mimicking KAL 015's echo to the point of making these two echoes indistinguishable. From the evidence we already have, we can reconstruct what must have happened. Each time the controller requested a change in transponder code, both echoes on the screen reacted in the same way, the transponder code changes being made simultaneously by both planes. Under these circumstances, the only other way left to the controller to determine which plane was which was to have KAL 015 maneuver in such a way that it could be unambiguously identified—that is, unless the other aircraft made a similar maneuver at the same time.

KAL 007 succeeded in maintaining the confusion until the controller asked KAL 015 to change its heading to 280 for confirmation of its identity. KAL 015, which was flying over the Pacific Ocean, did so, bringing it closer to Niigata, its mandatory waypoint. But this time KAL 007, which was flying on the other side of the Japanese islands, could not follow suit. To have done so would have turned it away from Niigata and made it impossible for the plane to reenter its assigned route on time. The different behavior of the two aircraft resolved the controller's problem. The controller positively identified KAL 015 on R-20 over the Pacific Ocean and cleared it to fly "direct Niigata." There may, however, be another reason why KAL 007 did not change heading to 280 degrees as requested by Tokyo Control. The request was made at 04:12:47. A few seconds later, at 04:13:16, there is on the Narita tape a call that may have been the last one made by KAL 007:

04:13:16 . . . ZERO FIVE ZERO, ZERO ONE FIVE . . .

At first it appears as if KAL 015 is calling KAL 050, but KAL 015 would have been too busy with Tokyo Control to chat with KAL 050. It is more likely that KAL 007, surprised by some unexpected event, transmitted a call to KAL 050 and KAL 015 at the same time. A message that was cut short. Was the call made at 04:13:16 the Mayday that KAL 007 never issued?

A few seconds later, as if sensing that something unusual had occurred, KAL 050 informed Tokyo that KAL 007 was not responding "this time."

04:13:51 (KE 050): TOKYO CONTROL, KOREAN AIR ZERO FIVE
ZERO UNABLE CONTACT KOREAN AIR ZERO
ZERO SEVEN THIS TIME.

When it informed Tokyo that KAL 007 was not responding to its call, KAL 050 took the precaution of specifying "this time." Was it implying that it had been able to contact KAL 007 previously? By then KAL 007 and KAL 015 had in all likelihood informed KAL 050 of their activities, and KAL 050 had helped KAL 007 simulate radio failure. Now, however, KAL 050 may have thought KAL 007's radio silence was disquieting. Its manner of conveying this information to Tokyo Control—specifying "this time"—may betray that worry.

There is no further trace of KAL 007 after (04:13:51) on the Narita tape. Perhaps it was at the moment the transmission was cut short that the Korean airliner was destroyed. That transmission might, however, have been initiated by KAL 015 and cut short for reasons at which we can only guess—the two aircraft could have shifted frequency to the chatter frequency. KAL 007's end could have come a moment earlier, when the Tokyo controller asked KAL 015 to change its heading to 280 degrees. His previous inability to distinguish between KAL 015 and its mysterious echo (KAL 007) suddenly ended, and he cleared KAL 015 to proceed "direct Niigata." There are two possible reasons for the end of the controller's problem. The first I have already mentioned—KAL 007's failure to adopt the 280-degree course when KAL 015 did make the turn. The second possible reason is more gruesome: KAL 007's radar blip may suddenly have disappeared. Even if neither of those hypotheses is correct and the airliner flew for a while after 04:12, it didn't fly far. We know it can't have reached Niigata, which was about eighteen minutes and 144 miles away.

In any event, by that time Soviet territory was three-quarters of an hour's flying time and four hundred miles behind KAL 007. How and why then was it destroyed? It is not plausible to think that the Soviets, who had ample opportunity to shoot down the airliner earlier, would have sent an interceptor beyond the end of its two-way range, and through lively Japanese air defenses, to destroy it. It is also implausible to suppose that KAL 007 flew four hundred miles at its assigned altitude, exchanging ambiguous but calm words with its fellow Korean airliners, already so gravely damaged that it would soon perish. All the way down the Hokkaido and northern Honshu coast, Japanese help was close at hand. To activate that help would have required no more than a word.

The Search for the Crash Site

T he radio transmissions between KAL 050 and KAL 007 showed that the plane was still flying normally at 04:12 hours (Japan time), forty-six minutes after it was said to have been destroyed by a missile. Flying at the speed of 456 knots indicated on its flight plan for this leg of the journey, the airliner would have continued to fly for another 350 NM or roughly 400 statute miles. We are certain KAL 007 was still flying normally at 04:12 because it contacted KAL 050 at that time, but it may have continued flying beyond then. All we know for sure is that the plane did not report its passage over Niigata, implying that the plane never made it that far.

Where exactly did KAL 007 crash? Examination of VHF radio waves, whose reception distance is a function of an aircraft's altitude, shows that at the time of its final radio message, forty-six minutes after the attack at Sakhalin, KAL 007 was somewhere south of the Tsugaru Strait, a few minutes from Niigata, its next waypoint on its assigned route to Seoul. KAL 007 could have been flying after 04:12 hours, although it didn't make it to Niigata, which it would have wanted to reach at 04:30. That gives us the basis for a somewhat extended probable impact area.

Tokyo Control had doubts about the identity of the echo of KAL 015 up until the time they authorized it to head directly to Niigata. After they instructed KAL 015 to make a thirty-five-degree change in heading, the bright spot on their radar screen that actually made the requested heading change was no doubt KAL 015. As far as the Tokyo controller was concerned, the other, unknown echo, which had been mimicking KAL 015's echo, was not a civilian aircraft under his control since he had no official information, i.e., no flight plan, about it. If it had disappeared, its disappearance cleared the confusion on his radar screen. Beyond that, and not knowing what it was—or had been—he was not in a position to take any action.

This may have been the moment of KAL 007's destruction. But in the absence of radio contact, Tokyo Control had no way of being certain that the unknown echo, which it had confused with that of KAL 015, had been that of KAL 007. Officially, and for all the Tokyo controller knew, KAL 007 was somewhere along Romeo-20, flying five minutes ahead of KAL 015. Of course, it hadn't shown up on the radar screen where it should have been and the controller was at a loss as to where it actually was.

If only KAL 007 had risked administrative sanctions and identified itself, the plane's position would immediately have been picked up over the Sea of Japan. There would have been problems once it landed in Seoul, of course, but the aircraft would have returned to a legitimate existence after its passage through a shadow world. Had KAL 007 availed itself of the protection offered by the official system of air traffic control, it might have escaped destruction.

Back to the Beach

The uncertainty about the exact time of KAL 007's destruction led to a corresponding uncertainty about the exact area of impact. Knowing that I had found debris from the plane on the beaches of Sai and Okushiri six years after the disaster, John Keppel suggested I return to the beaches to look for any signs that would help us better locate the area of impact. The Fund for Constitutional Government's investigation provided funding for the expedition. This time my objectives were, first, search the western coast of Honshu, south of the Tsugaru Strait, for the southernmost point where floating debris from the Boeing 747 had washed up on the beach. This would enable us to determine the plane's impact area with greater accuracy. Second, find a piece of debris that could clearly be identified as coming from KAL 007.

Some aviation experts felt that any debris that was found, though coming from a Boeing 747, had to be specifically identified as coming from the Boeing 747 used for Flight 007. Linking the debris to the very airframe in question (HL-7442) would provide dramatic proof of the jetliner's actual fate, although such a link was not needed to show that the 747 debris in the south came from KAL 007. In recent years, no other Boeing 747, and for that matter no other large transport aircraft, had crashed anywhere from which its floating debris could have reached the beaches that I was to search.

My plan was to begin from a point slightly south of what we then believed to be the probable impact point and walk north until I found the first signs of debris. My earlier search on Okushiri had shown me that debris could remain untouched on the beaches for years. It had also shown the likelihood of finding additional debris at some distance from the water, where it had been washed up by high tides and heavy storms. I planned to start at the Oga Peninsula. The peninsula's location south of the estimated impact area and its shape, a right angle that jutted into the Tsushima Shio current, made it an ideal spot to catch any debris that might have passed by.

I chose as my starting point the town of Akita, which is near the sea and south of the Oga Peninsula. Akita is the largest town in the area and the only one where I could consult the archives of a local newspaper. I had planned to spend the morning at the paper's office and then take the local train to Oga, where I would arrive in the afternoon. Using Oga as my base, I had calculated that I could walk the beaches around the peninsula in about five days and then proceed farther north. Things turned out differently.

I left Tokyo on August 5, 1990, by the night train and arrived in Akita at six in the morning. The local newspaper offices wouldn't open until 10:00 A.M., and I had four hours to spend. I had noticed on the map that the coastline south of Akita consisted of a long, straight beach nearly twenty-five miles long, which I had already scanned intently from the train. While looking at these wide and nice beaches, I had told myself that there was little chance of finding anything so far south, but I had four hours to kill and I might as well take advantage of the time. But what if I did find something? Finding any debris this far south, even a single fragment, would mean a complete change of itinerary, for there would be no point in continuing the search farther north. My carefully prepared plans would then become worthless. I would have to begin again from scratch.

On the Beach at Michikawa

Immediately upon my arrival at Akita, I took the local train and arrived at 6:44 A.M. at Michikawa, a small station in a small village, with barely a few houses here and there along the road. From the station, as small and cute as a child's toy, I quickly found a path to the sea through a pine wood on a hill that sloped gently down to the beach. In the quiet morning air I filled my lungs with cool air, feeling all the excitement of a scout during wartime. I soon arrived on the beach—an immensely long beach that stretched endlessly before me for miles and miles to the north and south. Before leaving Tokyo I had feared not only that all the hotels would be full at this time of year, but that the beaches would be mobbed with tourists and would be cleaned every morning, leaving me with virtually no hope of finding anything. For this reason I had brought a small metal detector with me.

But no sooner had my feet touched the sand than I saw piles of flotsam and debris deposited by the wind and waves. No one had touched them, no one really cared. It was exactly like the beaches at Sai and Okushiri. Any ordinary tourist would have groaned in horror. But I rejoiced, and the beach appeared more beautiful than ever. I started walking toward Shimohama, the next village and the next train station, whose roofs I could make out in the distance, eight miles north. I looked at my watch. It was 6:55. I was on schedule.

Walking was easy in the cool air. The beach was very wide, nearly a thousand feet in some spots. It was covered with flotsam from the edge of the water up to the pine groves, which bordered it along the interior. Newly arrived driftwood and flotsam were closest to the water's edge. The farther one got from the water, the older the debris was. High up on the beach were piles of flotsam that had been pushed there by the tides or exceptionally bad storms. Poking around, I found a stream of it about fifty feet wide, some distance from the water's edge. I had a hunch that this was the flotsam washed up about the time the airliner crashed, and I decided to follow my intuition.

The First Debris

After an hour, I began thinking about my expedition on the Okushiri beach nine months earlier. It was winter then, cold, windy, and raining. I said to myself that if I were back on Okushiri, I'd have found a piece of debris by now. Of course I wasn't on Okushiri and felt foolish for thinking it. Fifteen minutes later I found the first debris: a piece of honeycomb panel of the same type I had found on Sai. It was half-buried in the sand and barely visible. But the form of these honeycomb panels was so well anchored in my unconscious that I couldn't have missed it. The piece measured eight by four inches. I didn't jump in the air or cry out with joy. Just a kind of internal satisfaction and the impression that KAL 007 must have crashed farther south than we had suspected. I would have to change my plans. There was no need to go farther north. Now I had to go south, endlessly walking the beaches, in search of the last piece of debris I could find. To find the last, I had to know there were none farther south. That would be considerably more difficult. It is a lot easier to find something than to prove it isn't there.

Having left my camera with my bags at the station, I had no choice but to take the fragment with me and return later to take photographs of the spot where I found it. Now that my plans had changed, the local Akita newspaper could wait. It was less urgent to poke around their archives to find out if any debris had been discovered in the area since I had just found one myself. I carefully marked the spot with a piece of bamboo and was about to leave the beach when I saw another piece of debris in the sand, similar to the first, but much smaller. Ten minutes later I found the third piece, stuck between two enormous cement blocks that ran the length of the beach to prevent erosion. It was 7:55. One hour later I turned up a fourth piece, half-buried in the sand beneath a tire track. The face that had been exposed to the sun showed traces of an explosion and contained a large number of small holes, as if it had been hit by shrapnel. The side turned down was painted red, probably indicating the piece was part of an air cargo container. I left it where it was and continued on.

The sun was now high in the sky and it began to get hot. Not having my camera with me, I didn't see the point of looking for additional fragments. The fact that I had found any was in itself highly significant. I took a shortcut back to the road, meaning to return to Akita from the closest train station. Leaving the beach, at the foot of a small hill, I noticed an old and rickety wooden shack that appeared unoccupied. As I approached, I noticed, on one side of the shack, an old Coke machine! It was completely rusted, the paint had peeled off, and it looked like something that had been picked up at a flea market. It must have been there for years, and I wondered if it was still working. It would cost me a hundred yen to find out. I dropped my coin into the slot and listened as it fell with a dull sound. Time was suspended for a brief instant. Freeing itself from the mechanism that held it in place, the bottle shot out with a noise that must have been heard down at the water's edge. It was cold and refreshing.

I returned to Akita, knowing I would have to change my plans radically. First, I booked a room at the local inn in Shimohama. I then continued on to Michikawa where I had started out that morning and, taking my camera, returned to the beach, to photograph and pick up the debris I had left.

From a distance I could make out the spot where I had found the first debris that morning. I began walking. It was 3:15 in the afternoon when I recovered the last of the debris I had spotted in the morning. I started walking north and crossed a small stream. The beach grew wider, nearly a quarter mile wide in some places. The pine-covered hills gave way to sand dunes, which were protected by blocks of cement, indicating that the sea came at least this far inland. It was in one of these blocks of cement that I found the sixth fragment. This one was unpainted but was covered with a bloodlike substance that had run, dried, and blackened. Could it be blood?

The Bomb

I continued walking. I went pretty far inland but could still see pieces of driftwood. Suddenly I spotted a cylindrical object that resembled the head of a rocket. It was metallic gray and the letters CCC were visible in black, like the Soviet CCCP, but without the last letter. The cylinder was made of aluminum and measured roughly three inches wide by sixteen inches long. I picked it up carefully and saw some writing that had almost completely been rubbed away. I turned the cylinder in the sunlight until I could make out what was left of the marking:

TO ARM FOR HAND LAUNCHING
ROTATE COVER TO ARMED POSITION

I looked at the cover and my heart skipped a beat when I saw that it had been rotated to the armed position. I put it carefully back where I had found it. Then, mimicking bomb experts I had seen on films and television, I lay down on the sand with my head near the device and examined it up close. This way I could examine the cylinder without my hands shaking too much. I picked up the device again and looked through a small opening on the side. I saw an inscription that read:

meaning "U.S. Navy Bureau of Weapons".[1] I looked through another opening opposite the first and, this time, saw the following notice:

BATTERY WATER ACTIVATED

I breathed a sigh of relief. No missile, not even those launched from submarines, uses water-activated batteries. To my knowledge, the only devices containing batteries like this were the markers and radio units used for naval rescue operations. Though it had failed to fire, it was armed. This meant that the device I was holding might have been used for a rescue operation. I picked it up and took it with me. I had found the device not far from Shimohama.

I returned to the hotel and took a shower. After the euphoria of the morning's discovery I had to decide what to do next. I would naturally continue to look farther south. The only problem was that I was unable to find another hotel far enough south. I finally located a small inn, a good distance into the interior, from which I could make two- or three-day trips, sleeping on the beach and returning to the hotel to shower, have a decent dinner, put my notes in order, contact John, take care of the mail, and get a good night's rest. The village was called Oouchi and was near the Ugo-Iwaya station. There were few trains during the day, but a bus left the train station every hour. It stopped in a place called Chuo Gakko Mae, and from there it was a fifty-minute walk to the hotel.

I made the necessary arrangements by telephone and went down for dinner. After dinner, I took some photographs of the device I had mistaken for a bomb. I found the serial number, 437369014581954, and the lot number, LOT NR: 19025K00659. I would now have to call John and give him the information. He had been in contact with several senators in Washington, and there had been talk of opening at least a limited inquiry into the KAL 007 incident.

Ugo-Iwaya

The inn at Ugo-Iwaya was situated near the end of a deep valley surrounded by mountains on every side. It was the only building in sight except for a small stable next to it that held about two dozen friendly cows. The "inn" was nothing more than a farm in the mountains that took in boarders during the summer. I was the only guest and slept like a log.

I took advantage of the change in plans to return to the newspaper office in Akita. I was met by Mr. Nakaya, the paper's vice president. While his assistants went to the archives vault and looked for any report of debris having been found in the area at the time of the KAL 007 incident, he filled me in with details on the local hydrography. The current always flowed north and was at times extremely strong. The Oga Peninsula behaved like a giant vacuum cleaner, pulling in large numbers of floating objects, although some continued drifting all the way to Hokkaido. A dozen years ago a young man drifted from Shimohama, the spot at which I had found the first debris here, all the way to Matsumae in southern Hokkaido, 120 NM to the north, where he arrived unharmed.

Nothing in the archives indicated that debris had been found in the area at the time of the crash. But back then no one had expected to find anything. A find might have gone unnoticed. I took advantage of my trip to Akita to look for a more convenient place to stay than Ugo-Iwaya, though I liked the isolation of the mountain valley and the friendly cows. I finally found something in a small village called Konoura, not too far south and close to the train station. I could stay the week. The village was located on a promontory that jutted out from the coastline.

Konoura

In Konoura, the bus between the station and the hotel ran twice a day, morning and night. Fifteen hundred feet north of the station was a small fishing village protected from the sea by a jetty, which was itself protected by thick blocks of cement. Between the jetty and the cement blocks was a kind of deep alley about fifteen or twenty feet wide, filled with flotsam of all kinds that had been driven by the waves and wind and remained trapped there. Walking along the jetty I looked around rather mechanically, not expecting to find anything of value. I was wrong. I found the first fragment at three-thirty, the second two minutes later a few feet from the first, and the third a hundred and fifty feet from there. I left the village and continued on toward the south, to Kisakata.

Kisakata

Kisakata is a small fishing village again surrounded by jetties. These are protected by a wall of stacked cement blocks that left a wide, deep trench between the sea and the jetty. The waves pass through the spaces between the blocks and over them during storms, carrying debris. On the top of the piles of flotsam I found several pieces of honeycomb of the same kind I had found at other places and that had been identified in 1983 as coming from KAL 007 by the experts from Japan Air Lines, the Japan Defense Agency, and Korean Air Lines who examined the debris found by JMSA, the Hokkaido police, and returned by the Soviets.

My first reaction was to assume that the honeycomb was on top because it had arrived last. But upon reflection, I realized that its location in the pile had nothing to do with chronology but depended on the laws of physics. Every time a wave arrives, it submerges the piles of accumulated debris, and following Archimedes' law, the junk settles according to its density. The honeycomb fragments, being the lightest, always end up on top. I also realized that the same phenomenon was at work with the objects buried in the sand, which tends to act like a liquid. Heavy objects such as metal and rubber tires have a tendency to be buried deeper and deeper in the sand, while lighter objects such as honeycomb rise to the surface.

Approaching the end of the jetty at the entrance to the port, I saw a big chunk of aluminum panel that was between six and nine feet square. It was of the same pale blue used on the fuselage of Korean Air Lines planes. This time it wasn't honeycomb, but a sandwich panel consisting of two sheets of aluminum surrounding a sheet of black plastic. It was the first time I had discovered a piece of structural debris from the exterior of the Boeing 747. It appeared to be part of a fairing (aerodynamic covering) from the lower portion of the fuselage, which is painted this same pale blue. The sandwich was approximately two millimeters (one-twelfth inch) thick, and the aluminum sheets were eight thousandths of an inch thick, which is extremely thin. But the sandwich itself was rigid. Cutting off a small piece, I saw that it floated. Its density was only slightly lower than that of water, but it floated. Interestingly, a story I saw later printed in *Izvestiya* mentioned that the Soviets had recovered identical debris on Sakhalin, which they had identified as belonging to KAL 007.

Along this part of the beach, which was about a mile and a half long and ended in a cliff, I found a total of nine honeycomb fragments, the largest number of fragments to date in any one locality. The beach was situated at the beginning of a headland that jutted out into the sea. The high density of debris along this beach indicated that they had remained clustered together, implying that the point from which they began drifting was not far. As soon as I left Kisakata and continued south, however, the density of debris dropped sharply, from 5 fragments per mile north of the village to 0.5 per mile toward the south. I felt that I wasn't far from the impact area, beyond which no more debris would be found.

Fukura

By this time I was getting close to Niigata. I decided to explore Fukura, another small fishing village about eighty-five miles away. Fukura was the last train station close to the beach on this part of the coast. After Fukura the train turned toward the interior, and I would be unable to walk along the beach to the next train station as I had done until now. Through the window of the train I watched the coastline, trying to determine how difficult walking would be. North of Fukura the coast dropped away sharply in a series of vertical cliffs. Toward the south, however, there was a long, wide beach of white sand, roughly eight miles long and several hundred feet wide.

Arriving on the beach, I noticed streaks of flotsam, clearly separated from one another. The first was relatively close to the edge of the water and contained nothing of interest. The second, roughly in the middle of the beach, had a considerable amount of driftwood. The last was high up on the beach and quite spread out. Storms and high tides had left the majority of this debris. I decided to begin with it and explore the middle section on my way back.

My instincts were right. I found two pieces of honeycomb. By the end of the afternoon I had walked to the end of the beach without finding anything else. It was unbearably hot. I decided to rest awhile and jumped into the cool water. The beach was deserted as far as I could see in either direction. I let myself float on the surface of the cool water, grateful for the rest but conscious that I was still a long way from the end of my search.

Nezu-ga-Seki

I had chosen Nezu-ga-Seki as the next search area because it was far enough from Kisakata (47 miles) and had a long beach and an outcropping of rock that would retain any floating debris. The village was sixty-two miles from Niigata. I found a piece of honeycomb with some Korean writing, which was perfectly legible, and traces of corrosion primer on its aluminum panel. I then found a strange sort of badge that looked as though it had been glued to a businessman's attaché case. This piece of white plastic was shaped like an escutcheon, somewhat resembling a medieval coat of arms. Printed in blue was a stylized design that could have been a professional film camera, and within a lower half-circle was a Korean inscription.

Not far from the post office someone had pointed out a Korean restaurant. There I found an old Korean woman who translated the badge into Japanese. It read, DAI NI KAI "SCREEN" TAI KAI, "Second Major Screen Festival," or something to that effect. I was later told that this may have referred to the Second Seoul Film Festival of 1983. Possibly one of the participants had decided to fly on Korean Air Lines Flight 007.[2]

Murakami

My next stop was Murakami, closer still to Niigata. I found a single piece of debris here. It was gray, similar to those I had found at Okushiri. Was it the last? My next search area was Niigata itself.

The night before leaving for Niigata I made a table plotting the quantity of debris I had found against their distance from Niigata. The table is reproduced on page 102.

Taking into account the selective and somewhat arbitrary nature of my search method and the likelihood that I hadn't located all of the debris that made its way to the Japanese beaches, the table indicates that I was quite close to the impact area, which should not be far from Niigata.

Niigata

I had planned to take an early train from Murakami, which would put me in Niigata at eight-thirty in the morning. It was pouring outside. I took a bus from the station to the stop nearest the beach. I walked into the first open café I found. When the rain finally began to let up a bit, I left. I had walked a few feet when I heard someone call. The owner of the café was holding an umbrella in his hand. "Here, a customer left it a long time ago. You might as well get some use out of it."

It was still raining hard, but the umbrella helped, and it wasn't cold. The beach was long and straight and extended south as far as the eye could see. It combined the three most favorable characteristics for finding debris: a gently sloping, sandy beach, a jetty of cement blocks, and a back beach of small dunes covered with light vegetation. If any debris had found its way here, I would be sure to find it.

In spite of the rain, visibility was good and walking was easy if I ignored my shoes, which were now filled with water. I looked carefully everywhere that experience had taught me to expect debris. There were two false alarms: the first turned out to be nothing more than a flat stone, and the second, following a few perilous maneuvers to get to the object, was just a piece of plastic. By the end of the day I had been up and down the beach and was sure there was no debris to be found. After all my efforts, I had finally located the point beyond which there would be no more debris from the airliner. This made Murakami, just twenty-five miles north of Niigata, the southernmost point where debris was found. This agreed well with the chart I had drawn the night before (see below).

Location	Distance from Niigata	Number of debris
Shimohama	160 NM	6 + 1
Konoura	130 NM	3
Kisakata (North)	120 NM	9
Kisakata (South)	110 NM	1
Fukura	75 NM	2
Nezu-ga-Seki	35 NM	3
Murakami	25 NM	1

The Impact Area near Niigata

I had found the impact area but now I had to confirm it. There was no time or need to check every beach south of Niigata. Niigata is located inside an immense bay, one side of which faces north and the other west. Just opposite Niigata is the island of Sado Jima, well-known during feudal times for its gold mines. It was also the place where the shogun exiled his enemies. One aspect of Sado Jima was particularly important for my investigation. Situated directly in line with the Tsushima Shio, it ended in a large bay open on the southwest like an immense net stretched across the current. If any debris from the Korean airliner had found its way into the current south of Niigata, some of it would inevitably have drifted onto the beaches of Sado Jima. A thorough search of Sado Jima would give me a conclusive answer one way or the other. The message in the film cartridge that I had found with Mr. Kashima when I came across the first debris from Hotoke-Ga-Ura, in the village of Sai, had come from Sado Jima.

Sado Jima

An excellent hydrofoil service makes the trip from Niigata to Sado Jima in about an hour. From the port there is a bus to the village of Mano, deep inside the bay, where I would continue my search. I found a room not far from the village of Hamochi. The message I had found in the film canister came from a school nearby. The school's director, Mr. Noguchi, gave me a warm reception and confirmed that all the messages of his program had ended up somewhere up north. None had ever showed up south of the place where he had released them in the channel between Sado island and Niigata. This confirmed the direction of the current and indicated that the debris from Flight 007 found in the Tsugaru Strait came from the Sea of Japan north of, probably near, Niigata.

The beaches at Sado Jima were very much like the others I had examined, with white sand, occasional rocks, and jetties of cement blocks to fight erosion—a perfect trap to catch any debris. It was very hot, nearly 38° C (101° F). I still hadn't found anything by the time the sun finally began to set behind some clouds along the horizon. I returned to the hotel.

The following day, August 23, 1990, I continued my search along Mano Bay, in the extreme west of Sado Jima. A storm was approaching and the air was becoming oppressive. Some parts of the beach were easily accessible, others required the agility of a mountain climber. The immense Mano Bay is completely open to the wind and the dominant current and would inevitably have caught anything that passed within reach. If KAL 007 had crashed south of Niigata, fragments of debris would have found their way here, along the bay.

Because of the approaching storm, the sea was higher than usual and six-foot waves were breaking along the coast. After looking at the waves for a while, I came to an interesting conclusion. Along certain parts of the beach, the cliffs ended in a high, vertical rockface that dropped into the sea. The biggest waves could reach this height, however, and managed to dislodge bits of driftwood and other pieces of flotsam that had been there for quite some time, pulling them back into the open sea with the surf. Back at sea, this material continued drifting, pushed by the wind and current, and often ended up quite far from its starting point. On the other hand, where the beach was wide and sloped gently, any debris was pushed farther and farther into the interior of the island. This confirmed my previous observations that, because of their configuration, certain beaches held any debris that landed on them much longer than others. It was on these beaches that I had always located debris from Flight 007.

August 24, 1990, was my third day on Sado Jima. I had explored nearly all of Mano Bay and had found nothing. I was now almost certain that KAL 007 had not crashed south of Niigata. To be completely certain, however, I decided to explore Saboma Bay, which opens to the southwest, near the entrance to Mano Bay. If there was no debris at Saboma, I could be reasonably certain that Murakami was the southernmost point where any debris from the airliner had been washed up.

Saboma was very much like Mano Bay, with strong winds and high seas. I quickly located the spots where I had the best chance of finding anything. I looked around carefully, especially among the cement blocks of the jetties. By nightfall I was exhausted but satisfied. No debris had been washed up at Sado Jima. Murakami was definitely the southernmost point where debris from KAL 007 had landed. This meant that KAL 007 must have crashed within twenty-five miles north of Niigata.

I returned to my hotel. I had been exploring the Honshu beaches since August 5. I was worn-out and looking forward to a hot bath, a cold beer, and a good night's sleep. In spite of the fact that I had been forced to change my plans the day of my arrival at Akita and head south while my previous plans had been to go north, I had accomplished all of my objectives:

1. I had found debris that could only have come from Korean Air Lines Flight 007.
2. I had found the southernmost point to which debris from KAL 007 had drifted.
3. I had established that the impact area was between Niigata and Murakami.

As a kind of bonus, I had found a device belonging to the U.S. Navy, with its serial number intact. The device, which I had sent to John Keppel the day after I found it, turned out to be a smoke shell that could be launched from an airplane. These were often used by the Japanese US-1 seaplanes to mark the position of shipwrecks and verify the direction and force of the wind on the surface of the ocean when landing to rescue survivors. That the shell had wound up on the beach meant it had been used for a rescue operation somewhere in the Sea of Japan. Given the shape of the Japanese coastline and the narrowness of the Sea of Japan, rescue operations are generally performed by ship or helicopter, which do not use this type of smoke shell. US-1 seaplanes as a rule are used only in the Pacific.

The smoke shell I had found is a piece of American hardware that is also used by U.S. Navy planes. On the night KAL 007 was destroyed, a U.S. Navy plane, NAVY FB 650, was flying in the area and at 04:27 was at waypoint KADPO, a reporting point not far from Niigata, where it cancelled its IFR flight plan to continue patrolling along the surface of the water near the spot where KAL 007 must have crashed. NAVY FB 650 arrived there soon after the jetliner went down. It could have fired the smoke shell that I discovered seven years later on the beach.

KADPO and the KAL 007 impact area are interesting for another reason: on September 13, 1983, less than two weeks after the destruction of KAL 007, a squad of Japanese fighters intercepted four Soviet planes, including two reconnaissance planes, there. Why would Soviet planes have been flying in the area? The Soviet Navy had just completed a series of naval exercises not far away. Did they have information about where KAL 007 had actually crashed?

Before returning to Tokyo, I decided to return to the Tsugaru Strait and visit Uchiura Bay and the village of Kuroiwa, near Hakodate, where debris from KAL 007 had been found in September 1983. There I found two additional pieces of debris. The first was a piece of honeycomb that carried a perfectly legible marking in Korean, together with a serial number:

[ ]:70001444[ ]: [ ]   -89[ ]92C112   125   1-2

Although not in itself conclusive evidence that the fragment was from the Korean Air Lines Boeing 747, the Korean marking came as proof that the debris was of Korean origin, and not from one of the JASDF's target drones. It could have been a piece of paneling from the plane's galley, and this was suggested by the second piece of debris that I found nearby. It was a fragment of honeycomb painted beige, a color often used in airplane galleys. The fragment was distorted as though by an explosion. It was the most severely damaged fragment I had yet come across. It bore black impact marks from three objects that must have struck the panel with considerable force.

My second exploration of the Japanese beaches had brought additional evidence that KAL 007 had not crashed near Sakhalin Island. Together with the radio evidence I'd found, I felt it was conclusive.

The crash point of KAL 007 close to Niigata explained why no debris from the airliner had been found near Moneron at the time of its destruction. KAL 007 did not crash there. It explained why no debris had been found in the north for ten days: that is the time it took the debris to drift northward. Finally, it explained why debris had been found in the south: that is where KAL 007 did crash.

The only point that might be contested is the speed with which the debris drifted from near Niigata to the area around Moneron Island, Wakkanai, and Sakhalin. It traveled some 365 NM in just under ten days at an average speed of about 1.5 knots. That is fast but not unreasonably so since current speeds up to 2 knots have been observed in the Sea of Japan. Moreover, a few days after the shootdown, a storm in the Sea of Japan, lasting several days, contributed substantially to the speed with which floating debris must have been carried north.

PART THREE

THE SEARCH FOR THE WRECKAGE

The Witnesses Speak Out

The *Izvestiya* Investigation

Toward the end of 1990, the Soviet newspaper *Izvestiya* began a long series of articles on the 007 affair. Andrei Illesh, the lead reporter and the series's editor, interviewed many people involved in the disaster and the search for wreckage. Their testimony was edited and rearranged to tell the official one-intruder, one-shootdown story. Even so, the statements carried by *Izvestiya* were correctly quoted. They contain much real and revealing information.

Whatever the main purpose of the series may have been, *Izvestiya* mentioned my own investigation in articles that appeared on May 17 and 18, 1991. Drawing principally on my press conference in Tokyo on December 17, 1989,[1] Sergei Agafonov, the newspaper's representative in Tokyo, quotes me as follows:

> *The official version cannot account for the behavior of the Boeing on the Japanese radar screens. If we assume, however, that the aircraft Osipovich shot down was not the Korean airliner but a different plane, then the pieces fall into place, including the fact that KAL 007 continued its flight. . . . This also explains another mystery: the fact that the pilot of the Korean airliner transmitted a radio message fifty minutes after the "Boeing" had been shot down by the Soviet interceptor.*

Here Andrei Illesh, the series's editor, added:

> *This is no fantasy either. The radio conversations of the Korean pilots were recorded by both the Japanese and Americans. . . . These conversations occurred long after Lieutenant Colonel Osipovich shot down an aircraft. Correspondents from Asahi Television in Moscow showed me the results of the analysis of these conversations (independently conducted in the U.S. and Japan),[2] which prove that the voice belongs to the pilot of KAL 007.*

The correspondent for Asahi Television mentioned by Illesh is my friend Ryuji Osaki, who had gone to Moscow in search of documentary evidence. I had sent him spectrographs of KAL 007's late radio transmission so he could trade them with Illesh for documents we did not have. The May 18, 1991, issue of *Izvestiya,* which carried the article in which I am quoted, also printed a map attributed to the Japanese Maritime Safety Agency (JMSA), along with Illesh's assertion that the map shows my analysis to be wrong. However, the map is one *I* prepared. Before being published in *Izvestiya* it had been sent to Senator Kennedy in the United States and Senator Seya, vice president of the Japanese Diet. It was also published in France by *Aviation Magazine.* My name and the date I drew the map were clearly indicated. This information had been removed by *Izvestiya.*

The map illustrates four of the many different air encounters between Soviet interceptors and intruder aircraft. It also shows the track of the Korean airliner as it continued toward the south after passing the island of Moneron. That line was erased in the *Izvestiya* version. Illesh, who presumably published the map without realizing it was mine, used it to contradict my findings. But other Soviets, who prepared it for publication, must have known that the map was mine. They were aware of its meaning: Sakhalin airspace had been invaded by a squadron of intruding aircraft. They knew the map contradicted Illesh's ongoing contention that all that had happened was that the Korean airliner, a civilian passenger plane, had inadvertently strayed off course.[3]

Some members of the Soviet intelligence services and some members of the Soviet leadership surely knew what had really happened. When President Gorbachev visited Japan in April 1991, Sergei Agafonov traveled to Khabarovsk ahead of the president to cover the event. There he met people in the president's entourage, including a "high-ranking and powerful general who was a member of the government." Agafonov asked the general his opinion of my investigation. The general said, "Michel Brun has discovered part of the truth. The real story is more complicated than the official version of the event." The general told Agafonov that the wreckage at Moneron was "from military aircraft and there were three of them." It may have been the general's comments that prompted *Izvestiya* to mention my investigation, even though the editors tried to minimize its implications.

Despite the *Izvestiya* series's support for the official account of events, witnesses cited, including Lieutenant Colonel Osipovich, the pilot who the Russians claim shot down the Korean plane, and the undersea divers who worked on the wreckage, put the credibility of the official story in doubt. That did not escape the notice of the Soviet journalists. Referring to the dimensions of the black boxes found by the Soviet divers, Alexander Shalnev, *Izvestiya's* correspondent in New York,[4] wrote:

If the data [ICAO and Korean Air Lines] are correct, they contradict the information published in Izvestiya.

Andrei Illesh himself complained that "the facts do not fit together right."[5] Below, we shall see why when we study the series of more than fifty articles.

The series began with the "sensational revelation" that the wreck had been found by the Soviets.[6] Early in the *Izvestiya* series one of their correspondents asked Marshal Kirsanov, commander in chief of Soviet aviation, about my conclusion that the Korean airliner was not shot down near Sakhalin; it was destroyed four hundred miles to the south. The marshal said that was "absurd." The *Izvestiya* journalist then asked, "In that case why did Michel Brun question the location of the impact area of the Boeing?" This time the marshal replied, "I don't know exactly." He added, "We did locate ["a" or "the"] wreck, however."[7]

The *Izvestiya* journalists proceeded as though Marshal Kirsanov meant, "We located the wreckage of the Korean airliner." That is the way most news agencies around the world carried the story. But there are no articles *a* or *the* in the Russian language. Which one is intended is usually made clear by the context. Kirsanov's remark, however, was ambiguous, probably intentionally so.

Illesh, the series's editor, insists that a single wreck was found, that it was located by the oil-drilling ship *Mikhail Mirchinko,* and that all the divers involved were from Murmansk and under the direction of team leader Zakharchenko. But his own witnesses contradict that version of events.[13] Their statements describe several different recovery operations, as we shall see in the following chapters. At one point, in frustration Illesh writes, "There are as many different versions of events as there are witnesses."[8] He could instead have said, "There must be as many wrecks as there are different versions of events." That would have solved his problem. Fortunately for us, he published the contradictory statements anyway.

In his effort to prove that the only wreck around was that of the Korean airliner, Illesh gave all the credit to the civilian divers aboard the *Mikhail Mirchinko*. Perhaps that was because they had actually found the wreck of a Boeing—in this case an RC-135, which is a converted Boeing 707, but more about that later. In the process, Illesh was gratuitously insulting to the Soviet Navy. He drew an angry rebuttal. In a telegram to Tass about an undersea expedition planned by *Izvestiya,* Captain Kosik[9] contradicts him by saying that it was the Navy, not the civilian divers, which found the wreckage:[10]

I'm really not sure why Izvestiya *waited eight years for an undersea expedition since the Soviet Navy found the wreckage a long time ago and recovered everything there was to recover. If they wanted to see it, all they had to do was ask the Navy Oceanographic Service.*

Not accepting Kosik's rebuke, Illesh wrote:

No Navy diver was on the bottom in the area where the KAL 007 wreckage fell. At this time [autumn 1983] the entire recovery operation was conducted by the Mikhail Mirchinko *with the divers from Murmansk and Sakhalin, with help from the* Gidronavt *and its minisub* Tinro-2.

Yet, among others, the Soviet Navy had played an important role in the undersea recovery operations. Captain Girsh, commander of the *Tinro-2,* said that taking refuge at Moneron from a storm, he had talked to Navy divers who, working far from the area where he had been exploring a wreck, had themselves found a sunken aircraft with the tail standing upright among the reefs.[11]

Several wrecks had, in fact, been found and explored—at different times, with different participants, with different methods, in different depths of water. That *Izvestiya's* witnesses each spoke of the wreck on which they worked as though it were the only one may have reflected their political caution—certainly most of those who saw wreckage knew it had not come from a Boeing 747. But the very partial nature of their testimony also importantly reflected the fact that from the start the Soviet command had insisted on secrecy and the compartmentalization of information. That is to say, it tried to keep the individuals and the teams participating ignorant of what others were doing.

What lay behind this was the growing assertiveness of U.S. policy in the spring and summer of 1983 and Soviet reluctance to challenge the United States publicly. If it had become known that the Soviets had shot down a number of U.S. military aircraft, it was indeed probable that public opinion, ignorant of how the crash had come about, would have led the Reagan administration to retaliate. And the risk of nuclear war, which the KAL 007 operation had already created, would have been aggravated.

What is interesting in the *Izvestiya* articles are not Illesh's arguments with the Soviet Navy, but the witnesses he quotes. By comparing their statements with the documents we have collected, in particular the JMSA's operations log and situation maps, which mention the daily position of all the ships, we can compare the testimony of the witnesses and determine which wrecks they found, which groups of divers and ships were involved, and in what areas they were working. We can re-create the Soviet recovery effort from the first days of the operation. We can add to our knowledge of what happened during the air battle over Sakhalin. We can again demonstrate that what was presented as the crash of KAL 007 on Moneron was that, or rather those, of other aircraft. To make the almost incredible events of the KAL 007 affair credible, we need to show that the evidence of air logistics, of ocean currents, of floating and sunken debris, of search and recovery operations, of air-traffic-control communications, of transmitter profile and voice-print identification, of Japanese press accounts and Soviet communications transcripts, all points in the same direction. The *Izvestiya* articles provide much data useful in this effort.

Toward the end of the *Izvestiya* series the Japanese media also became interested in the story. In its October 15, 1991, issue the Tokyo daily newspaper *Yomiuri Shimbun* printed the testimony of Ivan Bilyuk, captain of the Soviet fishing vessel *Uvarovsk*. The October 17, 1991, issue of *Izvestiya* also picked up the same story. The following is a combined rendering of the two, together with my comments.

During the night of August 31 to September 1, 1983, the modern deep-sea trawler Uvarovsk, *skipper Captain Bilyuk, was returning to his home port of Korsakov, in southern Sakhalin, from a seven-month fishing expedition in the Indian Ocean. Around 06:30 Sakhalin time, [04:30 in Japan] the officer on watch indicated that an American warship was dead ahead.*

Captain Anisimov had observed one or more intruder aircraft on the radar of his patrol boat at 05:32 Sakhalin time, and that a Soviet interceptor fired a missile on an intruder at 06:24 Sakhalin time. In other words, the U.S. man-of-war was on the scene when the battle was still taking place.

Captain Bilyuk was quite surprised at the news because he had never seen an American warship in La Pérouse Strait before. Half an hour later, around 7:00 in the morning, Sakhalin time, after evading the American warship, which had been hampering their progress, Captain Bilyuk received orders to head for Moneron, passing west of the island. He was told to remain on the lookout for any objects or persons floating on the surface of the water. [This information agrees with Soviet ambassador Pavlov's statement when he informed the Japanese government that "the traces of an air crash" had been detected west of Moneron.] Bilyuk didn't find anything of interest west of Moneron and continued north of the island. Around 08:00 [Sakhalin time], after the sun had been up for nearly an hour, with his binoculars he noticed a large, milk white slick on the surface of the water roughly 200 meters [600 feet] across. He noted its position on the map, 46°35' N by 141°22' E.

This position was published in the Japanese newspaper *Yomiuri Shimbun* together with Captain Bilyuk's map, but not in *Izvestiya*. The spot indicated by Captain Bilyuk is barely 4 NM due east of the position of the *Chidori Maru* when the fishermen observed the explosion of an aircraft.

The slick was aviation kerosene, which had bubbled up to the surface. The sea in and around the kerosene patch was covered with thousands of pieces of debris, mostly honeycomb panels that looked as if they had been cut with a knife. That led Captain Bilyuk to assume that an airplane had been hit by a rocket. He also noticed a smoke signal still working with an orange flame burning.

Smoke signals used for sea rescue usually have a short life of just a few minutes, half an hour at the most. The aircraft that crashed at this spot may have been either of two aircraft: the one observed by Captain Anisimov at 05:33 Sakhalin time (03:33 Tokyo time) or another one, which the Soviets said was "stopped at Pravda at 06:24." Captain Bilyuk discovered the crash site at ten o'clock, in the first case four and a half hours or, in the other, three and a half hours later than the events. In either case, if the smoke signal had been activated by the fallen aircraft, it would have been extinct long ago. The obvious conclusion is that it was dropped by an airplane or helicopter to mark the spot for rescuers. The interesting question is, who dropped it, the Soviets or the Americans? We may infer that, if it were the Soviets, Captain Bilyuk, who had received orders from Soviet headquarters to look for a crash, would have, no doubt, been given the coordinates by radio. Which was not the case.

The Uvarovsk *remained at the site for two hours and collected approximately one ton of debris.*

This represents a substantial amount of debris given the extreme lightness of the material. In their article in *Izvestiya*, Illesh and Shalnev mention neither this honeycomb debris nor the smoke signal. According to them, the *Uvarovsk* received the order to leave the site immediately, which is incorrect. It did not leave until after it had been relieved by another ship, the *Zabaikalye*. Illesh and Shalnev mention only the existence of "civilian" debris floating on the surface, including fur coats and leather jackets. It is worth pointing out that the passengers left New York on August 31, when people are not expected to be carrying their winter clothing.

A short digression on the nature of this civilian debris is needed here. According to French investigative TV journalist Misha Lobko, who interviewed him in 1993, the first mate of the *Zabaikalye* said there were large quantities of pairs of shoes with their laces tied together as in a shoe store. Captain Bilyuk of the *Uvarovsk* told the Associated Press,[12] "My first impression was that they just took some things from a store and put them in the water. They were very new. They still had labels on them." There is no evidence that the baggage compartment of KAL 007 broke open. Floating debris from the airliner did not, of course, reach Moneron for another nine days.[13]

> *The* Zabaikalye, *under the command of Capt. Vladimir Alexeiev, was the largest vessel in Nevelsk. When he arrived at the site, Captain Alexeiev saw that the debris was concentrated in an area approximately one nautical mile square. "There was so much that we were overwhelmed," he recalled. The* Uvarovsk *let them recover the debris and headed for a point 46°35' N, 141°27' E, which was about seven miles east and closer to Sakhalin Island, where another airplane had apparently crashed. They joined three other ships already at the site, including a cargo ship that dropped two boats into the water to collect some large, heavy objects, while the JMSA patrol ship* Rebun *observed from a distance.[14]*
>
> *Captain Bilyuk received orders to drive the* Rebun *away. He hoisted the international signal indicating, "We have priority and are going to cross your bow." When he was questioned later, the captain of the* Rebun *had a vivid but disoriented recollection of the incident:*
>
> *"I wasn't exactly sure what was going on. I saw two Soviet planes flying low and directly above us in a circular pattern, and I thought they wanted to stop the Soviet fishing vessel. I tried to pick up the Soviet marine frequencies on the radio, but got nothing but static."[15]*

The *Rebun* changed direction and started patrolling at slow speed. At 17:00 hours it arrived in the area where the *Chidori Maru* had seen an airplane explode just above the surface of the water. The *Rebun* saw a Soviet vessel at the exact spot where the *Chidori Maru* had been earlier that day. This was the *Zabaikalye,* collecting the debris found by the *Uvarovsk.* The *Zabaikalye,* which had been joined by other vessels, remained in the area throughout the day and at nightfall continued working with the aid of searchlights. It is possible that the *Uvarovsk, Zabaikalye,* and other Soviet ships were able to collect most of the debris. But they didn't collect *everything* before the *Rebun* arrived in the area that afternoon. Otherwise why would they have continued working on into the night?

Neither the *Rebun* nor the JMSA, nor any Japanese or Soviet official, nor the U.S. Navy, spoke of this debris, although one of the parties involved had earlier marked the spot with a smoke signal. Already in the KAL 007 case we see three governments, those of the United States, the U.S.S.R., and Japan, withholding information, each for its own reason.

Ambassador Pavlov had immediately informed the Japanese government about the discovery of "traces of an aviation accident" west of Moneron. That was the first we had heard of a crash there.[16] The Japanese and Soviet ships were north of the island, where the smoke signal was. The Japanese stated they did not find any debris from the Korean airliner before September 9. They had found debris before this date, but it had nothing to do with KAL 007. As indicated in a previous chapter, the first fifty-four pieces of debris found by the JMSA came from military aircraft. The debris picked up by Captain Bilyuk's *Uvarovsk* and by the *Zabaikalye*, and marked by one of the parties involved with a smoke signal, evidently also came from military aircraft—at least the authentic debris did. But for years this was mentioned by no one.

Among the Soviet ships that showed up north of Moneron, one is particularly noteworthy. It was a KGB patrol vessel (the KGB was responsible for patrolling the country's borders), commanded by a Captain Anisimov. The ship had been on duty off Nevelsk when, between 05:32 and 05:33 hours (Sakhalin time, 03:32 in Japan), there appeared on its radar a blip that was crossing the sky at a speed of 800 km (500 miles) per hour. Within forty seconds the blip split in two, then three, before disappearing approximately 30 km (19 miles) from Moneron along an azimuth of 010 degrees from the island, at a point 46°33' N, 141°18' E, give or take a few miles to take into account some uncertainty about the azimuth. Captain Anisimov noticed on his radar screen a lone fishing vessel near that spot.

The position given above places it close to where the *Chidori Maru* was at 03:30 (46°35' N, 141°16' E) when it witnessed an airplane explode at sea level. There is, however, a three-minute time difference between the two accounts. The description of the two events also differs. The *Chidori Maru* captain's account indicates that the aircraft remained intact until the explosion and didn't break up until it hit the surface of the water. Moreover, the details provided by Captain Anisimov make us doubt that what he saw was a single airplane splitting up into two, then three parts. First of all, the split took place along the horizontal plane and lasted approximately forty seconds at a speed of 800 km (500 miles) per hour. It is hard to imagine an airplane losing a piece of its fuselage large enough to be observed by a marine radar and then continuing to fly for forty more seconds before losing another slightly smaller piece. The observation would more easily correlate with a group of fighters that separated from one another in what is a classic maneuver used by attack aircraft. By contrast, the *Chidori Maru*'s account indicates that a single fighter was passing directly overhead at the moment it fired a missile, just before the explosion of another aircraft, its target, which was at moderate range from it. That makes it seem likely that Anisimov and the captain of the *Chidori Maru* were describing two different events.[17]

Captain Anisimov's observations reveal something else of even greater importance. He observed what he interpreted as the "destruction of an aircraft" at 05:33 Sakhalin time. However, according to Marshal Ogarkov, an interceptor stopped an intruder plane above the village of Pravda at 06:24 hours Sakhalin time, roughly one hour later.[18] From this we understand that two aircraft were shot down with an hour interval between the two. That broadens our idea of the scope of the air battle of Sakhalin.

Anisimov also said he recovered approximately 100 kg (220 pounds) of debris, mostly honeycomb panels. He did not indicate where he collected them, except that he was "at sea off Nevelsk." The JMSA patrol boat *Rebun* mentions that day (September 1) sighting a group of Soviet vessels collecting debris, among which may well have been Captain Anisimov's patrol boat. According to the *Rebun*'s captain, the patrol boat took the cover off its cannon and pointed it at him, an effective way of telling him to stay away.

The interviews with the captains of the Soviet vessels *Uvarovsk* and *Zabaikalye* make it clear that the Soviets recovered floating debris in three different locations. There were, in fact, even more crash sites. To distinguish the different sites from each other and to show what can be learned from them, I will examine the evidence in some detail.

The Soviet Underwater Search (1)

The First Wreck, September 13

In presenting the testimonies he publishes in *Izvestiya* about the undersea search, Soviet journalist Illesh admits they are far from clear: "This is the most confusing part of the 007 incident—the search for the Boeing's wreckage."[1] Although he arranges his material as though he were talking about a single incident, and says or implies all the intruder aircraft were the one Korean airliner, Illesh, fortunately, publishes statements of participants that are sufficiently specific to show the source of their inconsistency. The persons speaking were talking about different wrecks found on different dates, in different places, under different conditions. Establishing the where, when, and who was involved was made possible thanks to the Japanese Maritime Safety Agency maps John Keppel and I had obtained. Without this invaluable tool, which recorded the daily positions and the actions of the vessels of all kinds involved in the search, reconciling apparently contradictory statements would have been a lot more difficult. With the exception of Japanese television reporter Iwao Koyama, who was at the scene during the whole search and recorded the salvage vessels' positions live from the JMSA daily briefings (see chapter 4), John and I are today the only investigators in possession of these invaluable documents. He obtained a first part during a trip to Japan, and I obtained the rest in Tokyo. Together, they constitute the most detailed and complete report on the search efforts by all the nations involved. They allowed me to find order where Andrei Illesh only saw confusion, to have a clear idea of how many wrecks the Soviet Navy Pacific Fleet found, and to see how it conducted its search.

The Pacific Fleet was under the command of Admiral Sidorov, who was responsible for the Soviet search effort. During a meeting in Moscow with the Families of the Victims held on March 11, 1993, Admiral Sidorov said that, once alerted, the Soviet Navy immediately sent a group of military vessels to the area where an aircraft was believed to have crashed. The area was easily located by the presence of debris floating on the surface. Boundaries were established and the area was marked out with buoys.[2] "Within twenty-seven minutes of the crash, small Soviet craft were on the scene and small effects were recovered, but no bodies."[3]

In order for the small craft to be on the scene within twenty-seven minutes, the crash site had to be fairly close to Nevelsk. If we count a minimum of ten or twelve minutes to alert the crews and have them join their boats, start their engines, and haul their anchors, that leaves only fifteen minutes travel time from Nevelsk to the crash point, which thus has to have been within a few miles of Nevelsk. There is precisely such a crash point, illustrated on the map that President Yeltsin handed representatives of Korea, the ICAO, and the U.S. next of kin in Moscow, on October 14, 1992. It is also indicated by the JMSA log and situation maps, which show that on the first few days after the disaster, an intensive search effort took place in a narrow, lens-shaped area, wholly within Soviet territorial waters, approximately 6 NM off the Sakhalin coast, and centered at 46°35′ N, 141°45′ E, along the 100-meter (300-foot) depth line. Oceanographic data show that the seafloor in this area is muddy; the water is extremely dirty, visibility is low, and there is no aquatic life. All of which agrees with the divers' comments as well as with the testimony of Nikolai Sergeievich Antonov, a captain from the fishing base at Kholsmk, quoted by *Izvestiya:*

> *I arrived in the search area five or six days after the Boeing was destroyed. I had been sent to replace the captain of the* Kareng, *a large, refrigerated trawler. There were already a large number of ships in the area—military ships and fishing vessels. There were fifteen or twenty fishing vessels. These had their nets out and were trawling in the search area. There was a thick layer of mud on the bottom and the nets broke frequently. The seafloor was dead, there was no sign of aquatic life. No one had ever caught any fish in the area. Finally the fishermen hooked the Boeing.[4]*

The Soviet Navy had soon realized that the aircraft that crashed there was reduced to pieces too small to locate with sonar and had decided to use the direct-contact method, dragging trawl nets and steel cables across the shallow bottom. Admiral Sidorov explained in more detail how the operation was conducted:

> *The fishermen rigged a trawl net so that it could be tugged by two trawlers. They covered its underside with leather so it would slide better [in the heavy mud]. They collected some paper and debris from the plane. The size of the search area was revised and now estimated to be 2 kilometers by 1.5 kilometers [1.2 by 1 mile]. It was divided into three sectors, where debris had been found by the fishing vessels, which caught them in their nets. . . . Around September 8 or 9, 1983, a trawl net got caught in a fuselage section, which it dragged for nearly a mile. Then we called in the* Mikhail Mirchinko, *but it had no divers on board.[5]*

The *Mikhail Mirchinko* arrived at the site on September 10, as indicated by the JMSA documents and by the testimony of its crew. The *Mirchink* is a sophisticated oil-drilling ship and diving base, able dynamically to stabilize her position precisely over a specific spot on the bottom without dropping anchor. The ship was to begin diving operations immediately. But because it arrived without its normal complement of civilian divers, the Soviet Navy had to call in their own divers from their main base of Sovetskaya Gavan on the Siberian mainland.

Zhan Andreievich Aleschenko was chief mate on board the *Mirchink* from September 10 to the end of the search operations. He was interviewed by Stanislav Glukov, a correspondent for *Izvestiya:* "There were a number of sailors from Sovetskaya Gavan on board ship. When they had located the search area [with cables and nets], they [the military divers] began searching the seafloor."

Illesh never admitted that several wrecks were found at different places and at different times by different teams of divers. He took no account of the conflicting testimony he himself provided in the eighth installment of the *Izvestiya* series:

> *During this time the divers—throughout the entire Soviet Union there were no more than fifty divers as skilled as the Murmansk divers—were resting in their quarters near Kholmsk, with nothing to do until the end of September. As their team leader, Vladimir Vasilievich Zakharchenko, commented, "We were rushed to Sakhalin by plane and sent to our quarters on the base. Then they forgot about us. We stayed alone in our dorms until the end of the month. . . . It was only at the end of September that a minesweeper brought us out to the* Mikhail Mirchinko."

By the end of September the *Mikhail Mirchinko* had moved to another crash site. The divers who were working the ship during the first days of the month then, of necessity, could not have been those from Murmansk, for at that time they were resting in their dorms, fighting their boredom. Aleschenko, chief mate on the *Mirchink,* gives us further detail of the Navy work on this first wreck:

> *The Soviet Navy had trawlers rake the seafloor and managed to bring up some debris this way. As the divers were able to discover later on, the trawl net got caught in the central part of the fuselage, which it dragged for nearly a mile. But we had to find the exact spot where the fuselage got tangled in the net. To do this we had to send them [the Navy divers] down to examine the bottom.*

Illesh continues the story in *Izvestiya* with a quote from Zakharchenko:

They decided to send a TV camera down to look at the bottom. During this time we were resting in Kholmsk, in our dorm. I'm simply relating what our colleagues [the Navy divers] were doing. At first they didn't find anything interesting. For a day or two we watched their progress with the TV camera. In my opinion what they were doing was useless, because the bottom was muddy and you couldn't see more than three meters [ten feet] in that dirty water.

We suggested they use a diving bell with observers in it. They sent down the diving bell with four divers: one who looked ahead, a second to look on the right side, a third to look on the left, and the fourth to look at the bottom, directly beneath it. The size of the observation zone increased immediately to 15 meters [50 feet]. And on exactly the third day they found the plane.

The *Mikhail Mirchinko* had arrived in the search area on September 10. The third day brings us to September 13, 1983. Aleschenko, chief mate of the *Mirchink*, provides more details:

The wreckage from the plane was severely damaged. It had been reduced to pieces. The largest pieces we saw were the pivot support structures, which are extremely solid. These were between four and six feet long, and twenty to twenty-four inches wide. Everything else was in small pieces.

V. Verbitsky, radio operator on the *Mirchink:*

Most of us were able to keep some debris as a souvenir. Some of us even made bowls out of the titanium pivots. . . . Yes, the plane must have hit the surface of the water with tremendous force to break the titanium pivots.[6]

This type of pivot is an essential structural element on any aircraft with a variable-geometry wing design, which is only used on supersonic aircraft. The wreck the Navy was working on was probably that of an EF-111, which the U.S. Air Force used extensively as an electronic countermeasures (ECM) aircraft.[7]

The JMSA maps and documents show that the *Mikhail Mirchinko* and the ships that accompanied it worked in the area of this first wreck until September 26. At six in the morning on September 26, the fleet accompanying the *Mirchink* consisted of eighteen ships, including seven trawlers. By noon only ten ships were left with the *Mirchink*. All the trawlers and their support vessels had left. What remained of the *Mirchink*'s fleet also left the territorial waters of Sakhalin for a new search area some forty miles to the west, an area 16 NM northwest of the island of Moneron where the U.S. Navy was engaged in a search for the wreck of an aircraft apparently of special interest to it. The crash site was far from where everyone else was working. The recovery operations for the first wreck of September 13 south of Nevelsk in territorial waters off Sakhalin thus ended September 26. They had lasted twenty-six days.[8]

The Second Wreck, September 16

While the *Mikhail Mirchinko* was working on the first wreck, a second wreck had been found by another salvage vessel on September 16, in international waters, north of Moneron Island, 15 NM to the west of the first wreck. Operating from minisubmersibles from the *Georgi Kozmin*, a salvage ship and diving base, Soviet Navy divers retrieved a 10-meter (30-foot) wing section—which obviously came from an aircraft other than the one Admiral Sidorov described as blown to bits. In its issue of September 18, 1983, the *Too Nippo*, a provincial newspaper from Aomori, reported:

On the morning of September 17, information was received at Wakkanai and JMSA headquarters in Otaru, indicating that an object, whose exact nature is unknown but which looks like a piece from an aircraft, was hauled up from the bottom by a Soviet ship observed by the Japanese patrol vessel Daisetsu. *The search area was located west of Sakhalin, in the area where the Korean airliner is believed to have disappeared.*

This is the first time the Soviets have been seen to bring up an object from the ocean floor. According to our sources, during the afternoon of September 16, 1983, at 21:00 hours [Japan time], Soviet vessels assembled at a point 46°34' north and 141°21' east, 31 kilometers [19 miles] north-northeast of the island of Moneron.[8] Among the Soviet ships were the Rudonski *and the 12,000-ton salvage ship from the Soviet Navy, the* Georgi Kozmin. *At 23:00 hours they hauled up a 10-meter [thirty-foot] long piece of the wreckage.*

At 03:30 in the morning on September 17 a minisubmarine able to drop divers on the seafloor was put in the water, along with two support boats. The minisub returned to the surface at 05:40, and at 06:30 was hauled back on board the mothership's bridge. At 06:55 the same day, another minisub, yellow this time and approximately 17 feet long, was put into the water by a 700-ton vessel and was observed as it began its descent. This occurred in international

waters at a depth of 164 meters [540 feet]. Although the patrol vessel
Daisetsu *was located 500 meters [1,600 feet] away, the Soviets sig-*
naled the ship to keep its distance in order not to endanger the
recovery operation.

The ten-meter (thirty-foot) piece of wreckage recovered on September 16 seems to have been part of an aircraft wing. It could not have come from the same airplane as the first wreck, which was too far away and was reduced to small pieces. Another aircraft would be found on October 17 or 18 a few miles to the south (see next chapter). I do not, however, believe that the wing section came from that aircraft. The *Georgi Kozmin*, with its support flotilla, including other specialized vessels like the *Rudonski*, mini-submarines, and the Navy divers who recovered the wing section, contin-ued to work intensively in the same area for two months—twice as long as the *Mirchink* spent on the first wreck. That was a major investment of time and equipment. It leads me to believe that the second wreck was a separate aircraft, unrelated to the airplane the *Mirchink* found a month later (see map, Figure 12, page 135), and that, in all likelihood, the *Georgi Kozmin* and its flotilla explored the wreck and recovered from it what they chose to recover.

The second wreck could very well have been the airplane that the *Chidori Maru* saw explode at low altitude over the water and the one at the crash site visited by Captain Bilyuk's *Uvarovsk*. The recovery operation lasted fifty-four days.[9]

The Third Wreck, *Tinro-2*

The *Tinro-2* is a minisubmarine from the Ministry of Fisheries. It was dispatched from Vladivostok to assist in the search and recovery operations. Oddly enough, however, its first dives did not take place where everybody else was looking, around Moneron, but far to the north. The *Tinro-2* arrived on scene on September 14 and by September 17 had conducted several dives and had located a third wreck. We know its location thanks to a coin-cidence. Admiral Sidorov tells us:

An American helicopter crashed far from the search area where the American fleet was working. They asked for our assistance. We pro-vided the coordinates of the spot where their helicopter crashed.[10]

Why would the Soviet Navy have known where an American helicopter had crashed when the Americans themselves did not know? Clearly it had crashed near a Soviet ship, far from the American fleet. The U.S. Navy after-action report confirmed this.[11] The report states that on September 17, 1983, following mechanical failure, an SH-2F helicopter from the frigate *Badger* crashed and sank in international waters at 47°01′ N, 141°13′ E. The four-man crew was recovered unharmed by the USCG *Munro* an hour and a half after the accident. The after-action report, para E1, recounts the incident as follows:

The most significant HSL event of SALVOPS was unfortunately the operational loss of the USS Badger*'s, HSL 37/2, SH-2F, due to an in-flight mechanical failure on 17 Sep 1983. Amidst the abrupt, rapid action, aerial emergency one "MAYDAY" UHF call was transmitted before the helo went down. This "MAYDAY" was copied by both an alert AWACs and surface-ship crew: the ensuing SAR successfully rescued the crew less than ninety minutes after the helo entered the water 35 miles from the closest surface ship.*

The position of the helicopter crash is approximately thirty-five miles north of the general search area where the American and Soviet fleets were working. What was an American helicopter doing so far from the spot where everyone was supposedly looking for the Korean airliner? The helicopter was based on the USS *Badger*, which was specially outfitted for electronic intelligence work, or SIGINT. It seems logical to assume that the *Badger*'s helicopter out on patrol was involved in the same sort of intelligence mission as was its mothership. And if this is true, what were they looking for, so far from the main search areas? An answer is found in the interview with Capt. Mikhail Girsh, who commanded the minisubmarine *Tinro-2*:

At first no one paid any attention to us because our mothership was only 1,000 tons and the yellow bands on its smokestack showed that it belonged to the Ministry of Fishing. But as soon as we opened the hangar doors and dropped the submarine, the Americans began to get excited . . . helicopters, the frigate Badger *. . . came in very close. They harassed us so much that sometimes it was impossible to get the submarine into the water. . . .*

One day, while I was diving, an American helicopter crashed into the water. I remember that the captain of the Gidronavt *[the mothership] told me over the special telephone, "Misha, be careful down there or a helicopter might fall on your head." I said to him, "What's going on? Are you joking, or what?" "No," he said, "it's serious. An American helicopter just crashed right in front of our eyes."[12]*

This shows that the *Gidronavt* and the *Tinro-2* were working on September 17 more than thirty-five miles north of the principal search area. During the dive on the seventeenth, when the helicopter nearly landed on top of the minisub, Captain Girsh found and photographed debris from an airplane. By reason of chronology I call this the third wreck, it having been found a few hours after the *Georgi Kozmin* recovered the wing section of another airplane thirty-five miles to the south. This northern crash site corresponds to the point where interceptor 163 may have shot down an airplane at supersonic speed at 04:42 (Japan time). It would have been a fairly small aircraft, which tends to be confirmed by an observation from Captain Girsh, who claimed he found little debris in the area. The recovery operations for the third wreck lasted six days.

On September 26, the Soviets turned over to the Japanese a first batch of what they said was floating debris from KAL 007. Most of it *was* floating debris, although it did not all come from KAL 007. Among the debris that did not were two life rafts (one for ten persons, the other for one man), structural elements like an air brake from a supersonic fighter, pieces of fuselage skin painted white, blue, and gold (U.S. Navy colors), and a wing-armament pylon. They were items of military debris presumably recovered at one or another of the three crash sites found on September 13, 16, and 17. Boeing 747s, like KAL 007, do not have life rafts (they use evacuation chutes instead). They are not painted white, blue, and gold—though some U.S. Navy aircraft are. They do not have air brakes and do not have wing-armament pylons, either.

By September 17 the Soviets had located three crash sites spread over an area of approximately thirty miles. The aircraft that would be discovered on October 18 by the *Mikhail Mirchinko* will be our next story.

The Soviet Undersea Search (2)

The Fourth Wreck of October 18

By noon on September 26, the flotilla accompanying the *Mikhail Mirchinko* had moved to a deep-water search area on the other side of Moneron, northwest of that island. That is where the U.S. Navy claimed to have heard the pinger from KAL 007's black boxes. The *Mirchink*'s move indicated the end of the search operations for the first wreck and prompted a rotation of the diving crew on board. The Murmansk divers, who had been waiting at their dorm in Kholmsk, boarded the ship on September 26:

> *They had forgotten about us. They left us on our own until the end of September. . . . It wasn't until the end of the month that a minesweeper brought us out to the* Mikhail Mirchinko *and we were officially given our "orders to find the [or an] airplane."*[1]

Four divers from the team entered the compression chamber on September 29. They remained under compression for a month, until October 26, when they were replaced by another group of divers, who remained under compression until November 6. Other divers from Sebastopol, Sakhalin, and of Sovetskaya Gavan must also have participated in the rotation of crews aboard other ships.

In its search for the September 13 wreck, the Soviet Navy had used the direct method, for the reasons that Admiral Sidorov described in the preceding chapter. The search that resulted in the October 18 find was conducted in a totally different way. An officer who "participated in the search for the Boeing," but requested anonymity, provided the following commentary. (The October 18 find may, indeed, have been a Boeing, though in this instance not a Boeing 747 like KAL 007 but a Boeing 707 configured as a USAF RC-135.)

> *The search for the Boeing could be referred to as a large-scale operation. We had data from Air Defense personnel, which we entered into a computer. Specialists calculated the coordinates of the impact point of the aircraft. We then queried the radar stations that had picked up distance and azimuth coordinates. After a few hours*

we had a mathematically calculated ellipse.[2]

In this instance the coordinates of the impact area were obtained only after "a few hours," using a mathematical procedure on a computer. By contrast, the impact area of the first wreck was "immediately determined by the presence of debris" and marked with buoys; several vessels had arrived within twenty-seven minutes of the crash. The officer describing the location of the fourth wreck continues:

> *A Navy officer, a navigation specialist, worked on the computer data. We immediately went to the search area. We used magnetic detection technology, similar to that used on minesweepers. There were ships all over the place and this hampered our ability to work. Our search vessels operated in three successive waves. First came the minesweepers with magnetometers. If I remember correctly, there were six of them. Then there were the hydrographic vessels with their search sonar. Finally, there was another group of minesweepers that used side-looking sonar. That way we could patrol the same area with three different types of ships. When all three types of ships had a confirmed echo, we sent down the divers. . . . We were aware that "the enemy" [the Americans] possessed excellent hardware, and we were envious of their ships. . . . Yet we were the first ones to locate wreckage, not them.*[3]

The search, in three successive waves, is illustrated on the JMSA's situation maps for September 9, 1983, where the first wave of the search, using six minesweepers, is clearly indicated. One of *Izvestiya's* witnesses tells a story, interesting in itself, which indicates the time schedule:

> *Admiral Sidorov ordered us to fool the Americans with a phony black box, which was very hard to distinguish from the real one. The false black box was thrown overboard in a depth of 620 meters [2,000 feet] of water. To add to their problems, the admiral ordered two groups of ships to simulate a search operation in the area where we had dropped the false black box, while the other ships continued looking in the true search area.*[4] *It was also suggested that two trawler captains head for the phony search area and start transmitting in clear [noncoded] language false radio information to fool the Americans. The fishermen cried out on the radio, "We've found the black boxes!" Shortly afterward the Americans invited the Western media on board their ships so they could be present for the recovery of the black boxes.*[5]

The Soviets may indeed, as they claimed, have planted a false black box in the water on September 26 in order to distract the Americans, who had been hampering their search effort. But the Americans said they had detected signals from a black box in the same search area (northwest of Moneron) by September 14, *before* the Soviets tossed their false black box into the water. Thus the first signals detected by the U.S. Navy did not come from the false black box. They probably came from the pinger of an airplane that had actually fallen in the area. The Soviet Navy kept a number of ships in that area, where they remained for more than a month, working in depths of more than 1,000 meters (3,000 feet). This would indicate that there was, indeed, a wreck there, containing real black boxes.[6]

However, the movements of the Soviet ships observed by the JMSA give credence to Admiral Sidorov's claim that he planted a false black box to distract the Americans. The September 26 map of the JMSA shows that, before noon, Soviet ships suddenly moved to the area 16 NM northwest of Moneron, where the concentration of American vessels was greatest. These Soviet ships were clearly those that dropped the false black box and simulated its location. At the same time, the main Soviet fleet was assembled around the *Mikhail Mirchinko,* north of Moneron, where, no doubt, it "continued looking in the true search area," in the words of the officer quoted above. This was where "the aircraft" would be found on October 18, which Illesh insists was the only wreck found. Capt. Ivan Varfolomeievich Shaydurov took part in that operation. He says:

> *They sent me to the search area to participate in the operation and put me in charge of the group of trawlers. . . . When I assumed my duties, the smaller trawlers and their support vessels had already left [the area of the first wreck]. They never returned to the new area, which was three nautical miles square. . . . I stayed there one month, from October 10 until November 10. . . . The* Mikhail Mirchinko *was anchored right on top of the Boeing's fuselage.[7]*

Captain Shaydurov's statement is confirmed by the JMSA documents. He says that the "smaller trawlers and their support vessels" had already left when he assumed his duties on October 10. The Japanese documents show that they had left on September 26. The JMSA log also shows that on September 30 most of the Soviet fleet, assembled around the *Mikhail Mirchinko,* was north of Moneron Island, where it would remain for several weeks in a narrow area no larger than three nautical miles square, as Captain Shaydurov stated.

Why did the Soviets send back the first group of trawlers? The small trawlers were well adapted to searching in the shallow, sheltered waters near Sakhalin Island. But this time, the work was in the deeper, rougher water north of Moneron. Search and recovery efforts on this new crash site were more difficult.[8] The Soviets sent the smaller ships they had used in the sheltered waters near Sakhalin back to port, replacing them with deep-sea trawlers under Captain Shaydurov's orders. The wreckage was finally located:

> *More than a month had passed since the shootdown when we got to the spot. In fact, almost two months. We found the airplane on the seventeenth or eighteenth of October. We spent the following days working on the bottom, which was crawling with crabs and all kinds of shrimp and fish. There were even some octopus.[9]*

The marine environment in which the October 18 wreck was found was completely different from the area of the first wreck of September 13, where the ocean bottom was covered with thick mud that broke the trawl nets, where visibility was extremely poor, and where aquatic life was totally absent. Illesh says:

> *In conducting my research I interviewed not only Mr. Zakharchenko, the head of the diving team, but some of the divers themselves, who spent six to eight hours a day working underwater. I spoke with Grigory Matveyenko, Vadim Kondrabayev, and Vladimir Kov, and I think it would be appropriate if readers had a chance to hear the transcription of our interview. This is the first time this information has been made public, and I have made no changes to the text. Let's hear what they have to say in their own words.[10]*

Illesh, however, only provided excerpts of his interview with the divers. From another source, I obtained the complete text and have incorporated here passages Illesh left out. In the following section, references to *Izvestiya* indicate the published version of the interview; *original text* refers to the unpublished parts of the interview.

Zakharchenko:	The depth was 174 meters [571 feet]. The bottom was hard and flat; it was sand with a layer of shells over it. It extended horizontally. *[Izvestiya]* [11]
Vadim Kondrabayev:	I never saw water that clear. Nowhere else was the water that clear. *[original text]* [12]
Vladimir Kov:	The water was so clear you could see everything very dis-

tinctly. You could see 50 meters [165 feet] in front of you. You could make out the individual grains of sand. It was breathtakingly beautiful. But it was cold.

Reporter: What depth?

Vadim: Between 160 meters [525 feet] and 173 meters [568 feet].

The divers: We saw a huge, empty, flat field and, suddenly, a landing gear. [Izvestiya] [13]

The divers' statements are confirmed by the JMSA situation maps. The *Mikhail Mirchinko* was stationed at 46°32′ N, 141°20′ E. The maps show that the depth at this location is 174 meters (571 feet). The bottom there is horizontal and flat, made of sand, and covered with a layer of shells. It is, in fact, the only spot in this entire region of the Tatar Strait where the Japanese Admiralty maps show a sand bottom covered with shells. This was, of course, different from the mud bottom at the site of the first wreck. Another contrast was the intense aquatic life. It was while fishing here that the *Chidori Maru* No. 58 observed the explosion of an airplane.

What type of aircraft was found this time? The unpublished statements of the divers are revealing. It appears that a large part of this plane's fuselage remained intact. The divers commented:

It took us two or three days to find our way around the wreck. . . . The plane was filled with all kinds of stuff, but there were no bodies. [14] . . . In some places the debris was one and a half meters [five feet] thick. [15]

Apparently this was a large aircraft, larger than the plane that had been found on September 13. But it wasn't a Boeing 747, at least not the Boeing 747 used for Flight 007, for the very good reason that there was no trace of any passengers. Nor of the row on row of seats that characterize the wreck of a civilian airliner. The divers remarked:

We didn't see any bodies on either the first or second day. [16] . . . We managed to find our way around the aircraft. [17] Later, I saw a hand with a black glove on it. [18] I participated in all the dives. I remember it very clearly: the plane was filled with all sorts of stuff, but there was absolutely no sign of any bodies. Why? I didn't see any human remains. There was no luggage, not even a handbag. . . . On the other hand there were lots of things you wouldn't expect to find on a passenger plane . . . reels, for example.

The original text provides additional information about these "reels":

Reporter: I understand that Vladimir Vasilievich recovered some computers. Were there any recording devices? Were there many of them?

Vladimir: Yes, I recovered miles of tape. I kept pulling at it. But those were my orders.

Vadim: They were the same kind of tapes you find on large typewriters, but much bigger. The Soviet Army uses this sort of thing, wound on large reels.

Zakharchenko and the divers provide more information pointing to the military origin of the aircraft:

We had several jobs to do. The first was to collect all the documents, all of them. Then we had to bring back the radio equipment, the consoles, etc. We also brought back the tape reels for the computers and the recording devices.[19] They only asked us to recover the electronic components, magnetic tape, documents, black boxes . . . magnetic tape recorders and similar hardware, photographic apparatus, recorders.[20] . . . They asked us to recover all the electric cables connected to the consoles and to the other equipment we had brought up.[21]

The divers continued, "We recovered pieces of the Boeing; they were from the outside covering. There was a piece of fuselage covering that had an emblem on it made of a circle and two commas."[22] Andrei Illesh commented, "This is apparently the Korean Air Lines symbol."

The logo of Korean Air, the new name assumed by Korean Air Lines after the 007 disaster, is the yin-yang symbol, which could roughly be described as two inverted commas inside a circle. However, in 1983, the logo of Korean Air Lines was a stylized image of a crane (the bird).[23] The piece of fuselage skin was thus not from KAL 007.

In the January 31, 1991, issue of *Izvestiya*, a witness is quoted as saying, "They recovered a life raft."[24] There are no life rafts on board passenger Boeing 747s. These airliners use the large emergency evacuation chutes, which serve as floating platforms if the plane has to ditch. The fact that a life raft was found is one more indication that the wreckage was not from the

Korean airliner. A further comment by Vladimir, which Illesh chose not to print, corroborates this. "I saw parachutes waving in the water like ghosts." Civilian Boeing 747s do not carry parachutes, either. Military aircraft do.

The divers said, "We put everything in a kind of big one-and-a-half-by-two-meter [five-by-seven-foot] basket."[25] Illesh did not mention how many baskets were brought up from the bottom. The number is in the original text:

How many baskets did you fill each day?
Ten, maybe more. . . . We worked for at least twenty days on the bottom. That would make about two hundred baskets.

The divers recovered two hundred one-and-a-half-by-two-meter (five-by-seven-foot) baskets, filled with documents and electronic equipment, from this one wreck. Finding such a large quantity of documents and electronic equipment points to an intelligence aircraft, such as an RC-135, which is crammed with top-secret documents (especially the codes used to encode and decode messages) and electronic apparatus.

Vladimir K., a diver who worked on the fourth wreck, said, "I was afraid one of those boxes was going to blow up in my face"—presumably a reference to weapons. There were other dangers. B. Kurkov, a Soviet Navy officer, said:

When the race for the black boxes began, the Americans became extremely insolent, especially around Moneron. They interfered with our trawlers, cutting right across their bow. They came into our territorial waters and even threatened the lives of the divers from the Mikhail Mirchinko, *using high-energy sound waves.*[26]

Vadim Kondrabayev, one of the divers who was injured during this incident, lost his voice and can only speak in a barely audible whisper. He relates the story as follows:

One day an American ship put a powerful acoustic device into operation to interfere with our work. . . . It was as if someone were hammering a nail into our eardrums. . . . We quickly returned to the deep-submergence vessel and were brought back to the compression chamber. . . . The antisubmarine frigate Sebastopol *succeeded in driving off the Americans, and we marked the search area with buoys and patrolled the area with our trawlers. It was the only way to protect ourselves from that unbearable pain.*[27]

Sergei Godorozha, another diver, was quoted in the same issue of

Izvestiya:

> *When our comrades were brought up, they were terrifying to look at: their eyes were red, their blood vessels had burst, they were as white as death.*[28]

One explanation that would absolve the U.S. Navy of wrongdoing is that they were merely using their sonars for detection. It may be so. But it may also not be so. Sonars, like radars, can work at various frequencies. Some have no effect on underwater life, fish or marine mammals such as whales or porpoise. Others are lethal to marine mammals and humans underwater. The modern navies of the world use special sonar frequencies under water for the protection of harbor and other vital installations from attack by combat divers.

The Soviet search pinpointed the location of the fourth wreck in the first part of September with the three successive waves of vessels with different means of detection. The salvage operations themselves began only after the *Mikhail Mirchinko* had finished its work on the first wreck and was in a position to be redeployed with a fresh team of divers entering the compression chamber. Although the location of the second wreck is close to that of the fourth wreck, there is reason to believe that the two were the crash sites of different aircraft. Figure 12 shows their locations, along with those of other sunken aircraft. The recovery operations for the October 18 fourth wreck lasted forty-six days.

The Fifth Wreck

In an article in the *Izvestiya* of January 26, 1991, Andrei Illesh gives rare, reasonably precise geographical data for a crash site, once more, of course, ostensibly that of the Korean airliner, but different from that of the fourth wreck, which the Soviets usually present as the sole one.

> *All this activity took place within a fairly small area, just on the edge of the 12-mile limit. The airplane fell near this invisible line that separates territorial from international waters. Sources say it was approximately 11 nautical miles from shore.*[29]

As we have seen, the first wreck fell within the Soviet territorial waters of Sakhalin Island (and not Moneron), approximately 6 NM from the shore. The second was found in international waters, approximately 18 NM from Moneron, the third at 45 NM to the north of that island, and the fourth at approximately 20 NM from it. None of these locations corresponds to the eleven nautical miles mentioned by Illesh. The JMSA maps show that the Soviets looked for the wreckage of an aircraft eleven nautical miles off the shore within the territorial waters of Moneron (not those of Sakhalin).

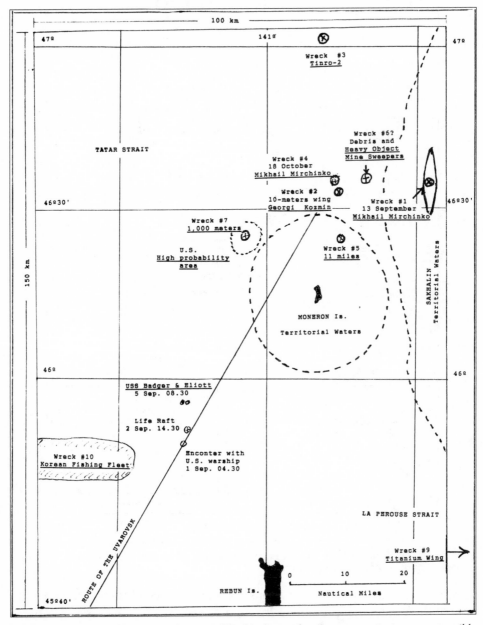

Figure 12. *Nine different crash sites off Sakhalin with an arrow pointing to a possible tenth just off the map. Evidence suggests one or two other water crash sites whose precise location cannot be established, as well as at least three on Sakhalin.*

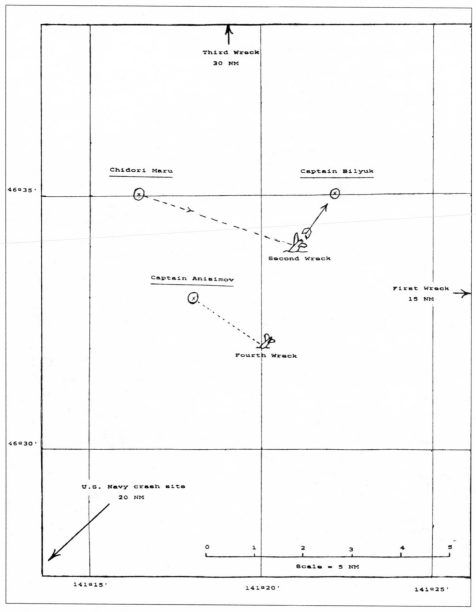

Figure 13. *The* Chidori Maru *and Captain Anisimov witnessed two different events in the first hour of the air battle of Sakhalin.*

Search and recovery operations for the fifth wreck lasted longer than any of the others—September 1 through November 10, seventy-two days in all. The Soviet search effort used many ships in the operation: the *Georgi Kozmin,* the *Mikhail Mirchinko,* together with the *Perseus,* the *Pegasus,* and the *Okeanolog,* the latter an undersea scientific vessel. Apparently only military divers were used. This may have been the wreck the Navy divers described as found with "the tail standing up among the reefs." Captain Girsh, of the *Tinro-2,* speaking of the Navy divers, said:

> *They found the fuselage, the part near the tail, with lots of debris. It was standing straight up among the rocks. First they lowered it down, then they went inside.*[30]

The fact that the divers, who were working underwater at a depth of 150 meters (500 feet), were able to lower the fuselage to a horizontal position indicates that the aircraft was relatively small but large enough for them to "go inside." It may have been a military aircraft that carried the serial number 65802124-903 painted in yellow on a gray camouflage background, which I saw on a video brought back from Moscow by a Japanese television crew. It could have been the plane shot down by fighter C of the JDA map, at 04:01 hours, which the Japanese initially believed had landed at Sakhalin.

The Sixth Wreck

Although five different wrecks have been identified, there are indications that the Soviets searched for and found several others. Some of the information concerning these other wrecks is found in the uncut version of *Izvestiya*'s interview with the divers.

Reporter: Were the minesweepers working in your sector?

Civilian divers: No, in an entirely different area. They found the [or a] fuselage. They recovered it and took the debris to Nevelsk. I saw what they unloaded. One was a piece of metal that weighed more than a ton with a lot of metal accessories. When we arrived on October 1, the debris had already been removed.[31]

The sixth wreck, from which debris was unloaded in Nevelsk before October 1, appears to have been a midsized aircraft. Please see Figure 12 (page 135) for its probable location, which is based on the following factors. The account of the *Uvarovsk*'s movements and observations, given by Captain Bilyuk, as well as the time schedule he indicates for his ship's movements on September 1, indicate an area of floating debris in international waters between the fourth and first wrecks. The JMSA situation map for September 1 shows that a cargo ship put two boats in the water here and retrieved a heavy object. That the area is relatively shallow makes the use of mine-sweepers plausible.

The Seventh Wreck

Captain Girsh mentioned yet another search operation:

We were working at a depth of between 250 and 270 meters [800 and 900 feet]. One day the Breeze *and the* Pegasus *[both equipped with autonomous undersea vehicles] were suddenly pulled out of the search area. They sailed behind the "hump" to work in water that was over 1,000 meters [3,000 feet] deep. They worked there for a long time. I have no idea why, or what they found there.*[32]

Water that reaches a depth of a thousand meters is more than thirty miles from where Captain Girsh and the *Tinro-2* were working north of Moneron. The area to which the *Breeze* and the *Pegasus* were sent could have been the crash site 16 NM northwest of Moneron on which the U.S. Navy had been working intensively. The Soviets had kept an eye on it right along. It is where Admiral Sidorov staged the episode of the false black box. The actions of the U.S. task force, which I will describe in more detail later, make it seem likely that it located the wreck of the aircraft that interested it most and recovered from it the sensitive equipment it wanted before it widened its area of operations in mid-October.

If the area 16 NM northwest of Moneron was in fact the area to which the *Breeze* and the *Pegasus* were sent, they could have been dispatched to take a look for themselves at the wreck the United States had been working on. There is also, however, deep water southwest of Moneron, to which the Soviet vessels could have been sent. In any event, there clearly was a wreck 16 NM northwest of Moneron (Figure 12, page 135, the seventh wreck).

Other Wrecks

Other information makes it likely that, in addition to the seven wrecks identified above, three or more other aircraft crashed in the water near Sakhalin Island that night. (As I have already mentioned, there is evidence that three crashed on Sakhalin itself—not listed in my number series.) Adm. Kessoku Konomu, who oversaw the JMSA search operation from its head-quarters at Otaru, told me he believed that debris landing on the beaches of the eastern end of Hokkaido shore on the Sea of Okhotsk probably came from a crash in the Sea of Okhotsk north of the peninsula on the eastern side of Sakhalin (Terpeniya Peninsula). Indeed, the communications of Soviet fighter 163 indicate that it engaged an intruder airplane there. (The eighth wreck, in the Sea of Okhotsk.)

The titanium wing section accidentally caught in the net of a Japanese boat fishing for sole and hauled up from the bottom of the Sea of Okhotsk on November 17, 1989, probably came from an SR-71 (Blackbird), a U.S. ultrahigh-altitude, ultrahigh-speed reconnaissance aircraft in service at that time. This has been denied by the head of the Lockheed "Skunk Works," which made it.[33] If, however, it did not come from an SR-71, it came from a similar high-performance U.S. military or intelligence aircraft. Because the titanium wing section was sunken debris, we have no direct evidence on when it entered the water. That, however, the wing section was found near Sakhalin, an area virtually littered with the crashes of military aircraft shot down at the time of the air battle over Sakhalin, makes it plausible that it came from one more casualty of that battle. (Figure 12, page 135, the ninth wreck, in the Sea of Okhotsk.)

Floating military debris entering La Pérouse Strait and the Sea of Okhotsk and reaching the northwestern beaches of Hokkaido seem likely to have originated in the mouth of the Strait or in the Sea of Japan south of Moneron. Other evidence suggests one or more crashes there: the small life raft found south of Moneron on September 2, the day after the disaster; the fact USS *Badger* and USS *Elliot* patrolled the area; the encounter of Captain Bilyuk's *Uvarovsk* with an American warship while the air battle was still taking place; and Captain Girsh's testimony that the *Tinro-2* made several dives south of Moneron and found wreckage there. (Figure 12, page 135, the tenth and perhaps other wrecks, south of Moneron.)

It is, of course, possible that one or more of the crashes I have mentioned were those of Soviet military aircraft. I have cited evidence identifying one wreck as almost surely that of an RC-135, debris from two different EF-111s (or, less probably, F-111s), debris that appears to have come from an E-2, and sunken debris from an SR-71 or a similar U.S. aircraft whose crash seems likely to have been part of the air battle of Sakhalin. Moreover, wrecks on which the Soviets made major recovery efforts seem unlikely to have been those of Soviet aircraft. This criterion suggests that the third wreck could have been Soviet. Recovery operations for it lasted only six days.

The Black Boxes

Since there is debris, oceanographic and communications evidence that KAL 007 crashed off Honshu, not off Sakhalin, there is no reason to suppose that the Russians ever had their hands on the Korean airliner's black boxes—that is to say, its cockpit voice recorder (CVR) and its digital flight data recorder (DFDR). Yet twice, once in November 1992 and again in January 1993, the Russian government gave the ICAO and others transcripts and other data said to have come from them. The two sets are different; and both contain their own internal evidence of misrepresentation or forgery. In addition, President Yeltsin stunned the South Koreans by presenting President Roh with battered black boxes of which the DFDR was missing its recording and the CVR's recording was unintelligible—a Korean said, "recorded backwards."

As a result, the story of the Korean airliner's black boxes forms an important part of the story of the cover-up, and I have dealt with it in the section of this book devoted to that subject. At the same time, what Illesh printed in *Izvestiya* about the black boxes that were found off Sakhalin and, according to him, came from the Korean airliner clearly adds up to a demonstration that they did not come from it, but were recorders or other sensitive electronic apparatus from military aircraft.

Like all large civilian aircraft, the Boeing 747 is equipped with two black boxes, one that records the last thirty minutes of conversation from the cockpit, and one that records the last twenty-five hours of flight data. The rectangular boxes measure twenty by five by eight inches. On Flight 007 the cockpit recorder was slightly shorter and measured thirteen by five by eight inches. The boxes are watertight and shock resistant. They are equipped with an underwater signal transmitter, or pinger, that enables them to be located under the water. On Boeing 747s they are normally located in the rear of the aircraft, at the fin root just under the tail section, which is the most secure spot on the plane in case of accident. In crashes, the tail section usually remains intact. Fragments from the tail fin from the Boeing used for Flight 007 were found, however. This would imply that the tail was fragmented by an explosion, and it is thus possible that KAL 007's real black boxes were destroyed.

The two black box recorders aboard a Boeing 747 are orange, rectangular, about the size of a video camera, almost of equal size, one only slightly larger than the other. Yet those described by Illesh's witnesses were of numbers, sizes, shapes, and colors different from the airliner's and different from each other. They were sent back to Moscow by different means, having been packed in different ways.

Admiral Sidorov, in charge of the Soviet search effort, said, "I recall very well. All [the boxes] were placed in rubber bags filled with distilled water containing 50 percent alcohol as a preservative. The bags were sent to Moscow on a special plane. There were nine of them."[34] Kurkov, a Soviet Navy officer quoted earlier, told *Izvestiya*:

> *Your paper wrote that there were only two black boxes on the Boeing. But according to our information [1983] there were seven. Three black boxes were sent to Moscow on an Il-76. I spoke to a man in headquarters who flew back with them. He told me that as soon as they landed in Moscow and the door was open, five Air Force generals rushed into the cabin and headed straight for the rubber bags.*[35]

Admiral Sidorov said the black boxes were packed in distilled water and alcohol. A Soviet Navy officer said he saw a black box recovered by the *Mirchink* being packed in a container containing seawater by aeronautics experts at Nevelsk. Zhan Aleschenko, chief mate of the *Mirchink,* described one as "a bright red ball, about the size of a volleyball."[36] An unnamed source told *Izvestiya:* "They looked like large round doughnuts."[37] In a televised interview one of the divers said, "They were shaped like a horseshoe." Some "boxes" were presumably instrument packages other than black box recorders.

Whatever all these objects were, and however many of them there may have been, they clearly did not come from a single airplane, and surely not KAL 007.

Mysterious Aspects of the Naval Search

I have not yet mentioned the fleet of Korean fishing vessels that for nearly six weeks kept a strange patrol along the southern edge of the Moneron search area. They arrived on the morning of September 5, when they first appear on the JMSA situation maps, as do USS *Badger* and USS *Elliot.* The arrival off Moneron of the Korean fishing boats was, incidentally, before the government of the Republic of Korea decided to participate officially in the search for the KAL airliner.[38] The mystery is thus who retained the fishing boats and what was their task.

There may be two answers to the latter question. They may initially have been looking for the sunken debris of an aircraft toward the western end of the area they patrolled, since they spent some time there (see Figure 12, page 135, the tenth wreck). For most of the time, however, they went back and forth on a west-east line seeming to form a picket line to prevent floating debris born north by the Tsushima Shio from reaching the official search area.[39]

In discussing floating debris from military aircraft, I have mentioned two pilot's ejection seats, at least one of which appeared to have been used. I said there that we had no evidence that any U.S. pilot reached the water alive. We do, however, have evidence that at the time the Soviet authorities thought pilots might have. In his book *The Mystery of the Black Boxes* Andrei Illesh quotes KGB captain Genadii Ivanov:

> *I vividly remember that night. It was my first day as a combat unit commander assigned to the protection of the border. It was early morning. I received an order by radio to search for the [or an] aircraft that had been shot down. In the telegram, there was a special paragraph with instructions to exert the utmost care because the pilots were armed with combat weapons. The search area we were assigned was south of Moneron Island. We found nothing there, however, and toward the end of the day, we received the order to go north.*

Misha Lobko, director of Dathanna International, French investigative TV producers, later interviewed Ivanov and heard the same story directly from him.

The mystery that struck the Soviet participants most strongly was the absence of the many bodies that would have characterized the wreck of a civilian airliner. Speaking of the fourth wreck, one of the divers said, "Normally when a plane crashes, even a small plane . . . there are always small suitcases, or at least handbags. . . . I saw no human remains. And we worked down there for nearly a whole month."[40]

In *Izvestiya*, Illesh said:

> *It appears that the divers had come to the same conclusion as everyone else, and which had also been picked up by the press: the plane was empty when it flew over Sakhalin; the whole KAL 007 story is a horrible fabrication made up of bits and pieces.*[41]

In the original text of the *Izvestiya* interviews, Vladimir, one of the divers who worked on the fourth wreck, said:

> *We talked about it among ourselves . . . there were no passengers on the airplane. It was all a fabrication, a hoax. I felt the same way. . . . There was no sign of any passengers.*[42]

Viacheslav Popov, an undersea researcher and observer on the *Tinro-2*, goes one step further. To him, not only were there no passengers on the planes that fell at Moneron, but there was a real crash of a real passenger plane somewhere else:

> *I must say I was relieved not to find any human remains in the wreckage. Not only were there no corpses, but no sign of any luggage either. This led us to wonder whether or not it was really a passenger plane.*[43] *Or was it a decoy? Among ourselves we tried to explain how it had happened. There was an accident involving a real Boeing somewhere, far from here, and they camouflaged the entire affair with this plane, a spy plane.*[43]

There is something extraordinary in this observer's account. Working on the wreckage in 1983, his conclusions mirror our own knowledge about the affair after years of investigation and raises an important question: Why would anyone want to camouflage an accident involving a real Boeing?

The U.S. Search Operations

For more than two months, from September 1 to November 6, 1983, the U.S. Navy's Task Force 71 (TF-71) engaged in search and rescue (SAR) and search and salvage (SAS) operations, ostensibly for the Korean airliner. The Navy worked dangerously close to Soviet territorial waters[1] and was often confronted by the Soviet Navy in a nearly hostile environment. Officially, the American Navy never located any debris. Nearly ten years after the event, two small television teams from Sakhalin and Japan would independently find the wreckage of a big aircraft on their first try and come back with underwater video footage. An examination of U.S. search operations provides insights into the Navy's behavior and possible answers to the questions it raises.

Information about the U.S. Navy search effort is contained in two documents, the *KAL Flight 007 After Action Report* prepared by the Seventh Fleet commander of surface combat forces and the *Final Report of Sonar Search for Korean Airlines FLT 007* by the supervisor of U.S. Navy Rescue Operations for Naval Ocean Systems Command.[2] These two reports contain several assertions:

- American forces were at the site within hours after the disaster.
- The search for surface debris was conducted between September 1 and September 13.
- No debris (floating or sunken) from the Korean plane was found.

All are probably technically true, but are singularly uninformative in the light of what the Navy obviously knew. Captain Bilyuk of the *Uvarovsk,* coming back home from the Indian Ocean, found a huge slick of oil on the surface of the sea, north of Moneron Island, at 08:00 Japan time, on September 1, with thousands of pieces of debris, mostly aluminum honeycomb. Other Soviet vessels, such as the *Zabaikalye* from Nevelsk, came to help retrieve the debris and worked into the night with searchlights. Heavy objects were retrieved from the sea by a cargo vessel. There is evidence, recorded by the JMSA interception of U.S. radio communications, that a small life raft was spotted south of Moneron by a U.S. Navy Orion P-3C on September 2.

The reader will also recall that Foxtrot Bravo 650, a U.S. Navy aircraft, began patrolling at low altitude in the area of waypoint KADPO, four hundred miles to the south off Honshu, at 04:27 hours Japan time, a few minutes after KAL 007 must have crashed nearby. There is evidence FB 650 may have fired a smoke marker of the kind used to facilitate landings at sea by rescue seaplanes. Moreover, at the time of the disaster, the USS *Badger* was off Vladivostok, half a day's journey from Moneron. The ship didn't arrive at the search and rescue area off Moneron until 08:00 A.M. Japan time, on September 5. Lacking evidence to the contrary, it is reasonable to speculate that USS *Badger* and USS *Elliot,* which arrived at Moneron with it, may have spent three or four days near the true impact area of the Korean airliner, north of Niigata, near waypoint KADPO. If this were confirmed, it would prove that the U.S. Navy knew the true impact point for Flight 007. It seems highly unlikely that it did not, given the fact that the largest U.S. signal intelligence station outside the continental United States and a U.S. airbase receiving all Japanese radar data were nearby at Misawa.

Even though the reports were long classified "secret," they presumably got fairly wide distribution within the government. Given what had actually happened, the Navy could hardly have been explicit about what it had really been doing without revealing the air battle of Sakhalin and the southern crash site of the Korean airliner. In so far as possible, it tried to sidestep the real issues. For the most part, its reports avoid references to the Korean airliner. The after-action report's transmittal letter refers to Task Force 71's search and rescue and search and salvage operations "in connection with Korean Airline Flight 007." Its "Executive Summary" states: "Nothing associated with KAL 007 was discovered." And: "Had TF-71 been permitted to search without the restriction of claimed Soviet territorial waters, the aircraft stood a good chance of having been found."

That is to say, when put on the spot by its false position, the Navy used evasions and misleading formulations and wound up blaming its apparent failure on the Soviets. It could hardly have admitted picking up floating debris from KAL 007 north of Moneron without stating the date on which it did so. And that, given the nature of the current, would have pointed to the airliner's southern crash site and revealed the military nature of the other debris. These Navy reports illustrate that large-scale clandestine operations such as the KAL 007 mission lead to false statements even in highly classified documents and corrupt even operational services.

The U.S. Navy Undersea Search—The U.S. High-Probability Area

The U.S. undersea search began on September 14 and continued through November 5. An area known as the "high probability" area, sixty nautical miles square (a circle with a radius of approximately 4 NM) was established with the information that the U.S. Navy had at the time. The area was centered about a point 46°25' N, 140°56' E, 16 NM northwest of the island of Moneron. On September 20, Task Force 71 already had an evaluation by the commander in chief of the Pacific Fleet (CINPACFLT) of the presumed impact area and information about the radar tracks that had been given by the National Security Agency (NSA) to NAVSEA personnel before their departure from Washington on September 10.[3]

TF-71's area of high probability is unrelated to any of the four impact areas observed by the Japan Defense Agency, the Soviets, and the fishing vessel *Chidori Maru*. These are:

- the area noted by the *Chidori Maru,* and Captain Bilyuk, at 46°34' N, 141°22' E
- the area noted by Captain Anisimov, at 46°32' N, 141°20' E
- the JDA Wakkanai radar point at 46°30' N, 141°30' E
- the JDA Wakkanai radar point at 46°30' N, 141°15' E

All these points are located north and east of Moneron, whereas TF-71's area of high probability is northwest of the island (see Figure 12, page 135). The logical conclusion is that the NSA, which gave its radar track to NAVSEA personnel, had intercepted tracking of an aircraft that crashed in a spot different from any of the others.

It is interesting, and revealing, that in its report, TF-71 stated it did not admit receiving the information about the *Chidori Maru*'s sighting until October 8 and the Japan Defense Agency's radar data from Wakkanai until October 14. That is more than a month after the information had been widely carried by Japanese English-language, U.S., and other newspapers, magazines, and television. We need an explanation, other than inefficiency, for which the U.S. Navy is not noted, for TF-71's claim it had not known of the sightings until October 8 and 14 and did not broaden their search area until after that.

An explanation of this behavior is probably that TF-71 initially put all its resources to work to recover sensitive equipment from an aircraft in the original high-priority area and was successful. Having done so, it was free to turn its attention elsewhere. Once it "received this information," TF-71 "extended its probability area" to take account of the new data (that of the *Chidori Maru* and the JDA), broadening it from 60 to 225 nautical square miles. That gave the Navy a total of three different impact areas to work with. But the Navy was not in a position to reveal the nature of either the sunken debris it no doubt recovered in its high-probability area or of the sunken debris the Soviets were recovering elsewhere.

The debris would be shown to be military, thus pointing to the air battle of Sakhalin. Or, alternatively, the Navy could have recovered planted debris ostensibly or really from KAL 007. In which case the alleged crash site would invite scrutiny, which would in all likelihood reveal its implausibility, thus pointing to the cover-up.

However, the Navy reports indicate that TF-71 was aware of the presence of wreckage at different places:

> *From September 5 to November 5, thirty-three different [Soviet] trawlers dragged the waters in both the U.S. and Soviet high-probability areas. Soviet trawlers were observed towing their nets in the Soviet high-probability area, presumably hoping to hook a piece of wreckage. They were also observed towing their nets in the area where the U.S. search was being conducted, probably hoping to locate any wreckage that was there or disperse it, so the U.S. ships couldn't recover it. The Soviets also used trawl nets in areas that were not considered to be of high probability.*

The U.S. Navy was particularly interested in the activities of the *Mikhail Mirchinko*. TF-71 saw it recover objects from the bottom.

> *Because of its continued presence in the [Soviet] high-probability area and its inherent capabilities [dynamic positioning, hoist capacity, support for diving operations], as well as Soviet susceptibility due to the proximity and observation of its activities by U.S. ships, the* Mikhail Mirchinko *was closely watched by American intelligence forces. The* Mikhail Mirchinko *remained in position in an area that was between 46°31′ N–46°35′ N, 141°14′ E–141°25′ E.[4] Activities observed on board the ship included the handling of objects on the bridge, using [100-ton capacity] cranes to lift objects from the seafloor, transferring unidentified objects to other ships, using drill rigs, and the takeoff and landing of helicopters for the transfer of personnel and cargo. Diving operations from other ships were observed in the vicinity of the* Mikhail Mirchinko *and could have been coordinated by the ship.*

Having observed the *Mikhail Mirchinko* recover things from the bottom, the U.S. Navy took advantage of its momentary absence from the spot over which it had stabilized its position to send its best observation vessel, the USCG *Munro*, to verify what the *Mirchink* had discovered there.[5]

On October 17 the Mikhail Mirchinko *left the position it had been occupying since September 26. The* Munro *searched the area using side-looking sonar equipment for twenty-one hours in this location; the contacts obtained were confirmed by an undersea camera and turned out to be coral and rock formations.*

The U.S. task force was better equipped than the Soviet Navy, with better-quality equipment and more qualified personnel. It is incredible that the *Munro* was unable to detect the large wreck in the relatively shallow water over which the *Mikhail Mirchinko* had been positioned. The *Mikhail Mirchinko* soon came back and resumed its recovery operations. The after-action report says:

On November 1 the Soviets made several dives in an undersea vessel. Several loads of unidentified objects were transferred from the Mikhail Mirchinko *to a barge anchored alongside.*

Finally, the *Mirchink* left for the second time, and the U.S. Navy, its report tells us, sent the *Munro* back for a more detailed search of the wreck.

On November 3 the Mikhail Mirchinko *left its location for the first time since October 17. The U.S. Navy performed a second series of searches in the area with side-looking sonar equipment above the point where the* Mikhail Mirchinko *had been positioned. Using side-looking sonar equipment, on several occasions the U.S. Navy made contacts, which were significant enough to warrant confirmation with an undersea camera. In each case these contacts turned out to be coral or rock formations. On November 4 the* Munro *completed its search with the side-looking sonar in the* Mikhail Mirchinko*'s area of operations. There was no significant contact. The only man-made objects detected were a shoe, some oil cans, an empty pan, an illustrated magazine, and a rag. No object associated with the KAL 007 aircraft was found.*

No significant contact? What about the fuselage the divers took several days to find their way about? What about the debris several meters deep? What about the big aircraft from which the two hundred "baskets" of equipment were retrieved? And was the Sakhalin television team that found the wreckage at its first try in July 1990 better equipped, or better qualified, than Task Force 71? Despite its usual reticence in the reports, the Navy seems to have followed the cynical old advice "lie when necessary."

One interesting point, however, is its admission that the sonobuoys used starting on September 5 by the USS *Badger* and USS *Callaghan* to locate the underwater signal of the black boxes were of a type appropriate for picking up military pingers. Sonobuoys appropriate for picking up the 37.5 KHz frequency of civilian localizers were not used until September 28, by which time the batteries of KAL 007's pinger would have begun to run down and the black box locators would have ceased to transmit their signals. The Navy's failure to supply its task force with sonobuoys appropriate to the mission it was ostensibly carrying out, that is to say the search for the Korean airliner, exhibits clumsiness in carrying out the charade its government had thrust upon it.

In concluding the after-action report, in its "Summary for the Commander," part B (U) *effectiveness,* the U.S. Navy has high praise for its own operations:

> *Performance of the Search Force was superb. Not since the search for the H-bomb off Palomarès had the Navy undertaken a search effort of such significance. The search effort is considered to have been highly successful. Although no wreckage of the aircraft was discovered, the operation established, with a 95 percent or above confidence level, that the wreckage does not lie within the probability area outside the 12-nautical-mile area claimed by the Soviets as their territorial waters.*

It would be interesting to know the true criteria used by U.S. Navy Task Force 71 to measure its "superb performance" and those that led it to consider the operation "highly successful." Perhaps they included the recovery of sensitive equipment from the U.S. aircraft that crashed in deep water in the U.S. high-probability area 16 NM northwest of Moneron.

PART FOUR

THE FLIGHT TO SEOUL

The Departure from Anchorage

P roof that KAL 007 was still flying forty-five minutes after the official account of events says it was shot down was supplied by Dr. Tsuboi, director of the Iwatsu Electric Company's laboratory in Kaguyama, near Tokyo.[1] When KAL 007 sent its radio reply to KAL 050 at 19:12 GMT, it was flying not far from Niigata and was on the verge of reentering the official air route system that would have taken it back to Seoul. The plane was on time. If nothing out of the way had happened, the plane would have entered Niigata airspace right on schedule. The airliner was no more than a few minutes away from Niigata when it was destroyed. This is extraordinary when one thinks about it. By the time it left the Alaskan mainland, the plane had been significantly off course and had been increasingly so ever since. Yet now, after flying off course for more than six hours at jet airliner speed, it was on the point of integrating its flight with its assigned schedule as if it had never been off course.

The Crew

Before KAL 007 took off from Anchorage, regulations had been broken. As a result the flight was technically illegal. The flight crew (pilot, copilot, and flight engineer) had not had a sufficiently long rest period on the ground between flights. They were not "airworthy," and if it were essential for them to return to Seoul on that particular flight, they should have traveled as passengers. Moreover, two complete flight crews were among the passengers that night, both of which were well rested, and one of which had previously flown to Anchorage with the twenty-member cabin crew. It should have been on the flight deck on the trip to Seoul instead of being relegated to the first-class cabin. Regarding the rest period of Captain Chun's flight crew, in its report of 1983 the ICAO claimed:

> *Rest in excess of the minimum required by the KAL Operations Manual was obtained by the flight crew of KAL 007. . . . There were rest periods of 22 hours on the first visit to Anchorage, 31 hours in New York, and 11 hours 43 minutes on returning to Anchorage.*

This short passage contains two errors. The first is probably a simple error of arithmetic. The report states that the crew spent 11 hours 43 minutes in Anchorage. But the rest period did not begin until 14:37 and ended at 01:50 (Anchorage local time). The difference is 11 hours 13 minutes and not 11 hours 43 minutes.

The second error is more serious. The KAL Operations Manual states that the minimum rest period must not be less than one and a half times the total flight time for the previous flight, unless the next flight is a charter flight or a cargo flight, in which case the minimum rest period must be at least equal to the duration of the previous flight. In addition, one hour following the last flight and two hours prior to the next flight are not counted as part of the rest period. Capt. Chun Byung-In[2] and the other two crew members of his flight crew had arrived at Anchorage from New York via Toronto on cargo flight KAL 0975, after 8 hours and 46 minutes in flight. Their rest period should have been one and a half times 8 hours 46 minutes, or 13 hours 9 minutes. The crew, which was responsible for the safety of the 269 persons on board KAL 007, was thus short of its minimum rest period by 1 hour 56 minutes.

A document from Anchorage airport that was telexed to Seoul and appears in the appendix to the ICAO report provides the official analysis of the rest period for the crew of KAL 007:

Capt Chun B.I. team
KE0975/30 YYZ ANC in 13:37
KE007/31 ANC SEL out 03:50
Anchorage ground time ttl 12 hr 13 min

Simply stated, this means Capt. Chun Byung-In and the other members of his flight crew arrived in Anchorage on KAL 0975 from Toronto on the thirtieth at 13:37 hours. They left Anchorage on board KAL 007 for Seoul at 03:50 hours. Total ground time at Anchorage was 12 hours 13 minutes.

If we do the math, we see that the difference between the departure time for KAL 007 (03:50) and KAL 0975's time of arrival (13:37) is 14 hours 13 minutes. The person who wrote the telex must have deducted the two hours before departure that are not counted in the rest period. But according to company regulations, one hour after the arrival time should also have been deducted from the flight crew's ground time. Did someone simply forget? As it was, the message showed KAL 007 short of its required rest.

A commercial jetliner is manned by two teams of personnel: the flight crew, responsible for flying the aircraft (pilot, copilot, flight engineer), and the cabin crew, responsible for taking care of the passengers (chief steward, hostesses, stewards). All planes, regardless of the nature of the flight, carry a flight crew. All passenger flights have both a flight crew and a cabin crew. Cargo aircraft, however, generally do not include a cabin crew, although some freight companies often have a single hostess or steward on board during long-distance flights.

Captain Chun and his flight crew arrived in Anchorage from Toronto on cargo flight KAL 0975. There was no cabin crew on board. When he took charge of Flight 007 in Anchorage, Captain Chun was supplied with a cabin crew. The cabin crew, which had been resting in Anchorage waiting for 007, did not arrive alone, however. They were accompanied by a flight crew, which had flown the plane they came in on. What happened to this flight crew? The answer raises several important issues. This flight crew followed them on board KAL 007, not to pilot the aircraft, as might have been expected, but as passengers in the first-class cabin.

Cockpit personnel and flight attendants form a complete crew on a passenger plane. The cockpit personnel for KAL 007, who were resting in Anchorage along with the cabin crew, were replaced by Captain Chun and the other members of his flight crew shortly before takeoff. The facts that KAL 007's originally intended flight crew was not only available but boarded the aircraft as passengers, and that Captain Chun's crew had not had the officially mandated rest period and were thus in violation of the regulations suggests that someone, for reasons that were not then apparent, wanted Captain Chun and no one else as pilot on the flight deck of KAL 007 that night.

The same is true of Capt. Park Young-man, the pilot of KAL 015, KAL 007's Los Angeles–originated companion flight on the Anchorage-Seoul leg. Park was an old friend and Korean Air Force colleague of Chun's. Documents in the docket of the civil KAL 007 case in the Washington, D.C., Federal District Court indicate that Park and the other members of his flight crew arrived in Anchorage on a cargo flight from Kansas City. On KAL 015 they displaced a rested and qualified flight crew, which then embarked, along with the flight crew Captain Chun had displaced, as the six supernumeraries on KAL 007 mentioned on page one of the text of the 1983 ICAO report. On two occasions later in the flight of the two Korean airliners, KAL 015's Park Young-man submitted KAL 007 position reports to Anchorage in which factors of time and procedure show that they cannot have been normal relays from his sister airliner. They misled later inquiries as to KAL 007's position.

The Flight Plan

The ten thousand pounds of additional fuel KAL 007 is said to have loaded before takeoff that night has been much discussed. The relevant documents are given in the appendix to the ICAO's 1983 report. These consist of the Operational Flight Plan, the Weight and Balance Manifest, and the Flight Release Sheet. The three documents were prepared by the KAL flight dispatcher in Anchorage and confirmed and corrected by Captain Chun, who signed them.

As its name indicates, the flight plan contains all the main technical data for completing the flight, including weight, flight path, and weather conditions. There are calculations for the amount of fuel needed on each leg of the journey and a detailed analysis of the route that will be flown, together with the anticipated speeds and estimated flight times between waypoints. The flight plan is calculated by computer at the request of the flight dispatcher, who includes it with the rest of the pilot's flight information. Captain Chun had examined the flight plan and made several revisions, including the estimated fuel consumption. Captain Chun accepted the computerized calculations of "trip fuel" consumption for the anticipated 7 hours 53 minutes of flying time, which was 206,400 pounds. However, he crossed out all the remaining figures, including all the calculations to determine the estimated reserve fuel, which the flight plan gave as:

Alternate	19,800 pounds
Holding	12,000 pounds
Contingency (10%)	17,600 pounds
Total	49,400 pounds

Crossing out this calculation, which was nothing more than a suggested analysis made by the flight dispatcher, Captain Chun redid the calculations on another document, the Flight Release Sheet, which added information that did not appear on the Operational Flight Plan, such as the flight times on which he based his estimates:

Fuel Reserves:

Alternate—0 hrs 40 min	17,300 pounds
Holding—0 hrs 30 min	11,000 pounds
Contingency (10%)—0 hrs 47 min	17,000 pounds
Total—1 hr 57 min	45,300 pounds

The most surprising thing about Captain Chun's calculations is that he reduced the total reserves from 49,400 to 45,300 pounds, a decrease of 4,100 pounds of fuel. It is highly unusual for a pilot to reduce the amount of fuel he has been assigned. On the contrary, pilots often ask for more fuel than the flight dispatcher recommends. Captain Chun's fuel calculations are immediately noticeable because they are so unexpected.

Like the majority of commercial airlines, KAL had a strict policy of cost reduction and offered bonuses to its pilots whenever they saved fuel. Reserve fuel, which is by definition not intended for use during normal flight, remains in the plane's tanks at the time of landing. Flight dispatchers consider it dead weight and always try to keep it to a minimum. Disputes about reserve fuel have been the biggest source of contention between flight dispatchers, who try to reduce it to cut costs, and cockpit personnel, who try to maximize it in the interest of safety. Any dead weight carried by an aircraft not only limits the amount of cargo that can be taken on board, but also results in additional fuel consumption and is, therefore, considered undesirable by most airlines.

By reducing his fuel reserves by 4,100 pounds, Captain Chun also reduced the amount of dead weight on the plane, which would result in a savings of 800 pounds of fuel over the flight. This is not significant given the total consumption of 206,400 pounds of fuel. Even if it didn't result in a bonus, it would certainly have merited approval from his superiors. Captain Chun reduced his fuel reserves by 4,100 pounds on the Flight Release Sheet, which is the first document, and sometimes the only document, that is examined by the Operations Office for statistical information. Strangely, however, he approved the estimated fuel consumption that was indicated on the operational flight plan, without deducting the 800 pounds of fuel that he had painstakingly managed to save by reducing his reserves.

The total of 251,700 pounds or "gate fuel" is the amount of fuel in the plane's tanks at takeoff. To this must be added the fuel needed for starting the engines and taxiing, which is 2,000 pounds. These 2,000 pounds are consumed before takeoff but are present in the plane's tanks at the ramp. That makes a total of 253,700 pounds of fuel. This part of the Flight Release Sheet appears as follows:

Fuel at destination, 1 hr 57 min	45,300 pounds
Burn off fuel, 7 hrs 53 min	206,400 pounds
Gate fuel, 9 hrs 50 min	251,700 pounds
Taxiing	2,000 pounds
Ramp fuel	253,700 pounds

Officially, KAL 007 was carrying 253,700 pounds of fuel. What was the plane really carrying?

The third document that appears in the ICAO's report of 1983 is the Weight and Balance Manifest. It indicates 263,700 pounds of total fuel before takeoff. This figure for "total fuel" should correspond to the 253,700 pounds of "ramp fuel" shown on the Flight Release Sheet. However, the two figures in this instance differ by 10,000 pounds, which has given rise to considerable speculation about the amount of fuel the plane was actually carrying on takeoff.

On the Weight and Balance Manifest, Captain Chun put a check mark next to the 206,400-pound figure of burn-off fuel, indicating that he agreed with the estimate. However, this figure does not take into account the savings of 800 pounds resulting from the 4,100-pound reduction in the fuel reserves. The Weight and Balance Manifest is used to calculate the takeoff parameters and, in particular, adjustment of the trim settings, which Captain Chun carefully checked and accepted, as indicated on the document by "TRIM = 7.0." We would think, therefore, that the amount of fuel indicated on this document was the actual amount of fuel KAL 007 was carrying in its tanks on takeoff. This implies the aircraft left with 263,700 pounds of fuel as indicated, 10,000 pounds more than shown on the Flight Release Sheet. But let us think through whether or not that was the case.

The Operational Flight Plan worked out by the Operations Office estimated 255,800 pounds of fuel, to which should be added 2,000 for start-up and taxiing, giving a total of 257,800 pounds. The difference between this figure suggested by the flight dispatcher and Captain Chun's corrected figure is only 5,900 pounds. In his book *Shootdown,* already quoted, R. W. Johnson mentioned a difference of 7,900 pounds, but the author apparently failed to take into account the 2,000 pounds needed for start-up and taxiing, which the Operational Flight Plan does not show. Captain Chun, then, would have left with 5,900 pounds more fuel than the estimate shown on the Operational Flight Plan prepared by the KAL flight dispatcher. This difference corresponds to less than fifteen minutes flying time. Why would Captain Chun have gone through all the figure-juggling for such an insignificant saving?

Neither Robert Allardyce nor any of the other experts, including those from the ICAO, commented on a more fundamental question. At 7:20 A.M. on September 1, 1983, KAL 007 was 1 hour and 15 minutes late at Seoul, and the flight was displayed on the arrivals board as "delayed indefinitely." A Korean Air Lines official told the anxious families who had gathered at the airport for the plane's arrival that at the time of takeoff at Anchorage the plane had enough fuel to remain in the air for twelve hours.[3] The Flight Release Sheet, however, shows 251,700 pounds of fuel at the gate, and a corresponding maximum possible flight time of 9 hours and 50 minutes. If we add the quarter hour from the additional 5,900 pounds of fuel, we arrive at 10 hours and 5 minutes of flying time. Where was the remaining fuel to come from?

A careful examination of the Flight Release Sheet suggests an answer. In the upper right-hand corner of the document appear several calculations involving the plane's weight. The first figure in the column indicates the maximum allowable structural weight: 759,000 pounds. The second line indicates the allowable weight as a function of weather conditions and the takeoff runway. Two figures are given from which the pilot selects one as he sees fit: 759,000 pounds for runway 06, with a ten-degree flap setting, and 744,100 pounds for runway 32, with a twenty-degree flap setting. Captain Chun checked off the first figure of 759,000 pounds, indicating that this was the weight and runway he would use. This did not necessarily represent the actual weight on takeoff, but simply the maximum allowable weight under the given conditions. In the margin, to the right of this figure, Captain Chun has written "–2,575." What does the figure refer to? Subtracting it from 759,000 pounds results in a weight of 756,425 pounds.

If we consider that to be KAL 007's actual weight on takeoff, we need to deduct the plane's Zero Fuel Weight, which is 460,967 pounds, to determine the amount of fuel Captain Chun appears to have been calculating KAL 007 might be carrying on takeoff. The remainder is 295,458 pounds, 31,758 pounds more than the figure given by the Weight and Balance Manifest and 41,758 pounds more than the figure shown on the Flight Release Sheet. The 41,758 extra pounds of fuel was equivalent to an additional 115 minutes of flying time. If we add this to the 9 hours and 50 minutes indicated by the Flight Release Sheet, we get a total of 11 hours and 45 minutes of flight time. That is close to the 12 hours of flight time announced by Korean Air Lines management personnel. It suggests that KAL management was familiar with details of KAL 007's loading at variance with the figures on the documents Captain Chun filed at Anchorage.

The figures correspond to the jottings seen on the Flight Release Sheet and to the statements made by Korean Air Lines. Thus, Captain Chun had probably planned on taking off from runway 06 with a ten-degree flap setting, and a weight of 756,425 pounds. But, as it turned out, the control tower had assigned him runway 32, which he accepted. For some reason he must have been willing to take off under less favorable conditions. Margins of safety are large enough so that takeoff under these conditions would not have presented unacceptable risks, except perhaps in case of engine trouble during the takeoff.

If we add to the 756,425 pounds indicated above the 2,000 pounds of fuel used for starting and takeoff, we obtain 758,425 pounds, which is very close to the maximum allowable weight of 759,000 pounds. There is thus the possibility that Captain Chun took off from Anchorage with his aircraft loaded to its maximum allowable weight of 759,000 pounds. The handwritten annotation of –2,575 would represent his estimate of fuel consumption for starting the engines and taxiing. It is greater than the 2,000 pounds estimated in the other documents and makes sense if the aircraft had been as heavily loaded as I estimate.

KAL 007 should have arrived in Seoul at 6:05 in the morning after eight hours and 5 minutes in the air. Twelve hours after takeoff would have brought the time to 10:05 in the morning, Seoul time. In *Shootdown,* R. W. Johnson remarked:

> *There is in a word something dreadfully fishy about the whole CIA report. One cannot but observe that it arrived in Seoul just as the passengers' relatives were becoming hysterical because they knew the plane must be out of fuel wherever it was.*[4]

By the "CIA report" Johnson was referring to the information attributed to the CIA saying that KAL 007 had landed safely on Sakhalin (see chapters 1 and 2).

If KAL 007 had left Anchorage much more heavily loaded than Captain Chun's stated figures on fuel indicate, it would be reflected in the plane's performance during flight. That turns out to be the case. An aircraft's weight has the greatest effect on its performance during the climb. This is why all commercial airliners begin their long-distance flights at a prescribed flight level, which they maintain until they burn off a sufficient amount of fuel to climb to a higher level. KAL 007 left Anchorage at 13:00 GMT and reached a cruising altitude of 31,000 feet twenty-nine minutes later at 13:29:28 GMT. In contrast, its companion KAL 015, which left Anchorage fourteen minutes behind 007, reached its cruising altitude of 33,000 feet in only twenty-four minutes, and it is likely that it had reached 31,000 feet in twenty-two minutes. The seven-minute difference between the two suggests that KAL 007 was much more heavily loaded than KAL 015.

The copy of the Operational Flight Plan left at the Anchorage air-traffic-control office by Captain Chun raises another much discussed question. It shows the following handwritten annotations: "ETP 1501 NM," "3 hr 22 mins," and "250 NM." The third figure was inserted between waypoints NEEVA and NIPPI. Most authors who have written on the subject believe ETP indicates "equal-time point." This is the point along an airplane's route at which, taking into consideration wind direction and speed, it would require as much time to reach the destination as to return to the starting point.

If we do the necessary calculations, however, we learn that, given the flight conditions on that particular day, the ETP was not located 1,501 NM from Anchorage, but 1,862 NM away. If ETP 1501 NM doesn't refer to the equal-time point, it must refer to something else. In aeronautics, where abbreviations are often standardized to avoid errors of interpretation, the letters ET within a three-letter abbreviation often indicate "estimated time of." ETP, therefore, would indicate estimated time of P. We need to find out what P refers to in the given instance. Closer examination of Captain Chun's figures gives us a better idea of the point to which he refers and at the same time reveals some remarkable coincidences.

The total distance from Anchorage to waypoint NEEVA is 1,251 NM. If we add to this the 250 NM that Captain Chun has inserted into his flight plan between NEEVA and NIPPI, we obtain 1,501 NM. From the position he reported as NEEVA[5] to the point where KAL 007, according to both the United States and the Soviets, reached Soviet airspace is 250 NM. The indication 250 NM, therefore, appears to refer to the distance between the point reported as NEEVA and the border of Soviet airspace at Kamchatka.[4] Captain Chun's jotted "1,501 NM" thus corresponds to the total distance between Anchorage and the border of Soviet airspace along the course both the United States and the Soviet Union say KAL 007 flew.

Also, if we add 3 hours 22 minutes to 13:00 hours (departure time from Anchorage), we obtain 16:22. The time of penetration by an intruder plane over Kamchatka given by the Soviets is 16:30, a difference of eight minutes. But it was on this part of its flight that KAL 007 lost nine minutes from the estimate given on its flight plan. If the plane had been on time, it would have arrived at a point 1501 NM from Anchorage (Chun's "ETP 1501") at 16:21, within one minute of the time on his flight plan. The 3 hours 22 minutes also coincides with the time a U.S. ferret subsatellite in polar orbit (1982 41C) came into position to register events off and over Kamchatka.[6]

In chapter 17, I will discuss the possibility that KAL 007 may not have flown over either Kamchatka or Sakhalin. I also discuss evidence suggesting the course that both the United States and the Soviet Union said it flew was actually flown by a U.S. military aircraft simulating KAL 007, while KAL 007 flew a more southerly course. In that case, the fact that Chun's marginal notes refer to the more northerly course and the timing of the flight of the aircraft that flew it would constitute an act interesting in itself.

The Passenger List

These are not the only discrepancies between KAL 007's actual and reported parameters. All the official announcements state there were 240 passengers plus 29 crew aboard, for a total of 269. The 1983 ICAO report and the airline's passenger list say so. However, the Weight and Balance Manifest signed by Captain Chun shows only 225 passengers plus 19 crew, for a total of 244. Were there 269 or 244 people on board the aircraft? Why the difference? Though I cannot yet offer a definitive explanation of the discrepancy, scrutiny of what we have been told about who was aboard the Korean airliner illustrates that in the KAL 007 case, almost no matter where you look, things are not what they at first glance seem.

Dr. Gilbert Millet is a deputy from the Gard region of France and mayor of Alès. He has a seat in the French National Assembly. On January 18, 1989, he submitted a written question to the Chamber of Deputies in which he drew the attention of the minister of transportation and maritime affairs to "the gaps in the investigation conducted by the International Civil Aviation Organization (ICAO) following the tragedy that occurred on September 1, 1983, involving the death of 240 people, some of whom were Canadians of French origin."

Deputy Millet's interest in the affair is obvious. One of his relatives, a Canadian of French origin, was on board Flight 007 that night. He was the brother of Philippe Robert de Massy, a lawyer in Montreal, who works for the government of Quebec and whose parents left France and settled in Canada. Philippe de Massy, who was, of course, distressed by the tragedy and believed that much of the story hadn't been disclosed, asked his French cousin Deputy Millet to do whatever he could to persuade the French government to become involved.

Deputy Millet claims there were 240 people in all aboard KAL 007. He does not indicate the source of his information. A handwritten annotation was made by the government, after consultation with Ambassador Costantini, French representative to the ICAO. The annotation says 250 persons were on board, 225 passengers and 15 crew members. The two figures add up to 240, not 250. Ignoring the government's oversight, the total figure of 240 people doesn't correspond to the 225 passengers and 19 crew indicated on the Flight Release Sheet, and even less to the total of 269 passengers and crew mentioned by KAL and others.[7]

John Keppel and I have a copy of the airline's list of KAL 007's passengers, supposed to be complete, with 240 names on it. If we add to this the three cockpit crew, the twenty cabin crew, and the six displaced crew members, we come to a total of 269. We have, however, no proof that the list of 240 passenger names is correct. There is evidence that at least three alleged casualties of KAL 007 were not aboard the Korean airliner.

In an interview of the Soviet divers who participated in the underwater search for the Korean airliner in 1983, one of the divers, identified by the nickname Beardy, said that he found a passport and photograph of a person named "Riukovtchiuk."[8] Although the name Riukovtchiuk is the Russian phonetic rendering of whatever original name it was, and although it suffered a phonetic transcription from Russian to Japanese, then from Japanese to English,[9] it is nevertheless recognizable as a name with a Slav flavor and is not among the 240 names on KAL 007's passenger list. No name on that list can be associated, even in the broadest sense, with that name. Some people in Japan and Korea, aware of the information, have come up with the probably mistaken idea that it might be a tortured rendering of a Korean name: Chung Riu-Ku (from Tchiuk-Riu-Kof). Anyway, a Japanese television team from TBS went to the head office of Korean Air Lines in Seoul. Korean Air Lines refused to tell the TBS journalists whether any such person had been aboard KAL 007. The airline said it was withholding the information on the orders of the Korean government.

Case two. Around September 10, 1983, on the Sea of Okhotsk beach of Hokkaido, not far from the town of Abashiri, a Greek ID card, written in Greek, with a photograph of a young man, was found by the Japanese police. It belonged to a Greek national by the name of Vayanopoulos. The name does not appear among the 240 names on the passenger list. According to page 6 of the ICAO report of June 1993, no Greek nationals were aboard KAL 007.

Case three. Another strange piece of evidence was presented by Japanese television (TBS) in October 1991. Among various items of debris allegedly from KAL 007 brought back from the bottom of the sea by the Soviet divers in 1983 was a Pan Am boarding pass. The Japanese commentator told us that it possibly belonged to a KAL 007 passenger who intended to go from Seoul to Tokyo aboard a Pan Am flight. I managed to get a copy of the video and made a still copy of the boarding pass. The passenger's name was not legible.[10] But the Pan Am flight number, 801, was clearly distinguishable. The flight originated at J. F. Kennedy airport in New York and was direct to Tokyo. That being the case, there is no reason why a passenger on KAL 007, from New York to Seoul, would have been in possession of a Pan Am boarding pass for a flight from New York to Tokyo. One would not have one unless one actually boarded and made the Pan Am flight.

It is, of course, true that someone could have been traveling aboard KAL 007 bound for Seoul with an obsolete Pan Am boarding pass from a previous flight to Tokyo in his pocket. In that case the boarding pass would not have wound up on the ocean floor off Sakhalin, because the Korean airliner crashed not there but four hundred miles to the south. But it is quite conceivable that he might have traveled from the United States to Tokyo on Pan Am and then have boarded an RC-135, a number of which are stationed in Japan, which crashed off Sakhalin. From the evidence presented by the Soviet divers, we know that at least one RC-135 did crash there.

The fourth case has a bizarre flavor to it, a mixture of human drama and the secret world of spies. The story begins in 1983, at the small border post of Perepytye, south of Nevelsk. The border post commander and political commissar was Lieutenant Belov. A French TV reporter of Russian descent, Misha Lobko, was on Sakhalin in June 1993, where he interviewed Lieutenant Belov. Lieutenant Belov remembered:

> *The orders were straightforward: destroy everything and confirm by a report. Then, shut up. Never give out any information. They came with a big ten-ton truck, a ZIL 131. They were sailors. They asked, "Where is the hole?" I showed them.*

They discharged the ZIL 131 truck into the hole with the help of my soldiers. They brought a forty-four-gallon drum of gas-oil, which they poured over it. Then they set fire to it. It burned for two hours. When everything had burned down, we brought in a bulldozer to crush and disperse what was left. Then we covered it with soil. I telephoned to higher-ups at Nevelsk and reported. I am sure the names and grades of the higher-ups I reported to were phony, but anyway I said, "It is destroyed." That's all.

I met Misha Lobko in Paris in February 1994, and he told me more. In November 1992, the hole at Pereputye was "found again" and opened. A government commission under the presidency of Mr. Stepanov came and ordered that all metal pieces with an identification number be taken out. The hole was then closed. It was opened again in January 1993, and all the remaining debris was taken out and stored in a hangar in Kholmsk, where the KGB sorted it and sent some to Moscow. In March of that year, the rest was buried again in the hole at Pereputye. In June 1993, the hole was opened for a third time, while Misha Lobko was there. This time, all the debris was taken out and sent to the same hangar in Kholmsk as before. Misha Lobko was able to film the debris there before the KGB sorted it and sent some to Moscow.

Because of his Russian parentage, Misha Lobko had been raised in the Russian language and culture. Some of the Russian officials he made friends with showed him the photograph of a little girl, about ten to twelve years old, apparently from Asia, which they agreed to let him film in exchange for a substantial payment. (See photograph on page 164). The original photograph was found inside a wallet that had been in the hole at Pereputye. Because the leather wallet was thick and tightly packed, it miraculously escaped destruction by fire. It was sent to Moscow with other items, including several passports. Misha Lobko was not allowed to film the passports. Later that year, on September 1, 1993, during a commemorative ceremony, a few items from the hole at Pereputye were handed over to the families of the victims. But the photograph of the little girl and the passports were not given to the families. Misha Lobko wondered why.

Because of its human appeal, the Japanese television station TBS, for which Lobko was working at the time, broadcast the little girl's photograph during its evening news program in prime time. It was also broadcast in Seoul. That evening, somebody telephoned the Seoul television station and identified the girl and her father. The girl was working as a secretary in Seoul. Her father, a military man, had disappeared in 1983. When TBS heard of the development, they immediately tried to learn more but were prevented from going further. They were stonewalled everywhere. Rumors surfaced that the father of the little girl had not been a passenger aboard KAL 007. He had been an officer with the South Korean Army, working with the intelligence service, the KCIA. He disappeared at the same time as the Korean airliner and had never been heard of since.

I wanted to verify the rumors and I asked the help of Dr. Sugwon Kang, professor of political science at Hartwick College in the United States and a friend of John Keppel's. Professor Kang has worked many years on the KAL 007 case and is presently writing a book on the subject. We had exchanged findings. Professor Kang has good contacts with the South Korean press and particularly with the *Joong Ang Daily News,* a Seoul newspaper. I had contact with the same newspaper, which, on October 30, 1992, published one of my articles about the forgery of the black box that President Yeltsin gave to the South Korean government. However, Professor Kang and I were unable to get any new information about the little girl or her father. This is strange since the girl's identity was already known, at least by the television station that received the first call. If the father had been an innocent passenger aboard KAL 007, there would have been no need to keep it secret.

Misha Lobko told me that the people with whom he spoke on Sakhalin believed that the story that the hole in the ground at Pereputye had been dug to dispose of debris from KAL 007 was false. Initially, they said, an aircraft had crashed there. It had been, they said, an RC-135. If that is true, it is possible that the little girl's father was aboard it as a language specialist. These sophisticated signals-intelligence collection platforms often have language specialists among their crews of twenty-five to thirty, although they are normally U.S. citizens.[11]

The list of the dead remains flawed. But some things are clear. If KAL 007 had not deviated from its assigned course and if U.S. military aircraft had not overflown Kamchatka and Sakhalin, those that died that night would, in all likelihood, still be alive. However many people were on KAL 007 and the other airplanes I have mentioned that may have been flying, one thing is clear. They all died as a result of a badly planned and ill-executed intelligence mission that should never have been undertaken in the first place. It deprived the next of kin of their loved ones. And once they were dead, the cover-up deprived their kin of their bodies and the truth of how they died. Whoever they were and however they died, each wholly unnecessary death hurt someone.

But I am getting ahead of our story. Let us return to KAL 007's flight across Alaska and the Bering Sea.

Figure 14. *The little girl from Pereputye. Her father's wallet was recovered from a crash by the Soviets. He was a Korean Central Intelligence Agency officer who disappeared at the time of the KAL 007 disaster and may have been aboard a U.S. military aircraft.*

The Flight

Two Korean Air Lines passenger flights were in Anchorage on August 31, 1983: KAL 015 from Los Angeles and KAL 007 from New York. Anchorage was only a refueling stop for these flights. The aircraft would take on fuel and change crews. KAL 015, having arrived twenty minutes earlier than KAL 007, should normally have left first. That night KAL 007 was the first plane to take off. Was there a significant reason for the change in the routine?

KAL 007 took off from Anchorage on runway 32 at 13:00 hours GMT. At 13:01:12, the control tower announced "radar contact." At 13:05:23, KAL 007 reached 5,000 feet, at 13:28:01 it reached 30,000 feet, and at 13:29:28, the plane reached its cruising altitude of 31,000 feet. Flight KAL 015 took off fourteen minutes behind KAL 007. It was initially assigned an altitude of 31,000 feet, the same as KAL 007, which seems to indicate that both aircraft were officially carrying the same weight and would be able to maintain the same speed.

However, when the control tower gave the authorization to climb to FL 310 (31,000 feet), KAL 015 put in a request to climb to 33,000 feet. There was no apparent reason why the plane couldn't have accepted the 31,000 feet. The fourteen-minute difference put the two aircraft 100 NM apart, which was enough to provide a generous margin of safety. Because both aircraft were Boeing 747s and performed nearly identically, the difference in time and distance between them should have been maintained all the way to Seoul. The extra unacknowledged weight, which I discussed in the previous chapter, could account for the fact that they did not.

KAL 015 took off at 13:14 hours GMT, and the control tower announced "radar contact" at 13:14:27, just 27 seconds after the official takeoff time. In contrast, it took KAL 007 a relatively long 72 seconds, or nearly three times more, to reach the altitude required for radar contact. From the beginning of the takeoff run, marked by the control tower's authorization to take off, it took KAL 007 2 minutes and 27 seconds to arrive at the point of "radar contact," while KAL 015 did it in only 1 minute and 7 seconds.

KAL 007's climb performance on takeoff thus lagged behind that of KAL 015, indicating that KAL 007 was more heavily loaded than its sister ship. That is also shown by the time it took the two aircraft to reach cruising altitude. It took KAL 007 29 minutes and 28 seconds to reach an altitude of 31,000 feet, and only 24 minutes 33 seconds, five minutes less, for KAL 015 to reach the higher altitude of 33,000 feet. All this favors the hypothesis that KAL 007 left Anchorage with considerably more fuel than was indicated on its flight documents—enough to stay in the air for nearly twelve hours.[1]

Soon after takeoff, KAL 007 was authorized to proceed "direct Bethel." That meant it was cleared to fly directly to the VOR beacon at Bethel,[2] at the western end of the Alaskan Peninsula, without having to follow the standard VOR track indicated on the maps as J-501. In this respect, the ICAO report of June 1993, page 42, paragraph 2.4.1, contains a statement that looks like an excuse. It says: "The clearance given [direct Bethel] indicated that the normal means for ensuring navigation on route J-501 west of Anchorage VOR/DME was not available." This statement is obviously here to lessen in the reader's mind the KAL 007 crew's responsibility for the initial deviation from its course since they cannot be faulted if the "normal means of navigation was not available." However charitable the intention might be, the information is misleading. Only the navigation aid at the starting point of the Anchorage-Bethel leg, namely the Anchorage VOR/DME (the VOR gives a position relative to it, the DME gives a distance), was temporarily out of service. But the midway point, the Cairn Mountain NDB (nondirectional radio beacon), and the Bethel VORTAC (VOR plus TACAN, a military DME) were working normally. KAL 007 could, or rather should, have used them for its navigation to Bethel.

In 1983, Korean Air Lines used the North Pacific Airspace Operations Manual as the basis for their guidance for flight crews operating in the North Pacific Route System. Particularly relevant were the procedures for checking navigation-system accuracy at the commencement of oceanic navigation. These procedures required careful overflight of the last external navigation aid, in this case, the Bethel VORTAC, and specific checks of the accuracy of the aircraft's inertial navigation system (INS) by comparing the coordinates displayed by the INS with the actual coordinates of the VORTAC beacon while flying overhead. For flying outbound, the procedures also required that the aircraft fly a specific track from the VORTAC and check the INS's accuracy against it while flying farther and farther away from the coast over the ocean. On page 43 of its report of June 1993, the ICAO blandly remarks, "These procedures, included in the KAL Operations Manual, were not observed since KAL 007 did not pass over Bethel VORTAC."

The ICAO did not examine, or indeed mention, the possibility that KAL 007 did not pass over the Bethel VORTAC because its flight crew chose to fly their own route, for their own purposes. Yet that surely was a possibility that an objective inquiry would have examined.

When KAL 007 told Anchorage that it was passing over Bethel waypoint, it was in reality 12 NM north of it and outside the boundaries of the airway. Given the accuracy of the aircraft's navigation systems and instruments and of the Bethel VORTAC, had it followed the rules and its instructions, it would have passed within a few feet of the beacon's vertical axis. That it was not overhead Bethel when it said it was must have been abundantly clear to the flight crew from several of the airliner's instruments. Its position report "at Bethel" was the first of KAL 007's misleading reports to air traffic control.[3]

The ICAO assumed KAL 007's deviation from its assigned course to be the result of one of a number of accidental and undetectable errors. This hypothesis is at variance with what I have said about KAL 007's position report at BETHEL, which indicates that the airliner's deviation was at least detectable. One of the best qualified students of the KAL 007 case, Robert Allardyce, a professional pilot, navigator, and flight engineer, has studied this phase of KAL 007's flight carefully. He concludes that as well as being detectable, the airliner's deviation from its assigned course was intentional.

He finds that the plane was guided by its inertial navigation system and followed a great-circle track, which led it from the Anchorage VOR to a point north of Bethel, and then on across the Bering Sea. This, he says, shows planning from the start. Captain Chun's character and experience also make it seem likely that he knew what he was doing. He was a meticulous man and an expert navigator—the back-up pilot on the president of the Republic of Korea's airplane.

Chun's speed on this leg is also of interest. To cover the 346 NM between Anchorage and Bethel, he had estimated a flying time of fifty-three minutes at a speed of 391 knots, with a headwind of 33 knots. As it turned out, he covered the distance in forty-nine minutes at an average speed of 427 knots, his headwind being only 11 knots. The plane's average speed was 36 knots greater than anticipated and the headwind was 22 knots less than predicted. The difference of 14 knots is not very significant since the stated wind velocity is the result of an instantaneous rather than an average reading, which might have differed to some extent. It's possible that KAL 007 accelerated during the Anchorage-Bethel leg by pushing its engines slightly, but the major reason for the four-minute gain (fifty-three minus forty-nine) is simply the result of the decreased wind velocity. Flying over nearly the identical flight path, KAL 015 gained eight minutes on its schedule, passing directly over the Bethel VOR at 14:01 instead of 14:09, as anticipated. The fact that KAL 007 gained only four minutes rather than the eight gained by KAL 015 once more reflects that one aircraft was much heavier than the other and did not accelerate as fast as indicated on its flight plan, which did not take into account the unauthorized extra weight.

After Bethel, KAL 007 began the transoceanic part of its flight. The plane was scheduled to arrive at the next waypoint, NABIE, 312 NM away, at 14:30 GMT, flying at a speed of 456 knots, with a 25-knot headwind.

Instead KAL 007 reported passing the NABIE waypoint (actually abeam it to the north) at 14:32 hours GMT, two minutes late, at an average speed of 435 knots, 21 knots less than scheduled. The headwind abeam NABIE was 59 knots, 24 knots greater than had been forecast. Because the two figures off-set one another to within 3 knots, it is possible that KAL 007's delay along this leg of its flight path was simply the result of the winds.

When KAL 007's passage over NABIE was announced, Chun did not contact air traffic control directly. The radio message was relayed by KAL 015 at 14:35:02 GMT. The fact that KAL 015 relayed KAL 007's position would seem to indicate that 007 was unable to contact Anchorage directly. Because the plane's radios were working properly, the most commonly accepted theory is that KAL 007 was too far off course to communicate with the relay station on St. Paul Island. VHF radio has line-of-sight characteristics and is thus limited in range by the curvature of the earth. If the plane had remained on Romeo-20, its assigned route, it would have been in VHF radio range of the relay station on St. Paul, which would have enabled it to contact Anchorage control.

There are problems with KAL 015's relay, however, for the tape recorded at Anchorage contains no trace of a request from KAL 007 to KAL 015 or, at least, had KAL 007 really been out of range, no response from KAL 015. If events had proceeded normally and KAL 007 had wandered off course with-out realizing it, the aircraft would have called Anchorage several times. Even if Anchorage for some reason did not pick up the calls, KAL 015, which was flying fairly close to its sister aircraft, could not have failed to hear them. After not receiving an answer from Anchorage, KAL 007 would have called KAL 015 to ask them if they were in radio contact with Anchorage. An affir-mative response from KAL 015 would have shown up on the tape. KAL 007 would then have asked KAL 015 to relay its position report to Anchorage. Here, too, an affirmative response from KAL 015 would have appeared on the Anchorage tape. KAL 007 would then have transmitted its position report to KAL 015, which would have relayed it to Anchorage. Ordinarily KAL 015 would have read the message back to KAL 007 word for word, to ensure it had been understood correctly and contained no errors.

KAL 015 transmitted KAL 007's position report at 14:35:03, only three minutes after KAL 007 passed the waypoint. It usually takes two or three minutes for an aircraft to transmit its position report to air traffic control. Thus there was not enough time for a relay procedure to have taken place between KAL 007 and KAL 015. Even if, as seems unlikely under the cir-cumstances, part of the relay had been conducted between the two Korean airliners on a chatter frequency unrecorded at Anchorage, the time between KAL 007's reported passing of the waypoint and KAL 015's "relay" was too short for the necessary procedure to have been followed.

Shortly before KAL 015 called Anchorage to transmit KAL 007's position report, and while Anchorage was trying to raise KAL 007, three transmissions in Korean appear on KAL 007's assigned frequency on the tape recorded at Anchorage—here translated below and written in lower case. One might suppose that KAL 007 was giving a position report to KAL 015. On the other hand, in a suit brought against Korean Air Lines by the victims' relatives, which was tried in the United States District Court in Washington, D.C., KAL 015's copilot testified under oath that all or most of the transmissions were from him while he was speaking to KAL 007. However, neither appears to be the case.

On pages 25 and 26 of its Information Paper No. 1[4] the ICAO report of June 1993 attributes the three messages to KAL 007 and is so affirmative in identifying the traffic as coming from KAL 007 that it says the calls were made with KAL 007's VHF radio set #2. This raises several important questions. That messages from KAL 007 were recorded loud and clear at Anchorage implies that the airliner was within VHF range and perfectly capable of transmitting its NABIE position report without the need for a relay by KAL 015. The ICAO should, at the very least, have mentioned the point. At the same time, the fact that KAL 007's interlocutor in these communications was not recorded on the Anchorage tape means that the plane was located far to the north of airway Romeo-20 and out of range of the Anchorage VHF en route antenna on St. Paul Island.[5] The interlocutor was, of course, not KAL 015, whose transmissions were recorded at Anchorage. Here again, the ICAO should have been prompted to raise pertinent questions. Instead it chose to cover it up by closing its eyes to them with a politically conformist eyelid. The transmissions are as follows:

14:33:53 Anchorage:	*KOREAN AIR ZERO ZERO SEVEN, ANCHORAGE CENTER, HOW DO YOU READ?*
14:34:17 KAL 007:	*Please shut it off [stop it] as you proceed. (in Korean)*
.... Unknown:	*................*
.... KAL 007:	*Please call again. (in Korean)*
14:34:37 Anchorage:	*KOREAN AIR ZERO ZERO SEVEN, ANCHORAGE CENTER.*
14:34:50 KAL 007:	*Three three zero won't do. (in Korean)*
.... Unknown:	*................*
14:34:54 KAL 007:	*We have three three zero. (in Korean)*
........Unknown:	*................*

14:35:02 KAL 015:   *ANCHORAGE, KOREAN AIR ZERO ONE*
                       FIVE.

The Korean transmissions appear to consist of two separate exchanges between an aircraft that was picked up on the Anchorage tape and another whose replies were not recorded. The first exchange occurs at 14:34:17. The aircraft that is speaking (in all likelihood KAL 007) appears to have been asking the airplane that is not heard to shut off (or stop) something as they proceed. We don't know what the other speaker said in reply, but the first aircraft then suggested he call again. Several authors who have examined this radio conversation have translated the Korean as "please try again." That is incorrect. The original sentence includes the Korean formula for addressing another person and the Korean verb *pullo,* meaning to call. The ICAO has it partly correct when it interprets it as "try to call."

The second exchange is separated both in time and by a call from Anchorage. The words *three three zero* in the second exchange in Korean were almost universally interpreted to mean FL 330, an altitude of 33,000 feet. The ICAO interprets this part as follows:

KAL 007 (VHF #2): Unable to get Flight Level Three Three Zero....
KAL 007 (VHF #2): We are maintaining Flight Level Three Three Zero.

It is not clear what the ICAO was thinking about when it offered this transcription without comment. It is hard to believe that someone would say he is unable to get Flight Level Three Three Zero and in the same breath declare he is at Flight Level Three Three Zero. Moreover, as the ICAO knew well, at this stage of its flight KAL 007 had been assigned FL 310, which it said it maintained for another hour and a half, until 16:03:53 UTC, when it was cleared to climb to FL 330.

In view of the ambiguity of the data, I asked Dr. Tsuboi, the director of the Iwatsu Laboratory, to analyze the transmissions in Korean on the tape. None of the speakers was KAL 015, the voice prints of whose pilot and copilot Dr. Tsuboi had previously identified. The first transmissions at 14:34:17 GMT were identified by Dr. Tsuboi as coming from an unknown aircraft, but in all likelihood were from the VHF transmitter of KAL 007's pilot (VHF #1). The second transmissions, at 14:34:50 and 14:34:54, were identified as coming from the VHF transmitter of KAL 007's copilot (VHF #2). That the KAL 007 transmissions were recorded at Anchorage proves that it was within radio range of St. Paul Island. One reason KAL 007's NABIE position report was "relayed" for it by KAL 015 could have been a desire to convince Anchorage that KAL 007 was having problems with VHF transmission. That might have made the subsequent radio breakdown they simulated with Tokyo more plausible. There is another possible reason, which I will come to in a minute.

The plane to which KAL 007 was talking in Korean was a third aircraft. Since it was not heard, little is known of it except that it was far enough north of the airways to be out of range of Anchorage. This third aircraft seems to have been neither Korean nor civilian. The only two commercial jetliners on this part of Romeo-20 were KAL 007 and KAL 015. Moreover, this ghost plane was not under control of FAA's Anchorage Center and was able to operate relatively unrestrictedly in the Alaskan Defense Identification Zone. There is a good chance, therefore, that it was a military aircraft. But not just any military aircraft. At least one of its crew members spoke Korean and was in contact with KAL 007. Why would a military aircraft, some of whose personnel spoke Korean, be in radio contact with KAL 007 that night?

More than six hundred miles away, American military controllers, who seem in this instance not to have been in on the secret, were observing air traffic over the Bering Sea and the northern Pacific. Evidence of this was discovered by Lawrence L. Porter, who mentioned it in his report "Acoustic Analysis of Air Traffic Communications Concerning Korean Air Flight 007."[6] At 14:34:01 GMT, sixteen seconds before the first transmissions in Korean, an unidentified voice could be heard in the FAA Anchorage control room. It was unintentionally picked up by Controller DeGarmo's microphone and recorded on the tape of transactions at his position. Porter believes it came from a speakerphone.

First voice *(presumably military controller at Elmendorf AFB):*	*Okay, you guys got someone bumping into the Russians' air defenses over here.*[7]
Second voice *(FAA controller DeGarmo):*	*Oh, you're kidding. A person should warn him.[8] That's why you should've given the information here, instead of waiting.[9]*

Robert Allardyce, who discusses the incident in his unpublished study, believes the first voice belongs to a military controller who contacted the Anchorage civilian controller following the standard procedure for flight-plan correlation established by the U.S. Department of Defense. Larry Porter, who knows him, says that the second voice is that of DeGarmo, the FAA controller.

Did DeGarmo believe that KAL 007 was heading for Soviet-controlled airspace without authorization and was thus in grave danger, and do nothing about it? If so, did someone tell him to keep his fingers out of things he didn't understand? Was it KAL 007 or the Korean-speaking military plane that the military controller at Elmendorf AFB was speaking about? If the Korean-speaking plane had flown from Anchorage (Elmendorf AFB), why would the military controller not have known that? Why would he have implied it was a civilian aircraft and thus FAA's responsibility? DeGarmo himself would have seen it on radar (civilian and military, to which he had limited access) over at least part of its route. What was he thinking about when he unquestioningly accepted KAL 015's "relay" of KAL 007's NABIE position report, which should have sounded odd to him? There are, as the reader will see as we go along, some questions in the KAL 007 case that can only be answered as the shape of the larger events becomes clear.

Allardyce did not have access to the Iwatsu analyses and didn't realize that KAL 007 was within range of the VHF antenna on St. Paul Island. He concluded that KAL 007 was too far from St. Paul to be heard and had asked KAL 015 to relay the message for them. In tracing a probable route for 007, he determined a zone of uncertainty that would have located the plane somewhere between 205 and 220 NM off course. This put the plane within 206 NM of St. Paul. Allardyce estimated the maximum range of the St. Paul VHF antennas at 205 NM and saw this as confirmation that KAL 007 was out of VHF radio range.

In trying to understand KAL 007's behavior, it is important to know whether the plane was or was not out of VHF radio range. Dr. Tsuboi's spectrographic analysis proves that the plane was within it. Allardyce's calculations appear to indicate that it was not. I checked Allardyce's calculations and found an error in his computation of the VHF range. The formula that is used to calculate the distance of the visual horizon is $D = 2.1 \sqrt{h}$, in which D (the distance in nautical miles) is equal to the square root of the height, h, of the eye (or an antenna) in meters, multiplied by 2.1. For an aircraft at 31,000 feet, the horizon is located 204 NM away. The antenna at St. Paul Island was 657 feet high. Applying the same formula, we get a distance of 30 NM for the horizon of the antenna. The two values are added to determine the maximum distance at which an aircraft flying at 31,000 feet could still see the point of an antenna 657 feet high and receive its signal. This gives 204 + 30 = 234 NM.

Allardyce simply added the 657 feet of the antenna to 31,000 feet altitude and calculated a single horizon based on a height of 31,657 feet. He found this to be 205.6 NM. Since on the basis of other evidence, he had estimated, probably accurately, that KAL 007 passed within 206 NM of St. Paul Island, he was convinced the plane was out of radio range, although barely. When I checked Allardyce's VHF range calculations and realized they were incorrect, I asked John Keppel to inform him of my findings. Allardyce graciously admitted he had made an error and that the range was indeed 234. The ICAO report of June 1993, page 45, paragraph 2.7.3, indicates that at NABIE, KAL 007 was approximately 60 NM north of its route. Since at that point, the route is 140 NM from St. Paul NDB, it follows that, according to the ICAO, KAL 007 was approximately 200 NM from the St. Paul antenna. The ICAO failed to note that it was within VHF range—although it indicated as much by its attribution of the 14:34 UTC transmissions in Korean to KAL 007. The conclusion then, is that KAL 007 was within VHF range.

Why then did KAL 015 transmit KAL 007's position report at NABIE for it rather than let KAL 007 report for itself? It had the effect of making those who later examined the Anchorage tape think that KAL 007 was out of radio range of the en route antenna and thus farther north than was the case. This is, however, as good a place as any to say that from its position abeam NABIE all the way to where it was destroyed off the west coast of Honshu, we have no conclusive evidence as to the course KAL 007 actually flew.

We have a U.S. map supposedly representing intercepted Soviet radar tracking data on the course of the Korean airliner, and two Russian sets of course data said to have come from KAL 007's digital flight-data recorder—all three of which differ from each other. For its 1993 report, the Russians also gave the ICAO data that included two different radar tracks approaching Kamchatka, both of which were presented by the ICAO as having been flown by the Korean airliner. All of these data, U.S., Soviet, and Russian, however contradictory, are useful. They almost certainly represent the courses flown at the time by one or another aircraft of interest to us. The data can often be pieced together with other evidence to tell us something valuable. In the present instance, however, the question is, which, if any, of these tracks is that of KAL 007?

Pending the reliable evidence we shall one day get that will resolve the question of KAL 007's course across the Bering Sea and the northern Pacific, there are two broad alternatives. One is that from its position abeam NABIE the airliner flew a sufficiently northerly course to arrive north of Shemya and southeast of Karaginski Island, where Marshal Ogarkov (somewhat ambiguously) said it was picked up by Soviet radar and rendezvoused with a U.S. RC-135, flew across Kamchatka, the Sea of Okhotsk, and Sakhalin—and then, which Ogarkov did not say, turned south and flew down the coast of Japan. The other alternative is that KAL 007 held a more southerly course across the Bering Sea and the northern Pacific, passed south of Kamchatka, crossed the Kuril Island chain and the Sea of Okhotsk, passed through La Pérouse Strait between Sakhalin and Hokkaido, and then turned south. In that case it would not have overflown Soviet territory.

In chapter 17, I will review the evidence suggesting that KAL 007 followed the more southerly of these two routes. In the present chapter we have already met evidence that makes this plausible. Abeam NABIE, KAL 007 gave the impression it was out of VHF range of St. Paul Island when it was not. At the same time, it appears to have been talking in Korean with a military airplane to its north that was out of VHF range of St. Paul. KAL 007 thus cannot have been on the northerly course while the Korean-speaking military airplane apparently was.

We have also seen that the VHF position report at NABIE was submitted for KAL 007 by KAL 015, and we will see that it happened again at waypoint NEEVA. Though both reports claimed that KAL 007 was on course, the fact KAL 007 itself did not submit them implied, incorrectly as we have seen, that it was out of range to the north.

After the VHF NABIE position report, KAL 007, or the other aircraft speaking for it, made a few transmissions on HF to Anchorage and Tokyo, which were recorded there.[10] Unfortunately, Dr. Tsuboi did not have these transmissions in his database when he made his analysis. Objective spectrographic and voice-print analysis should, in particular, be done of KAL 007's HF NIPPI position report. The official account of events puts KAL 007 at that time as just having crossed Kamchatka and leaving its airspace for international airspace over the Sea of Okhotsk.

If this NIPPI position report, whoever sent it, was in fact sent from the place the official story puts KAL 007 at the time (17:08 GMT), it would no doubt have been recorded and the position of the aircraft located by direction-finding by the Soviets. If sent from this position, the NIPPI position report would in all likelihood have been intended to put the Soviets on notice that one of the aircraft approaching it over the Sea of Okhotsk might be a passenger-filled civilian airliner.

I am getting ahead of my story. Let me now return to the progress of the aircraft, whichever it was, KAL 007 or its simulator, on the northern course across the Bering Sea. To avoid intolerable complexity during the balance of this chapter, I will refer to the aircraft flying the northern course as KAL 007. Many of the factors affecting the progress of the aircraft on this route were the same regardless of whether KAL 007 or a simulator was flying the route.

When it transmitted 007's NABIE position report, KAL 015 also provided the plane's estimated time of arrival (ETA) at NEEVA, which was 15:49 hours. Yet less than ten minutes later, at 14:44:09 GMT, KAL 007 called Anchorage directly on its HF radio, which carries much farther than VHF. At that time it retransmitted its entire position report, which is quite unusual. Even stranger is the fact that it revised its ETA at NEEVA to 15:53 hours.

Although the distance between NABIE and NEEVA is 593 NM, a four-minute delay after ten minutes flying time is impossible. An explanation might be that the first estimate given Anchorage by KAL 015, in the name of KAL 007, was made on KAL 015's own authority, and was made according to KAL 007's computerized flight plan without coordination with KAL 007. Caught by surprise, KAL 007, which in the meantime had made a change in its estimates, had to revise its ETA upward.

KAL 007's ETA at NEEVA, "relayed" by KAL 015, was the exact time indicated in the computerized flight plan, which assumed a 35-knot headwind. The actual wind over the position KAL 007 reported as "NABIE" was coming from 250 degrees at 65 knots, which gave them a headwind component of 60 knots. This would decrease their average speed (which had been calculated for a 35-knot headwind) by 25 knots and lead to a delay in arriving at "NEEVA" of exactly four minutes. Realizing this, 007 corrected its ETA at NEEVA to 15:53 GMT. This supports the idea that the NABIE position report relayed by KAL 015 did not originate with KAL 007, for it would have calculated its ETA at NEEVA using the actual wind conditions.

KAL 007 did not, however, report passing NEEVA at its corrected ETA, but after an additional five-minute delay, at 15:58 GMT. This was in addition to the four-minute delay it had already announced, and in addition to the two minutes KAL 007 had been late at NABIE in relation to its computerized flight plan. Once more KAL 007's position report was relayed by KAL 015. Once more there is something strange about the relay. KAL 015 called Anchorage at 16:00:39 to report its sister ship's passage of the waypoint at 15:58. Two minutes and 39 seconds is not enough to complete the relay procedure I have already outlined. In this instance, however, I believe we must accept that the substance of the report was provided by KAL 007. The reported nine-minute delay since NABIE was too strange for the report to have been a canned message sent by KAL 015 on 007's behalf without consultation.

As shown above, four minutes of this delay can be attributed to the stronger than anticipated headwind, which KAL 007 took into account in calculating its corrected ETA. But what about the other five minutes? They are the result of an additional decrease in ground speed of 23 knots, which cannot be attributed to meteorological conditions. KAL 007 reported passing NEEVA at 15:58. KAL 015 passed it at 16:02. The fourteen-minute difference between them at the time of takeoff from Anchorage had fallen to twelve minutes at Bethel and eleven minutes at NABIE. Now, at NEEVA it is no more than four minutes.[11] It would appear that 007 intentionally slowed its speed over this leg of the flight.

The Soviets said that before penetrating Kamchatka airspace, the intruder plane flew wing to wing with an RC-135. Marshal Ogarkov gave a detailed description of the rendezvous and showed the flight path of the two aircraft on his map, during his September 9, 1983, news conference for Western journalists.[12] Ogarkov said:

I want especially to call your attention to the fact that the South Korean plane entered the zone of detection of Soviet radar systems in an area that is constantly patrolled by American reconnaissance planes, particularly RC-135s. This time we detected an RC-135 in this area at 2:45 A.M. local [Kamchatka] time on September 1. As registered by Soviet radar systems, for two hours it conducted a somewhat strange patrol here. At 4:51 A.M. Kamchatka time, [15:41 GMT] another plane with a blip analogous to that made by an RC-135 plane was detected in the same area and at the same altitude—8,000 meters. The planes approached each other [up to the total merger of the blips on the screen] and then proceeded together for some time [about ten minutes]. Then one of them, as has been repeatedly observed earlier, headed for Alaska, while the other one headed for Petropavlovsk-Kamchatsky. Naturally, Soviet Air Defense Forces command posts drew the conclusion that a reconnaissance plane was approaching the U.S.S.R.'s airspace.[13]

The two planes flying sufficiently close together to appear in a single radar blip for ten minutes suggest an aircraft that needed fuel and a KC-135 tanker refueling it.

Various observers have speculated on the reasons for KAL 007's delay on its NABIE-NEEVA leg. The Soviets suggested that the forty-minute delay with which KAL 007 left Anchorage in relation to its original schedule was done to effect coordination with successive passes off Kamchatka and Sakhalin of a U.S. electronic intelligence satellite in polar orbit, which they called Ferret D and in international terminology appears to have been 1982 41C. The movements of the satellite do not seem a likely cause of KAL 007's delay (or that of an aircraft simulating it) on its NABIE-NEEVA leg. They were entirely predictable. Had coordination with them been an object, adjustments could have been worked into the aircraft's schedule before it left Anchorage as the Soviets suggested was done.

It has also been suggested that KAL 007's delay in its NABIE-NEEVA leg was introduced in order to effect coordination with the RC-135 discussed by Ogarkov and admitted by the United States to have been in the area for some time "on mission orbit" and to have crossed the path of KAL 007 twice. On the face of it, if adjustment of the schedule of the two aircraft had been necessary, it would seem easier for the RC-135 to have terminated its orbiting earlier rather than to have required KAL 007 to delay its flight for the four minutes on the NABIE-NEEVA not accounted for by wind.

However, we do not necessarily, or even probably, have a complete account of the U.S. aircraft and their operations in the area southeast of Karaginski Island and north of NEEVA. In military operations unforeseen events often lead to unexpected delays. In this connection, it may be relevant to note that on KAL 007's next leg, NEEVA-NIPPI, it reported an arrival at NIPPI that showed a speed in excess of that foreseen in its flight plan. It seems to have been making up for time lost on the previous leg.

It has also been speculated that KAL 007 slowed down intentionally on its NABIE-NEEVA leg in order to look like an RC-135 to Soviet radar. If that were the case, there would have been at least equal reason for KAL 007 to have flown at RC-135-like speed, 430 knots, rather than its own normal speed of 480 to 500 knots, on at least the 250 NM segment of its next leg between NEEVA and the Soviet air frontier. The time and distance factors in KAL 007's position reports must have been accurate or very nearly so if, as we know it was, the airliner was about to arrive on time at NIIGATA when it was destroyed. Had the Korean airliner flown at the speed of an RC-135 over the first 250 NM, slightly less than half the total distance of its next (NEEVA to NIPPI) leg, we would expect to have evidence of it in the airliner's speed reflected in its position report at NIPPI. But Chun's position report at NIPPI indicates an average ground speed over the leg of 480 knots despite a fifty-knot headwind, well in excess of the 463 knots called for on the leg by his flight plan.

There is little reason to doubt, however, the Soviets' statements that they interpreted the aircraft heading for Kamchatka mentioned by Ogarkov as an RC-135. For one thing, it was flying at 8,000 meters (26,000 feet), an altitude the RC-135 in mission orbit had been holding, rather than the 31,000 feet KAL 007 had been at, or the 33,000 feet to which it had been cleared shortly after NEEVA. Moreover, the oncoming aircraft was flying at the speed of an RC-135 rather than at the speed of a Boeing 747.

Although the other of the two aircraft Ogarkov mentioned rendezvousing southeast of Karaginski Island no doubt, as both he and the U.S. said, "headed back for Alaska," one should not think that what the Soviets saw during the next half hour was a single southwest-bound aircraft heading for Kamchatka. The 1993 ICAO report, on pages 48 and 50, prints two Soviet maps, each showing the radar track of an aircraft approaching Kamchatka from the east. One of these airplanes is labeled "KE 007," and the other is also by implication the Korean airliner, considering the thrust of the report—that is to say, the one-intruder, one-shootdown story.

The maps are drawn to different scales. When you reduce them to the same scale, it is obvious that the two radar tracks of the aircraft approaching Kamchatka are different and cannot refer to the same plane. That is, however, not all. As will be made clear in chapter 15, when you analyze the maps carefully, you see that they yield evidence of three or four different aircraft approaching or crossing Kamchatka. Of these, two flew at speeds that KAL 007 could not have attained, one bordering on the supersonic and the other clearly supersonic. On one of the maps the two tracks shown are both labeled with a tracking number, 6065, which, it is clear from other evidence, means "military, possibly hostile."

There are reasons to conclude that none of this radar evidence refers to KAL 007. It may have been on the northern course, have approached Kamchatka, and have overflown it. But we have no evidence that it did. In either case, in KAL 007's departure from Anchorage and its flight across the Bering Sea, we have seen several things that require explanation. Why was its cockpit crew inserted at Anchorage despite the fact that one was already available? Why didn't it send its own NABIE position report when it was in range of the VHF en route antenna on St. Paul Island? Why abeam NABIE was it talking in Korean to an aircraft to the north of it that appears to have been military? Why didn't it send its own position report at NEEVA? The one hypothesis that the ICAO reports failed to examine is that KAL 007's off-course flight was intentional from the beginning.

Kamchatka

If KAL 007 penetrated Kamchatka airspace at 16:30 GMT as alleged, it is hard to believe that it could have done so unescorted without being detected, intercepted, and shot down. Had it done so, it would, for thirty-eight minutes, have flown across a highly strategic Soviet area, heavily defended by radar and antiaircraft missiles, without being intercepted. That stretches credibility a little too far. During its transit of the peninsula, KAL 007 would have flown close to, not only the Petropavlovsk airbase, but also an important nuclear-submarine base and a number of top-secret missile bases as well. Yet in comparison to the aircraft and cruise missiles that the Soviet defenses were designed to counteract, the Boeing 747 was an extraordinarily large and relatively slow target. In fact it is probably the largest radar target in the sky. A Boeing 747 literally splashes across the screen. It is reasonable to wonder why and how a radar target of this magnitude could have flown undisturbed for thirty-eight minutes across one of the most heavily defended regions of Soviet territory. In addition, Soviet fighters, capable of reaching the Boeing's cruising altitude in less than a minute, were scrambled from an airbase near Petropavlovsk, eight minutes before the intruder flew close to the base, but were unable to locate it.

Commenting on the Russians' failure to intercept the intruder, the United States said it was the result of "bad radar, bad planes, and the bad Soviet pilots"—and added to the list years later a recent storm that was said to have destroyed much of the Soviets' radar. The result, the U.S. said, was that the Soviet interceptors never got within 20 NM of the Korean jetliner.[1] However, the United States never claimed to have, itself, observed the Korean airliner while it was over Kamchatka. They "watched the Russians watching the plane."[2] That is to say, the United States intercepted the Soviets' radar tracking. But if the Russians had known that their fighters were within 20 NM of their prey, approximately one minute of flying time, well within not only radar but also visual range, they couldn't have failed to intercept the aircraft.

Moreover, the navigation and anticollision lights on an aircraft can be seen from a long way off (50 to 80 NM) during the dead of night with a cloudless sky, which were the prevailing conditions over Kamchatka at the time. If the Soviet fighters had been only 20 NM away from the Korean jetliner, they would certainly have been able to see the plane, if only with the naked eye. Even from the ground, the plane would have been perfectly visible to the naked eye, assuming, of course, that its navigation lights were on. The fact that neither the fighters nor people from the ground saw it can only mean that the plane, whether it was KAL 007 or another plane, had its lights extinguished. And this in turn indicates that it was not innocent. If it had been an airliner, it should have had all its position lights and particularly its anticollision beacon on.

If KAL 007, or a simulator, overflew Kamchatka successfully, only the presence close by of EF-111 ECM (electronic countermeasure) antiradar aircraft (the same planes that were used during the raid on Tripoli and fooled Iraqi radar during the Gulf War) could explain the fact that it wasn't intercepted over the peninsula. These antiradar aircraft capture the detection signals emitted by enemy radar, doctor them, and send them back to the originating radar in such a way as to show false echoes where there is no aircraft, while the real aircraft is protected from detection.

The Kamchatka towns, villages, and airports were all well lighted and clearly visible from the sky. That would have alerted the crew of KAL 007 that they were flying over land when they were supposed to be flying over water. There is a turbulence ridge over Kamchatka that would also have told KAL 007 that it was not flying over water.[3] We do not know whether KAL 007 overflew Kamchatka or not. If it did, it is hard to believe that it would not have realized it was dangerously off course. It is still harder to believe it would not have been shot down there without the simultaneous presence of military antiradar aircraft. We doubt that it was there. If it was not, its simulator probably was.

During his news conference on September 9, 1983, Marshal Ogarkov stated that after having flown wing to wing with another plane, the intruder penetrated Kamchatka airspace at 16:30 GMT at an altitude of 8,000 meters (26,000 feet). Russian interceptors scrambled to head off the aircraft at 16:37 hours and unsuccessfully tried to force it to land. The intruder plane left Kamchatka at 17:08 GMT at an altitude of 9,000 meters (29,000 feet).

A Soviet rear admiral later gave a substantially different account of the overflight of Kamchatka.[4] Analyzed carefully, his and other Soviet accounts of events at this time imply that on the night in question there was an extensive U.S. presence in this highly strategic region:

> *There were often two or three aircraft carriers in the vicinity of the Commander Islands, which sent their aircraft in the direction of our airspace. It was a constant war of nerves. That night, August 31, I was at my post and watched as it happened. A plane was flying a mission off our coast. Another aircraft approached. Everybody assumed it was a tanker plane approaching a reconnaissance plane.*

But to our surprise, the tanker, instead of turning north, headed south and continued flying along the international route [Romeo-20], and the reconnaissance plane stayed where it was. Then it suddenly disappeared from our radars. The aircraft probably dived beneath radar cover, at around 3,000 meters [9,000 feet].[5] Obviously it was intentional.

The radars picked it up again near the Kronotsky Reserve.[6] There is a mountain chain in the area and the aircraft must have picked up altitude to avoid it. One of the officers sounded the alarm and two interceptors were scrambled, flying east to head off the intruder, who was coming from an easterly direction. They were able to pick up the intruder on their radars, but lost him when he turned above the mountains and were unable to find him again. A second pair of interceptors was scrambled to help the first two, which had reached the limit of their flying range. But the intruder escaped in the direction of the Sea of Okhotsk.

Another witness to the events, Alexei Kretinin, who served at a command post in Kamchatka, gave a report of the incident in *Sibirskaya Gazeta:*[7]

What we thought was a tanker plane appeared on the radar screens at 04:59 [15:59 GMT]. On the military maps it was identified as number 6065. At 05:25 [16:25 GMT] it approached the border. At 05:33 [16:33 GMT] it penetrated our airspace. A second pair of interceptors was scrambled [which implies that a first pair was already in the air] but didn't find the intruder.

The intruder plane disappeared suddenly from the radar screens as soon as it had penetrated our airspace. The plane reappeared thirteen minutes later. During the last minutes of its overflight of the peninsula, while it was visible on the radar screens, the aircraft was pursued by a third pair of interceptors.

The three accounts, Ogarkov's, the admiral's, and Kretinin's, imply that more than one aircraft approached and overflew Kamchatka. While superficially similar, they differ in important details. Before we try to draw at least general conclusions on the basis of all the available evidence as to what happened at Kamchatka at this time, let us see what the two Russian radar maps printed on pages 48 and 50 of the 1993 ICAO report (see appendix and chapter 14) add to our stock of evidence.

Before turning to Kamchatka itself, it is worth noting that the map on page 48 of the report shows events southeast of Karaginski Island quite different from those shown on the diagram Ogarkov used at his September 9,

1983, press conference. Ogarkov's diagram showed an RC-135, which had been in mission orbit, flying wing to wing for ten minutes with the southwest-bound intruder that had been picked up by Soviet radar at 15:51 GMT. In contrast, the map on page 48 of the report shows an RC-135, which, after terminating its orbiting, headed south and crossed the track of the southwest-bound aircraft forty minutes before that aircraft arrived. As I said in chapter 14, what actually happened in the rendezvous area was in all likelihood more complex than our evidence permits us to describe comprehensively. The point makes it easier to understand the meaning of the valuable but confusingly presented evidence the Soviets made public regarding events at Kamchatka.

The map on page 48 also shows the track of a southwest-bound aircraft picked up on Soviet radar at 15:51 Z (Z = GMT = UTC), as was the one Ogarkov described, flying a somewhat wavy course that terminates abruptly off the east coast of Kamchatka shortly after 16:26 Z, the last position-time given. At that point it was still over international waters and heading slightly south of west. This aircraft is not elsewhere represented on either the map on page 48 or the map on page 50. The track is labeled "KE 007" but cannot be that of the Korean airliner because the average speed of the aircraft it describes verges on the supersonic.[8]

The map on page 48 of the report shows a second radar track, clearly belonging to another aircraft, picked up by Soviet radar at 16:32 Z, near but behind where the first terminated, flying generally southwest, crossing the Kronotsky Peninsula on the east coast of Kamchatka, and after a brief flight over water, turning inland north of Petropavlovsk. Its track terminates at the coast of Kamchatka, which on this map, in defiance of the rules of good cartography, is printed black, thus obscuring the further course of the aircraft. The course this aircraft was following could be continuous with the second (southwesterly) of the two tracks shown on the map on page 50 of the report. The latter starts on the east coast, then crosses the Kamchatka Peninsula on a southwesterly course, and enters international airspace over the Sea of Okhotsk. The maps thus already illustrate the complexity of what happened at Kamchatka.

But there is more. Events on this second page-50 radar track, like all the other events noted on that map, are marked in Moscow military time from 19:51 to 21:28. That is 16:51 to 18:28 GMT. Thus the events described on the map took place an hour later than those marked in Z time (GMT) shown on the page-48 map, which run from 15:51 to 16:28 GMT. Although I do not trust the way data on the page-48 map are presented, on balance I think the second tracks on the two maps are not continuous and represent two different aircraft flying in two successive hours.

I must here explain that, despite consistent mistranscription by the 1993 ICAO report, Moscow military (standard) time is three hours later than

Greenwich time, not four hours later, as the ICAO would have it. The ICAO must be basing its misrepresentation on the theory (excuse) that on August 31 the Soviet military was using summer time. That is not true. I will return to the subject later in this chapter and again in chapter 16.

The track of the second (southwesterly) aircraft shown on the page-50 map, slanting across the Kamchatka Peninsula in a southwesterly direction, cannot be that of KAL 007. The speed of the aircraft tracked is sometimes as low as a very slow 240 knots, but twice it accelerates to a supersonic 720 knots, once north of the Elizovo airbase, and once more over the Sea of Okhotsk west of the Soviet airbase on the Kuril island of Paramushir. This, of course, suggests a flexible military aircraft, perhaps a swing-wing (anti-radar) EF-111, making no effort to look like either KAL 007 or an RC-135, and twice using its speed to shake off pursuit. Once more the evidence indicates events radically different from the official account of a lone intruder, the unwittingly off-course civilian airliner.

The first (northeasterly) track on the map of page 50 shows an aircraft on a SW heading picked up by Soviet radar at 19:51 Moscow military time (16:51 GMT), which is the same minute as, but an hour later than, the time at which the first aircraft on the page-48 map was picked up by Soviet radar. The course of neither of these two aircraft heading southwest is entirely straight (as the course of a civilian airliner being flown by its inertial navigation system, its usual mode of navigation, would have been between way-points). However, as I have said, the two courses—once reduced to the same scale—are clearly those of different aircraft. Like the second track on the page-50 map, the first track on that map is given the generic tracking number 6065, which is to say "military, possibly hostile."

Once more we see the apparently contradictory nature of the evidence—and the complexity of the events it describes. Like the second track on the page-48 map, the first track on the page-50 map crosses the Kronotsky Peninsula, almost but not exactly an hour later than the other, but then, unlike it, curves south away from land before disappearing from radar at 20:41 Moscow military time (17:41 GMT). This curve to the south away from the land sounds like the (first) aircraft described by the admiral but presumably was made by an aircraft an hour later than the event he describes. The events he describes sound like part of the sequence starting at 15:51 GMT, not the events of a second hour.

Of the four (or three) aircraft shown on the two 1993 ICAO report maps, only one is shown crossing the Kamchatka Peninsula and entering international airspace over the Sea of Okhotsk on a course that would have taken it to Sakhalin. The one falsely labeled "KE 007" appears to have dived down under Soviet radar off the east coast of Kamchatka, with no indication where it went from there. It may have then crossed the Kamchatka

Peninsula, but, if so, we have no radar track for its doing so on either map. The first (northeasterly) track shown on the page-50 map, as I have mentioned, crosses the Kronotsky Peninsula and then curves out to sea. We thus have aircraft arriving at Kamchatka some of which do not appear to have gone to Sakhalin. And, as the reader will see in chapter 16, we have aircraft arriving at Sakhalin some of which cannot have previously crossed Kamchatka.

On these two ICAO maps of Russian origin, we have aircraft disappearing from radar, presumably by dropping down below 9,000 feet, and not again appearing on the maps, as well as aircraft popping up to radar level with no visible precedent on the maps. It is quite easy to produce such effects if you are playing games. An aircraft can fly below 9,000 feet and suddenly climb up to radar level. Two aircraft can fly sufficiently close together to appear in a single blip. There may thus have been more aircraft over or off Kamchatka at this time than we have evidence of. The Russians probably have other radar data than what they chose to give the ICAO: on the surface at least, the evidence they put forward was presented in such a way as not directly to contradict the official (one-intruder, one-shootdown) version of events. At the same time, radar-spoofing by U.S. aircraft may at times have seemed to present the Soviets with more oncoming aircraft than were in fact there.

Recognizing these elements of imprecision, what can we say about aircraft crossing Kamchatka on the basis of the statements I have quoted and the radar maps I have discussed? First, it seems likely that an aircraft on a southwest course flew from a position southeast of Karaginski Island and north of waypoint NEEVA and entered Soviet airspace off the east coast of Kamchatka about 16:30 GMT, then crossed the Kamchatka Peninsula, exited Kamchatka airspace about 17:08 GMT, and entered international airspace over the Sea of Okhotsk headed for Sakhalin. That is what the official Soviet and U.S. stories say KAL 007 did. The first part of such a track is consistent with what the first (northeastern) aircraft shown on the page-48 map did, although it flew at greater speed than Ogarkov indicated, or of which KAL 007 was capable. In November 1992, President Yeltsin gave the U.S. next of kin and the South Korean government documents supposedly relating to KAL 007 including a Soviet map said to be based on digital flight-data-recorder course data showing an aircraft flying from Anchorage (probably Elmendorf AFB) to mid-Sakhalin, where it was presumably shot down.[9]

A second and, less probably, even a third southwest-bound intruder aircraft may have flown a generally similar course and crossed the Kamchatka Peninsula at roughly the same time, that is to say, in the 16:00 GMT hour. With some differences of detail, suggesting that they were describing different aircraft, both the admiral and Kretinin described aircraft doing this. It is suggestive that Kretinin, who is given to specifics, gives times at which the aircraft he describes was picked up by Soviet radar and crossed the air frontier (15:59 GMT and 16:33 GMT respectively) that are different from those cited by Ogarkov (15:51 GMT and 16:30 GMT respectively). The admiral's intruder (or his second intruder) reappeared on the radar screens while it was overflying the Kronotsky Reserve, relatively close to the coast, whereas Kretinin indicates that the plane reappeared after thirteen minutes, which places the aircraft 94 NM from the east coast of Kamchatka, well beyond the Reserve.

Incidentally, I take the references that both Kretinin and the admiral make to the (at least the first) aircraft they discuss as "a tanker" to mean an aircraft initially thought by Soviet air defense to be a tanker. Neither of them, I am sure, think that anyone would send a tanker across the Kamchatka Peninsula under such conditions, a senseless thing to do. To send one or more RC-135s, accompanied by one or more EF-111s, would be another matter, although itself displaying a high level of hostility.

I have already mentioned evidence that there was a second hour of events at Kamchatka (17:30 GMT on as well as 16:30 GMT on, that is). This second hour of events at Kamchatka took place at the same time as the first hour of intrusions at Sakhalin. That fact certainly impressed the Soviet higher command with the seriousness and scale of the action being undertaken by the Americans. As a further indication that there was in fact a second hour of events at Kamchatka, I will describe events taking place at that time for which we have both radar data and an eyewitness account.

If we look at the map on page 50 of the 1993 ICAO report, we see, just south of the small bay on which Petropavlovsk is located, a complex tangle of intersecting radar tracks, spread out along an east-by-north/west-by-south axis. They are marked as the tracks of Soviet interceptors 544 and 543. Interceptor 544, which took off first, reached the level at which it was picked up on radar just before 20:46 Moscow military time, its first position-time recorded. That this means 17:46 GMT, not 16:46 GMT, and is thus related to intruders in that hour and not the previous one, is indicated by the following eyewitness account.

The story is related by Andrei Illesh in his book *The Mystery of the Black Boxes*. It not only helps to fix the hour but is of considerable interest in itself.

> *Major Kazmin was a pilot in Kamchatka, stationed at the Elizovo airbase, near Petropavlovsk. He received his orders for takeoff just before dawn [emphasis added].*

That is consistent with 544's first recorded position time of 17:46 GMT, and Kazmin's further comments indicate that he may have been the pilot of 544. If not, he was clearly sent up at very much the same time. Dawn on Kamchatka that day was about 18:00 GMT on the ground, and 17:40 GMT at 8,000 meters. An hour earlier rather than some minutes prior to 17:46 GMT would *not,* repeat not, have been "just before dawn."

Kazmin was in the air within three minutes. Course 120, toward the Pacific Ocean, altitude 8,500 meters. After having crossed the shoreline, Kazmin heard through his radio that pilot Emilianov was taking off and that the reserves had been put on alert. Kazmin had his radio tuned to the flight controller's frequency and was able to monitor the takeoff order. But he also wanted to contact ground control for instructions, and he asked his navigator to do it through his own radio.

Here we see that Kazmin was flying a MiG-31, which, unlike the MiG-23 or the SU-15, has a crew of two. At the time the MiG-31 was the very latest, still-secret fighter with state-of-the-art electronics. It was some years before the Soviets would acknowledge that the MiG-31 existed.

When Kazmin was 220 kilometers from his base, he saw a dark, cigar-shaped silhouette in front of him. It had no lights. Kazmin signaled it with his navigation lights. As a normal procedure, he had been flying with his navigation lights dampened to 30 percent power to economize on battery power as well as not to affect his night vision adversely. He put his lights to 100 percent power several times in succession but with no response from the intruder. He then maneuvered his landing lights and flashed them at the plane, but again without effect. Finally Kazmin asked the ground to illuminate the intruder with searchlights, but got no answer from the ground to his request. He was running low on fuel and had to turn back without having been able to take any positive action. He saw the intruder for only twenty to thirty seconds.

The next day, after the debriefing by the high-ranking people from Khabarovsk, there was a phone call from Marshal Ogarkov, who asked him, "Why didn't you shoot it down?" Kazmin answered, "Because I had no orders." Marshal Ogarkov got angry and said, "I did not ask you whether or not you had any orders, I am asking you why didn't you shoot it down."

Marshal Ogarkov was Soviet chief of staff at the time. He knew the full complexity and threatening nature of the events that had taken place at

Kamchatka at the time of the encounter and felt that Kazmin should have shot at any intruder he had a chance to shoot at. Why Kazmin treated the cigar-shaped aircraft that suddenly appeared before him the way he did is more complex.

In the first place the "cigar-shaped silhouette" appeared in front of him suddenly; he saw it for only twenty to thirty seconds. That is to say, he saw it visually and not on his radar. Obviously he was surprised to see it. That is to say, his ground controller had told him nothing about it. He did not know what it was and treated it like an unknown aircraft that could, conceivably, have been friendly. He told the marshal that he "had no orders," by which in all likelihood he meant that he had no orders with regard to that specific aircraft.

Clearly he and Emilianov had been given specific orders of some sort. If they were the pilots of interceptors 544 and 543 whose radar tracks are shown on the page-50 map, running back and forth on an east-by-north/west-by-south line of quite definite length just south of Petropavlovsk, their mission was no doubt one of being on airborne alert to protect that important naval base. That is to say, their mission had nothing to do, initially at least, with the second intruder aircraft, to their north, shown on the page-50 map. The controller handling the two interceptors protecting Petropavlovsk may well not have been the one handling the intruder initially well to the north of the city of a northeast-to-southwest course.

On a turn at the end of a leg to the west, interceptor 544 may well have unexpectedly glimpsed the intruder coming at him nearly head-on at 21:06 Moscow military time (18:06 GMT). The intruder some four minutes earlier had accelerated to supersonic speed and would have flashed past. The place, however, was not the "220 kilometers from his base" that Kazmin mentioned to Illesh. Moreover, the "cigar-shaped silhouette" Kazmin mentioned sounds like an RC-135, a Boeing 707, and the 707 cannot, of course, fly at any such speed. As I have suggested, the supersonic intruder aircraft on the page-50 map may well have been an EF-111, which is not cigar-shaped.

If the close encounter shown on the map did not happen to Kazmin, and he was not the pilot of 544, then he had a similar experience somewhere else at much the same time with another intruder of the second Kamchatka wave.

During my investigation I interviewed a reserve officer in the Soviet Armed Forces, Colonel Privalov, who served on Kamchatka with the general who commanded the military region at the time of the KAL 007 affair and was a friend of his. When I talked to him, Privalov was in Paris as a correspondent for *Pravda*. He quoted his friend, the commander of the military region, as saying that Soviet intelligence evaluated the U.S. effort that night as "rehearsal for a massive invasion." The reader will see in later chapters some of the other elements that led the Soviets to this evaluation. But what happened at Kamchatka—involving as it did surprise and deception, coordination with a ferret satellite, overflights and other border violations, signals-intelligence and antiradar aircraft, and events spread over two hours—was very much part of the threatening picture the Soviets saw.

The Air Battle of Sakhalin

One of the hardest things for Americans to admit, even those who do not believe the official account of events, is that a substantial clash occurred between U. S. military and Soviet aircraft, involving American casualties, which has been kept secret for twelve years. Their hesitancy is understandable. But it does not accord with what has come to light in my investigation. In chapter 10, I discussed debris and crash sites that indicate such a clash. In this chapter I will cite and explain in detail the evidence of interceptions and shootdowns over Sakhalin.

In *The Target Is Destroyed,* Seymour Hersh says KAL 007 left Soviet airspace at Kamchatka at 01:58 Tokyo time, which is to say 16:58 GMT, although he does not cite the source of his information.[1] Since he accepts 16:30 GMT as the time of penetration, his figure implies that KAL 007 crossed Kamchatka at an average ground speed of 586 knots. With a headwind of 50 knots[2] over the peninsula, that would mean that the airliner had flown at 636 knots, the equivalent of the supersonic Mach 1.058, obviously impossible for a Boeing 747. If the exit time given by Hersh refers to a real aircraft, it can only have been a supersonic, hence military, aircraft; or else two different aircraft were involved, the entry time referring to one aircraft and the exit time referring to another. Having exited Kamchatka, KAL 007 is said to have crossed the Sea of Okhotsk and once more violated Soviet airspace, at Sakhalin. But the whole course KAL 007 flew from the Bering Sea to the Sea of Japan off the west coast of Honshu remains uncertain. What is clear is that a number of aircraft violated Soviet airspace at Sakhalin, some having crossed the Kamchatka Peninsula and others having crossed the Kurils to its south.

In chapter 3 we saw that what happened over Sakhalin according to the U.S. government was very different from the account of the same events given by the Japanese government. That led us to understand that several intruders were involved and that what happened was a complex event. Our information has broadened since the early days of the investigation and now comes from the following sources: the Japanese statement about an explosion at 18:29 GMT and the accompanying JDA radar map, the *Chidori Maru* testimony, the American statement about a disappearance from radar at 18:38 GMT and the Kirkpatrick tape, the *Izvestiya* series of articles and its many quotations from witnesses, and finally, the Russian transcripts appended to the June 1993 ICAO report.

The Japanese and American statements generally, and particularly the JDA radar map and the Kirkpatrick tape, are so different that they could not initially be reconciled. The *Izvestiya* articles seem to tell the official U.S.-Soviet story. However, the richness of detail in the witnesses' statements permits us to distinguish several pursuits and shootdowns by different fighter pilots, and the recovery of several different wrecks by Soviet divers in different parts of the sea around Sakhalin. It is, however, the Russian documents handed over to the ICAO for its 1993 report, appended to it as Information Paper No. 1,[3] that give us the most dramatic evidence of the scope of the Sakhalin events and allow us to understand the apparent contradiction between the Japanese and American data.

Most of the Russian documents are transcripts of communications between various command posts on the ground at Sakhalin, from the commander in chief of the Soviet Air Force Far East Military District, General Kamenski, down to lower-ranking officers. What is truly revealing in the Russian documents is that the action begins at four o'clock Sakhalin time and continues uninterrupted for nearly three hours, until the sun rises at 06:49 hours. Pilot Osipovich, as well as fighter 805's pilot, both having shot down an intruder minutes earlier, land just before sunrise. The Russian transcript give us evidence of multiple intrusions, interceptions, and shootdowns over a long enough period for Soviet AWACs and fighter reinforcements to have been sent from the Siberian mainland in time to enter the battle. That is to say, the transcripts give us evidence of a major air engagement, the intensity of which is confirmed by evidence I cite in other chapters, much of it physical or documentary. The veracity of the broad outlines of what happened are thus secure.

But when we set out to write a connected narrative of what happened that night over Sakhalin, we undertake a difficult task. Despite the amount of it, our evidence is fragmentary. Moreover, the times cited in the transcripts have been substantially falsified. They present a sequence of events that in fact stretched over a period of nearly three hours as having happened in a two-hour period. This permits a substantial number of interceptions of intruders to be presented, nominally at least, consistent with the impression that they might all have been that of the one Korean airliner. The falsification has been done in two ways: first, by draconian editing in the Russian ground-communications transcripts, together with the misstatement of times to obscure the largest cuts; second, by the ICAO's mistranslation into UTC (GMT) of the Sakhalin times used in the air-to-ground transcripts and of the Moscow military (standard) times used in the ground-communications transcripts.

In every instance, Russian and ICAO falsifications have the effect of minimizing rather than exaggerating the clash that took place. Even if the

Russians suppressed information about half the battle, they left enough to document the other half.

Although it is at times difficult to decide whether a particular event took place in the earlier or the later period (the minutes cited appear to be correct, the hours may or may not be), there is usually enough data in one place or another to permit an event to be put in its proper place. That is illustrated by the following example.

At 17:48 UTC (04:48 Sakhalin time) Lieutenant Colonel Novoseletski, having just arrived at his command post at Smirnykh, receives information from Lieutenant Kozlov at Sokol that fighter 805 has taken off from Sokol and that target 6065 is 200 km east of Cape Terpeniya, tracking 240 degrees. He is also informed that "Deputat's" radar cannot observe the target on its equipment and they cannot draw anything on the situation board because the plotters haven't yet arrived. They just go by reports.[4]

At supposedly the same time, the same fighter 805 receives from the same Deputat information that the target is on an azimuth of 60 degrees from Deputat (at Sokol) and at a distance of 440 km from it.[5] We wonder how Deputat could have sent this report since its equipment could not observe the target and it could not even do the plotting since its plotters had not yet arrived. Also, this puts the target at 264 km from Terpeniya instead of 200 km, and to the northeast instead of to the east.

The mystery is cleared up when we look at the time of Deputat's transmission: 05:48 Sakhalin local time. That is 18:48 UTC and one hour later than Kozlov's telephone conversation with Novoseletski at 17:48 UTC. Not incidentally, we find fighter 805 flying two missions an hour apart, pursuing two different intruders. As we shall see below, it will by no means be the only fighter to do so.

The Russian documents also contain a transcript of the air-ground communications that Ambassador Kirkpatrick presented to the Security Council of the United Nations, the so-called Kirkpatrick tape. But with a difference. The Russian air-ground transcript is given in Sakhalin time. Its transmissions are one hour later than the same events given in GMT on the Kirkpatrick tape. Where the Kirkpatrick document has fighter 805 announce "target destroyed" at 18:26:22, the Russian transcript has the same "target destroyed" report by fighter 805 at 06:26:01 hours (19:26:01 GMT). Since fighter 805 landed at 06:45 hours (19:45 GMT), just four minutes before the sun rose at 06:49 (19:49 GMT), the Russian time is correct and the Kirkpatrick time is wrong by one hour. Presented as the story of the shooting down of the Korean airliner, it records events that in fact happened one hour after KAL 007 left the Sakhalin area.

Now we understand why the American story is so different from the Japanese story: it happened one hour later. For simplicity's sake let us call the events on the Japanese radar map "the first hour" and those on the Kirkpatrick tape "the second hour," although their combined duration is about three hours. Understanding that we are dealing with two sets of events gives us the key to unscrambling the complicated and conflicting testimonies and lets us reconstruct the events in the air battle of Sakhalin.

(Note: the times mentioned in the reconstruction below are all in Sakhalin local time. To get Japan time, subtract two hours. To get GMT (UTC), subtract eleven hours. For example, 05:00 hours Sakhalin time is 03:00 hours Japan time and 18:00 hours GMT (UTC).)

The *Izvestiya* series of articles contains detailed testimony by participants in or witnesses to the events. A first glimpse of what happened at Sakhalin that night is given by Ivan K., a colonel in the reserves. He was in command of the PVO (the Soviet Air Defense Force) post on Sakhalin. We must remember that the Soviet witnesses are quoted only on some of the events, and then as if there had been only one intruder, KAL 007. Once more we have selected real events compressed into a scenario compatible with KAL 007's flight schedule. Comparison with other evidence allows events to be put into their proper place. Ivan K. says the following:[6]

> *On the night of August 31 to September 1, 1983, V. Ponomarev was the duty officer on Sakhalin. When an intruder left Kamchatka, additional forces were put on alert. When the intruder was over the Sea of Okhotsk, it was located by an Oborona [Air Defense] radar facility on Sakhalin. A Level One alert had been declared, and interceptors were prepared to take off at two airbases.[7] The first two interceptors were scrambled from Smirnykh and approached the Boeing while it was still night. The pilots were unable to determine what type of aircraft it was. The fighters from Smirnykh had run low on fuel and, because of fog, had to land at Yuzhno-Sakhalinsk. At this moment another pair of fighters was scrambled from Sokol to replace the first two. One of these was piloted by Gennadi Osipovich.*

It is strange that the two fighters from Smirnykh, which were MiG-23s, would run low on fuel so early—at 05:46, the time the Russian transcript gives for Osipovich's takeoff—after so short a mission and make an emergency landing at Yuzhno-Sakhalinsk, more than 300 kilometers (186 miles) from their home base, especially since they had been equipped with additional fuel tanks, as we shall see below. The characteristics of the MiG-23 are well-known. Of all Soviet aircraft it is the one the West is most familiar with. More than ten thousand were built, and many of these were exported throughout the world. The MiG-23 is a variable-geometry (swing-wing) aircraft of sophistication and long range. Author Bill Gunston, a British pilot, described the MiG-23's characteristics as follows:

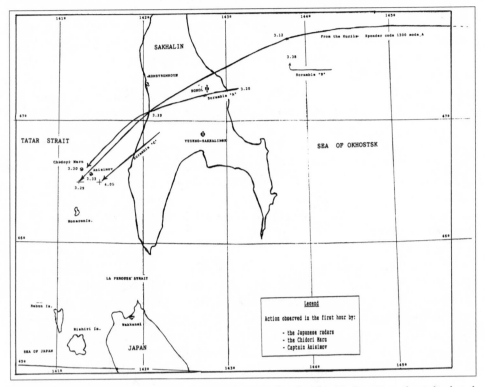

Figure 15. *Some events of the first hour of the air battle of Sakhalin. For others disclosed by the Russian communications transcripts, see Figure 18 (page 222).*

- Combat range, when equipped with four air-to-air missiles, is 530 miles.
- With an 800-liter ventral reserve tank, under the same conditions, it's range is 700 miles.
- The plane's combat range includes the time needed to climb to a given altitude at full speed without use of the afterburners, ten minutes of combat in the area with use of the afterburners, the time to fire its missiles, and the time to return to base.
- The 800-liter ventral tank is only used to take off and climb to the plane's given altitude. The tank is dropped shortly after takeoff.
- The MiG-23 can also be equipped with wing tanks, which considerably increase its range but impose severe restrictions on its speed and ability to maneuver. They must be jettisoned before folding back the wings.

It is these fuel tanks that are of interest. The MiG-23s that took off from Smirnykh were equipped with all three of them. We should thus bear in mind that they had considerably more range than the PVO colonel's account in *Izvestiya* implies. Assuming a takeoff without the ventral tank, the MiG-23's range of 850 kilometers (530 miles) means the aircraft can fly 530 miles to its destination, engage in combat for ten minutes (using its afterburners), and fly 530 miles back to base with some reserve fuel in its tanks. That would give them at least two hours in the air. With all three tanks, as was the case here, they could have flown for three hours. From this we see that they must have taken off around 02:45.

We have confirmation of the landing at Yuzhno-Sakhalinsk from other sources. In his book, Illesh quotes a flight engineer at Sokol:

> *When I reported for duty at 09:00 A.M. on September 1, 1983, I was astonished to see that all the fighter aircraft had disappeared and the parking area was empty. I asked a private on duty, who told me that aircraft had been shot down during the night[8] and that two MiG-23s from Smirnykh had landed at Khomutovo, the airport at Yuzhno-Sakhalinsk.[9]*

As for Osipovich, the world has heard of him from the *Izvestiya* series of articles. He replaced Major Kazmin in the role of the pilot who shot down KAL 007. Osipovich was not the pilot of fighter 805, which was also specified as the interceptor that shot down the Korean jetliner, but was flying a brand-new MiG-31, number 804.[10] Fighter 805 was probably also a MiG-31 rather than the SU-15 it is usually claimed to have been.

Osipovich began his interview with *Izvestiya* by recalling a recent violation of Soviet airspace by armed U.S. military aircraft. On April 4 of that year (1983), two squadrons[11] of fighters from the carriers *Midway* and *Enterprise* violated Soviet airspace at Zeleny Island in the Kurils. They penetrated more than thirty kilometers (nineteen miles) into Russian territory, and for fifteen minutes conducted practice bombing runs on ground targets. That time Soviet interceptors did not scramble. Sensing that this was a deliberate provocation, the base commander kept his planes on the ground. General Tretyak, Soviet air defense chief for the Far East (he was also in command during the KAL 007 overflight), questioned the commander about this:

"Why didn't you scramble your planes?"

"I didn't want to start a war. This could have turned into a general conflict, and I didn't feel I had the authority to risk a full-scale war."

"Someone else wouldn't have had as many reservations as you."[12]

The base commander had a point about the dangers of World War III involved in U.S. behavior in the western Pacific. The overflights Osipovich mentioned were part of broader operations. In the spring of 1982 a two-carrier battle group sailed by in front of Petropavlovsk. U.S. naval elements were put into the Sea of Okhotsk, the home of the missile-firing submarines that were the backbone of the U.S.S.R.'s deterrent force. In the spring of 1983, a U.S. three-carrier battle group, accompanied by B-52 bombers, AWACs, F-15 fighters, submarines, and submarine-patrol aircraft, were for the first time put into the normal patrol area of the Soviet submarine fleet. USS *Midway,* blacked out, on radio silence, and with all other monitorable electrical systems shut down, was put into Soviet territorial waters (twelve-mile limit) near Petropavlovsk.[13]

The base commander wasn't punished for his actions. There is evidence that multiple and sustained overflights by U.S. carrier aircraft again took place in June in the same general area. We cannot be sure what lessons the United States may have drawn from these incidents and the lack of Soviet response. Perhaps they thought that there would be no response to the greater provocation of August 31. If so, they badly misunderstood the lessons that the Soviets drew from the events of April and June. By August 31 they had deployed MiG-31s to the area, had given controllers and pilots permission to ditch their aircraft to increase their combat range, had taken other measures preparatory to effective action, and were resolved to react energetically to further provocations.

When Osipovich came back from vacation on August 16, his regiment was on alert and was no longer using the MiG-23s but the new and more powerful MiG-31s. At the time, the MiG-31 was the most modern of all the Soviet fighters. Capable of attaining speeds up to Mach 3, three times the speed of sound, it was equipped with sensitive radar equipment that enabled the plane to attack both ground-level and aerial targets, as well as cruise missiles. For ten years the Russians were unwilling to admit publicly that the MiG-31 existed.[14] Osipovich, an experienced pilot, completed his training in four instruction sessions and was operational on the new plane.

On the face of it, Osipovich's testimony when he says he had converted to a MiG-31 should be sufficient in itself. There is, however, so much disinformation on the subject, by the United States, the ICAO, and Russia, which each for its own reasons wants us to believe that Osipovich was flying an SU-15, that additional testimony to support Osipovich's is in order.

An interview with another witness, Col. A. Zakharenko, appeared on page 6 of the May 23, 1991, issue of *Izvestiya* as part of Illesh's series. In 1983, Colonel Zakharenko was the bureau chief of the military newspaper *Krasnaya Zvezda (Red Star)* for the Far East. A few hours after the disaster, he received orders from Moscow not to send any further unscrambled communications but to continue gathering information until it could be safely transmitted. On the afternoon of September 4, 1983, he received a cable from Capt. V. Firsov, head of the newspaper's Information Service, who asked him to get in touch with the chief of staff for the Far East Military Region, where an encoded message was waiting for him. It was from the chief of the general staff, giving him permission to interview a pilot and his targeting navigator, who together had brought down an intruder aircraft.

An important piece of information is here—the mention of the targeting navigator. In 1983 the MiG-31 was the only two-seater combat aircraft whose crew consisted of a pilot and a targeting navigator. The MiG-23 and SU-15 are one-man aircraft. A fifty-two-minute video edited by Illesh and screened by Russian TV in 1992, filmed at Sokol after the event, shows Lieutenant Colonel Osipovich standing among rows of planes on the airfield. The planes are all MiG-31s.

The First Hour

On August 31 then, Osipovich took the night watch with his MiG-31. His rank made him second-in-command of the regiment. He was also the most experienced pilot on the base. He decided to put himself on Level Three alert, meaning he didn't have to wear his flight gear. He could remain in the barracks but had to be ready to take off within ten minutes. After dinner he watched television for a while and slept briefly. While Osipovich sleeps, the clock ticks, the intruders close in, and we can follow the course of events.

02:45 (approximately). Two MiG-23s equipped with long-range wing tanks take off from Smirnykh and fly northeast over the Sea of Okhotsk. The time I cite here is based on the amount of fuel they initially carried and the time we knew they were out of fuel (see below). At 02:45 the SW-bound intruder Ogarkov mentions southeast of Karaginski Island had not yet been picked by Soviet radar. A map included with the Soviet annex to the 1983 ICAO report shows an RC-135 in the north of the Sea of Okhotsk. RC-135 missions may be as long as twenty hours. If an RC-135 was over the Sea of Okhotsk by the 02:00 hour Sakhalin time, the two MiG-23s might have taken off in this context rather than responding to events at Kamchatka, where our evidence suggests no intrusions for another forty-five minutes.

04:00 Alert code Zero Zero is put into force over the whole island of Sakhalin. In chapter 15 we have seen that one or more intruder aircraft had entered Soviet airspace off the east coast of Kamchatka at 03:30 or 03:33 and crossed the peninsula on a NE-SW course. By 04:00 an intruder would have been abeam the naval base at Petropavlovsk and the Elizovo Air Force base. While alarming in itself, an intrusion by a single aircraft would scarcely explain a full alert at Sakhalin nearly a thousand miles away. The alert presumably reflects multiple incursions at Kamchatka and other U.S. behavior that the Soviets considered threatening. Perhaps broader factors—U.S. ships and submarines at sea, aircraft in the air, and satellites in space—led higher commanders to take the developing situation seriously from the start. Admiral Sidorov told Misha Lobko he was in his office (in Vladivostok) by 03:00 that morning.

04:22 Captain Kutepov, combat control officer at the combat control center of the fighter division at Smirnykh, tells Major Kostenko, operations duty officer at the same combat control center:

> *The target 60-65 has now been designated a "type unidentified target, that is, without identification signal."[15] It is "now tracking 240, somewhere over the Sea of Okhotsk. It crossed Elizovo[16] going to the Sea of Okhotsk, roughly toward us. I've looked at the plan, we have to check routes of our long-range aircraft. Is someone there flying one of those long-range aircraft or not? Could that airplane be ours? It's already somewhere abeam Noglikov."[17]*

04:27 Major Kostenko, operations duty officer, combat control center of the fighter division, wakes up General Kornukov, commander of the Sokol Air Base and of the Second Fighter Regiment:

> *Excuse me for waking you. We have, well, an alert code Zero Zero at four o'clock. There was a border violation in the Elizovo area, an RC-135 now tracking 240 over the Sea of Okhotsk, moving toward us. That's all for the moment. Distance somewhere around 500 kilometers, abeam Noglikov, but closer to Elizovo.[18]*

We note that a few minutes earlier, at 04:22, the target was labeled 60-65 and "unidentified." Here, there is no reference to 60-65 and the target is clearly identified as an RC-135.

> — *Okay, brief the officer on duty.*
> — *The officer on duty has been briefed. Car number 02 is on its way to you.*
> — *Okay, I'm getting dressed. That's all.*

04:30 At around this time, Osipovich wakes up to inspect the sentries. He was barely dressed when the telephone rang. It was Lieutenant Astakhov. He told Osipovich, "Colonel, they want you on Level One alert!" For a Level One alert a pilot had to be suited up and in his plane, ready to take off at a moment's notice. Osipovich wondered why he was being assigned to a Level One alert when another, younger pilot of lower rank was already standing by on Level One alert. Reluctantly Osipovich headed for his MiG-31. He made radio contact with the controller, who confirmed the order to Level One.

04:32 The following conversation takes place between Colonel Burminski, deputy commander of the fighter division at Smirnykh, and Captain Solodkov, the Sokol Air Base Command Post duty officer:

— *Comrade Colonel, now we will calculate the tracking in the Elizovo area from twenty-one minutes.*
— *Yes.*
— *For the time being, we have a presumed border violation by the target, type not yet identified, in the area of Elizovo.*[19]

The target we had been hearing about was not in the area of Elizovo at around 04:21, the time from which Captain Solodkov is calculating the tracking, but half an hour earlier, between 03:35 and 04:08. The intruder he is discussing with Colonel Burminski is evidently another intruder.

04:42 The two MiG-23s that took off from Smirnykh and headed out to sea to intercept an intruder are closing in on their target.

A few minutes earlier in Tokyo, it is 02:30 A.M. Alarming indications of aircraft heading toward Sakhalin have been detected by the Japanese intelligence services at the same time the Soviets were detecting them. Initially they probably got the information by intercepting Soviet radio communications, later by their own radar as well. The Japanese have six major radar installations on the coast of Hokkaido, as well as signals-intelligence surveillance aircraft that fly twenty-four hours a day over La Pérouse Strait. The Japanese intelligence services judged the unfolding of events so serious that the members of the Air Self-Defense General Staff were roused from their beds and ordered to an urgent meeting. I learned of this in articles in the Japanese press of September 1, 1983, which stated that by 05:10 A.M. (07:10 in Sakhalin) the chiefs of staff of the JASDF had given orders to review all data collected by their radars on Hokkaido and northern Honshu. Since the Japanese make decisions by consensus, a relatively slow process, discussions must have been under way well before 05:10.

We can assume that discussions among the chiefs lasted at least an hour before a decision was made at 05:10. We can also assume that it would have required roughly an hour and a half to get everyone out of bed and prepared for the meeting, to send the cars to pick them up, and have everyone assembled at headquarters in Tokyo. This means that by 02:30 (Japan time) in the morning (04:30 Sakhalin time), the JASDF high command was considerably anxious. Would the Japanese general officers have been dragged out of their beds in the middle of the night if the situation hadn't been judged an issue of national importance?

On page 63 of his book, Andrei Illesh reconstructs the events as follows. His account once more illustrates that the Russians, as well as the Americans, were squeezing into one hour and one interception the events of nearly three hours and several interceptions, cutting out those that didn't lend themselves to the effort. Even so, Illesh's account gives us useful details not included in Colonel K.'s somewhat similar account summarized earlier in the chapter.

When the Boeing approached Sakhalin, it was at first headed toward Yuzhno-Sakhalinsk. Two MiG-23s were sent up from Smirnykh, equipped with additional fuel tanks. They flew toward the intruder. The intruder was still unidentified. In order to identify it, the two MiG-23s jettisoned their fuel tanks. They reported back that the intruder looked like an RC-135 and they escorted it for some time. But then, the RC-135 changed course and escaped toward Japan. The MiG-23s began to run low on fuel and were ordered to come back since there was no point in escorting an aircraft that was going away from Soviet airspace. But when the MiG-23s were heading home, the aircraft changed course again toward Sakhalin. This is when Osipovich came in. The Boeing entered Sakhalin airspace with Osipovich trying to intercept it. The two MiG-23s resumed the pursuit,[20] and one of the MiG-23s requested permission to shoot down the intruder. But the ground could not issue the order. Not the command post nor the regiment, not even the division. I think that is because they were getting confused.

At this time, Osipovich was asked to identify the intruder.[21] He approached it to between one and a half and two kilometers. The target then began to exit Sakhalin airspace. The MiGs could not prevent it because the SU-15 of Osipovich was between them and the target.[22] The command posts from the regiment and the division were silent. Finally, Osipovich heard the command: "Destroy the target." But Osipovich couldn't fire because he was too close. So he maneuvered and he fired from five kilometers away. He witnessed two explosions. The Boeing immediately lost altitude and entered a spin. Osipovich was ordered to go back to base. The two MiG-23s landed at Khomutovo, near Yuzhno-Sakhalinsk.[23] On the ground, after he landed, Osipovich's mechanic, astonished that his aircraft had no more missiles, asked him, "What happened with your missiles?" [24] *Osipovich was not in a good mood and simply waved him off with his oxygen mask. He then went to the telephone to make his report to the regimental command post. That is what really happened.*

According to the Soviet pilots' testimony mentioned by Illesh, two MiG-23s took off from Smirnykh, followed, when they were low on fuel, by Osipovich. We have seen that even without wing tanks a MiG-23 can fly from two to three hours without landing. Colonel Ivan K., mentioned earlier in this chapter, tells us that Osipovich took off after the two MiG-23s had landed at Yuzhno-Sakhalinsk for refueling. This gives us an approximate time for Osipovich's takeoff, 05:45–06:00, roughly three hours after the first two MiG-23s had taken off from Smirnykh. But that must have been the start of Osipovich's second mission because the two MiG-23s took off around 02:45, Sakhalin time. Osipovich was in his cockpit, ready for takeoff at 04:42 for his first mission.

04:44   The Soviet radar at Burevestnik on the island of Iturup in the Kurils locates an aircraft over the Sea of Okhotsk, headed for Sakhalin.

In his book, Hersh says that the National Security Agency (NSA) told Congress in a secret briefing that the Soviets located KAL 007 at 17:44 GMT, (04:44 Sakhalin time) while it was over the Sea of Okhotsk.[25] The plane, Hersh says, was 225 nautical miles from Sakhalin Island and flying west at eight miles per minute. It was picked up by a Soviet radar at the Burevestnik Air Force base on Iturup Island, as well as by two radar facilities on Sakhalin. According to the Japanese press on September 3, 1983, the maximum distance at which the Burevestnik radar could observe an aircraft flying at 10,000 meters (33,000 feet) was 245 NM. A plane crossing Kamchatka on the course and at the time the Soviets and the United States said KAL 007 did would have been 270 NM from the Sakhalin coastline by 17:44 GMT, not 225 as the aircraft Hersh described was. In addition, it would have been out of range of the Burevestnik radar. The plane Burevestnik saw was apparently an aircraft coming from the North Pacific by way of the Kurils.

04:45   Osipovich takes off from Sokol and heads toward an intruder six hundred kilometers away.

Osipovich told about his first takeoff, about 04:45 Sakhalin time, in an interview he gave to Yuri Zenyuk of *Novosti Agency,* published in English by the *U.S. Armed Forces Journal International* in October 1989, and also in

Russian by *Krasnaya Zvezda,* the newspaper of the Soviet armed forces, of March 13, 1991, in an article by Lt. Col. A. Dokuchayev:

> *I was put on alert, and approximately fifteen minutes later I received the order to take off in the direction of the Sea of Okhotsk. When I was approximately 600 kilometers [373 miles] from the base, I was warned that an enemy plane was ahead of me, and I received instructions from ground control. When I was within 28 kilometers [17 miles] of the aircraft, I saw him on my radar and continued my approach. At a distance of 13 kilometers [8 miles] I reduced speed and followed the plane. I saw a light blinking, but I was unable to determine anything because even military planes use them in peacetime.*

Osipovich doesn't mention seeing the aircraft's silhouette, in contrast to his second mission, when it was beginning to grow light. While he was engaged in that early mission, other fighters also took to the air.

04:48 Fighter 805, a MiG-31 like Osipovich's, takes off from "Point Two" (Sokol) and heads toward an intruder spotted by the radar at Cape Terpeniya two hundred kilometers to the east of it, tracking 240 degrees.

04:55 General Kornukov, commander at Sokol, reports to General Kamenski, commander of the Soviet Air Force Far East Military District at Smirnykh:

> *I will be at the command post. [A] target 6065 is in the air. Provisionally an RC-135. Two fighters have gone up below minima. Postovaya has been brought to readiness.*[26]

At 04:22, a target 6065 (military, possibly hostile) was "unidentified" as to type of aircraft. At 04:27, the target was not labeled 6065 but was identified as an RC-135. Here the target is both 6065 and "provisionally an RC-135." These are presumably three different targets, as can be surmised by the fact that "Postovaya is brought to readiness." Postovaya is a main fighter base near Sovetskaya Gavan on the Siberian mainland, on the other side of the Tatar Strait and far away from Sakhalin. It would not have been brought to readiness for a single intruder, which the Sakhalin command had more than enough means to deal with as is evidenced by the following orders given by Lieutenant Colonel Novoseletski, acting chief of staff of the fighter division at Smirnykh:

04:55 First, send [fighters] 121 and 805 to intercept target 6065, a military target. If the border is violated, destroy the target.[27]

This order to "intercept and destroy the target" clearly shows that Sakhalin had no need for reinforcements from Postovaya as far as that intruder was concerned. But the situation was clearly more threatening than that.

04:55 An intruder is spotted by the Cape Terpeniya radar station, 140 kilometers from the state border, tracking 240 at 20 kilometers from the boundary of the 100-kilometer waters.[28]

There is little information to help us attribute that target to any one fighter. However, being so close to the boundary, it was probably not Osipovich's target, which was, we recall, 600 kilometers from Sokol. It may, however, have been the target for fighter 805, which was 200 kilometers from Sokol seven minutes earlier.

05:00 (approximately) Sakhalin command requests two AWACs in reinforcement from Vanino, on the Siberian mainland.

Later on, during the "second hour," we will learn from Osipovich's comments that two "battlefield surveillance aircraft" (AWACs), call signs *Tanker* and *Suchogruz,* from Vanino were engaged in the Battle of Sakhalin. Taking into account the time it takes to scramble these heavy aircraft and the transit time to fly from Vanino to Sakhalin, the request would have had to be placed by the Sakhalin command by about 05:00.

05:05 Air Marshal Kirsanov stated that the intruder's flight [by implication that of KAL 007] had been coordinated with the passage of the Ferret-D satellite, which appeared over Sakhalin at 18:05 GMT, the moment when he said the intruder plane penetrated Soviet airspace.

As we shall see, several intruder aircraft were approaching Sakhalin at this time. They were within the satellite's range to record electronic signals (and perhaps also take infrared photographs).

05:05 General Kornukov asks radar operators at Plantatsia near Smirnykh if they are observing another target:

— *Are you observing the target?*
— *We are issuing another warning.*

05:07 Ensign Loginov, at the Plantatsia radar station, gives Captain Solodkov the coordinates of the new target:

Reading from Plantatsia, bearing to target 60, 65 [degrees], 340, distance 340 [kilometers], tracking 200 [degrees]. You have the cable downstairs now.

05:07 Captain Solodkov, command post duty officer at the Sokol Air Base, confides to Migal, chief of the rescue services, about yet another target:

This border intruder looks like our TU-95. I hope nothing bad has happened. It is painfully suggestive, the altitude and track and speed.

05:10

— *I called the zone. They say there is nothing of ours in the air.*
— *Roger. Well. Where is it going?*

05:11

— *It is going in the region of Makarov, about one hundred kilometers, straight like this. Include everything you can, short-range radio navigation system, because, well, an intruder can't operate that way . . . that's according to us, you are fine sitting below. . . .*
— *Well, it's not fate the way it turned out, in that case we have here . . .*
— *It hasn't bombed us . . .*[29]

Makarov is a harbor on the east coast of Sakhalin, roughly two hundred miles north of Sokol. That intruder 100 kilometers from Makarov and tracking 240 degrees is a different intruder from the one tracking 200 degrees and located 340 kilometers from Plantatsia. The conversation between these officers at two separate command posts 250 kilometers (155 miles) apart suggests the concern felt by the people on the ground while a battle was going on over their heads. Several minutes later (05:18), another conversation between Captain Morozov and Tania Grishkova, wife of Stanislas Ivanovitch Grishkov, a high-ranking officer, probably a general, mentions another aircraft of which we hear here for the first time:

— *It went through the Kurils.*
— *Has it already passed?*
— *Looks like it.*
— *Who is speaking?*

— Grishkova.

— Ah, Tania, excuse me, Morozov, may I speak with Stanislas Ivanovitch?... Good morning, Stanislas Ivanovitch.

— ... So, all the commanders are here. I would of course recommend coming here.

— ... Something has happened, the situation there [in the air] is complicated.[30]

The aircraft Morozov is discussing crossed the Kurils at that time (05:18) or shortly earlier. This is the second intruder mentioned as coming in from the North Pacific through the Kurils. The first was the aircraft picked up by Soviet radar at Burevestnik at 04:44, which must have crossed the Kurils some thirty minutes earlier, thus generally abeam the intruder(s) crossing Kamchatka and heading for Sakhalin (see below). The meaning of the remark "something has happened" is not clear—it may be confirmation that the intruder Novoseletski at 04:55 ordered shot down was in fact shot down soon after crossing the air frontier. At 04:56, Burevestnik Fighter Regiment Commander Gerasimenko confirmed that he had given the order.[31] It is also to the point that six intruders have been observed heading for Sakhalin simultaneously (see below).

05:11   Colonel Novoseletski, acting chief of staff of the fighter division at Smirnykh, to Captain Titovnin, fighter controller at the combat control center of the fighter division:[32]

—Titovnin, give me the tracking data [from Smirnykh].
—Bearing 45, range 110 kilometers, altitude 9,000 meters.

05:12   The Japanese radars at 18:12 GMT (03:12 Japan time) observed an aircraft at 47°40' N, 143°45' E, flying southwest at 430 knots, altitude 10,000 meters, and transmitting transponder code 1300 on Mode A.[33]

Its tracking data from Sokol are bearing 65, distance 81 kilometers, evidently a different intruder from the one observed one minute earlier at 05:11, flying at a different altitude. It begins its transit of Sakhalin on a heading of 257 degrees and will make a pronounced turn of 22 degrees halfway across to a heading of 235 degrees.

Between 05:12, the time of this observation, and 04:44, the time of the Burevestnik observation, is twenty-eight minutes, corresponding, at a speed of 430 knots, to a distance of 201 NM. If that distance is plotted backward along the route of the aircraft observed by the Japanese, it corresponds to the position of the aircraft observed by Burevestnik. It shows, however, the aircraft as coming not from Kamchatka but as having crossed the Kuril Islands and coming from the North Pacific from a position on or close to Romeo-20, KAL 007's assigned route. A speed of 430 knots is equivalent to 7.2 NM per minute, exactly the 8 miles[34] per minute of the plane to which Hersh and NSA were referring. The aircraft observed by the Japanese radar at 05:12 and the one seen by Burevestnik at 04:44 were thus, in all likelihood, the same. It was transmitting on transponder code 1300, which is appropriate for an aircraft leaving Japanese airspace but is improper for an aircraft flying toward Japanese airspace, as was the case with KAL 007. In addition, Mode A is used by the military. KAL 007 should have been using transponder code 2000 in Mode C.[35] This fact should have told the Japanese that it was not the Korean airliner.[36]

I will review these sightings to give the reader an idea of the picture Soviet commanders on Sakhalin were looking at. They saw six intruder aircraft coming at them virtually simultaneously. At 05:05, a first intruder had entered Sakhalin airspace. At 05:07, a second intruder was spotted 340 kilometers to the ENE of Plantatsia, tracking 200 degrees. Four minutes later, at 05:11, a third intruder, looking like a TU-95, was sighted. Its altitude and behavior made Soviet observers worry that it might be a Soviet aircraft. They checked Soviet flights and found that it could not be one of theirs. It was south of Terpeniya, tracking 240 degrees, straight toward Makarov 100 kilometers away from it, where it was feared it might bomb but didn't. At the same time, a fourth intruder was observed on a bearing of 45 degrees and at a distance of 110 kilometers from Smirnykh. Still at the same time, a fifth intruder was observed crossing the Kurils. And at 05:12, the Japanese radars spotted a sixth intruder, some 150 kilometers south of Makarov and 420 kilometers south of the target observed by Plantatsia.

Under these circumstances it is not hard to see why the Soviet commanders decided to shoot intruders entering Soviet airspace without going through the time-consuming warning procedure that 805 and Osipovich used during the second hour. Faced by multiple intruders, which they had identified as "military, possibly hostile," they presumably merely followed standing orders applicable in such circumstances. By the second hour, someone in Moscow, possibly Andropov, may have passed the word down that if an intruder had its lights on, an interceptor should go through a warning procedure before firing and try to get the intruder to land.

General Kornukov, chief of the Sokol Defense Area, gives his orders to destroy a target on command:

05:14 Kornukov:

Be ready to fire, bring everything to ready status. I will give Osipovich the order in two minutes or even less. In a minute and a half, I will give the order to open fire. Bring Tarasov[37] into the same area. And watch very closely, 163[38] is also there at point one. . . . Guide him from interception radar, issue the command from interception radar. . . .[39] Be careful, behind the target and our fighter, we still have the MiG-23 from Smirnykh.

Ivlichev:[40]

I have given the order to Litvinov [in 163] to ready his weapons. He is ready.[41]

05:16   An intruder penetrates Sakhalin airspace at 18:16 GMT and is intercepted by a Soviet fighter.[42]

At precisely this time, Kornukov orders Gerasimenko,[43] commander of the Burevestnik Fighter Regiment, to take control of 163:

05:16

Gerasimenko, the commander orders you to take control of 163 from Smirnykh. Do you see him?[44]

05:17   A target has now violated the state border and General Kornukov orders that it be destroyed:

Kornukov:

Seventeen thirty-one, [seventeen minutes thirty-one seconds], target sixty-five violated the state border of the U.S.S.R. I order you to destroy the target.[45]

Gerasimenko:

I issued the order to destroy the target [through the chief of staff, to the controller and to the pilot].[46]

At 05:17 hours, the order to destroy the target, issued by General Kornukov, descending the chain of command, reached the fighter pilot who was in a lock-on position, the thumb already on the firing button, awaiting that order. That target was destroyed there and then.[47]

05:18   Immediately thereafter, Kornukov orders Gerasimenko to destroy another target:

Kornukov:

So, at eighteen thirty-one [eighteen minutes thirty-one seconds] target sixty-five violated the state border of the U.S.S.R. I order you to destroy the target.[48]

05:19   The Japanese radars observe the intruder they spotted at 05:12 accelerate from 430 to 450 knots.

05:20   (18:20:20 GMT) KAL 007 announces to Tokyo Control it is leaving FL 330 (33,000 feet), at which it had been flying, for FL 350 (35,000 feet).

At the same time as KAL 007 reported its climb to Tokyo Control, the aircraft observed by the Japanese radar dived to 26,000 feet. A few minutes earlier, at 05:15, the aircraft observed by the Japanese radars had made dramatic changes in altitude. At 05:12, its altitude was 35,000 feet. At 05:15 its altitude was 29,000 feet; between 05:15 and 05:23 its average altitude was 29,000 feet; and at 05:23 its altitude was 32,000 feet.[49] These changes of altitude no doubt took place. But they are nonetheless misleading. That is one of the reasons I think they are real. Because they are presented in such a way as to make one think they are less dramatic than they actually are. For example, with the aircraft at an altitude of 29,000 feet at 05:15 and at 32,000 feet at 05:23, it could not have been at an average altitude of 29,000 feet in between. The average between 29,000 and 32,000 is 30,500, not 29,000. In order for the airplane to have been at an average of 29,000 feet, it had to have dived down to 26,000 feet at around 05:19, then climbed again to 32,000 feet. Had KAL 007 made such dramatic altitude changes, it would have been lying to Tokyo Control about the nature of its climb and the flight level it was flying. The Japanese press was quick to catch the point when it got the information.[50] We, of course, know that KAL 007 was not the plane the Japanese were tracking: the Japanese's plane was shot down at 05:29 while the Korean airliner was not.

05:20   The Japanese observers see a Soviet MiG-23 fighter appear on the radar screen, flying at 8,000 meters at a speed of 450 knots. It is 36 NM (41 miles) behind the intruder and flying at the same speed since at 05:19 A.M. the intruder had accelerated to 450 knots.

05:21   The fighter division command post at Smirnykh advises somebody in the chain of command:

Do not talk by loudspeaker. Bring to readiness the rescue squadrons at Sokol and Khomutovo.[51] Khomutovo through civil, through the KGB.[52] Bring Khomutovo to readiness one. Use of missiles in the air ...do not give...[53]

From this cryptic communication, it is clear that missiles have been fired at an intruder at least as early as 05:21, probably before then. From the location of the rescue squadrons mentioned, on the eastern and southern parts of Sakhalin, both inland, it seems possible this early shootdown took place either over the Sea of Okhotsk or over Sakhalin itself. The order "do not talk by loudspeaker" may have been given to avoid alarming people not directly involved in the action. It seems justified if more action was expected, i.e., more intruders were in the air. Otherwise, the one shootdown would have put an end to the lone intruder, and such a news blackout would have had no point.

The *Hokkaido Shimbun* in its September 1, 1983, issue mentioned that an intruder plane had been seen on radar at 03:23 Japan time crossing Sakhalin in a westerly direction 97 NM from Wakkanai, at an altitude of 32,000 feet. Although this plane was sighted near the village of Pravda, it is not the one Marshal Ogarkov said "was stopped over the fishing village of Pravda at 06:24." The *Hokkaido Shimbun* plane was spotted at 05:23, one hour earlier—at least if we are to take Ogarkov's 06:24 (Sakhalin time) to mean just that, 19:24 GMT rather than 18:24.

05:23 KAL 007 reports to Tokyo Control that it reached FL 350 (35,000 feet) at 18:23:05. At the same time, an aircraft "looking like the Korean airliner" was observed by Japanese radar flying at 32,000 feet.

Why did the plane observed by the Japanese, the one that was transmitting transponder code 1300 in Mode A, change altitude so suddenly? On page F-6 of the appendix to the 1983 final report of the ICAO, there is a weather report for the night of August 31–September 1. That night, cloud cover over Sakhalin was ten octas (an octa is one-eighth of the visible sky), five octas of which (slightly more than half the sky) consisted of low clouds, with their base at 1,500 feet and their summit at 9,000 feet, and five octas of high cirrus clouds, with their base at 29,000 feet and their summit at 32,000 feet. The aircraft was trying to take cover in the clouds, which would have given it limited protection against infrared guided missiles, which function poorly when there is heavy cloud coverage.

05:25 The MiG-23 observed by the Japanese radars, having accelerated to

751 knots, crosses sideways the flight path of the intruder that made the dramatic altitude changes, at a point 47° N and 142° E, but 40 NM behind its tail and 2,000 meters (6,000 feet) below it.

When the fighter crosses its flight path, the intruder that had been flying steadily at 450 knots is there no more. It had been there three minutes earlier, but at the time of the crossing, it was 40 NM (46 miles) away from the fighter (see Figure 16). From that distance, it was, of course, impossible for fighter "A" to fire its missiles at the intruder. Fighter A was not after that intruder but another one.

05:27 KAL 007 starts to report passage of waypoint NOKKA, which it had estimated passing at 18:26, GMT (05:26). It calls Tokyo Radio using routine procedure, waits for Tokyo to answer its call, and calls again routinely to transmit its NOKKA position report. But its call then becomes weak and unintelligible[54] (see chapter 7).

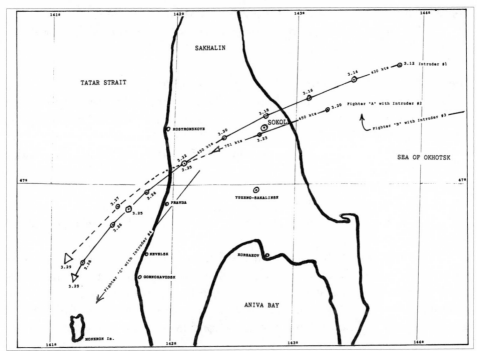

Figure 16. *Radar map of the interception of an intruder by fighter A. Analysis of the data shows that two interceptors shot down two different intruders at virtually the same place and time.*

05:29 The Japanese radars at Wakkanai observe the aircraft squawking transponder code 1300 in Mode A explode at an altitude of 10,000 meters and disappear.

At the same time, the other intruder, flying parallel to the above but 2,000 meters below it, and the MiG-23 "fighter A" on its tail, both disappear from the radar screen. Moments later the MiG-23 is observed making a climbing turn. This suggests that two different intruders may have been shot down at this time.

05:30 The 99-ton Japanese squid-fishing vessel *Chidori Maru* No. 58 observes an explosion low over water, about 1,500 meters (1,640 yards) away in an east-southeast direction.

05:32 Captain Anisimov of the KGB is patrolling the Soviet sea frontier off Nevelsk. On the radar screen of his patrol boat he observes an aircraft cruising at eight hundred kilometers per hour at low altitude break into three pieces over forty seconds. Alternatively what he saw may have been three aircraft flying in tight formation separate.

05:38 An RC-135, escorted by "fighter B" a MiG-23, changes heading, turning north, and disappears from Japanese radar, probably shot down and crashing at 05:39.

05:40 Reassured that the RC-135 they were escorting had ceased to be a menace, the two MiG-23s that had taken off nearly three hours earlier and were now low on fuel head toward Yuzhno-Sakhalinsk, closer than their home base of Smirnykh. As they head in, fighter 805 takes off from Sokol for the second time at 05:42, directed toward an intruder, the same or another.

05:45 Having succeeded in shaking off the two MiG-23s that were after him, the RC-135 again changes course and heads toward Sakhalin.

It is probably at this time that the Sakhalin Command requested reinforcement fighters from Postovaya near Sovetskaya Gavan, on the mainland, already on alert. At least two of these Postovaya fighters, 731 and his wingman, two MiG-31s, will arrive too late to participate in the first hour of the battle, but will be on hand for the second hour.

05:45 At approximately this time, Osipovich shoots down an RC-135 as he explained to Lieutenant Colonel Dokuchayev in his interview with *Krasnaya Zvezda:*

When he [an intruder] penetrated our airspace, I received the order to intercept the plane. I flashed my lights and fired four warning bursts across the front of his aircraft. But he didn't react and I received the order to destroy the plane. We were approaching the west coast of Sakhalin and I fired two missiles. I knew it wasn't a fighter and was convinced it was a reconnaissance plane, an RC-130 or RC-135, because of its speed, its altitude, and other characteristics.

05:45   Reporting to General Strogov, deputy commander of the Far East Air Force, General Kornukov commented:

> — *The pilot is Lieutenant Colonel Osipovich, deputy commander of the regiment. He fired two large missiles.*
> — *Which ones?*
> — *He fired two R-98s.*[55]

05:52   KAL 007 briefly answers a call by KAL 015. Just four cryptic words in Korean, which were enough to reassure KAL 015, who answered, "Roger," and ceased to call.

This communication was recorded at the Tokyo Narita Control Center, indicating that not only was KAL 007 still flying normally over the Sea of Japan at the end of the first hour, but also that it was within VHF range of Tokyo.

The Second Hour[56]

05:42   Fighter 805, a MiG-31, takes off for the second time and is followed closely by fighter 121, another MiG-31, which also takes off from Sokol, at 05:45.

05:46   Fighter 163 takes off from Smirnykh in northern Sakhalin on what was, no doubt, his second mission of the day.

The details of that mission have been reconstructed here from information on the Kirkpatrick tape and on the transcript of communications of Soviet fighters and their ground controllers appended to the ICAO report of 1993. The two sources are very much, but not exactly, alike. Unlike the ground-to-ground transcripts, which gave us fragmentary, if often invaluable, snatches of dialogue, in the case of 163 at least the air-to-ground transcript gives us a long, apparently nearly continuous, sequence of transmissions by the pilot. They give us a fuller idea of what one Soviet interceptor, in this instance the MiG-23 163, was doing during the second hour. We learn elsewhere that the pilot was Litvinov. Bear in mind that what happened was not a video game. The three Soviet interceptors, 805, 121, and 163, and the two to three U.S. aircraft involved were all manned by young men, three or four of whom were dead by the time the sequence ended. Osipovich also shot down an intruder during the same period.

Fighter 163 soon encountered an intruder plane north of the Terpeniya peninsula. At 06:08 it jettisoned its auxiliary fuel tanks, although they were still full, and began a series of violent maneuvers, diving from 25,000 to 12,000 feet, then climbing almost straight up to 23,000 feet, while making abrupt heading changes. The intruder must have been small and maneuverable, perhaps the same aircraft that had zigzagged through the Kamchatka mountains.

A fighter's auxiliary fuel tanks are expensive, and no pilot will deliberately drop them—especially when they are still full—unless he is preparing to engage in combat. Fighter 163 seems to have been scrambled in pursuit of an intruder that had penetrated Sakhalin airspace 250 miles north of the events I have been discussing hitherto. The aircraft he pursued crossed Sakhalin heading southwest, while trying to shake off the interceptor on his tail. But the interceptor had locked on his quarry. Judging by the relative calm that followed the two planes' violent maneuvers and the fact that at 06:17:15, 163 had to contact ground control to ask his position relative to his base, the battle may have ended in his favor, probably somewhere over the mountains that border the Leonidovo airbase on the east. Fighter 163 continued on a 230-degree heading and at 06:19:44 signaled that he was 25 kilometers (15 miles) behind another intruder.

Two minutes later, at 06:21:51, the radar blip split in two and 163 now appeared to be following not one but two aircraft, which were 10 and 15 kilometers (6 and 9 miles) in front of him. The two aircraft were accelerating. Two minutes after this, at 06:23:49, the two intruder aircraft moved closer together again, until they were nearly touching wings, and accelerated again to supersonic speed. At 06:27:29 fighter 163 began another series of violent maneuvers to keep up with the intruders and changed heading from 180 to 150 degrees. At 06:28:35 the fighter told the ground he was carrying out an order (which we cannot hear, the ground-to-air communications not being given us). It was perhaps to fire his missiles.[51] He suddenly made an abrupt change of heading from 150 to 210 degrees, while climbing from 7,500 to 8,000 meters (25,000 to 26,000 feet).

But the battle was not over for fighter 163. After shooting down the first of the two targets he was pursuing, at 06:29:05 the pilot asked the distance to the (second) target. Although he had been following a 210-degree heading, fighter 163 turned sharply north, to a heading of 360 degrees, which brought him back toward Sakhalin. At 06:32:22 he changed direction again, this time to the south, on a 210-degree heading, and asked the controller to give him the intruder's altitude. At 06:34:02 fighter 163 informed his controller that two of his four missiles remained. A few seconds later he announced that he had only two thousand liters of fuel left and requested instructions. The plane suddenly banked sharply to the right, from a 210- to a 60-degree heading. Six minutes later, at 06:40:04, fighter 163 was still flying on a 60-degree heading, closely watching the cloud cover below him for signs of an aircraft. But he couldn't find what he was looking for. There then followed a period of confusion, at which time he asked who was being ordered to turn 10 degrees to the right. The pilot couldn't understand why the controller was asking him to approach from the left on a 60-degree heading when he was already flying a 60-degree heading. The controller's orders had been intended for fighter 121, which had been instructed to assist fighter 163 against this third intruder. At 06:41:44, fighter 163 carried out a new order from ground control, probably to fire his remaining two missiles.[57]

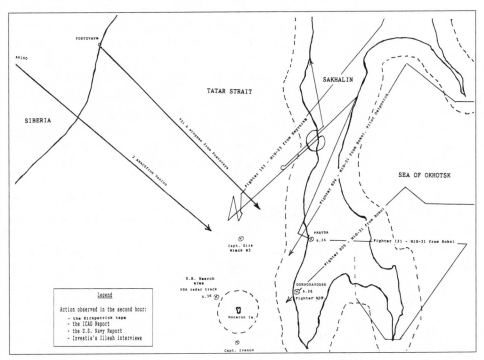

Figure 17. *Events in the second hour of the air battle of Sakhalin, probably involving the shootdown of four military intruders. The data are taken from the Kirkpatrick tape and transcript, which present them as taking place in the first hour and relating only to the interception of KAL 007.*

A minute later, at 06:42:58, fighter 163 made a long, sweeping turn to the right, bringing the aircraft around full circle. At 06:45:43 the fighter was still in its turn. At 06:46:05 the plane came out of the turn at a heading of 60 degrees, in the direction of Shakerst airbase. Fighter 163's own base was fogged in.

06:00 Fighter 805 turns behind an intruder.

Fighter 805 intercepted an aircraft that must have been an RC-135, which hadn't overflown Kamchatka but had come directly from the Pacific, that is, directly from route Romeo-20. The two planes, pursuer and pursued, crossed Sakhalin in a southwesterly direction, on a 240-degree heading. At 06:20:49, fighter 805 fired four warning cannon bursts. At 06:22:02 the RC-135 slowed suddenly in the hope of throwing off his pursuer. The Soviet fighter pilot later told a Moscow television station that this was a customary maneuver for an RC-135. Extending its flaps all the way out, the plane brakes sharply so that the fighter, which is incapable of flying as slowly, shoots past. While the fighter is maneuvering to get behind the target again, the RC-135 heads for the border and international airspace.

06:00 In Japan, the JASDF commanders at the Air Self-Defense Forces headquarters in Tokyo declare a DEFCON 3 alert, one step below general mobilization, for the Japanese Air Force Northern Command. A total of seventy-two fighters, half the Japanese active force, and two military rescue squadrons assemble at Chitose, on Hokkaido, facing Sakhalin and poised for combat.

The first U.S. wave had entered Sakhalin airspace between 02:30 Tokyo time (04:30 Sakhalin time) and 03:46 Tokyo time (05:46 Sakhalin time) while the general officers were still on their way to the meeting. The second wave is now just about to begin, and it is likely that, from now on, the JASDF chiefs of staff will be monitoring events by radar and signals intelligence "in real time," that is to say, as they happen.

06:00 (approximately 3 P.M. EDT) Most, if not all, of the B-52s at the U.S. Strategic Air Force Base near Pensacola, Florida, take off and remain in the air for a number of hours. This apparent emergency airborne alert of an important part of the U.S. long-range bomber force is observed by a Pensacola resident accustomed to the normal pattern of B-52 activities at the base.

06:00 Osipovich takes off again from Sokol (or is assigned a second mission without landing).

The circumstances surrounding Osipovich's second flight, which began at 06:00, are very different from those surrounding the first. It was daybreak, which shows that we are dealing with the second hour. Osipovich says he knows nothing about the controllers from Deputat, Trikotazh, and Karnaval, which the Kirkpatrick tape makes clear were controlling Soviet interceptors 805, 163, and 121, also in the air at the time of Osipovich's second mission. Osipovich, then, was in a different control network from theirs.[58] A number of other aircraft of which we had not previously heard, including the two AWACs from Vanino on the mainland, were also in the air at the time of the second mission. Osipovich's target in his second mission, too, was different. In his first mission he said his target was an RC-130 or an RC-135; in the second he said its silhouette was like that of a TU-16. From his two interviews it is clear that he shot down at least one aircraft on each of the two missions.[59]

In his interview with *Izvestiya,* Osipovich said that he received the order to take off at 06:00 hours. It is noteworthy that this takeoff took place after the aircraft destructions observed by the Japanese radars at Wakkanai (05:29) and by the crew of the *Chidori Maru* (05:30), and after Captain Anisimov's observations (05:32–05:33)—after, that is, the events of the first hour of the air battle of Sakhalin. The battle was thus still going on. By the time Osipovich had started his engines, gone over the checklist, and taxied to the entrance of the runway, his lights turned on in the still-dark night, it was 06:02. He was told to head east toward the Sea of Okhotsk at an altitude of 8,500 meters (27,600 feet).

06:10   After eight minutes in the air, pilot Osipovich receives a message from the controller: "Enemy [aircraft] dead ahead. It's about to violate our airspace . . . heading straight toward your aircraft."

However, immediately thereafter, to Osipovich's surprise, instead of directing him toward the intruder, which was now directly in front of him, the controller switched his orders and sent him after a target that was already behind him. Osipovich banked to the left and made a U-turn, exposing his tail to the first target, and, after changing altitude, went after the second aircraft. That aircraft, still over the Sea of Okhotsk, couldn't, of course, have been the Korean airliner, which, by that time, was over the Sea of Japan a few minutes north of Niigata. I mention this because it is precisely this target, merged with 805's to its south—just as Osipovich is merged with 805's pilot—that the official U.S./ICAO/Russian account of events says was Korean Air Lines Flight 007.

Shortly afterward, Osipovich noticed a small black dot in a cloud. Its anticollision lights were on. Keep in mind that at this time the sun hadn't risen yet. At an altitude of 8,000 meters (26,000 feet), the sun wouldn't rise until 06:30. Yet there was some daylight, for dawn had broken at 05:52. Twenty minutes after the beginning of dawn, Osipovich was able to distinguish the small black speck ahead of him:

The intruder was flying at approximately 1,000 km/hr [600 miles an hour]. I got him on my radar and followed from a distance of 13 km [8 miles]. Suddenly the controller began nervously asking me what my heading was, the target's heading, and his altitude. We had entered an area of radar silence, which the other plane must have known about, but which came as a complete surprise to me. I had flown in the area many times before, and this was the first time this had happened. The controller later explained that the echo of both planes had completely disappeared from the screen.[60]

After this statement by Osipovich, Illesh reproduces an excerpt from the tape of the Soviet pilots' conversations that Mrs. Kirkpatrick had presented to the United Nations.[61] The following words appeared in the excerpt:

— 805, is that you calling?
— Who's calling 805?

These lines were read to Osipovich, who commented:

Yes, that was me asking the questions. The voice seemed strange, though. As if someone had broken into our communications. A foreigner who spoke Russian, who had cut into our frequency to create confusion and give contradictory orders. To protect ourselves from this kind of interference, we use a secret, four-digit code. That's why we asked the unknown voice to call back using the code. If he didn't know the code, he couldn't respond.[62]

The Kirkpatrick tape suggests that the unknown caller never called back; at least his response doesn't appear on the tape. Presumably he didn't know the code. It wouldn't have been a Soviet pilot, but could very well have been an operator on board an RC-135 in the vicinity. An RC-135 is capable of transmitting on all frequencies used by the Russians and can interfere with radar and radio frequencies, military or civil.

At 06:22:02 hours, Osipovich said he had received an order to fire warning shots at the intruder and force it to land.[63] He said he fired 243 warning shots. But, he added, "I didn't have any tracers, only armor-piercing shells." Osipovich's statement generated controversy. Many saw it as refuting Marshal Ogarkov's claim that the interceptor had fired four warning bursts, for a total of 120 tracers in all. The Ministry of Defense of the Russian Federation stated that at the time the cannons of interceptor aircraft were routinely loaded with a mixture of rounds so that every fourth or fifth was a tracer. That kind of loading was not intended as a warning for the target but to help the attack pilot aim his fire. For practice exercises there were also strings of pure tracers.[64] Possibly Osipovich and the journalist misunderstood each other as to what constituted a burst of tracer shells. More to the point, however, may be the number of rounds fired and the time at which they were fired.

On the Kirkpatrick tape the fighter that fired the cannon bursts is number 805. His shots were fired at 06:20:49 (Sakhalin time). In his interview with *Izvestiya*, Osipovich times his firing of warning shots with an event that occurred at 06:22:02 on the Kirkpatrick transcript. This indicates that two fighters fired warning shots at very much the same time. Osipovich fired a total of 243 "armor-piercing shells" and 805 several cannon bursts, presumably the warning burst or 120 rounds Marshal Ogarkov mentioned.

Osipovich continues:

> *I received the order to force him to land. I took up position behind the plane and began firing warning shots. It was at this moment that he began to slow down. . . . There was an extraordinary commotion coming over the radio and I couldn't get in a word. I remember that there was a MiG-23 behind me that couldn't have been going too fast because he was still carrying his reserve tanks. He wouldn't stop shouting, "I see a dogfight! I see a dogfight!" I had no idea what dogfight he was talking about.*

The Kirkpatrick tape puts the sudden slowdown at the time when fighter 163 reported that an intruder was 25 kilometers (16 miles) ahead of him. At the time Osipovich had not yet fired either warning bursts or his missiles. Clearly, if there was a dogfight at that moment, neither Osipovich nor 163 (Litvinov) took part in it. The words Osipovich heard do not appear on the Japanese transcript, or on the Kirkpatrick tape either.

If we examine the Kirkpatrick tape, we see that at the time Osipovich heard the commotion on the radio (06:24 Sakhalin time) the tape shows almost no activity, with four calls per minute.[65] What happened to the other transmissions that were part of this amazing commotion? Were they cut out of the tape? Osipovich could hear them, why can't we? Spectrographic analysis on the Kirkpatrick tape done at the University of Washington shows splice lines and other evidence of deletions. Ambassador Kirkpatrick told the United Nations the tape had been made by a voice-actuated recorder with no deletions. Osipovich said that many other aircraft were in the sky that night: Osipovich's teammate, a plane from Smirnykh, and two AWACs surveillance aircraft from Vanino on the mainland, to name a few. Sakhalin is an important strategic location with close to twenty military airbases.

There is a good chance that at least one AWACs was stationed on the island. The fact that the AWACs *Tanker* and *Suchogruz* were sent in from the mainland to assist gives some idea of the scope of the intrusion.

Osipovich went on to say:

I signaled with my lights, but instead of obeying and preparing to land, the other plane tried to shake me off by reducing speed. The plane slowed down to 350 km/hr (217 miles per hour). My aircraft couldn't fly less than 400 km/hr (248 miles per hour) without stalling, which meant I would have to catch up with him again. We were near the border, and in order to stop him I would have to maneuver my plane behind him again, which would have given him the time to get away. I found myself in line with the other plane and above him.

I dived sharply and banked to the right, which brought me 5 km (3 miles) behind and 2,000 meters (6,500 feet) below the intruder. I turned on my afterburner and pulled back on the stick to lift the nose of the plane a little until my fire-control radar locked on the target. I fired right away. When I was near the other plane, I had a chance to get a good look at it. It looked bigger than an IL-76, but the silhouette reminded me of the TU-16.

The TU-16 is a Soviet bomber, reconnaissance, and transport plane, with a long, slender fuselage resembling a pencil. Osipovich, who had made more than a thousand interceptions in the sky above Sakhalin, was capable of describing a target if he could see it, which he could in the dawn now appearing.

The first missile hit the tail and there was a large orange flame. The second carried off half the left wing. The lights went out immediately.

Osipovich stated that the first missile, the one that hit the tail and produced an orange flame, was guided by an infrared homing device. Infrared guided missiles fly toward a source of heat. This means the aircraft he hit had one or more engines in the tail section. A Boeing 747 (KAL 007) or Boeing 707 (RC-135) has neither an engine nor fuel in the tail.

When the lights went out in the plane I had fired at, I turned right and returned to my base. I then heard the controller guiding "Migalk" to a target. "The target's descending," said the controller. "I can't see it." Migalk cried out, "The target's descending, it's at five thousand meters [16,000 feet]." And Migalk again, "I can't see it."

The target to which Migalk was being guided by the controller does not seem to be the same target Osipovich had just hit. Migalk does not seem to have been Osipovich's wingman. Because he was running short of fuel, Osipovich abandoned the target after he saw the fire in its tail. As wingman, Migalk would have been able to see the target as clearly as Osipovich and would have continued to track it without assistance from the ground. The fact that the controller guided Migalk to a target without referring to Osipovich suggests that he was directing him to a different target in another part of the sky.

Osipovich continued:

Turning toward my base, I looked at my instruments and saw that I had only ten minutes of fuel left. I was still 160 kilometers [100 miles] from the base, and to add to my worries the fog had rolled in. My airport was completely fogged in. I thought I might not be able to reach it, and flying over a piece of swamp, I thought I might have to eject. I somehow managed to land. I was welcomed like a hero at the base, and my commander, Colonel[66] Kornukov, told me to get ready to receive a new star [a promotion to a higher rank].

I had shot down an enemy spy plane. . . . These RC-135 are always circling around us. All this business about a civilian airliner didn't start until later on. They found a wreck but no passengers. The only human remains found was the black-gloved hand of the [or a] pilot. No matter what they say, I'll stick by my words: the plane I shot down was no passenger plane; it was a spy plane.

Later in an interview with Soviet and Japanese television, Osipovich said he followed the intruder on a course from the small island of Tyuleniy (south of Cape Terpeniya) to north of Nevelsk. Pravda is north of Nevelsk. Osipovich thus shot down an aircraft looking like a TU-16 near the village of Pravda at approximately 06:24. His target may or may not have been the plane of which Ogarkov spoke when he said, "The fighter stopped the flight of the intruder plane at 06:24 over the village of Pravda." There is, however, no clear official record of Osipovich's mission. That is because of the editing done in the Russian transcripts to merge Osipovich's second shootdown with 805's second shootdown and to make Osipovich look like the pilot of 805.

The clearest documents we have are interviews Osipovich gave various newspapers and television networks. I have assigned 06:24 as the time of Osipovich's firing because Osipovich said that right after he fired his missiles he broke off the attack and turned to a heading of 300 degrees, and the only reference we have of a turn to 300 degrees is 06:23:45. The coincidence with the stopping of an intruder at Pravda at 06:24 is quite strong. However, we must bear in mind that Osipovich also said that when he broke the attack, he had barely ten minutes' fuel left. He feared he wouldn't be able to land and might have to eject. Since Osipovich was reported "on approach for a landing" at 06:42, he must have landed at 06:45. He reported on the phone to Kornukov at 06:51, immediately after landing. There is thus a possibility that Osipovich's firing took place at around 06:36 or 06:37. In that case, the 06:24 Pravda shootdown would not be Osipovich's but someone else's.

06:25 The following conversation takes place between General Kornukov and Captain Solodkov, his duty officer at the Sokol Command Post:

> *The crew has been guided in for the attack, in the area of Kostroma, about fifty kilometers. Tell your rescue squadrons they must go to readiness one. It is heading south on course 210 degrees. A missile has been fired in the air [by a fighter]. Oguslaev is our flight-control officer. That's all I have.*[67]

06:25:31 Under control of Deputat, combat control center at Sokol, in this instance flight-control officer Lieutenant Borisov, fighter 805 fires two missiles at an intruder. The infrared guided missile explodes in the tail. The left wing is not damaged. At 06:26:01, the pilot announces, "Target destroyed."[68]

06:26:25

> *Captain Solodkov. Emir Command Post. At twenty-six minutes twenty-five seconds, article 37*[69] *fired one missile at the target. How do you read?*[70]

In less than a minute, three different shootdown sequences have taken place, one under flight-control officer Oguslaev, one by fighter 805 under the control of Deputat, and the other by an "article 37" (MiG-31) under the control of Command Post "Emir." If we have little information about the Oguslaev and Emir shootdowns, there seems to be too much about the 805 shootdown—presumably because the tapes' editors were trying to make 805's shootdown look like the only one by working in material belonging to other sequences (Osipovich's, 163's, etc.).[71]

After the RC-135 in front of him slowed down suddenly in an attempt to have him zip by, fighter 805 got back into firing position quickly. At 06:26:20, according to the U.S. version, above the town of Gornozavodsk, he fired two missiles. One second later, according to the Japanese version of events (two seconds later according to the United States), he announced, "Target destroyed." The Russian transcript, however, has it twenty seconds earlier at 06:26:01, as noted above. The latter change brings the detonation time on the air-ground communication tape into line with the detonation time on the digital flight-data recorder tape allegedly from KAL 007 also given to the ICAO by the Russians in January 1993.

Although the Soviet chain of command stated that the fighter fired his missiles from a distance of four kilometers, the ICAO maintains that fighter 805 fired his missiles from eight kilometers (five miles). At the speed the missiles were traveling, it would have required twenty-five seconds for them to reach the target. Does this mean the tape was altered? Or did another aircraft, and not fighter 805, announce "target destroyed" to Soviet ground control?

John Keppel, who speaks Russian, points out that, according to Hersh, interceptor 805 used the Russian word *zapustkal* (I let it fly) in saying he had fired his missiles, whereas the Kirkpatrick tape at that time has 805 use the phrase *pust proizvyol* (I have accomplished the launch). They mean the same thing but may have been said by two different pilots. In discussing the transmission that he quotes, Hersh says, "It was then, presumably, that the phrase 'The target is destroyed' also was heard."[72] *Presumably* is a funny word to use in this context. Recall that on the Kirkpatrick transcript the two transmissions are two seconds apart, one second apart on the Japanese transcript—in neither case the twenty-five seconds 805's missiles would have taken to reach the target.

The explanation may well be that in the description by a U.S. intelligence officer to Hersh of 805's shootdown, the former mixed 805's transmissions with those of an almost simultaneous shootdown somewhat farther north over Pravda by Osipovich. Explaining to Hersh how U.S. intelligence was supposed to have woken up to the seriousness of the incident, the officer may have goofed and played him the part of the tape of the shootdown that contained the *zapustkal* (I have launched) but not the "target is destroyed" phrase. Its absence would explain Hersh's strange remark about its "presumably" having been said at that time.

06:33:56 Fighter 805 heads for its base[73] and is still at 5,000 meters.

Once more Osipovich's narrative makes it clear that he was not flying fighter 805. After having fired his missiles, Osipovich had only ten minutes of fuel left and was preparing for a difficult landing at the fog-shrouded airport. If Osipovich had been 805's pilot, his firing time would have been 19:26:20 GMT (06:26:20). Under these circumstances, at 06:33:56 he would not still have been at 5,000 meters.

I asked Dr. Tsuboi at the Iwatsu laboratories to analyze the voices of the pilot of fighter 805 and Osipovich and compare them. As the spectrograms below show, the voices are of two different individuals.

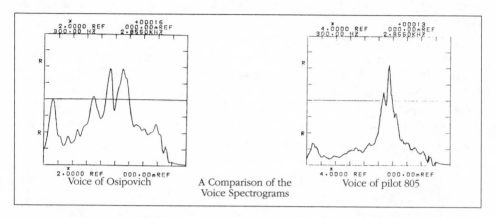

Voice of Osipovich

A Comparison of the
Voice Spectrograms

Voice of pilot 805

Figure 18. Osipovich and the pilot of 805 were two different people. Comparison of their voice spectrograms shows they are not similar. Done at the Iwatsu Electric Company laboratory outside Tokyo.

06:35 Soviet fighters come from the mainland.

The recording on the Kirkpatrick tape mentions four interceptors, only three of which, fighters 805, 121, and 163, seem to have taken an early role in the interception of intruders during the second hour. The fourth aircraft, fighter 731, appeared on the scene late, after the others had shot down their targets. Yet this plane used as much fuel as the other three fighters, which implies that it was in the air just as long. Between 06:33 and 06:35, fighter 731 was flying east on a 120-degree heading, at an altitude of 23,000 feet. Fifteen seconds later it was flying west on a 200-degree heading, this time coming from the left. It appears the plane was trying to intercept still another target.

06:35 Fighter 731 is on a 260-degree magnetic heading, flying due west, at 23,000 feet.

06:37 Osipovich may have fired his missiles at this time as possibly implied by his landing time (see below at 06:42).

06:38 Fighter 731 suddenly climbs from 23,000 to 30,000 feet. It may have shot down an aircraft at this time and climbed to 30,000 feet to keep clear of the debris. Two minutes later, at 06:40, the pilot indicated he had only two thousand liters of fuel remaining, the minimum necessary to land somewhere on Sakhalin.

Fighter 731 and Its Wingman, a Patrol of Two MiG-31s from Postovaya

From the ICAO report of June 1993,[74] we can see that fighter 731, said to be a MiG-21—but, as we shall see, in fact a MiG-31—must have been a patrol of two fighters. We also know that they took off, not from a Sakhalin airbase, but from Postovaya across the Tatar Gulf on the Siberian mainland. Postovaya is a Soviet Air Force base associated with the Soviet Navy base Sovetskaya Gavan, on the coast six hundred miles northeast of Vladivostok.

At least two interceptors that we know of (731 and his wingman) came from Postovaya. And—we know from Osipovich—two Soviet AWACs were sent from Vanino, also on the mainland. The AWACs appear to have been used as (airborne) combat control centers, each handling fighters. *Tanker* was handling 731. All this implies that more than two fighters were sent from Postovaya. Some twenty air bases were on Sakhalin with fighters and interceptors in sufficient numbers to repel any likely intrusion, let alone one by a single off-course civilian airliner. The call for reinforcements from the mainland illustrates the seriousness of the situation in the eyes of the Soviet command.

It takes a good half hour for fighter aircraft to cross the Tatar Gulf and get to Sakhalin. MiG-21s, as 731 and his wingman were said to be, are short-range aircraft. Besides, the MiG-21 is a pretty old aircraft, having replaced the MiG-19 in 1959. Thus in 1983 it was already twenty-four years old. Young for a man but retirement age for a fighter. The Soviet command evidently felt that they should be replaced in strategically sensitive areas, as Sakhalin and the Kurils clearly were. Our investigation shows that in 1983 just before the KAL 007 disaster, the MiG-21s remaining at Burevestnik air base on Iturup in the Kurils had been withdrawn and replaced. In his book Andrei Illesh tells us that starting on August 1, 1983, two squadrons of new MiG fighters had been sent from Postovaya to Burevestnik and the MiG-21s withdrawn, via Sokol on Sakhalin, to Postovaya.[75] Illesh does not specify the kind of new MiGs supplied, but it is not hard to establish their identity: Osipovich told us they were MiG-31s.

Postovaya was the main Soviet fighter base in eastern Siberia. It would surely have kept some MiG-31s for itself. It is clear that 731 and his wingman were not MiG-21s. For one thing MiG-21s were too short-range to be used as reinforcements for Sakhalin. For another, had they been MiG-21s, higher headquarters would not have wanted to retain them on Sakhalin as insurance against future incursions. General Kamenski, commander of the Soviet Far East Air Force, specifically ordered that 731, and no doubt the other fighters from Postovaya, were to be retained on Sakhalin when their mission was completed.

The fact that 731 and his wingman showed up late in the action at Sakhalin under control of a Soviet AWACs, call sign *Tanker,* strongly suggests that they had spent much of their mission over the Tatar Gulf. That in turn suggests action there as well as over Sakhalin and that incursions into Sakhalin airspace had in all likelihood come from the west as well as the east, at least in the second hour.

Fighter 731 appears to have shot down a target at 06:38. It could have been the one that U.S. intelligence services and listening stations observed crashing in the Tatar Gulf within a circle four miles in radius, 16 NM northwest of Moneron Island. This conclusion is arrived at by putting together two facts. The first is that fighter 731's actions, its sudden climb from 23,000 to 30,000 feet and other maneuvers, reflected combat. The second is that in his initial announcement, Secretary Shultz said that the airliner disappeared from radar at 18:38 GMT—which may imply that a U.S. Air Force or Navy aircraft was shot down at that time.[76] The radar track given by NSA to the U.S. Navy task force before its commanders left Washington was the basis for establishing the intensive search area 16 NM northwest of Moneron, the site at which the U.S. Navy concentrated its efforts.

06:42   Osipovich is on approach at Sokol.[77]

06:43   Fighter 805 lands at Uriuk.[78]

06:45   Osipovich having landed at Sokol is debriefed on the phone by General Kornukov:

— *What missiles were you carrying, "pencils"?*
— *Yes.*[79]

Note that on his first mission, one hour earlier, Osipovich had fired "large missiles," type R-98.

Immediately after Osipovich's landing at Sokol, General Strogov, deputy commander of the Soviet Far East Air Force, and General Kornukov converse on the telephone, from which we have the following fragment:

06:46 Strogov:

"It's already light there, at your location."[80]

And there is the following conversation between Lieutenant Colonel Novoseletski, chief of staff of the fighter division, and Captain Titovnin, fighter controller at a combat control center:

06:47 Novoseletski:

You don't have the sunrise yet?

Titovnin:

No, it will be in about thirty minutes.[81]

According to these remarks, dawn was breaking and the sun would rise in another thirty minutes, or about 07:17. The ICAO report of June 1993 puts it exactly at 20:13 UTC (page 9), which is 07:13 Sakhalin time. Although these numbers match well, we have a problem. The ICAO report of 1983 gives the sunrise at 06:49 (19:49 UTC). This is confirmed by the time of the sunrise in Tokyo, which that day was at 04:54 local Tokyo time or 06:54 Sakhalin time. Japan and Sakhalin are at the same longitude and eleven degrees apart in latitude. Accordingly, the sunrise in Sakhalin should be three to four minutes earlier at around 06:50. That is an astronomical consideration that we can trust.

Accordingly at 06:47, Titovnin could not have said that the sunrise would be in another thirty minutes. It is more probable that he said "three minutes," which gives a sunrise time of 06:50. *Three* and *thirty* sound more alike in Russian than they do in English. Moreover, General Strogov wouldn't have said that "it is already light" half an hour before sunrise, although it would be natural to say so three minutes before sunrise. We can trust that the sunrise was 06:49/06:50 at Sakhalin. Osipovich thus landed a few minutes before sunrise, a fact he confirmed in an interview with Misha Lobko.

Why did the 1993 ICAO report put sunrise late by twenty-four minutes? I asked the chief of the Accident Investigation and Prevention Section, Air Navigation Bureau, at the ICAO, who was the head of the 1993 KAL 007 investigation team. He told me he did not know where the number came from, but that reference to the sunrise had been made in order to show that it was still night at the time of the shootdown. This is an admission that the ICAO investigators studied various scenarios based on the amount of light according to the time of dawn and sunrise and tried to fill in the gaps.

06:50 The sun rises at Sakhalin.

06:52 Fighter 121, pilot Tarasov, lands at Sokol.

06:55 One MiG-23 lands at Sokol.

06:59 The two MiG-31s from Postovaya on the mainland, 731 and his wingman, are on approach for a landing on Sakhalin (at Sokol).

1) 18.07 - Time and distance factors have this intruder match with the Japanese rad
spotted at 18.32 pursued by fighter "B" and which turned north at 18.38 before e
pattern pretty well matches the flight pattern of the RC-135 U.S. reconnaissance
report of 1983 indicates that an RC-135 aircraft was flying in the area of the 1

9) 19.25 - Based on time and distance factors, this target, 50 km from Kostrom cann
19.25, 805's target was only 20 km south of Kostrom. It cannot be the intruder o
(see: 5-2) because at 18.25, it was at 47º N/142º E. and, of course, the time wa

At 19.25, there is a report of a "missile fired in the air" at a target headin

At 19.29 there is also a report by the "Emir" Command Post that "article 37 fi
26 minutes 25 seconds" - Ref. Page 153.

At 19.25.31 (6.25.31) fighter 805 reported to "Deputat" Command Post firing a
heading of 240 degrees and at 19.26.01 (6.26.01) he reported "Target destroyed".
That makes for three different missile firing in this short period.

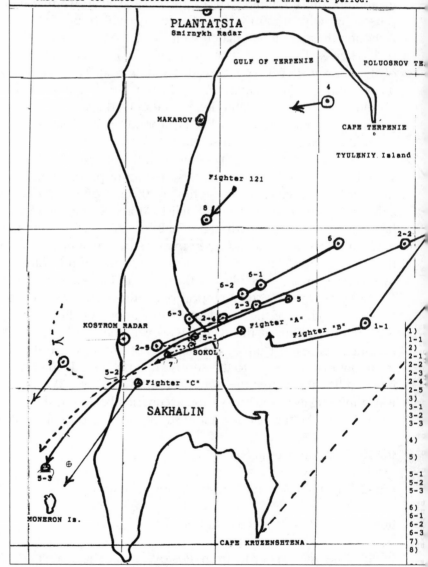

Figure 19. *Nine different intruders at Sakhalin as tracked by Soviet radar. From data in the Russian communications transcripts. Up to six of these intrusions took place in the first hour.*

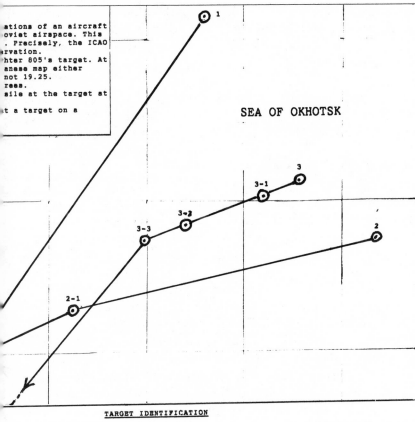

ations of an aircraft
oviet airspace. This
. Precisely, the ICAO
arvation.
hter 805's target. At
anese map either
not 19.25.
rees.
sile at the target at

t a target on a

SEA OF OKHOTSK

1

3
3-1
3-2
3-3

2

2-1

TARGET IDENTIFICATION

arence is to relevant pages of Information Document NO 1. ICAO 1993 Report)

JTC - From Plantatsia, bearing 65, distance 340 km, tracking 200 - Ref. Page 149
TC - Appear on the radar screen - Ref. Japanese radar observation
JTC - (5.48) From Sokol, azimuth 60, distance 440 km - Ref. Page 50
UTC - (6.00) From Sokol, bearing 55, range 250 km - Ref. Page 117
JTC - (6.06) From Sokol, bearing 55, range 160 km - Ref. Page 121
JTC - (6.13) From Sokol, range 45-50 km - Ref. Page 124
JTC - (6.17) Target violated the State Border - Ref. Page 126
JTC - (6.21) Target 20-30 km west of Uriuk with 805 - Ref. Page 151
JTC - 200/250 km east of Terpenie, tracking 240 - Ref. Page 183
JTC - 200/230 km east of Terpenie, tracking 240 - Ref. Page 183
JTC - Target approaching him 180 km to Terpenie - Ref. Page 83/114
JTC - Observe Terpenie 140 km, from border heading toward Cape Kruzenshtena,
       tracking 210/220 - Ref. Page 102.
UTC - 100 km south of Terpenie, heading straight toward the island, Tracking 240 -
       Ref. Page 149
UTC - Flying 430 knots, 10,000 meters, Xponder Code 1300, Mode A -
       Ref. Japanese radar observations and official announcement
UTC - Japanese target north of Sokol - from plotting
UTC - Target 47º N/142º E - Ref. Japanese official announcement
UTC - Disappear from radar, explodes at 10,000 meters - Ref. Japanese observations
       and official announcement
UTC - Bearing 45 degrees, range 110 km, altitude 9,000, no lights - Ref. Page 85
UTC - Target 30 km from State Border - Ref. Page 103
UTC - Target 20 km from State Border - Ref. Page 104
UTC - Target 20 km north of Sokol - Ref. Page 104
UTC - The target is 20 km from Sokol, going away - Ref. Page 128
UTC - (6.31) 121, the target is 25 km in front of you, going away - Heading 210 -
       Ref. Page 75
UTC - Target in the area of Kostrom about 50 km tracking 210 - Ref. Page 52

07:00 After evading an American warship in La Pérouse Strait, Captain Bilyuk of the *Uvarovsk* is ordered by radio to head for Moneron, passing west of the island, and to be on the lookout for any people or debris on the water.

07:00 At about this time, early morning, at the end of a long night, Captain Ivanov on his border-patrol ship receives by radio an order to search for the pilots of an aircraft that had been shot down south of the island of Moneron. The message warns that "the pilots are armed with combat weapons and may offer resistance."

07:10 It is 05:10 in Japan. The active phase of the overflights is over. The chiefs of the Air Self-Defense Forces staff, who had been following events as they happened, order a review of radar data from all the radar sites on Hokkaido and northern Honshu.

On the basis of a very partial Soviet communications record, we have identified nine or more different intruders at Sakhalin (see Figure 19). From *Izvestiya* and other accounts we have identified some ten crashes at sea and three on land. That some of the planes shot down were American we know from photographs and other evidence. Where in all this carnage was the Korean airliner? From time and distance factors we know that it was in the area of Sakhalin during the first hour and thus cannot have had anything to do with the events of the second hour. We know it was not destroyed over Sakhalin. None of the intruders we have identified fit it in shape, time, speed, or maneuverability. Could KAL 007 have been over Sakhalin but escaped? The only governmental statement that might fit is the first (of several) the U.S.S.R. made, the Tass statement read without comment on the Soviet evening news program on September 1, 1983. Among other things, it said:

> *The intruder plane did not react to the signals and warnings from the Soviet fighters and continued its flight in the direction of the Sea of Japan.*

In Tokyo, the Japanese air chiefs of staff were intensely interested in the events that had just unfolded at their doorstep. Hokkaido was an advanced listening post for Japan. Its radars peer across the Sea of Okhotsk and over Sakhalin. With events taking place so close to their borders, it's easy to understand why the Japanese officers insisted on an early analysis of the Hokkaido radar observations. But why also those from radars in the north of Honshu?

In his book Seymour Hersh tells us that U.S. air defense monitors, on what were termed *Rivet Joint* missions, routinely flew across the Sea of Okhotsk, through La Pérouse Strait, and then turned south and flew down the Sea of Japan coast of Hokkaido and Honshu. He says that such a mission was scheduled for August 31/September 1 but was canceled as events in the Kamchatka, Sea of Okhotsk, Sahkalin area developed.[82]

From their radar observations it was clear to the Japanese that one aircraft had done just that and had then disappeared from radar north of Niigata. In the light of what had happened over Sakhalin, and Tokyo's loss of communications with KAL 007, it was urgent to identify the aircraft that had flown south.

Escape from Sakhalin and Destruction off Honshu

We have looked for Korean Air Lines Flight 007 among the intruders at Kamchatka and Sakhalin and did not find it. In chapter 14, I suggested a hypothetical course for it that would have taken it over neither. That route would have crossed the Bering Sea somewhat north of R-20, its assigned route, but well south of the course the official account of events says it took. This hypothetical course would have taken it through the Kurils, across the Sea of Okhotsk, through La Pérouse Strait between Sakhalin and Hokkaido, and then south over the Sea of Japan toward Niigata—overflying no Soviet territory.

Until KAL 007 came within VHF radio and radar range of Tokyo Air Control Center (Tokyo ACC) at Narita Airport, we have no direct evidence that it flew any of this route. But it is worth noting that early U.S. and Japanese news stories, based on governmental sources, do have it passing through the Kurils south of Kamchatka. In chapter 3, I referred to the September 1, 1983, *Mainichi Shimbun* story that says so. On its front page, the September 2 *New York Times* carried a map showing KAL 007 passing through the Kurils. It cites the Department of State and the Federal Aviation Administration as sources.

Also relevant is a remark said to have been made shortly after the Korean Air Lines disaster by a high-ranking U.S. Air Force electronic-warfare officer. The officer said that the United States had recently lost an Air Force plane while it was simulating a civilian airliner. Initially I thought that it must refer to an incident other than the KAL 007 tragedy. But now I am not so sure.

We looked for the Korean airliner at the rendezvous with the RC-135 and over both Kamchatka and Sakhalin and did not find it. But we do have evidence of a Korean-speaking U.S. military aircraft abeam of waypoint NABIE and sufficiently far to the north to be out of range of the VHF antenna on St. Paul Island. Moreover, if KAL 007 was not at the rendezvous with the RC-135 southeast of Karaginski Island, another southwest-bound, presumably U.S. military, aircraft was. Time and distance factors make it plausible that it could have been the same plane as that which, north of NABIE, communicated with KAL 007 in Korean. If KAL 007 did not overfly Kamchatka and Sakhalin, more than one U.S. military aircraft did, one of which could have been our Korean-speaking aircraft, simulating KAL 007 along the lines the electronic-warfare officer mentioned and getting shot down for its pains.

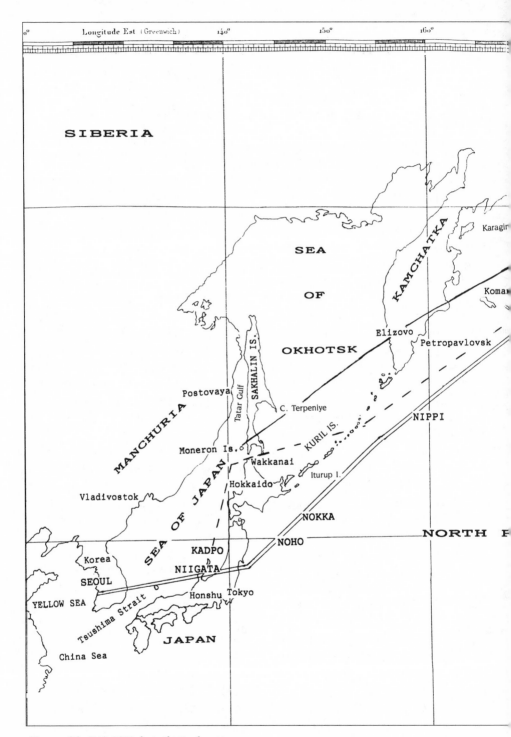

Figure 20. KAL 007's hypothetical route.

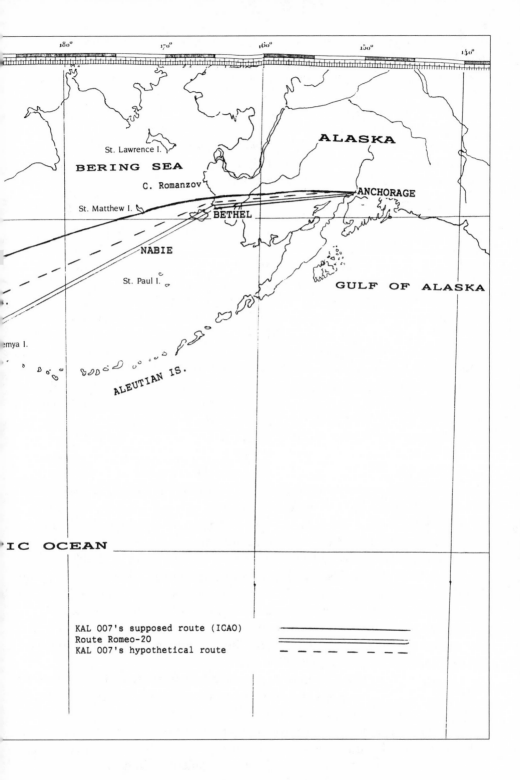

It is also worth noting that among the documents that President Yeltsin handed over in October 1992 to the U.S. next of kin and a representative of the South Korean government was a map said to have been based on data from the Korean airliner's black box. It shows the aircraft flying from Anchorage, across the Bering Sea and the Kamchatka Peninsula, and terminating in the middle of Sakhalin Island. The course is generally similar to the course described in the official account of events put forward by both the Americans and the Russians. This map shows the aircraft in question taking off from Anchorage at 12:58 GMT, not 13:00 GMT as we know that KAL 007 did. This, too, could have been the aircraft the electronic-warfare officer described, in this instance having taken off from Elmendorf Air Force Base rather than from Anchorage International Airfield as the Korean airliner did. Along with the map Yeltsin handed over was a 1983 Soviet experts' analysis of the black box's DFDR data, which says that the plane flew a constant magnetic heading of 249 degrees. The track on the map is consistent with this finding. Why would a military plane fly the Bering Sea using this relatively inefficient means of navigation except to simulate KAL 007, which the cover story says did so by accident?

If a plane simulating it flew the course that the official story says KAL 007 flew, it is reasonable to suppose that KAL 007 itself flew some other course. Abeam NABIE it may have been in contact with the simulator. In any event, it had an exchange in Korean with an aircraft, probably military, well to its north. That KAL 007 reported winds along the more northerly course described in the official story is not conclusive evidence that it was there. There is no evidence proving that it was and a good deal to suggest that it was not. All this concerns events as far as Sakhalin but no farther. Does what we know about the Korean airliner's course south from Sakhalin tell us anything relevant to the course it had taken previously?

As I have said earlier, KAL 007's position reports, while misleading as to the aircraft's geographical position, in time and distance factors must have corresponded very closely to those called for by its flight plan. If they had not coincided, when destroyed, the airliner would not have been on the verge of rejoining its assigned course at NIIGATA on time. Ever since BETHEL, when it was over land and under radar observation, the waypoints it reported had merely been designated points in the ocean. The civilian controllers had no means of verifying the airliner's reports of passing over them. NIIGATA, however, was different.

Captain Chun had the means to know where he was. In heading for NIIGATA, which from debris and radio evidence we know he did, he no doubt hoped to rejoin his assigned course without anyone realizing—or, perhaps more accurately, being able to prove—that he had ever been off course. But NIIGATA, like BETHEL, was on land and had radar. His arrival there would have been a matter of record. His flight plan called for him to arrive there at

19:30 GMT. Had KAL 007 not been destroyed first, he would have made it.

Based on this mandatory arrival time, if we backtrack from Niigata a distance of 485 NM corresponding to KAL 007's estimated route between NOKKA and NIIGATA, we are surprised to see that, had KAL 007 been true to its estimates, it could not have arrived at the point where fighter 805 of the American story is said to have fired his missiles at 18:26:20. If Captain Chun had wanted to abide by his NIIGATA ETA of 19:30, and I assume that he did, then at the time of its NOKKA ETA, 18:26, it would have been over La Pérouse Strait, over international waters between Sakhalin and Japan. It would not have been over Sakhalin in a position to have been shot down by a Soviet interceptor. Even before I obtained clear evidence that 805's shootdown sequence, like the other events on the Kirkpatrick tape, took place in the second hour, at 19:26 GMT, not 18:26, I realized that the time and distance factors of KAL 007's flight south toward Niigata were one more piece of evidence that 805's target could not have been the Korean airliner. Either KAL 007 had not overflown Sakhalin or it passed over the island nine minutes ahead of any other aircraft, which, to put it mildly, is improbable. Had it done so, it would have been shot down there.

The same reasoning applied to Kamchatka indicates that KAL 007 would have had to leave Kamchatka nine minutes earlier than previously announced. That is, at 16:59 GMT rather than 17:08 GMT.[1] Here, too, either KAL 007 crossed Kamchatka nine minutes ahead of the other aircraft or it didn't cross the peninsula at all.

KAL 007's transmission at 18:27 GMT has usually been thought to have been its last transmission and a distress call. In chapter 7, I made it clear that it was neither. The transmission started as a routine position report to say that KAL 007 had passed waypoint NOKKA, for which it had previously submitted an ETA of 18:26 GMT. After its initial call-up of Tokyo, and after receiving Tokyo's permission to go ahead with its message—all of which was routine procedure and none of which would have been done in an emergency—the airliner's transmission became almost indecipherable. That was because the balance of the transmission was unintentional and reflected sounds in the airliner's cockpit.

At the exact moment when the pilot was going to give his position report, an alarming transmission was heard on a loudspeaker in the KAL 007 cockpit on a frequency to which one of the airliner's radios was evidently tuned. Taken by surprise, the Korean pilot, who had not understood what was said because he was talking with Tokyo at the time, seems to have asked the sender to repeat the transmission, but forgot to change frequencies. That is why the sequence over the open mike can be heard on the Narita tape: "Repeat conditions . . ." and "Blood bath, really bad . . ."[2]

Three minutes later, at 18:30:05 GMT, on its assigned frequency, KAL 007 transmitted a lone "Roger." Was Captain Chun aware that his transmitter was still set to Tokyo Center's frequency? From this moment on he no longer returned calls from Tokyo ACC and continued on toward Niigata simulating radio failure.

The official explanation of why KAL 007's 18:27 transmission was cut short is, of course, that Soviet interceptor 805 had hit the airliner with a missile at 18:26 GMT. We have seen, however, that KAL 007 was not destroyed off Sakhalin but 400 miles to the south, off Honshu, that the allegedly 18:26 GMT transmission from 805, "I have accomplished the launch," was said at 19:26 GMT, not at 18:26 GMT, and that 805's target thus cannot have been the Korean airliner. We have also seen that at 18:30:05 KAL 007 transmitted a lone "Roger," and that it made two short series of transmissions, the first at 18:52 to KAL 015 and the second beginning at 19:09 to KAL 050.

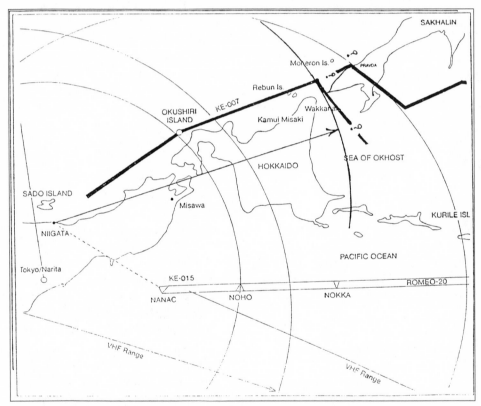

Figure 21. *KAL 007 may not have overflown Sakhalin. The airliner's position north of Niigata when it was destroyed and the speed it maintained to get there at that time suggest that it passed through La Pérouse Strait and could not have overflown Sakhalin.*

That the latter transmissions (19:09, 19:10 GMT) were recorded at Narita Airport by Tokyo Control shows that at the time KAL 007 was at an altitude and sufficiently far south to have been in line-of-sight range of it. That these transmissions, while identifiable by logic, ear, and voice-print analysis, avoided self-identification indicates that Captain Chun meant to leave Tokyo uncertain where it had been once it rejoined its assigned route at NIIGATA. So does the fact that on its trip south from Sakhalin, KAL 007 did not use the transponder code it should have used—2000 in Mode C as a civilian aircraft approaching Japanese radar-controlled airspace from an oceanic region—but appears to have mimicked KAL 015's transponder.

In Tokyo, to judge by his actions, the controller must have seen two aircraft on his radar screen converging toward Niigata. Both planes had called to report passing NOKKA about an hour ago, but only one of them—KAL 015—was correctly positioned on its route over the Pacific Ocean. The controller had great difficulty in identifying these two echoes on his radar screen. He suspected they were from the two Korean airliners, which should have been flying a few minutes apart on the same route. He had, however, lost radio contact with KAL 007; and when he asked KAL 015 for transponder code changes, both echoes appear to have responded to his request in the same way. The controller had already asked KAL 015 for three transponder code changes in rapid succession and had still not been able to resolve the ambiguity. One transponder code change would have been sufficient to identify any normally behaving aircraft.

Meanwhile, acting according to regulations, Tokyo ACC asked other aircraft in the vicinity of KAL 007 to try to contact it. At 18:54:48 GMT, KAL 007 answered, cryptically and in Korean, a call from KAL 015. KAL 015 answered, "Roger," indicating it understood, and didn't call back. It also failed to inform Tokyo that it had been able to contact KAL 007. It was now 19:06:30 GMT (04:06:30 Tokyo time, 06:06:30 Sakhalin time), early in the second hour of the air battle of Sakhalin up north. For the past thirty-nine minutes KAL 007 had failed to respond to calls from Tokyo since its interrupted communication of 18:27 GMT.

A half hour after an aircraft fails to respond, Air Traffic Control must issue an INCERFA. As its name indicates, an INCERFA is a phase of uncertainty, which assumes that the plane with which contact has been lost is flying normally and following its flight plan. For KAL 007, an INCERFA was issued at 18:56 GMT, a half hour after the plane's ETA at NOKKA, when it failed to complete its call to Tokyo reporting passage of the waypoint. Because of Teletype delays the INCERFA didn't go into effect until 19:05 GMT. When an INCERFA is in force, the aircraft's route is protected, and if necessary, other aircraft are rerouted to avoid possible collision. That was done with KAL 050. At 19:12:55, KAL 050 requested to be cleared from its present position "direct NOHO."[3] The Tokyo controller answered:

Korean Air Zero Five Zero, expect direct NOHO after reaching Flight Level Three Niner Zero, due to, uh, we have INCERFA traffic, your company Korean Air Zero Zero Seven. He is maintaining Flight Level Three Five Zero.

According to the INCERFA procedure, the Tokyo controller had to assume that KAL 007 was still flying normally at FL 350 and asked KAL 050 to climb first to FL 390 before authorizing it to proceed "direct NOHO," so as not to interfere with the assumed flight path of KAL 007.

As early as 19:07 GMT or barely two minutes after the INCERFA went into effect, the telephone rang in Tokyo ACC at Narita. "This is Sector One. Did you receive a call from the Rescue Center?"

"No!"[4]

Within the context of civil aviation procedure, nothing at this point justified a call from the Rescue Center. Normally that wouldn't happen until much later. After an INCERFA, ATC issues an ALERFA, or alert phase, which authorizes the civil aviation authorities to prepare search and rescue (SAR) activities that will be implemented during the distress phase, or DETRESFA. In the case of KAL 007, an ALERFA was issued at 19:22 GMT and a DETRESFA at 20:50 GMT. It is noteworthy, and still unexplained, that Sector One asked about a call from the Rescue Center at this time. The Rescue Center was part of the JMSA, the Japanese Maritime Safety Agency, which didn't receive word of the DETRESFA until it was declared by Air Traffic Control at 20:50 GMT. But word was, no doubt, informally getting around that something extraordinary was happening over Sakhalin.

A few moments after the telephone call by Sector One, KAL 050 succeeded in contacting KAL 007 and passed on to it a message from Tokyo Control asking it to contact Tokyo on "one one eight decimal niner" (118.9 MHz), as explained in chapter 7. Then, for three minutes, they talked cryptically in Korean. Obviously, KAL 007 did not want anyone to know that it had answered the call. It seemed caught between the desire to minimize radio contact and to calm the fears of other KAL people who were trying to contact it.

As we have seen in chapter 7, KAL 007 did not contact Tokyo as requested in the message passed on by KAL 050. With the possible exception of a call to KAL 015 and KAL 050 jointly at 19:13 GMT, KAL 007's transmissions to KAL 050 at 19:09 and 19:10 were its last. We do not know exactly when it was suddenly destroyed. It had to be in the next twenty or so minutes, before it would have identified itself to Tokyo and reported passing waypoint NIIGATA. After that, as an identified airliner on Japanese civilian radar, it would surely have escaped destruction. I found its debris on the Honshu beaches as far south as Murakami, 25 NM north of Niigata. If Murakami was abeam its crash point, KAL 007 would at the time have been less than four minutes from the waypoint, and (counting two or three more minutes to formulate its position report) six or seven minutes from safety.

Over the Sea of Japan not far from Niigata, KAL 007 was by no means alone. On the sea, the frigate USS *Badger,* and possibly other ships like USS *Elliot,* were not far away. According to the Soviets, *Badger* was on an intelligence-gathering mission off Vladivostok. But geography being what it is, Niigata is the point on the Japanese coast closest to Vladivostok and directly facing it on the shores of the Sea of Japan. In other words, "off Vladivostok" is simply another way to say "off Niigata." And in the sky at 19:13:54 GMT an American airplane, U.S. Navy Foxtrot Bravo 650, which had been flying under civilian air traffic control, was told by Tokyo that radar service was terminated. It asked permission to descend to FL 190 (19,000 feet) and gave its ETA at waypoint KADPO as 19:27 GMT, thirteen minutes later.

There were in all likelihood other aircraft in the sky off Niigata. Japanese P2J submarine surveillance aircraft patrol the Japanese coast twenty-four hours a day, 365 days a year. A little earlier that night the Japanese Air Force Northern Command had been put on high alert, DEFCON 3, one step below general mobilization. Seventy-two fighters, half the active fighters in the Japanese Air Force, had been assembled at Chitose air base.[5] On a much lower level of alert, two pairs of fighters are usually scrambled and sent out to the area perceived as threatening.[6] This time, in view of the commotion in the sky over Sakhalin, one or two squadrons of up to twelve aircraft each may have taken to the air. To judge by normal Japanese Air Self-Defense Forces procedure when fighters are scrambled in response to aircraft registered as threatening by the Badge System, some of the seventy-two fighters in this case may have been sent on airborne missions directly from their home bases before landing at Chitose. To this we should add any American fighters sent out from the U.S. bases of Yokota and Misawa.

At KAL 007's altitude, it would still be night for another minute or two: dawn would begin at 04:16 local Tokyo time or 19:16 GMT. At 19:14:56 GMT two carrier frequencies were heard over the radio, without any voice transmission, as if someone were trying to get a message through. At 19:16:23 GMT the Tokyo controller, in an effort to identify KAL 015's radar echo, asked for another transponder code change and a 35-degree heading change (from 245 to 280 degrees) "for confirmation."[7] That worked. Having positively identified KAL 015, Tokyo authorized it to continue "direct Niigata."

At 19:28:50 GMT, Navy Foxtrot Bravo 650 told Tokyo it had reached waypoint KADPO, canceled its IFR (instrument flight rules) flight plan, and left FL 190 (19,000 feet) for a lower altitude. It also left the civilian radio network and maintained communications exclusively with the military radio network. FB 650 then began patrolling in visual conditions just above the waves. But patrolling for what? And looking for what? It was barely dawn at sea level. The KADPO waypoint is located above the Sea of Japan, north of Niigata. It is also on the direct route from Sakhalin. That the KADPO area was significant in the KAL 007 case is consistent with the fact that, two weeks later, on September 13, 1983, two pairs of Japanese fighters were sent to intercept Soviet airplanes over KADPO. That the Japanese Defense Agency thought the place as well as the incident was important is indicated by the fact that JDA drew it—rather than the scores of other interceptions Japanese fighters were making all the time—to the attention of the international press.

What was FB 650's mission? We first hear it call Tokyo at 19:13:54 GMT giving its ETA at KADPO. That is close to the earliest time at which KAL 007 could have been destroyed and, in all likelihood, some minutes earlier. The Tokyo controller had his doubts about the identity of KAL 015 until 19:16:23 GMT, when he authorized it to fly "direct Niigata." That his uncertainty about KAL 015's identity was removed at that time could have been because KAL 007 had just then disappeared from his radar screen. Or it could have been because KAL 007 chose not to fly the dogleg the controller had demanded. That would have turned it away from NIIGATA, which it was intent on reaching without delay. The two empty carrier frequencies at 19:14:56 and the third at 19:24:05 seem, particularly in view of the interval of time between them, less likely to have marked KAL 007's sudden distress than to have been a covert means of communication by it, presumably intended for KAL 015.

U.S. Navy Foxtrot Bravo 650 was thus headed for KADPO before KAL 007 met its still unknown nemesis. How could FB 650 have known that there would be something of interest on the surface of the water? And that it would be of sufficient importance to look for it in very uncertain light? Or, while FB 650 was on its way to KADPO, was its mission modified by someone with real-time, or virtually real-time, knowledge of the disaster?

The radio silence of KAL 007 did not seem to affect KAL 015 unduly. Asked by Tokyo Control to try to contact its flight companion, KAL 015's attempts to contact KAL 007 did not display a sense of urgency; and as if unconcerned with the issue, it never questioned Tokyo Control about 007's whereabouts. Yet the two pilots were friends. Captain Park, the pilot of KAL 015, had been Chun Byung-In's squadron leader when they were both serving in the Korean Air Force. Did Park's friendship suddenly fail in a moment of weakness, or did he think that his friend was in no danger? The coolness, bordering on indifference, shown by KAL 015 toward the fate of KAL 007 reached its peak at 19:44:40 GMT when Tokyo called KAL 015 to tell it they still hadn't been able to contact KAL 007 and asked the pilot if he had been able to contact the missing plane. KAL 015 answered dryly, "Negative contact. This is KAL 015." Then, when signing off with Tokyo Control before contacting Taegu Control, KAL 015 had this curious departing comment: "Roger, take it easy."

At first sight this seems a heartless remark. It may show, however, that KAL 015 assumed at the time that KAL 007 was no longer in danger and was calmly flying toward Seoul. Park may have thought that Chun wanted to maintain radio silence all the way to Seoul.

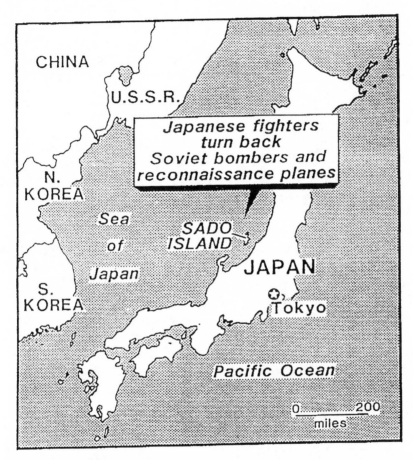

Figure 22. Waypoint KADPO, where FB 650 began its low-altitude patrol and near where I have located KAL 007's crash. The UPI caption reads: "Japanese fighters scrambled on September 13, 1983, to turn back two Soviet bombers and two reconnaissance planes that flew 100 miles off Japan shortly after Soviet warships ended an exercise in the Sea of Japan where a Korean airliner was shot down."[8]

By contrast, KAL 050, which seems to have had no advance knowledge of KAL 007's odd activities, was genuinely concerned about KAL 007's whereabouts. At 19:42:33 GMT, twelve minutes after KAL 007 failed to report passing Niigata, KAL 050 asked Tokyo Control if they had any news about 007:

TOKYO CONTROL, THIS IS KOREAN AIR ZERO FIVE ZERO. DID YOU CONTACT, AH, RADAR CONTACT, ZERO ZERO SEVEN NOW?

Tokyo, of course, replied that it had not.

What happened to KAL 007 between 19:12 and 19:30 GMT? The plane was out of range of Soviet interceptors, so a shootdown by the Soviets north of Niigata seems unlikely. Catastrophe as a delayed result of damage sustained at Soviet hands farther north also seems unlikely. KAL 007 had been communicating, normally if ambiguously, with other KAL planes long after it left Sakhalin. It never sent a distress message and never signaled any problem. It vanished suddenly, minutes before reaching Niigata, without any apparent reason.

Among the several things that could have happened to it, two are suggested by analogy and by facts that came to my attention in my investigation. One, the airliner was shot down by the Americans under the mistaken impression it was a Soviet aircraft bent on retaliation for what had happened up north. Or, it was shot down by the Japanese under the mistaken impression it was a Soviet aircraft threatening Japan in a widening conflict.

The *Vincennes* Syndrome

Could KAL 007 have been destroyed by mistake, under the same conditions that led to the destruction of the Iranian Airbus by the crew of the USS *Vincennes*? Critics of this theory might remark that a Boeing 747 is a large aircraft and would be immediately obvious on a radar screen. How could a large civilian airliner be confused with an enemy attack aircraft? The tragic death of 293 passengers on the Airbus shows that it could. Captain Rogers of the USS *Vincennes* shot one down thinking it was an F-14 on its way to attack his ship. The *Vincennes* was equipped with the Aegis radar detection system, the most modern in the American fleet, which is to say, the most advanced in the world.

The Airbus had taken off shortly before from Bandar-Abbas, a civilian airport. Although it was an Iranian airplane at an Iranian airport, it carried out all its communications with the control tower in English. The *Vincennes* was monitoring these communications in real time and knew the airplane taking off was a civilian airliner. The plane was then in a slow climb over the Persian Gulf, in the center of an international airway. It displayed all the characteristics of a commercial airliner, and nothing in its behavior threatened the warship. It all happened in Captain Rogers's mind, and he gave the order to fire on the plane. His judgment was clouded by fear of reprisal for his earlier attack on Iranian patrol boats. Although the plane in the sky was a big, peaceful passenger plane, Captain Rogers saw a small and aggressive F-14. Even though the radar indicated that the plane was climbing normally, he saw it go into a dive. And when the radar showed that the plane was flying steadily in the center of an international air route, he thought the plane had turned and was heading for his ship. When the Airbus was twenty miles away, he fired his missiles, killing all 293 aboard.

The American military presence in Japan was substantial, with Air Force bases at Misawa and Yokota and a naval base at Atsugi. At the time KAL 007 was destroyed, the United States no doubt had aircraft in the air and vessels at sea that were not a direct part of the air battle of Sakhalin. Was KAL 007 a victim of the *Vincennes* syndrome? The circumstances are similar: a commercial airliner appears in the sky shortly after some form of armed aggression in the vicinity (in this case the overflight of Sakhalin). A threat is perceived by a defense system that fears reprisals. The civilian plane is assumed to be an attack plane, though cooler heads would have identified it as an airliner.

Debris N3

The hypothesis that KAL 007 might have been shot down in error by a friendly missile may be supported by material evidence: debris N3, which was first described as the aileron of a small plane. This debris was found at the same time, and in the same current stream, as a debris from the Korean airliner. That suggests it fell into the water near and was contemporaneous with the airliner's destruction.

As I described in chapter 5, in November 1989 friends in the JMSA showed me a photograph of the piece of debris in the greatest secrecy and for a few moments only. This enabled me to form a more accurate idea of the nature of the debris. It carried traces of fingerprints on the fresh soot with which it was covered. The mark N3 appeared clearly on the lower right-hand corner, indicating a non-Soviet origin. A letter shaped like our *N* does not exist in the Cyrillic alphabet. The general shape of the debris convinced me that it was more likely to be a rudder than an aileron. Later I examined other photographs of N3. I was shown three pictures, one of which was of the other side of the debris, which I had not seen before. It clearly revealed the trim tab's control mechanism, composed of a circular actuator attached to the rudder by six bolts and a small rod connected to the trim. The mechanism extended about an inch from the surface of the rudder and must have been protected by a streamlined fairing. I was still unable to see the serial number 7111032 (mentioned on the sketch in the JMSA report we had previously been given),[9] either because the marking was too small to see or, as I had begun to suspect, because another, identical piece of debris bore the serial number.

That N3 was highly sensitive in the minds of the Japanese was confirmed by two admirals of the JMSA, one retired, the other on active duty. At the time of the shootdown, Admiral Kato was on duty in Hokkaido and took part in the search operation. He had recently retired when I met him in Tokyo, where he agreed to see me in the offices of the company of which he was vice president. As soon as I arrived, Admiral Kato told me he wasn't surprised by my visit. He had been informed of my progress on Hokkaido and my visits to the various JMSA bases. I wondered why this retired admiral was so interested in my investigation. When I mentioned debris N3, he told me he knew about my interest but added that the debris didn't exist, that nothing like it had been found by the JMSA. When I insisted and showed him the JMSA report and the sketch, he told me that the person who had drawn up the report had made an error. But I had already seen the photographs of N3 and knew the admiral wasn't telling the truth. Why would he want to convince me that N3 didn't exist? Why was it so important?

Adm. Kessoku Konomu, whom I also asked to see, was still on active duty and commanded the Second region of the JMSA at Yokohama when I met him. He gave me a warm reception at JMSA headquarters there. When I spoke to him about N3, he told me at once that he had personally seen the fragment, which appeared to be the rudder of a supersonic aircraft, "probably Soviet." But he added that it had nothing to do with KAL 007. It was an old piece of debris that had been floating in the water for a long time and had been covered with seaweed when found. Having seen the photographs, I thought it obvious that the admiral was trying to belittle its significance. The fragment wasn't covered with seaweed and hadn't been in the water long. The fresh soot on its surface proved this. And the presence of the letter *N* showed that N3 had not come from a Soviet aircraft.

I didn't discuss my doubts with the admiral, but asked him if he knew where the debris was now. Since it hadn't come from KAL 007, it shouldn't have been returned to Korean Air Lines. Without hesitation the admiral said, "Both of them are at the Chitose air base." He paused and I kept silent. The admiral realized he had said too much. He rummaged around in my documents, which were on the table, and pulled out the copy of the JMSA report. "Of course there were two! It says so right here." I was secretly delighted because the admiral's comments supported my own conclusions. There were two N3 fragments. Seeing that the report only mentioned one N3 fragment, the admiral now reversed his position and said he had been mistaken, there was only one fragment.

Later, after several months of haggling, and after having received authorization from a "very high level," JMSA headquarters in Tokyo provided me with an official photograph of N3. I had been promised a set of photographs, but one picture was better than nothing. I had it enlarged so I could study it. Even with a magnifying glass it was impossible to see the serial number 7111032. But the N3 marking was obvious.

Upon closer examination the photograph showed a number of details that revealed N3 wasn't an airplane rudder but the rear fin of a missile. What had been taken for a trim tab was the missile's rudder. But a small rudder, no more than twenty-one by nine centimeters (eight by four inches). The soot that covered the fragment was deep black and oily, and the fingerprints of the JMSA personnel who had handled it were easily visible. This oily soot had not come from a missile explosion. It was from burning kerosene. That implied the fin had been covered with it during the few seconds it had passed through the wake of a jet engine. The missile would thus have been piloted by an infrared guidance system. The rudder was bent toward the right at an angle of roughly ten degrees. The missile must have just made a slight change in its trajectory, then exploded in flight upon impact with its target or in close proximity to it.

Figure 23. *The N3 debris. The JMSA photograph eventually given to me with high-level Japanese government clearance shows the debris to be part of a missile fin.*

Admirals Kato and Konomu must have known the importance, and the implications, of N3 because both of them tried to hide it. One by denying its existence, the other by denying its origin. The JMSA was fully aware of the nature of the debris. After having registered the recovery from the sea of what was described as the aileron of a civilian light airplane, the report, initially written to be made public, had in fact been kept secret. JMSA personnel were forbidden to mention it or display the photographs. Also, both JMSA headquarters and the Japanese government were aware of my attempts to identify the debris, and the JMSA knew exactly what it was doing when it turned over the photograph of N3 to me after receiving authorization.

While recognizing the importance that the Japanese government obviously attaches to the N3 fragment, John Keppel has reservations about its authenticity as part of a missile that struck KAL 007. For one thing, perhaps as a result of sweeping done by the line of Korean fishing boats south of Moneron, KAL 007 floating debris was not found by JMSA due north of Moneron as the N3 piece was. Another thing that bothers him and me is that we have not been able to find a surface-to-air or air-to-air missile in use in 1983 likely to have been used off Japan by either the United States or the Japanese that fits the N3 fragment. Another problem with regarding the debris as part of the missile that destroyed KAL 007 is that it was a heat-seeking missile. The vertical fin of the tail assembly of the Korean airliner fragmented, but a Boeing 747 has no engine in the tail. How would a heat-seeking missile have hit the tail? All this being said, and even if the N3 debris is wholly unrelated, it remains possible that one or perhaps two missiles from a U.S. naval vessel or aircraft, fired in error as in the *Vincennes*/Airbus disaster, destroyed the Korean airliner.

A Japanese Pilot?

The day after Asahi Television's Saturday, March 23, 1991, broadcast of "The Scoop," devoted to KAL 007, it received a number of calls from viewers. Among them was an anonymous caller, a man who claimed to know who had shot down the Korean airliner. "All your stories are nonsense. At that time I was in the Air Self-Defense Force and serving at the Chitose Air Base in Hokkaido. We're the ones who shot it down. I know the pilot who fired the missile. He was in our regiment. He's retired now, working as a taxi driver."

The man refused to say more and no one took his story seriously. No one except my friend Osaki. While preparing for the broadcast, we had worked together for more than a month and had been together at the Iwatsu laboratories. And it was to Osaki, when he was in Moscow, that I had sent the fax of the voice prints to be given to Andrei Illesh, with whom Asahi TV wanted to trade favors. Osaki was familiar with Dr. Tsuboi's work and persuaded the Iwatsu lab to perform the analysis. He knew Flight 007 fell near Niigata. And he also knew that the anonymous caller's story was plausible. Osaki investigated and discovered a taxi company in Tokyo staffed by retired members of the armed forces. Unfortunately that was as far as he got, and the mystery of the anonymous caller remains unsolved.

However, we know that before KAL 007 was destroyed, half the

Japanese fighter force had been moved north to Chitose as an emergency measure. Some of it was, no doubt, airborne. In the light of JASDF procedures, it is entirely plausible that two pairs of fighters would have been directed by the Badge System to intercept the aircraft flying south off the west coast of Hokkaido and Honshu. The Japanese might not yet have been able to identify that aircraft as KAL 007 or as perhaps KAL 007. It is conceivable that JASDF commanders might have ordered their interceptors to destroy it.

What do we know that may be relevant? One consideration is troublesome. Six of the Japanese fighters at Chitose came from Komatsu. The direct route from Komatsu to Chitose passes above Niigata and Waypoint KADPO. The armed fighters were in the area where KAL 007 was destroyed at the time of its destruction. We also need to consider the relationship between the means of attack and the damage KAL 007 suffered. It seems unlikely that a heat-seeking missile would have hit KAL 007's engineless tail. A radar-guided missile fired from behind could have, but it would not have resulted in the damage to KAL 007's tail. Pieces of the lower part of the vertical fin, which bore the airliner's registration number, were found by the Hokkaido police on a Sea of Okhotsk beach and at the same time by the Russians south of Nevelsk. The Japanese press photographs of the largest piece show it to be bowed outward. This indicates pressure from the inside. A radar-guided missile, whether or not it had a proximity fuse (which would have exploded it some fifty feet from the aircraft), would have applied external, not internal, pressure to this part of the vertical fin.

We should, however, recognize that the anonymous telephone caller who said that the JASDF did in fact shoot down the airliner gains credence from the fact that what he said was in effect a public admission—the call was made to a TV station—of the air battle of Sakhalin. If KAL 007 were known to have been destroyed off Honshu, the wreckage up north would have been seen to have been that of military aircraft. It was the unacknowledged disappearance of the airliner in the south that made possible the cover-up of the disaster in the north. That neither Japan nor the United States wanted the truth to come out argues against the possibility that the call was intentional disinformation.

A Bomb?

Col. Fletcher Prouty, a retired U.S. Air Force intelligence officer of wide experience, has said that the United States intentionally destroyed KAL 007 by activating a previously planted explosive charge. He says that the Korean airliner never left its assigned course, was destroyed off the Pacific coast of Japan over the Kuril Trench, and now rests in this deepest part of the world's oceans.[10] It is technically feasible for the airliner to have been destroyed by a radio-activated bomb. On its route south from La Pérouse Strait, KAL 007 was continuously within line-of-sight radio range of U.S. installations at Wakkanai[11] and Misawa. But Colonel Prouty is surely wrong in saying that the airliner was destroyed over the Pacific. The debris and oceanographic evidence I have discussed in chapter 4 makes it unequivocally clear that it was destroyed over the Sea of Japan.

At this stage the data are insufficient for me to decide the proximate cause of the airliner's destruction. What is at stake is far too serious to decide on the basis of less than conclusive evidence. There is, however, no such uncertainty as to the ultimate cause. Had KAL 007 flown R-20 and the normal route across Honshu to Niigata, there is no question that the abnormal fate it suffered, however it came about, would not have happened.

The Need for a Public Investigation

What I have said with respect to both the N3 debris and the anonymous telephone call illustrates a number of the technical aspects of the airliner's destruction that should be responsibly and rigorously studied by a U.S. public investigation. The Russian Federation, Japan, and the Republic of Korea would in all likelihood cooperate with one if they were convinced it was undertaken seriously and with determination. It could, among other things, help to determine the proximate cause of the airliner's destruction.

Experts should study the nature of the damage to the airliner's tail. In my discussion of the Japanese pilot, I drew attention to the fragmentation of the vertical fin. It is unusual. Tail assemblies often survive a crash—even a bombing, as was the case with the Boeing 747 Pan American 103, which was destroyed over Lockerbie in Scotland in 1988.

The tail assembly of the Japanese short-range 747 that crashed in 1985 separated from the aircraft as a result of the sudden surge of pressure inside the tail when the rear pressure bulkhead failed. The section of the tail assembly that was open to pressure from inside the aircraft was aft of the pressure bulkhead. Explosive pressure released by the bulkhead failure rushed into this aperture and blew off most of the tail assembly. After the 1985 crash this opening to the tail assembly on 747s was sealed off from pressure from inside the aircraft.

An amateur photographer took a picture, carried by the press, of the Japanese 747 in the air after it had lost the bulk of the tail assembly. The photograph showed that, in contrast to what happened to KAL 007, on the Japanese 747 the leading part of the vertical fin remained intact and remained attached to the aircraft. It is structurally separate from the rest of the tail and firmly attached to the fuselage. The area is normally the most secure part of the aircraft. That is why the black boxes aboard KAL 007 were located in a rear part of the cabin ceiling, just below the leading edge of the vertical fin. That on the Korean airliner this section of fin was broken into substantial pieces that were bowed outward suggests localized and relatively moderate explosive pressure from inside that part of fin.[12]

What is needed here is to determine the exact nature and location of the explosive pressure that fragmented the vertical fin. Was the pressure indeed from inside the aircraft, and if so, how did that come about? What were the severity and the breadth of the explosive pressure in the tail? Would they account for the nature of other damage the airliner appears to have suffered at the time? There are two relevant points here. The cockpit crew may have been knocked out at the same time as the explosion in the tail. But much of the fuselage seems to have remained intact. The question raised is, of course, whether KAL 007 may have suffered two simultaneous or virtually simultaneous explosions.

As to the fuselage, after or during the disaster there clearly was some access to the cabin. Identification cards from two persons known to have been aboard KAL 007, and a business card from a third, were found on a Hokkaido beach on the Sea of Okhotsk. However, most of the aircraft's fuselage seems to have remained intact, imprisoning its victims. No bodies from the airliner were found. That nothing from the baggage compartment was found implies that it was not broken open.

What suggests that the cockpit crew may have been knocked out at the same time as the tail fragmented? It is the fact that we do not have anything convincing in the way of a postexplosion radio transmission from the cockpit crew. They would almost surely have sent one if all that had happened to the airliner had been a localized explosion in the tail. Under such circumstances the airliner would have remained relatively airworthy. The pilot of the Japanese 747, of which the bulk of the tail assembly had been blown off, was able to crudely maneuver his aircraft for twenty minutes before trying a grazing crash landing on wooded land, with disastrous results.

While we have the possible KAL 007 joint call to KAL 015 and KAL 050 at 19:13 GMT, and the two voiceless carrier-wave signals at 19:14:56 and a third at 19:24:05, none of these seem convincing as a postdisaster distress call. In the light of the KAL 007 debris as far south as Murakami, the 19:24:05 carrier wave would be a candidate were it not for the two others ten minutes earlier, which may have been signals of another type. It is, of course, possible that a final distress call has been removed from the Narita tape. But if so, KAL 015 would have heard it and would not later have been so lighthearted about its sister ship.

A public investigation should not, of course, confine itself to the question of how the airliner was destroyed. Why is also to the point. Many aspects of the airliner's behavior demand examination to show whether its cockpit crew was wittingly taking part in the ill-advised and disastrous intelligence and provocation mission the United States staged that night. In establishing the relationship between the two disasters, the air battle of Sakhalin and the destruction of KAL 007, the investigation would have an advantage my own has not had—the ability to question under oath people who took part in the intelligence operation, its planning, approval, execution, and cover-up. I mention the latter for good reason. The destruction of the airliner did not mean the end of improper and no doubt illegal activities in connection with KAL 007.

The Case for Truth

On the morning of September 1, 1983, Secretary of State George Shultz was on the verge of tears as he announced the destruction of the airliner and the alleged Soviet atrocity. No doubt Shultz spoke from distress over the 269 airline passengers and crew who had died on KAL 007 some nineteen hours earlier. By the time he spoke, however, he must have realized that the twin disasters, the air battle of Sakhalin and the destruction of the airliner, were the result of a U.S. clandestine operation that had gone dreadfully wrong. It had been directed against his own policies as well as against the Soviets.

From the beginning, important elements of the Reagan administration had sought a renewed Cold War. Secretary of Defense Caspar Weinberger, Director of Central Intelligence William Casey, and National Security Adviser William Clark emphasized confrontation rather than détente: to win congressional approval of a large military budget, to isolate the Soviet Union internationally, and to roll back Soviet influence in the Third World. No doubt Shultz shared many of these goals. But he also tried to maintain some moderation in U.S.-Soviet relations. That effort was now in jeopardy.

The operation planned in conjunction with KAL 007's flight must have appeared as logical to its planners as it was provocative to the Soviets. They faced a battery of intruders including, they were led to believe, a civilian airliner. If they tried to stop them, they risked committing an atrocity. If they allowed them to pass through unharmed, they would be conceding American air supremacy over a highly strategic part of Soviet territory.

The operation was a bold exercise in the new doctrine of "lateral escalation." Advocates of this doctrine held that the United States could respond to Soviet actions in one place—say, Europe or the Middle East—by exploiting vulnerabilities elsewhere. The U.S. could, moreover, deter undesirable Soviet initiatives by demonstrating such capabilities in advance. Few areas were more sensitive than the Kamchatka Peninsula, the Sea of Okhotsk, and Sakhalin Island, home base of the Soviets' missile-firing submarines essential to their nuclear deterrent. A successful large-scale U.S. overflight of this territory would make its vulnerability clear to both sides and would give the United States presumptive superiority in future crises.

But assuming the U.S. planners did not intend the actual results, including the death of the civilian airline passengers, the operation shows a level of miscalculation equal to its boldness. The miscalculation lay in putting too large a military overflight in a strategically sensitive area and coupling the whole with the flight of a civilian airliner. We do not know exactly how many U.S. airplanes were involved in the initial wave that hit Sakhalin at the time the Korean airliner, we believe, passed through La Pérouse Strait just to the south of Sakhalin Island. Clearly, there were several. That caused a substantial Soviet response.

Two factors may have deprived the U.S. military of the information it needed to understand what the Soviets were doing. The National Security Agency, it is true, intercepted the Soviets' radio communications and reported on them immediately. But the distribution of the NSA summaries appears to have been wider among U.S. forces in the Pacific (CINCPAC) than the few, if any, recipients who had been fully briefed on the operation. This invited misunderstanding of the Soviet response. Moreover, since the operation was clandestine, it presumably operated under the control of the National Security Council and Casey through supersecret "back channels." If it had been run through the normal military chain of command, that would, of course, have led the U.S. forces to understand what the Soviets were reacting to.

Elements of the U.S. forces, not understanding what the United States itself was doing, appear to have interpreted the Soviets' reactions to the intruding aircraft as reflecting aggressive intentions that did not in this instance exist. The number of aircraft casualties the United States suffered at Sakhalin—recall that there were ten or more crashes at sea and some three on land—makes it seem likely that CINCPAC committed additional forces to what was already a battle. The affair threatened to spin out of control. In his book Hersh writes:

> *Some senior Air Force and Navy officers in the Pacific, who were provided with summaries of the NSA cable traffic, "got emotional," as one officer recalled, and began formulating actions for retaliation against the Soviet Union, actions "that could have started World War III."* [1]

No doubt. But the planned operation itself was in line with Reagan administration military policy in that it put the burden of prudence entirely on the Soviets. After the U.S. overflights of the Kurils earlier in the year, the Soviets had resolved they would not let another U.S. provocation go unopposed. That, however, the operation did not result in World War III was due at least as much to the Soviets' prudence in limiting the scope of their reaction as it was to any good sense the United States may have generated at the last minute.

How could a U.S. action of that degree of folly have been conceived, planned, and set in motion? Its genesis may have been much more normal than the final product. It seems likely to have started with the U.S. military's wish to utilize its U.S.'s new capabilities in space to improve intelligence gathering and communications networking. They were looking for a way to send information from reconnaissance satellites directly to cruise missiles and strategic bombers approaching the Soviet Union.

Previously, information from reconnaissance satellites had to be dropped by canister and parachute over Hawaii and Big Pine in Australia, recovered, and analyzed. Only then could it be transmitted to the user. But by August 1983 the United States could for the first time process global battlefield intelligence information in real time. On the night in question two Ferret satellites were in position to collect information on Soviet air-defense activities and communications and could send it on via Tracking Data and Relay Satellite No. 1 (TDRS One) and military communications satellites in elliptical orbit high over the pole. The Shuttle STS-8 *(Challenger),* also in orbit at the time, may or may not have had a role in the exercise that was planned.

Something, however, was needed to turn on the Soviet air defenses and communications. Satellites were predictable, and if all that was going on was that one was passing overhead, the Soviets could leave their aircraft on the ground and their radars switched off. We have no hard evidence on the point, but it seems likely that Casey told the National Security Council that, in conjunction with Clark and a few others of the NSC staff, he would take care of any planning and execution that were needed to get Soviet air defenses to operate in a big way. The planning of the operation may thus have started with a relatively normal military wish to develop new capabilities. But with Casey, Clark, and some other hard-liners involved, the broader (and supremely unwise) strategic provocation objectives seem to have taken over.

Regardless of the operation's goals, it went terribly wrong in execution, leading in the eyes of the Reagan administration to the need for immediate remedial action. As a result of emergency work done by CIA during the evening and night of August 31, when it had a chance to review the intelligence information on the disaster, the U.S. government was able to transform what threatened to be a major political setback into a global propaganda success. The transformed account of events discredited the Soviet Union, contributed to the subsequent passage of the U.S. military budget (which had been in some trouble) through Congress in maximal form, overcame objections to the emplacement of Pershing II and cruise missiles in Europe, and did much to break the back of the peace movement in Europe and the United States. All this, based on the blunder of the operation and the big lie of the cover-up.

Taken together, the blunder and the lie committed the U.S. government to a decade of deceiving its own public and the world. The Departments of Defense, Transportation, State, and Justice were involved in the deception, sometimes illegally. The governments of Japan, South Korea, France, and Russia were drawn into the cover-up. Two investigations by one of the U.N. specialized agencies, the International Civil Aviation Organization, were suborned, and the solemn approval of the forty governments represented on its council of the two ICAO reports, which in effect embodied the U.S. cover story, was obtained.

But when did the cover-up begin? When Secretary Shultz read the bold and mendacious statement CIA had prepared for him? Possibly. But if so, we would need to accept that the cornerstone of the cover-up had been partly accidental—the destruction of KAL 007 before it reached Niigata and before its position had become a matter of Japanese government record. If the Korean airliner, which seems likely not to have overflown any Soviet territory, had not been destroyed in the south and that fact had not been suppressed, the Soviets could not have been accused of an atrocity. And the search for military debris in the north could not have been presented as a search for the Korean airliner. The ugly facts of the military overflights and the air battle of Sakhalin would have come out. The alternative to the accidental destruction of the airliner is, of course, its intentional destruction as the first step in the cover-up.

Once the decision had been made to suppress the truth, whatever it was in this instance, a substitute for it had to be put forward. Shultz's statement committed the United States to the main lines of the cover story. The Korean airliner had been hit by a missile from a Soviet interceptor at 18:26 GMT. By 18:30 it had descended to 5,000 meters. It had crashed into the sea off Sakhalin at 18:38.

An early step was to get the statements made by Japan, which had first-class radar and signals intelligence of its own, in line with the American position. That initially presented some problems. Evidently, soon after the events, themselves, the Japanese had been talked into telling the story of a single intrusion, interception, and shootdown—that is to say, they had been talked into burying the truth about a dangerous battle that, without coordination with them, had been conducted on their doorstep.

But, as we have seen, their initial statement told the story of an interception and shootdown significantly different from the one described in the American version of events. The Japanese implied that a Soviet interceptor had fired at an intruder, which "looked like the Korean airliner," shortly before 18:25 GMT and said that the intruder had exploded at altitude at 18:29—clearly not the missile-firing at 18:26 and the crash into the sea at 18:38, also allegedly of the Korean airliner, of which the American story told.

It took a week of U.S. pressure, applied through the Foreign Ministry, the chief cabinet secretary, and other civilian parts of the Japanese government, to overcome the resistance of the Japanese military, and to get the government of Japan to switch to the American version of events. Once the government of Japan was securely committed to the American cover story, it could not use its knowledge of the truth as a bargaining chip in its dealings with the United States. What went into the manufacture of this straitjacket?

The American position was largely based on the tape of the intercepted voices of the Soviet pilots over Sakhalin that Ambassador Kirkpatrick released to the U.N. Security Council on September 7, 1983. It had been, she said, recorded by the Japanese. When, however, Japan gave the original tape, which was more than two hours long, to the United States, the U.S. had promised not to make its origin public.

Although Mrs. Kirkpatrick told the Security Council that the tape she played had been recorded by a voice-actuated recorder and had not been edited, electronic analysis done at the University of Washington shows that neither was the case. The shutdowns between transmissions, allegedly caused by the voice-actuated recorder, were too clean to have been made by a transistor, which would not have cooled so rapidly. Spectrographic examination of the tape showed other splice lines.[2]

In reneging on its promise to keep its acquisition of the Japanese tape secret, in extracting from it only the second hour, in misstating its time by an hour, in taking from the second hour the 805 shootdown sequence as the centerpiece of the cover-up, and in inducing the Japanese publicly to adopt these falsifications in their own position, the United States put the Japanese administration in a position where disclosure of the truth would have been politically damaging to it. It would have looked like the U.S.'s running dog. Equally important in binding it to silence was the fact that a passenger-filled civilian airliner, which Japan had the means to identify, had crashed just off its coast and no search-and-rescue operation for it had been mounted.

For different reasons, much the same thing happened with the USSR, later Russia, though in this case acceptance of the U.S. position took place in two stages, of which the second was not completed for ten years. The first stage took place at Marshal Ogarkov's September 9, 1983, press conference when he told the story of the shootdown of an aircraft other than KAL 007 in sufficiently ambiguous terms so that the world took it for an admission that the USSR had shot down the airliner. The second stage was completed in January 1993 when Russia handed over to the ICAO a new version of black-box recordings allegedly from the Korean airliner, which this time had the airliner struck by a missile at 18:26 GMT, as the Americans insisted, rather than at 18:24, which had until then been a constant in the Russian version of events.

In the beginning the force bearing on the Soviets was the not unjustified fear of war with the United States. Subsequently that was replaced by the Soviet Union's, then Russia's, need for the U.S.'s economic help, through such institutions as the International Monetary Fund, and in the world market.

As we have seen in the *Izvestiya* articles and in the communications transcripts given the ICAO in 1993, Soviet submission to the U.S. will was accompanied by details in the fine print that contradicted the official story. Were these revealing details intended as support for a possible future switch of position and revelation of what actually happened? Or were they intended to be understood by the CIA as a form of pressure on the United States, whose help the USSR/Russia badly needed? Or were they reflections of internal conflicts stemming in particular from the Soviet military's resentment at being publicly blamed for an atrocity they had not committed? Perhaps a little of all three.

The United States had lost ten or so aircraft on the night of August 31/September 1. Why did it choose Soviet interceptor 805's shootdown rather than one of the others to represent the destruction of KAL 007? We do not know. Perhaps because the sequence was dramatic and could be used effectively on TV by President Reagan and in Ambassador Kirkpatrick's high-tech presentation before the U.N. Security Council. Perhaps because, once the time had been falsified by an hour, it could be plausibly connected up with KAL 007's communications and flight schedule and with the 18:38 crash of which Secretary Shultz spoke.

That crash was, no doubt, the one 16 NM northwest of Moneron on which U.S. Navy Task Force 71 concentrated its search despite the Soviets' obvious raising of debris from other crash sites. A plane, perhaps an E-2 Navy AWACs, whose electronic gear was considered even more sensitive than that of an RC-135, lay on the bottom there. The important thing was to have the world believe that the aircraft that crashed northwest of Moneron was the Korean airliner and that it had crashed at 18:38. Since KAL 007 had crashed the same night, no one would notice the substitution so long as it had vanished and would stay that way and so long as it could be denied that anything had been found on the bottom. While there were obvious loose ends in this part of the cover-up, it was good enough for the media, which seem to have felt that prudence dictated a minimum of curiosity.

After successfully aligning the Japanese with the U.S. story of the airliner's alleged shootdown over Sakhalin, and after Ogarkov had signaled that the U.S.S.R. did not intend to challenge the U.S. directly over what had happened, the United States still felt that some form of international approval for its account of events was necessary. For this purpose it chose the ICAO, perhaps the U.N.s' specialized agency most securely under its influence. The

ICAO had, moreover, limited investigative capabilities of its own and had to rely on evidence given it by national governments.

In late December 1983 the ICAO completed its first report on the KAL 007 disaster. With the authority of the United Nations, it laid out the main elements of the cover story—the airliner had gone off course unwittingly as a result of an undetected navigation error and had been shot down by the Soviets. In saying this, the ICAO demonstrated its fundamental lack of independence from the United States.

Getting the ICAO to front for it was in line with the cautious measures of self-protection U.S. intelligence took after its initial boldness. Prominent among these were to make an absolute minimum of governmental statements of a factual nature; to arrange for statements in defense of its position to be made almost exclusively by others (e.g., by the ICAO and "the Truth Squad," see below); to use the factual data of other states rather than introduce any of its own (e.g., the Kirkpatrick and Narita tapes, both Japanese); and to have the falsification of the record appear in the material of other states (e.g., the black-box recordings given the ICAO by the Russians—see below). In the event of disclosure, the hand of the United States in the falsification would not show or would at least be plausibly deniable.

Although U.S. intelligence has followed its in-house rules for self-protection, the history of the KAL 007 cover-up has been marked by instability, and over the years a pattern became apparent. The United States arranged, as safely and noncommittally as possible, for a necessary minimum of "information" to be made public. Sooner or later this "information" came under scrutiny by writers and other critics, who, despite their very limited numbers, raised embarrassing questions. U.S. intelligence, rightly or wrongly, felt that these should not be left unanswered. It again arranged, again indirectly, for more "information" to be made public—and we were off on another cycle. There have been four stages of the process.

Once released, the 1983 ICAO report was hailed as definitive by the United States and was accepted without questions by the media and, on the surface at least, by the public, although many individuals had their private doubts. A few careful and scholarly critics, notably R. W. Johnson of Magdalen College, Oxford, and David Pearson, then a Ph.D. candidate at Yale, wrote useful books throwing doubt on the official story, which were passed over in silence by the ever-cautious media.

In 1985 the Japanese inquiry group's members in the Diet were successful in getting the Nakasone government to release speed and altitude data supposedly relating to the Korean airliner, which did not match the official U.S. and ICAO story. To placate its parliamentary critics the Nakasone government also released the Narita tape of air-traffic-control communications with KAL 007, KAL 015, and KAL 050. The tape contained initially unexamined but explosive information on KAL 007's radio transmissions that occured after the official story said the airliner had been shot down. Also worrying to the American intelligence officers was, I believe, the 1989 Tokyo press conference in which I discussed evidence pointing to the air battle of Sakhalin and KAL 007's destruction in the south.

Apparently early in 1990, *Izvestiya* undertook groundwork for its series on KAL 007, which started in earnest early in 1991. The changed political atmosphere in the U.S.S.R. under Gorbachev no doubt played an important role in stimulating *Izvestiya*'s ostensibly sensational exercise in glasnost (openness). So did pressure for information on the airliner and its victims from four U.S. senators (Bradley, Kennedy, Levin, and Nunn), aware that elements of the official story were open to question and writing on behalf of the U.S. next of kin.

The Department of State, which obviously wanted Gorbachev to do something that would dispose of the KAL 007 case once and for all, was urging him to release the official 1983 Soviet government report on the case. There may also have been less visible influences exerted by the U.S. extreme right and U.S. intelligence. According to the *Washington Times* at least one American citizen, James E. Oberg, played a role in the preliminary *Izvestiya* investigation.[3] Oberg was a prominent member of the small group of people referred to privately by one of the few U.S. reporters who followed the case carefully as a member of "the Truth Squad," which argued the case in support of the official account of events.

On December 21, 1990, *Izvestiya* carried an article by its New York correspondent, Alexander Shalnev, concerning the U.S. senators' letters and foreshadowing the newspaper's forthcoming series on the airliner. Shalnev said that an investigation into the Soviet handling of the KAL 007 incident would not endanger the U.S.S.R.'s national security and "might show that we made a monstrous mistake" in shooting down the airliner. He mentioned a January 14 *U.S. News and World Report* article that said the Soviets had found the airliner's wreck in one hundred feet of water off Moneron and that "Moscow then ordered the bodies of the 269 victims destroyed in a local crematorium." That incensed the Soviet military, and a repudiation of the charge was printed in *Izvestiya*. After a pause *Izvestiya* resumed its coverage of the case. The series caught the world's attention and ran for many months. Despite its surface endorsement of the official line, in the fine print a mass of previously unknown data was put into the public domain.

The problem for the managers of the cover-up was to keep the flow of news from upsetting the acceptance by the media and the public of the official account of events. In this the cover-up had several factors working for it. From the start, as we have seen, the Soviet government, and then its successor the Russian government, refrained from directly challenging the

United States and tailored its statements to be compatible, on the surface at least, with the single-intrusion, single-shootdown scenario, which was the heart of the U.S. cover story. Andrei Illesh, the editor of the *Izvestiya* series, inherited this policy and edited his witnesses' statements to tell the story, ostensibly at least, of the shootdown of KAL 007 by the Soviets. Much of the work of the managers of the cover-up was thus done for them before the news in the *Izvestiya* series had left Soviet hands. The world media reported the ostensible meaning of the series and overlooked the many contradictory details it contained.

Pressure continued to be exerted on the Russian government, primarily by the United States, to confess to the crime neither it nor its predecessor had committed, to hand over the airliner's black boxes, which it never had, and to tell what it had done with the bodies of the passengers, which, for good geographical reasons, it had never found. This urging of the authorities in Moscow to confess may not have been necessary and, as it turned out, probably involved worse dangers than it sought to avoid. But fine tuning was difficult. In the United States, as in Russia, disparate elements with differing objectives (e.g., the four senators, the next of kin, the extreme right, and CIA) each had a hand in the game.

Bowing to pressure, and no doubt hoping to win wider political acceptance and financial support from the West, on October 14, 1992, the Russian president, Boris Yeltsin, handed over to a group of the U.S. next of kin and to a representative of the South Korean government documents that he said concerned the Korean airliner's black boxes and had long lain dormant in the KGB's files. He did this with some ceremony in St. Catharine's Hall in the Kremlin. He may not, however, have looked carefully at the package he presented, having, of course, delegated its preparation to others. It contained a stunning collection of booby traps for the cover-up.

Not only did the documents, in their 1983 form at least (some touches had been added), have nothing to do with the Korean airliner, Yeltsin's packet had enough data in it to make that clear beyond doubt. What was supposed to be the transcript of KAL 007's cockpit voice recorder was made up of radio transmissions recorded by listening stations outside the aircraft, together with pure fiction as to cockpit chatter and cabin announcements recorded inside the aircraft. Three different drafts showed different stages of the forgery's assembly. What was supposed to be KAL 007 course data from the airliner's digital flight-data recorder and from Soviet radar tracking described the flight and crash of two, probably three, different aircraft. (See the item on the black boxes in the appendix.)

It is hard to believe that this was not intentional on the part of at least some of those who put Yeltsin's packet together. As a member of the Soviet political elite in 1983, Yeltsin must have known that KAL 007 had not crashed off Sakhalin or Moneron. He thus knew that, in that sense at least, the documents he presented as relating to the airliner were forgeries. But did he know just how revealing the forgeries were? Probably not.

On November 18, 1992, on a state visit to the Republic of Korea, Yeltsin presented President Roh Tae-wu with what he said were KAL 007's black boxes. Ten days after his surprise presentation, the South Korean government, expressing its "embarrassment," announced that one of the black boxes, the digital flight-data recorder, was just an empty container of corroding metal without any recording. The other, the cockpit voice recorder, contained a recording, which, however, was unintelligible. Where did that leave the transcripts made public on October 14? From what had they been transcribed? The cover-up, whose inconsistencies were thus dramatically exposed, threatened to come completely apart, and the intelligence officers called in their political principals.

On December 8, 1992, representatives of the governments of the United States, Russia, Japan, and South Korea met in Moscow to repair the damage. They decided that "the original recordings" from the black boxes should be given to the ICAO. They requested the ICAO to "complete its [1983] investigation" and "in the first instance to have the recordings examined by competent experts from an ICAO member government." That, in this instance, meant France, as had been decided in 1983 at the time of the naval search off Sakhalin.

These decisions reflected a degree of confidence on the part of American intelligence that France's decoding of the black-box recordings and the ICAO interpretation of them could be kept compatible with the cover story. The key to success lay, of course, in the recordings themselves. But above all, real black-box recordings had to be physically given over.

On June 14, 1993, when the ICAO made its second report on the airliner public, we saw the nature of these recordings and what the ICAO had done in its interpretation of them. CIA's confidence in its capabilities had been justified. The report was, indeed, in line with the cover story, now with black-box tapes to back it up.

But the data from what was ostensibly a single set of recordings had changed substantially between October 14, 1992, when Yeltsin first made them public, and January 8, 1993, when the Russians gave the tapes to the ICAO in Paris. The ostensibly Russian black-box data now seemed very American. They had changed from showing that KAL 007 had been hit by one or two missiles at 18:23:14 GMT, as the Russians had until then maintained, to showing the missile hit taking place at 18:26:02 as the Americans insisted.

Surprisingly, however, the DFDR no longer showed that the aircraft had flown a constant magnetic heading of 249 degrees as the October materials had indicated, which would indeed have taken it over Sakhalin. It now showed that the aircraft had flown a constant magnetic heading of 245 degrees, which would not have taken it over Sakhalin at all, but rather over Sapporo on Hokkaido. How are we to explain that, in this respect at least, the new black box materials were less plausible than the old? My answer is speculative but fits the evidence we have.

In 1983, probably in the planning stage of the KAL 007 operation, U.S. intelligence decided that inadvertently leaving the magnetic compass coupled to the autopilot would be the most plausible explanation of the Korean airliner's going off course and overflying Kamchatka and Sakhalin, as the cover story was to assert it had done. After the details of 805's second-hour shootdown of its target had been ascertained, and as backup evidence in case of need, the United States had a simulation of KAL 007's alleged course flown. Let us call this the after-the-event simulation. This simulating aircraft, however, followed a constant magnetic heading of 245 degrees rather than the 249 degrees that would have taken it to Sakhalin. The Cold War was decidedly still on at the time; 245 degrees was the most northerly course that would not have taken the aircraft over Soviet territory and run the risk of getting it shot down.

Let us take the exploration of the meaning of the evidence one step further. Why have I suggested that a constant magnetic heading was decided on during the planning stage? Among the documents Yeltsin handed over in October 1992 was a map, allegedly showing KAL 007's course, but in fact showing the course of an aircraft taking off from Anchorage at 12:58 (not 13:00 as was the case with KAL 007), following a constant magnetic heading of 249 degrees, and terminating in mid-Sakhalin.

Earlier in the book I have discussed the possibility that this may have been a U.S. military aircraft simulating KAL 007 in order to persuade the Soviets that a passenger-filled airliner was mixed in with the first wave of military aircraft. Let us call this one the simultaneous simulation. Please note that in this analysis we are positing two different flights simulating KAL 007—this one, flown at the time with a constant magnetic heading of 249 degrees, and the one I mentioned earlier, a simulation flown after the event, with a constant magnetic heading of 245 degrees. Fletcher Prouty, who knows something about such things, once told John Keppel not to expect intelligence deceptions to be simple. We pay very intelligent people to think them up.

The decision to have this simultaneous simulation aircraft fly a constant magnetic heading must have been made in advance. It and KAL 007 were to fly across the Bering Sea and the Sea of Okhotsk at the same time. Why, if not to simulate a supposedly unwittingly off-course airliner, would a competent U.S. military pilot have used such a relatively inefficient means of navigation on a long overwater flight?

Some weeks after the disaster, while the 1983 ICAO report was being written, it was decided that a "finger error" in programming the airliner's inertial navigation system would be a more plausible explanation for its deviation (or that of its simulator) from its assigned course. And the constant magnetic heading, and with it the DFDR recording from the after-the-event simulation, were shelved. For nine years the cover story was maintained without having to come forward with a black-box recording to back it up. But after the events of October and November 1992, as I have said, it became clear that the only way to stabilize the situation was to reopen the ICAO investigation and to use black-box recordings as the basis for the ICAO's findings. The only way this could be done in a hurry was to take the 1983 after-the-event simulation's DFDR recording off the shelf, implausible 245-degree magnetic heading included, and use it.[4]

As it turned out, with the ICAO's help, that was good enough to get by the uninquisitive press. To see where a constant magnetic heading would take you, you must factor in the winds at the time and the magnetic deviations along the flight path. Just so long as publishers and editors could be dissuaded from assigning an investigative reporter to the case, everyone else was too busy to do the work necessary.

It comes, of course, as no surprise to the reader that the current version of the cover story, that put forward in the 1993 ICAO report, is false. For two reasons, however, I wish to mention some of the indications that this is so. First, it is instructive to see how vulnerable to analysis a cover story based on lies becomes over time. Walter Scott's "Oh, what a tangled web we weave, /When first we practice to deceive!" is as true as ever. The second reason is to inquire, How in countries where there is supposed to be freedom of information can such egregious contradictions be passed by in silence for so many years? It is important for their citizens to know. Acceptance of official lying breaks down the fabric of responsible government.

One incident may illustrate the instability of the official record. The last phrase of an important radio transmission from the Korean airliner, recorded on government tape, has changed three times. The changes have involved both the Japanese and Russian governments but were probably made at the initiative of the United States to protect the cover-up.

The cockpit voice recording given the ICAO for its 1993 report by the Russians is similar to the CVR transcript Yeltsin made public in October 1992, though without the component drafts that made it clear how the forgery was assembled. This time, however, a tape of the final composite—the "original recording" in the language of the cover-up—was put together for the purpose and given to the ICAO. It was this CVR recording that the French experts transcribed. The ICAO published the transcript but withheld the tape from the public.

I happened to hear a fragment of it that had been rerecorded in a

French videotape documentary on the transcribing and decoding work they had done. It included the last phrase of KAL 007's 18:27 GMT transmission, the transmission long thought to have been its last. The phrase was not the way I had previously heard it.

The Narita tape given the Japanese Diet in 1985 by Premier Nakasone, quite audibly and intelligibly, has this phrase as "Blood bath, really bad," a fact of which the public has yet to be told. In 1983 the ICAO had said its "best rendering" of the phrase was "Descending to one zero thousand."[5] Over time the "best rendering" qualification was dropped and the "descending to one zero thousand" became part of the official story. It was carried on the transcript released by the Russians in October 1992. So far as I know, however, until January 1993 that rendering existed only on paper. In the French documentary it caught my ear that "Blood bath, really bad" had been dropped and "descending to one zero thousand" had now been substituted as the official auditory record.

The DFDR recording decoded by the French, the backbone of the ICAO's 1993 report, is, as we have seen, presumably the one recorded by an after-the-event simulation, presumably the flight flown in 1983 referred to above. This recording offers an even richer lode of contradictions than the CVR recording.

The DFDR data do not match the data on the CVR recordings, which were partly made up of real radio communications. The outgoing radio communications on the two tapes are not the same in number or as to the times at which they were sent. See "Black Boxes" in the appendix. The DFDR recording cannot physically have come from KAL 007: the tape is twenty-seven hours long. That aboard KAL 007 was only twenty-four hours forty-eight minutes long. The DFDR tape lacks the serial number it should have had. The handwritten number written on the tape cover could have been added by anyone. The tape fails to include several of the parameters KAL 007's DFDR would have recorded. Perhaps the most important of those missing is time—its lack means that the tape could have been recorded at any time, which is to say that a simulation could have been flown at any time.

Also revealing is the fact that the DFDR recording registers the parameters of only two engines, rather than the four engines powering KAL 007. For technical reasons it is clear that the two registered must have been those of a two-engine aircraft, and that the lack of the other two was not due to some failure of registration by the DFDR.

As I spell out in detail in the black-boxes appendix item, the performance, flight maneuvers, and outgoing radio transmissions recorded by the DFDR are not consistent with the behavior of KAL 007.

- The details of the DFDR aircraft's landing at Anchorage, supposedly at Anchorage International Airport, are not consistent with the physical characteristics of that airport.[6] Following the headings indicated on the tape, on its way to the gate at Anchorage International Airport after exiting its landing runway, the DFDR aircraft would have had to pass through a building.
- The details of its subsequent takeoff from Anchorage are not consistent with the details of KAL 007's takeoff sequence, which we know from its radio transmissions and other data recorded by the U.S. Federal Aviation Administration at the airport.
- On landing and takeoff the DFDR aircraft made radio transmissions that we know KAL 007 did not make.
- The record of outgoing transmissions from the DFDR aircraft showed radio capabilities that KAL 007 did not have.

That all this passed unremarked upon by the media in the United States and, with some brief exceptions, other Western countries indicates to my mind a serious problem. A reasonably well functioning information system surely lies at the heart of responsible government. Its failure to function, on at least some important issues, means that we are sailing without a compass and can arrive where we very much do not want to go.

The human meaning of the twin disasters, the air battle of Sakhalin and the destruction of the Korean airliner, also needs to be pondered. The passengers aboard KAL 007 were killed without reason, their relatives and loved ones have been deprived of understanding how they died and, in important measure, of compensation for their loss.[7]

We know from the evidence and from the logic of the circumstances that there were no survivors from the airliner. That may well also be true of the thirty or more servicemen aboard the U.S. Air Force and Navy aircraft shot down that night by the Soviets over or near Sakhalin. But we do not know it with the same degree of confidence. The possibility, however slight, that there were U.S. military survivors is a subject that must be treated with circumspection and seriousness. The next of kin of service people who may have died that night are entitled to know what we know, but only if at the same time we make it clear what we do not know.

The data that initially misled the Japanese radar operators at Wakkanai to think that KAL 007 might have landed intact at Yuzhno-Sakhalinsk must have concerned a military aircraft. But the data could have reflected either a safe landing or a crash landing that no one survived. We have other evidence, photographic and anecdotal, of several other crashes on land. Some of the men from these aircraft might have parachuted successfully, though we have no evidence of this.

- In 1992 a prominent man from the state of Washington was on Sakhalin on business. Walking one day with the governor of Sakhalin he came on a place where there had obviously been some sort of explosion. He asked the governor what had happened there. The governor said it was "where an airplane crashed during the KAL 007 affair."
- On September 1, 1992, some Japanese KAL 007 next of kin and a few members of the world press were shown the hole in the ground at Pereputye, south of Nevelsk, to which I have referred in chapter 13. Russian officials said it was where debris from KAL 007 had been burned. In all probability, however, it was originally the crash site of a military aircraft that had burned on impact with the ground. Local residents said an RC-135 had crashed there.
- The course plotted on the DFDR map made public by Yeltsin in October 1992 (presumably that of the simultaneous simulation) terminates in mid-Sakhalin. The aircraft probably crashed there. To judge by its speed and other capabilities, it could have been an ELINT version of the DC-10. The parallel radar track to its south, which ends at a crash site near Nevelsk in Soviet territorial waters, in all likelihood is that of an accompanying aircraft, probably an EF-111.

Also to the point, we have photographs of debris at the sites of two different land crashes (from a set of eighty-two photographs given on March 11, 1993, by the government of the Russian Federation to families of the KAL 007 victims). One photograph shows that an aircraft, smaller than a Boeing 707, with a fuselage about three meters in diameter, less than half that of a Boeing 747, exploded in flight and its debris impacted vertically on the ground with tremendous force. The other aircraft, of about the same size or even smaller, appears to have tried to make an emergency landing and glided on the ground, losing its landing gear and other parts in the process.

Another reason for weighing the possibility of military survivors is that among the photographs of floating military aircraft debris recovered by the Soviets and the Japanese after the air battle of Sakhalin are those of two pilot's ejection seats, of which the propulsive charges had been fired, and several of small life rafts, clearly military. We know that the Soviets at the time thought that some American airmen might have reached the water alive (see chapter 11). We do not know whether or not any of them did. Nor do we know whether, if any did reach the water alive, they were subsequently saved.

In his speech to a joint session of the U.S. Congress on June 17, 1992, President Yeltsin said:

There will be no more lies—ever. The same applies to biological weapons experiments, and the facts that have been revealed about American prisoners of war, KAL 007, and many other things.

Prior to Yeltsin's departure for the United States and in press conferences in Washington during his visit, there had been Soviet statements about the possibility that there were still U.S. prisoners of war in the U.S.S.R.—though U.S. reporters and others interpreted them, if they existed at all, as coming from early overflights, the Korean War, or the Vietnam War. It was nonetheless suggestive to hear Yeltsin mention prisoners and KAL 007, albeit as separate subjects, in the same breath.

After Yeltsin's visit, a joint U.S.-Russian group looked into the possibility that U.S. military prisoners were still alive in the U.S.S.R. and concluded that there was no evidence to that effect. That is probably true. But given the fact that neither the U.S. nor the Russian government wants the truth about the air battle of Sakhalin known, it is not necessarily so. In a July 15, 1986, rebuttal of what President Reagan said to the European Council in Strasbourg about installing a hot line between the American and the Soviet military, Prof. Shôzo Takemoto wrote:

We can establish hundreds of different procedures, put in place as many crisis systems as we want, and install a thousand hot lines. As long as civilian airliners are used to carry out secret intelligence missions, as long as emergency warnings remain unsent, and as long as people in power are willing to use the lives of the innocent as pawns in a global chess game, there is no way to prevent future tragedies of this kind.

At the time, the Japanese government was considering building a stele at Wakkanai to commemorate those who died on the airliner. Professor Takemoto supported the project and suggested the text of an epigraph for it. The monument was built at the summit of a hill facing Sakhalin and Moneron, which you can see on a clear day. But it had another epigraph. The Ministry of Foreign Affairs, fearing American and Soviet objections, rejected his. At the end of the text he suggested, Professor Takemoto addressed his wife and eldest son:

Dear Departed. We condemn Korean Air Lines, who cruelly deprived you of the enjoyment of your remaining years, and the United States and the Soviet Union for their total disregard of human life. We swear that we will reveal the truth hidden behind the destruction of the plane that carried you. So that your death will not have been in vain, we call upon people across the earth, in your name, to reaffirm their respect for human life and the peace of the world.

Appendix: The Black Boxes

Their Characteristics

Black boxes are electronic devices that record the main parameters of an aircraft's performance in flight. These parameters, made available to investigators in the postmortem analysis of an accident, help them to understand what caused the crash. That in turn facilitates correction of the problem that caused the accident. Although they are called black boxes, they are in fact bright orange to make them easily visible among the wreckage at a crash site. There are usually two of them: the DFDR (digital flight-data recorder) and the CVR (cockpit voice recorder).

As its name implies, the DFDR records the technical flight parameters. It records with high accuracy the speed, altitude, magnetic heading, angle of bank, pitch, as well as longitudinal, vertical, and lateral load factors. It also records the actuation of the various controls and of each of the radio transmitters, the cabin pressure and the status of each of the four engines.

The other black box, the CVR, records voice communications in the cockpit on an endless (looped) tape on which only the last thirty minutes of conversation is available. It has four channels. Channel 1 records incoming and outgoing radio communications at the copilot's position. Channel 2 records the same at the flight engineer's position, plus announcements over the public address system. Channel 3 records conversation between crew members and other cockpit noises through the so-called ambient microphone in the cockpit. Channel 4 records incoming and outgoing radio communications at the captain's position. Although KAL 007, like any civilian Boeing 747, had only three radio transmitting positions—those of the captain, the copilot, and the flight engineer—it had five different radio transmitters: three VHF line-of-sight transmitters and two long-distance HF short-wave transmitters. Any one of these five transmitters could be selected from any one of the three different stations in the cockpit; but no more than three transmitters could be used at any given time.

The two black boxes aboard KAL 007 were located in the aft part of the fuselage, in the ceiling, just below the root of the vertical fin. That is the most secure place in the aircraft and the most likely to remain intact in a crash. To help in their recovery should the aircraft crash at sea, the black boxes are equipped with an underwater locator operating on a frequency of 37.5 kHz, powered by a water-activated battery large enough to operate it for a month.

The 1983 Russian Data, as Amended

As stated by an Associated Press dispatch from Moscow:

On October 14, 1992, Russian president Boris Yeltsin handed over to the American and South Korean delegations in Moscow documents concerning the destruction of a South Korean Boeing 747 by Soviet fighter planes. The documents included a transcription of the tape from one of the two black boxes, the cockpit voice recorder (CVR), which contained the crew's conversations and radio communications. They also included the investigation reports prepared at the time of the shootdown and the map of the Korean aircraft's route.

John Keppel obtained an Associated Press translation of the Russian documents. I analyzed this information carefully. While I was doing this, Philippe Robert de Massy obtained an English copy of what was supposed to be the same material from the Canadian government. I compared it with the Associated Press translation. The two documents were different, two versions of the same material. Their comparison told me a lot. The "transcription of the magnetic tape of the cockpit voice recorder" was not from KAL 007. Not only that, the material was not even from a CVR. The transcription had been compiled from communications between KAL 007, KAL 015, and Tokyo control intercepted from outside the airliner. To this had been added snatches of what was presented as miscellaneous conversation on the flight deck.

When President Yeltsin handed the Soviet documents over to the U.S. and South Korean delegations, he announced that Russia had revealed everything it could reveal about the incident. Yeltsin's spokesman V. Kortikov said, "The president considers that it would be useful to collect all the documents existing in other countries, including the United States and South Korea, into one bundle; and then it would be possible to attach the black boxes [the recorders themselves, that is] to it as material evidence." President Yeltsin's next move came as a surprise. He simply gave what he described as the airliner's "black boxes" to the South Koreans. This took place on November 19, 1992, on the official visit to Seoul that Yeltsin had been forced to cancel a month earlier. One of the boxes, the one containing the DFDR, was missing the magnetic tape on which the data was recorded. The box was nothing more than an assembly of rusty sheet metal. While the CVR did contain a tape, it was unintelligible. The governments of the United States, Russia, Japan, and South Korea, evidently feeling that emergency action was called for to save the cover-up, decided to meet in Moscow. After forty-eight hours of deliberation, they agreed to ask the ICAO to reopen its inquiry into the KAL 007 disaster. Russia promised to supply the ICAO with "the original recordings" from the black boxes and any other documents in its possession. The other nations promised their full cooperation.

The promised recordings were handed over by the Russian representative to the ICAO's office in Paris and were decoded in France by the Accident Investigation Bureau of the Flight Test Center at Brétigny-sur-Orge in January and February 1993. The results were given to the ICAO investigators. The ICAO interpreted the data and completed its report on May 28, 1993.

The 1983 DFDR

Among the documents President Yeltsin handed over in 1992 was an analysis of KAL 007's black boxes that had been performed by Soviet aviation experts in 1983. The report is signed by the head of the Experts Group, Lieutenant General (Corps of Engineers) Tikhomirov; Major General (Corps of Engineers) Didenko; Major General (Air Force) Stepanov; Major General (Air Force) Kovtun; and Mr. Fedosov, a member of the U.S.S.R. Academy of Sciences. Dated November 28, 1983, the report was originally classified top secret.

It contained data from the decoding of an aircraft's DFDR said to be KAL 007's and a CVR transcript that allegedly represented the last thirty minutes of conversations in the KAL 007 cockpit. Accompanying the report was a map showing the flight path of an aircraft from the time of its takeoff at Anchorage, given as 12:58:38 GMT. That is different from the takeoff time of KAL 007, which was 13:00 GMT. The flight path, reconstructed from the aircraft's DFDR, terminated in the middle of Sakhalin, after a flight that took it over Kamchatka and lasted five hours twenty-six minutes and eighteen seconds. On the map, the latter part of the DFDR course line is paralleled by the track of an aircraft (the same one or another flying parallel to it) observed by the Soviet defense radar. The radar track continues to a point in Sakhalin territorial waters to the north of Nevelsk, where the observed aircraft crashed at 18:24:56 GMT.

The Soviet analysis of the DFDR data said that the airplane maintained a speed of 910–920 kilometers per hour (565–570 miles per hour) and followed a 249-degree magnetic heading, from which it never deviated until its destruction. A missile exploded at 18:23:14, one minute forty-two seconds before the end of the recording. The aircraft, said by the map to have been KAL 007, was destroyed when it crashed at 18:24:56 GMT. This sequence is said to have been confirmed by photographs of the PVO radar screens.

The Soviet CVR of 1983

The transcription of the CVR is said to have been done by a group of officers from the GRU, Soviet military intelligence—Lt. Col. P. Doroshenko, Majors Yuri Andrianov and S. Luchkin, and Capt. Ye. Siganov—and signed by them on November 12, 1983. At six minutes and thirty seconds from the beginning of the tape, there is an announcement in the cabin in Korean, English, and Japanese:

It is now 0300 hours local time. We land in three hours. We will be providing breakfast.

This sequence is fictional on two counts. First, transoceanic aircraft usually cross several time zones in a single flight and do not use local time en route. The time given in public address announcements is always that of the destination airport. Second, on an oceanic night flight, passengers are never awakened for their breakfast three hours before arrival. The maximum is an hour and a half. The Soviet intelligence officers who put together the CVR transcript may have intended this fiction. They probably meant to prompt investigators to have a second look at the CVR documents. I did, and others probably did, too.

The CVR documents comprise three series of papers, only one of which is labeled "Content of Magnetic Recording on the On-Board Voice Recorder of the South Korean 'Boeing 747' on Flight 'Korean Air 007.'" The other two documents are labeled "Radio Exchanges of the Crew of the Boeing 747 with Each Other, Other Aircraft in the Air, and with the Air Traffic Control Service."

At first sight, the three sets of documents look identical and one wonders why we have three of them. A closer look, however, is revealing. They are not identical. The two series labeled "Radio Exchanges" show a number of minor variations, most of them apparently due to the fact that one of the series had better reception quality than the other since on it the communications are complete in passages where the other series shows ellipses or an "unreadable." Another difference is that most communications attributed to KAL 007 in one series are attributed to KAL 015 in the other series. The third document, labeled "Content of Magnetic Recording," is a combination of the other two documents.

None of these documents could have come from the Korean airliner's CVR or from any CVR for that matter. Two of them were separate recordings of KAL 007's radio transmissions made at different listening posts, one with better reception than the other. The one with better reception was probably an airborne listening station, possibly a Soviet AWAC. The one with lesser reception was probably a listening post on the ground. It might have been the air base, radar, and listening station of Burevestnik on the island of Iturup. The third document is a consolidation of the radio exchanges of the first two documents, to which has been added wholly fictional cockpit chatter and cabin announcements. In January of 1993, President Yeltsin handed over to the ICAO recordings theoretically from the same black boxes. They, however, are different in a number of important respects, particularly as regards the DFDR. The CVR transcript is a slightly "improved" version of the composite I have discussed above.

The 1993 ICAO Decoding

On June 14, 1993, during the 193rd session of the ICAO Council, Secretary General Philippe Rochat submitted his second report on the investigation into the Korean Air Lines Flight 007 tragedy. It states the conclusions of the reopened ICAO investigation following the return of the black box recordings by President Yeltsin. It is, therefore, not surprising that the main focus of the report is the analysis of the contents of the black boxes and the conclusions drawn from them. The report, number C-WP/9781, consists of two principal documents, the main body of the report, entitled "Report of the Completion of the Fact-Finding Investigation Regarding the Shooting Down of Korean Air Lines Boeing 747 (Flight KAL 007) on 31 August 1983," and Information Paper No. 1, which contains transcripts of Soviet communications and the transcript of the cockpit voice recorder that allegedly came from the Korean airliner. Information Paper No. 2 contains the Russian texts of the air-to-ground and ground-to-ground communications that the ICAO translated into English in Information Paper No. 1.

The report itself concludes that, without the pilot's knowledge, the Korean airliner flew a constant magnetic heading of 245 degrees, bringing it more than three hundred miles off course and causing it to overfly Kamchatka and Sakhalin. It claims that the airliner was shot down by an infrared-guided missile that exploded in the plane's tail at 18:26:02 GMT. Following the explosion, the plane suddenly climbed to 38,000 feet at a speed of 7,000 feet per minute. It then began a slow, spiraling descent. The two black boxes, the CVR and DFDR, are said to have stopped operating simultaneously (and for no apparent reason) at 18:27:46 GMT. On the face of it, this time should have indicated the destruction of the airliner.

From there on there is no direct indication that the aircraft was still flying. The ICAO, however, said that "radar data showed that the aircraft flew at least nine minutes in a descending spiral after the attack—and radar contact was lost at 5,000 meters at 18:35 hours." This appears to be an adaptation of the alleged Japanese radar track showing a nine-minute spiral 18:29 to 18:38, which the Japanese miraculously found twelve days after the event. The alleged track was part of the Japanese politically motivated transition to the American position that the airliner was destroyed on impact with the water at 18:38. (See chapter 3.) No substantiation is offered as to why this particular Soviet radar sighting was KAL 007. The ICAO does not specifically state the time of KAL 007's destruction. It says only that "at 18:26:02 hours the aircraft was hit by at least one of two air-to-air missiles. . . . As a result of the attack, KAL 007 collided with the sea and sank off the southwest coast of Sakhalin Island."[1]

The ICAO report is largely based upon the decoding of the DFDR and CVR. Examination of the ICAO's presentation of this material leads to the following conclusions, which will be substantiated below:

1. The DFDR and the CVR were not from the same aircraft.
2. The DFDR did not come from KAL 007.

1. A DFDR is used to record a number of technical parameters that describe an aircraft's behavior and the activation of its various communications devices. If the data have not been tampered with, the time of outgoing radio communications recorded on the CVR should appear on the DFDR tape. The CVR supplied to the ICAO recorded the final thirty-three minutes thirty-six seconds of flight and apparently stopped functioning at exactly the same time as the DFDR. A comparison of the time track on both devices shows that they do not coincide as to either the number or the time of outgoing transmissions.

a. The radio communications are not the same.

During the period in question, page 28 of the report shows that the DFDR recorded a total of twenty-nine radio communications, distributed as indicated below. Yet during this same time, pages 3 to 16 of Information Paper No. 1 show that the CVR recorded a total of only six outgoing radio communications. A comparison of the transmissions recorded by the two devices is as follows:

DFDR	CVR
9 on HF 1	4 on HF 1
4 on HF 2	none on HF 2
4 on VHF 1	none on VHF 1
4 on VHF 2	none on VHF 2
8 on VHF 3	2 on VHF 3

Transmitting a voice message obviously involves speaking into a microphone. This sound is then recorded by the CVR, the cockpit voice recorder, on at least two different tracks: a track for the microphone from which the communication originates (pilot, copilot, flight engineer); and a track for the cockpit mike (the voice speaking into the microphone can be heard throughout the cockpit and is captured by the cabin microphone). If the DFDR shows that twenty-nine radio communications took place but the CVR only recorded six of them, we can only conclude that the two devices were not on board the same aircraft at the same time.

b. The reference times are not the same.

A CVR recording contains a second-by-second time signal, but nothing on the tape can be used to correlate it to a specific time (or to a given day). In this instance we can check the times given for the same radio transmissions on the air-traffic-control tapes. In spite of the skill of the technicians who attempted to "synchronize" the data, the CVR still contains a number of chronological discrepancies with the recordings at Tokyo and Anchorage, and many of these are greater than five seconds.

2. The DFDR did not come from KAL 007.

My conclusion is based on the following factors:

- lack of a serial number
- physical characteristics of the recording tape
- number of parameters recorded
- performance and maneuverability data recorded
- radio transmissions

Lack of a Serial Number

All equipment used for aviation purposes is identified by a serial number. It is remarkable that in the case of KAL 007 no serial numbers were on the black box recordings. The metal boxes themselves, on which serial numbers were presumably engraved, were turned over by Yeltsin to the South Korean government. South Korea never turned them over to the ICAO and never made them public. We have no way of knowing if the metal cases are genuine or not. (If they were to be genuine, questions would arise as to who raised them from the seafloor, where, and when.)

The ICAO received only the tapes and the drive mechanism. KAL 007 was equipped with a Sundstrand DFDR, model 573A, type 981-600009-010, which carried the serial number 3069. The ICAO was able to verify that the mechanism in its possession was a Sundstrand model 573A, but was unable to identify the type of device. Nor was it able to determine the serial number. The number 3069 was written by hand on the tape cover, but this could have been added by anyone. It cannot stand as proof of a serial number.

Physical Characteristics

The DFDR on KAL 007 contains a Vicalloy recording tape. The tape, made of a special metal alloy, is eight hundred feet long, contains four one-quarter-inch tracks, and records sequentially at a speed of 0.43 inches/second. This provides six hours twelve minutes of recording time per track, for a total of twenty-four hours forty-eight minutes, as explained on page 27 of the report. However, on page 30, paragraph 1.14.3.7.1, we learn that the tape decoded by the Accident Investigation Bureau of the Flight Test Center in Brétigny-sur-Orge contained 27 hours of recorded material broken down as follows: a 5.5 hour segment for the last flight until the destruction of the aircraft; two complete flights, said to be a round-trip flight from Anchorage to New York and back to Anchorage for a total of 15 hours; and a final 6.5-hour flight supposedly prior to landing at Anchorage. This makes a total of 27 hours of recorded material on a device that can physically contain no more than 24 hours and 48 minutes of data. Clearly something is wrong. Because the tape speed is regulated with extreme accuracy to enable the reconstruction of the flight to better than one-second precision, we know that the tape was 852 inches too long. Was the tape originally longer than the tape on KAL 007, or was the additional footage added after the fact? In either case the tape could not have come from the DFDR on KAL 007.

Number of Parameters

The number of parameters appearing on the DFDR tape examined by the ICAO does not correspond to the DFDR that was on board KAL 007. In particular, page 29 of the ICAO report states that, according to Korean Air Lines, the following parameters, among others, were recorded by the Korean airliner's DFDR:

- engine-pressure ratio for the four engines
- UTC (extremely important in placing events within the time stream)
- VOR/ILS localizer and glide slope (navigation and instrument landing)
- GPWS (ground proximity warning system)

None of these parameters appear on the ICAO's DFDR. It provides engine-pressure ratios for only two engines instead of four. This implies that the DFDR used by the ICAO is from a twin-engined aircraft and not from a Boeing 747, which is a four-engined aircraft. The absence of universal time is also significant. It allows plenty of latitude for synchronizing the DFDR with the most convenient time scheme available and makes it relatively easy to create false data.

Performance and Maneuvering

The aircraft performance and flight maneuvers recorded by the DFDR are not consistent with the behavior of KAL 007. Page 26 of the report details the takeoff parameters at "Anchorage." I have put the word in quotes because nothing in the data tells us at which airport the aircraft carrying the DFDR landed prior to this takeoff. However, the landing sequence shows it was not Anchorage International Airport (though it may have been Elmendorf Air Force Base, which is also at Anchorage). I have compared the data from the DFDR concerning the aircraft's landing with a detailed map of the Anchorage International Airport in 1983. They do not match. Following the headings indicated by the DFDR, on its way to the gate after exiting its landing runway, the aircraft would have had to pass through a building.

It is also instructive to compare the data we have on the DFDR aircraft's takeoff, allegedly from Anchorage International, with the data we have on KAL 007's actual takeoff from that field. We can reconstruct the DFDR aircraft's actions from the DFDR data on the graph of page 26 of the ICAO report, "Chart 6. Flight KAL 007. Takeoff at Anchorage." At the same time, we know in detail how KAL 007 maneuvered at Anchorage because we have a record of the aircraft's communications with the control tower.

Comparison of Takeoff Maneuvers	
DFDR Aircraft	KAL 007
Begins to taxi without authorization 5 minutes 30 seconds before takeoff.	Requests authorization to taxi 4 minutes 53 seconds prior to takeoff.
Taxis for 4 minutes 45 seconds.	Taxis for 2 minutes 54 seconds.
Fails to contact the control tower and does not stop at the entrance to the runway.	Stops at the entrance to the runway and announces, "Ready for takeoff."
Begins takeoff without authorization.	Begins takeoff after receiving authorization at 12:58:13 GMT.
Rolls for 52 seconds before taking off.	Rolls for 1 minute 47 seconds prior to takeoff, which takes place at 13:00.

The above comparison shows that the data are from two different aircraft. The DFDR aircraft turned onto the runway without prior authorization (there is no trace on the DFDR of any communication before initiating the aircraft's runway operations) and rolled for only fifty-two seconds prior to takeoff, which indicates that the aircraft had significant reserve power. The other aircraft, KAL 007, always requested permission before any ground operation, as shown by its communications with the control tower on pages 17 to 19 of Information Paper No. 1. It rolled for one minute forty-seven seconds prior to takeoff, confirming that the aircraft was heavily loaded. The DFDR data indicate that the aircraft took off at a speed of 175 knots, which is high for a Boeing 747, whose takeoff speed is normally between 130 and 140 knots.

The Climb

After taking off at a speed of 175 knots, the DFDR aircraft shows rapid acceleration to 260 knots. After stabilizing briefly around 5,000 feet, it then began another period of rapid acceleration to 310 knots, a speed that the aircraft attained before reaching 10,000 feet. Three factors stand out in this scenario. First, a speed curve such as this is difficult to obtain with a heavily loaded Boeing 747, which will climb slowly. Second, an aircraft never climbs at its cruising speed. For reasons of safety it always climbs at a speed that provides the best rate of climb, which is around 230 knots for a Boeing 747. Third, also for reasons of safety, a regulation limits speed to 250 knots at altitudes below 10,000 feet to avoid the risk of collision with the large number of smaller or slower aircraft flying at these flight levels. The DFDR aircraft ignores the regulations, accelerating to 310 knots. It should be pointed out that military aircraft do not observe such restrictions.

The Turn to Heading 220

On page 31 of its report, paragraph 1.14.3.9.1, the ICAO states that "23 seconds after liftoff, a turn to the left was initiated onto a magnetic heading of about 220°." The report is referring to KAL 007, although the data are from the aircraft that carried the DFDR. This is revealing because KAL 007 did not begin a turn to the left until *after* it received instructions to do so from the control tower at 13:00:40, which it acknowledged at 13:00:50, fifty seconds after takeoff and not twenty-three seconds as indicated by the DFDR. An airliner in bona fide operation could not have turned earlier for it would not yet have received its heading instructions of 220 degrees from the controller and would not have known it should turn to that heading.

The Flight

Graph 6 on page 26 of the ICAO report shows a cruising speed of 310 knots indicated airspeed (IAS), which corresponds to a true airspeed (TAS) of 518 knots, or Mach 0.882. This is much higher than the cruising speed KAL 007 was required to fly in order to conform with its operational flight plan, which was Mach 0.84.

Radio Communications

The most revealing aspect of the radio communications does not involve the final flight but the preceding flight and, more specifically, the landing phase that appears on the DFDR. Graph 6 on page 26 of the report shows that during the last phase of the landing, there occurred, within the space of a few minutes, no fewer than fifty-three radio communications, most of which took place *simultaneously* on five radio transmitters, the two HF and the three VHF transmitters. This raises several important issues:

- There is no reason for such a large number of transmissions in such a short period of time by a commercial airliner.
- The final phase of a landing is always the most difficult part of a flight, and the crew is too busy to spend much time on the radio.
- On a Boeing 747 there are only three radio stations. These can be used to transmit simultaneously on, at most, three separate channels, assuming that both pilots and the flight engineer have nothing more important to do than spend their time on the radio. On a standard Boeing 747 it is impossible to transmit simultaneously from five radio transmitters. The outgoing communications registered by the DFDR tape that the ICAO was given must have been made by other members of a larger crew, operating from separate radio consoles, as would be the case on an RC-135 or a number of other large military aircraft.
- The indicated landing was supposed to have taken place at Anchorage International Airport after a civilian passenger flight from New York. Why would the aircraft have made twenty-five short-wave radio transmissions simultaneously on both HF units, HF 1 and HF 2? At the time of landing the Korean airliner was in contact with the control tower using only its VHF radio. The HF, or long-distance short-wave radio, is used exclusively for long-distance communications, especially over water. HF is *never* used over the American continent by civilian aircraft, and this plane was sup-posed to have flown from New York to Anchorage. Based on the DFDR data, we are led to believe that during landing the aircraft communicated extensively for several minutes with a distant station (a ship at sea or an airplane in flight), which it was unable to contact by any other means.

DFDR Aircraft	KAL 007
HF 1, two transmissions	HF 1, none
HF 2, three transmissions	HF 2, none
VHF 1, two transmissions	VHF 1, none
VHF 2, thirteen transmissions	VHF 2, eight transmissions
VHF 3, six transmissions	VHF 3, none

As the table shows, the communications recorded by the DFDR can-not belong to KAL 007.

Radio transmission during the takeoff phase of the DFDR aircraft shows similar characteristics. From the time the engines were switched on until two thousand seconds after takeoff, the DFDR aircraft communicated twenty-six times, using each of five transmitters. During this same time, KAL 007 made eight transmissions in all, all of them on VHF 2 (i.e., were spoken by the copilot on VHF). The table on page 277 illustrates the differences between the two sets of data.

The DFDR of the ICAO of 1993 and the Yeltsin DFDR of 1983

The Soviet analysis of the black boxes in 1983 was done by an experts' group headed by Lieutenant General of Aviation Makarov. Its report indicates that the missile detonated at 18:23:14 GMT. The 1983 ICAO analysis says the missile exploded at 18:26:02, three minutes later than the earlier report.

The 1983 Soviet analysis indicates that the aircraft was destroyed at 18:24:56 GMT, a time it said had been confirmed by photographs of the Defense Forces' radar screens. The ICAO analysis does not indicate a specific time for KAL 007's destruction and merely says it continued flying for at least nine minutes after the attack.

The map accompanying the analysis Yeltsin made public in October 1992 shows the location of an aircraft that was destroyed at 18:24:56 GMT within the territorial waters of Sakhalin, north of Nevelsk. On page 19 of the ICAO report, it states that the principal wreckage of KAL 007 was located at 46°33' N, 141°19' E, in international waters, 17 NM north of Moneron. Not only do the two locations not coincide, they are nearly thirty-one miles apart.

The 1983 Soviet analysis indicates that the aircraft followed a magnetic heading of 249 degrees. On the map, the route followed by maintaining that constant heading has been reconstructed from the takeoff at Anchorage until the plane's destruction north of Nevelsk at 18:24:56. The course ends over land, in the center of Sakhalin Island. In its 1993 report the ICAO said that the DFDR aircraft had followed a constant magnetic heading of 245 degrees, not 249 as the 1983 Soviet analysis had stated. Four degrees may not seem like much, but over the course of several thousand miles, the difference becomes significant.

In fact a constant 245-degree magnetic heading, which the ICAO and its supporters now ask us to believe the Korean airliner followed, would not have brought the aircraft over Sakhalin at all, but over Hokkaido, above the city of Sapporo. In 1983, ICAO experts had toyed with the idea of a constant magnetic heading, and at one point suggested that a 246-degree heading came closest to matching KAL 007's route. The idea was subsequently rejected because it would have put the aircraft 80 NM (92 miles) south of the spot where the attack was said to have taken place. A 245-degree heading puts the plane even farther south, more than 100 NM (115 miles) away from the site of the shootdown. In other words it was impossible, starting from Anchorage, to overfly Sakhalin by maintaining a constant magnetic heading of 245 degrees.

The 1983 Soviet analysis indicates that the aircraft maintained a speed of 910–920 kilometers per hour (565–570 miles per hour). The DFDR indicates a speed of 310 knots, for a true airspeed of 1,008 kilometers (626 miles) per hour. In light of these comparisons it is worth asking how the ICAO in 1993 and the Soviets in 1983 obtained such different data from what is supposed to have been the same black box.

Lieutenant General Makarov's 1983 analysis of the black box also contradicted the American scenario that Ambassador Kirkpatrick presented to the United Nations. The Kirkpatrick version states that KAL 007 was destroyed on impact with the water at 18:38, whereas the 1983 report claims it was destroyed fourteen minutes earlier at 18:24:56. That may be one of the reasons why, on October 16, 1992, less than forty-eight hours after the release of Yeltsin's documents, Bob Gates, director of the CIA, arrived in Moscow to confer with his Russian counterparts. While it is impossible to know exactly what transpired during Gates's stay in Moscow, the Russian position on the black boxes from KAL 007 suddenly changed, bringing it into closer agreement with the American version of events.

Ever since the first days after the tragedy, the official Soviet position had been that the intruder aircraft was "stopped" at 06:24 Sakhalin time over the village of Pravda. The first Soviet analysis of the black boxes, conducted by Lieutenant General Makarov in 1983, holds this position. It was reaffirmed during Marshal Ogarkov's news conference on September 9, 1983. It figures prominently in the Soviet report appended to the 1983 ICAO report, and it had been reaffirmed in the documents made public by President Yeltsin on October 14, 1992. The ICAO, analyzing data from what were allegedly the same black boxes, concluded otherwise.

What all this implies is that the DFDR analyzed by the ICAO is different from the DFDR analyzed by the Soviets in 1983, and that neither of them came from the Korean airliner. In contrast to the 1983 Soviet analysis of the "old DFDR," the ICAO report of June 1993, based on the "new DFDR"

- has the plane following a 245-degree magnetic heading rather than a 249-degree heading, a 4-degree difference that would have resulted in KAL 007 flying over Japan instead of over Sakhalin.
- says that the destruction of the aircraft took place at 18:37 GMT rather than 18:24 GMT, a difference of thirteen minutes.
- says that the crash occurred in international waters north of Moneron Island instead of inside the territorial waters of Sakhalin north of Nevelsk.

The DFDR analyzed by the ICAO in 1993 does not match anything that is known of the incident at Sakhalin—not the Japanese radar data, the transmissions of the Soviet pilots, the Soviet ground-to-ground communications, or the observations of the *Chidori Maru*. It seems to be a separate incident of its own. It tries to combine into a single story separate events that happened one hour apart and were not logically related to each other. This could have been possible only with black box recordings specially made for the purpose.

As to the CVR, the October 1992 materials that Yeltsin made public gave us an insight into this process of "making." They do the same for the making of the DFDR recording in that they cite a constant magnetic heading, 249 degrees, which would have taken KAL 007 from Anchorage to Sakhalin, where it was supposed to have been shot down. When the October 1992 materials were dropped and "the original recordings" were given the ICAO in their place, we find a DFDR recording indicating that the plane followed a constant magnetic heading of 245 degrees. As I have indicated above, 245 degrees would have taken KAL 007 over Sapporo on southern Hokkaido, rather than over Sakhalin.

Why in this respect are "the new black boxes" less plausible than "the old black boxes"? The reader will find a discussion of this subject in chapter 18.

121—A fighter from Sokol. Said to be an SU-15 but most probably a MiG-31, Pilot Tarasov.

163—A fighter from Smirnykh. Said to be a MiG-23, Pilot Litvinov.

464—A reserve fighter from Sokol. Probably a MiG-31.

731—A fighter from Postovaya on the Russian mainland. Probably a MiG-31 and his wingman.

804—A fighter from Sokol. A MiG-31, Pilot Osipovich.

805—A fighter from Sokol. Probably a MiG-31.

808—A reserve fighter from Sokol. Probably a MiG-31, Pilot Tarasov II.

Afterburner, also postcombustion—A high-power mode for jet engines.

Airways—A route in the sky marked by radio beacons.

ALERFA—In civil aviation, an alert procedure for an aircraft that has failed to report for more than thirty minutes after a mandatory checkpoint.

Alert code Zero Zero—A military alert code for the island of Sakhalin.

Alert Level One—An alert level for individual pilots in the Soviet Air Force where the pilot in question has to be seated in his cockpit, ready for immediate takeoff.

Alert Level Two—An individual alert level in the Soviet Air Force where the pilot does not have to be seated in his cockpit, but must be ready to take off within two minutes.

Alert Level Three—An individual alert level in the Soviet Air Force where the pilot can rest in the pilots' lounge but must be ready to take off within ten minutes.

Anisimov—Captain of a KGB border-patrol boat.

Asahi Shimbun—A major newspaper in Japan with a circulation of more than 6 million.

ATC—Air traffic control, a civilian agency controlling aircraft in flight.

AWACs—A battlefield surveillance aircraft and airborne command post with sophisticated electronic equipment.

Azimuth—The bearing of an object relative to a reference point.

Bearing—The direction in which one sees an object.

Bering Sea—A body of water north of the Aleutian Islands between Alaska and Siberia (including Kamchatka).

Bethel—A radar-controlled mandatory waypoint on the airways out of Anchorage.

Burevestnik—An important Soviet air base on the island of Iturup in the Kurils.

***Chidori Maru* No. 58**—A Japanese squid-fishing vessel that witnessed an aircraft explode low over the water at 03:30, September 1, 1983.

Chitose—A major Japanese military air base on Hokkaido, on a field also used by civilian airlines.

Code 1300—A transponder code to be used by all aircraft leaving Japanese radar-controlled airspace for the Pacific Ocean.

Code 2000—A transponder code to be used by all aircraft before entering Japanese radar-controlled airspace from the Pacific Ocean.

CPO—Command post officer.

CVR—Cockpit voice recorder. One of the two black boxes aboard an aircraft.

DEFCON 3—A military alert level for Japanese and U.S. forces in Japan, just below DEFCON 4, general mobilization. DEFCON 5 is a state of war.

Deputat—Call sign of a controller of aircraft of the fighter regiment based at Sokol.

DETRESFA—The highest alert mode in civil aviation procedure. It is implemented upon receiving a Mayday, when an aircraft with which radio contact has been lost has failed to land and has used up all its known fuel reserve, or when it is otherwise feared that human life may be at risk.

DFDR—Digital flight-data recorder. One of the two black boxes aboard an aircraft.

Diet—The Japanese parliament.

DME—Distance measuring equipment.

Elizovo—The Soviet military air base near Petropavlovsk, on Kamchatka.

ETA—Estimated time of arrival.

Ferret mission—A clandestine electronic-intelligence mission conducted by aircraft or space assets.

Fighter "A"—One of the three Soviet fighters observed by the Japanese radars in the first hour. A MiG-23.

Flight level (FL)—The altitude of an aircraft read on a barometric altimeter set on standard atmospheric pressure and expressed in hundreds of feet. For example an altitude of 35,000 feet is expressed as FL 350. Note that the word altitude is reserved for aircraft below FL 150 and is expressed in feet. Thus, altitude 9,000 feet but FL 190 (for 19,000 feet).

Georgi Kozmin—A Soviet salvage vessel that found a piece of wreckage, part of an aircraft wing, on September 16, 1983.

GMT—Greenwich mean time, also called UTC (universal time) and Z time.

Ground speed—The speed of an aircraft relative to the ground.

HBC—Hokkaido Broadcasting Company.

Heading—The direction toward which the nose of an aircraft points. Because of wind, it is usually different from the course from which it differs by the amount of draft.

Hersh, Seymour—An American investigative journalist, author of *The Target Is Destroyed*.

HF—High frequency. Designates short-wave radio.

Hokkaido—The northernmost island of Japan.

Hokkaido Shimbun—The main newspaper on the Japanese island of Hokkaido.

Honshu—The main Japanese island.

ICAO—International Civil Aviation Organization, a United Nations specialized agency with headquarters in Montreal.

ICBM—Intercontinental ballistic missile.

Illesh, Andrei—A Soviet journalist, editor of the *Izvestiya* series of articles about KAL 007, and the author of two books on the subject.

INCERFA—In civil aviation procedures an initial alert level for an aircraft with which radio contact has been lost.

Information Paper No. 1—A document appended to the ICAO report of June 1993 containing the ICAO's English translation of Russian communications transcripts.

INS—Inertial navigation system. A self-contained navigation system, in 1983 the primary mode of navigation used by aircraft on long overwater flights.

Iturup—A Soviet island in the Kuril chain.

Izvestiya—A major Soviet (Russian) newspaper with a circulation of 10 million.

Japan time—The official time zone in Japan, nine hours ahead of GMT and two hours behind Sakhalin time. Sometimes also called Tokyo time.

The Japan Times—An English-language Japanese newspaper printed in Tokyo.

JASDF—Japanese Air Self-Defense Forces. Officially, Japan has no regular armed forces.

JDA—Japanese Defense Agency. Having, theoretically, no regular army, Japan has no ministry of defense as such.

JDA radar map—A map of the radar traces of an intruder and three Soviet fighters over Sakhalin made public by the JDA at its 21:10 Japan-time press conference on September 1, 1983.

JMSA—Japanese Maritime Safety Agency. A kind of coast guard, in charge of all safety operations at sea. A civilian agency of the Japanese government, it uses naval rank and has armed vessels.

KADPO—A waypoint over the Sea of Japan on the airway out of Niigata.

KAL 007—Korean Air Lines Flight 007, from New York to Seoul via Anchorage.

KAL 015—A Korean airliner, flight companion to KAL 007.

KAL 050—A Korean airliner that contacted KAL 007 a few minutes before its destruction.

Kamchatka Peninsula—A part of Siberia closest to the Aleutian Islands.

Kazmin, Major—For years, wrongly presented as the pilot who shot down the Korean airliner. He was replaced in that role (again wrongly) by Lieutenant Colonel Osipovich. Major Kazmin was actually stationed on Kamchatka.

KE 007—The designation Flight 007 used in radio transmissions and other air-traffic-control references.

KGB—The Soviet secret police and foreign intelligence agency, also in charge of the border police.

Khomutovo—Designation of the civilian airport at Yuzhno-Sakhalinsk, also used by the military.

Kilometers—When it was created by a French scientist, the one ten-thousandth part of a quarter of a meridian. A kilometer is one thousand meters. There are one hundred centimeters in a meter, ten millimeters in a centimeter, and one million microns in a meter. The beauty of the metric system is that one can go from one unit to the other simply by shifting the decimal one place.

Kirkpatrick tape—The tape of the radio transmissions of the Soviet pilots over Sakhalin to their ground control, recorded by the Japanese and presented by Ambassador Kirkpatrick to the Security Council of the United Nations on September 6, 1993. Although said by Ambassador Kirkpatrick to be unedited, electronic and textual analysis shows substantial deletions. Time on the U.S. transcript of the tape is misstated by one hour.

Knots—Nautical miles per hour. Originally a measure of length, with a value of 15.43 meters. That is 1/120 of a nautical mile. Said differently, it is equal to half a second of latitude (see *Nautical mile*). In the days of the sailing ships, the speed was measured by putting a piece of wood vertically in the water. To it was attached a long string. On the string, a knot was made at each 1/120 of a nautical mile so that the number of knots passing through the sailor's hand in thirty seconds (the distance covered in the water in thirty seconds) was equivalent to the number of nautical miles made good by the ship in one hour. (There are 120 thirty-second intervals in an hour.) Thus a vessel doing so many knots is doing so many nautical miles per hour. Since the speed is measured by the number of knots counted in thirty seconds, it is always incorrect to say "knots per hour." One should always say "so many knots."

Kostroma—A radar station on the west coast of Sakhalin.

Koyama, Iwao—A Japanese journalist, former station chief for the Japan Broadcasting Company (NHK) at Wakkanai, and author of a book on KAL 007.

Kurils—A chain of islands that separates the North Pacific Ocean from the Sea of Okhotsk.

La Pérouse Strait—A narrow strait between the Japanese island of Hokkaido and the island of Sakhalin, called the Soya Strait by the Japanese.

Litvinov—Senior lieutenant, pilot of MiG-23 163 from Smirnykh.

Lobko, Misha—A French journalist of Russian origin who went to Russia and Sakhalin investigating the KAL 007 case. He interviewed pilot Osipovich. He independently came to the conclusion that there had been an air battle and heard of the author's investigation only after his return to France.

Mach—An expression of speed relative to the speed of sound, from the name of an Austrian scientist. An aircraft traveling at Mach 1 is traveling at the speed of sound.

Magnetic heading—The heading of a vessel on the magnetic compass, where north is oriented on the magnetic pole. Magnetic deviation is the difference between a magnetic heading and a true heading. Magnetic headings vary substantially from place to place.

Mainichi Shimbun—A major Japanese newspaper with a circulation of several million copies.

Makarov—A city on the east coast of Sakhalin on the shores of the Gulf of Terpeniya and toward which one of the intruders was headed.

Makarov, Lieutenant General—Soviet lieutenant general of Aviation.
Mayday—The voice equivalent of SOS From the French m'aider (help me).

Meter—The one thousandth part of a kilometer.

MiG-21—An obsolete Soviet jet fighter.

MiG-23—A Soviet swing-wing interceptor, capable of Mach 2 plus.

MiG-31—A powerful Soviet interceptor, Mach 3 capable.

Mikhail Mirchinko—A civilian Soviet oil-drilling vessel with sophisticated capabilities such as dynamic positioning and deep-water submergence. It was used for the recovery of several aircraft wrecks off Sakhalin and Moneron Islands.

Mode A—A mode of operation for a transponder, used by both military and civilian aircraft, with a short pulse duration of only eight microseconds and no altitude encoding.

Mode C—A mode of operation for a transponder in which the altitude of the aircraft is automatically encoded with the identification signal.

Moneron—A small island in the Tatar Gulf, to the west of Sakhalin, called Kaiba Tô when it was under Japanese rule.

Moscow standard time—The official time in Moscow, three hours ahead of GMT. Used by the Soviet military as Standard Military Time throughout the Soviet Union.

Narita tape—The recording of radio communications between KAL 007 and the air-traffic ground control in Tokyo, handed over by Prime Minister Nakasone to the Japanese Diet on July 10, 1985.

Nautical mile (NM)—Universally used in sea and air navigation because it is equal to one minute of latitude on a meridian. On a navigation map distance is measured in degrees and minutes of latitude. A nautical mile can thus be used for any navigation problem without conversion. Another advantage is the expression of speed in knots: one knot is one nautical mile per hour.

NEEVA—A waypoint on airway route Romeo-20, north of Shemya Island, not radar-controlled.

Nevelsk—A town and harbor on the west coast of Sakhalin.

Niigata—A town and harbor on the Sea of Japan and a waypoint on KAL 007's assigned route to Seoul. KAL 007 was destroyed just north of Niigata.

NIPPI—A waypoint on airway route Romeo-20.

Noglikovo—A Soviet air base south of Elizovo.

NOKKA—A waypoint on airway route Romeo-20.

NSA—The U.S. National Security Agency, which handles the interception of communications and radar emissions.

Okushiri—A small island in the Sea of Japan, just north of the entrance of the Tsugaru Strait. Much KAL 007 debris was found there several years after the incident by the author. On July 27, 1993, it was visited by Emperor Akihito and Empress Michiko following a devastating earthquake of 7.8 on the Richter scale

Osipovich, Lt. Col. Gennadi—A Soviet pilot incorrectly said to have shot down KAL 007.

Pan, Pan, Pan—In civil-aviation radio procedures, a standard and mandatory way to ask for help. It is one degree of urgency below Mayday (SOS). From the French panne (breakdown).

Pearson, David—Author of a book, *KAL 007: The Cover-Up*.

Plantatsia—Designation of the command post and radar station at Smirnykh air base.

Position report—A radio communication by an aircraft to ATC made at all mandatory waypoints, in which an aircraft gives its position, its ETA at the next waypoint, the wind aloft, and other pertinent information.

Postovaya—An important Soviet air base on the Siberian mainland close to Sovetskaya Gavan, a major Soviet Navy base.

Pravda—A small fishing village on the west coast of Sakhalin where the Soviets said they "stopped the flight of an intruder" at 06:24 Sakhalin time on September 1.

PVO—The Soviet Air Defense command.

RC-135—A U.S. signals-intelligence-collection aircraft, a Boeing model 707.

Rivet Joint—A type of electronic-intelligence-collection mission flown by an RC-135, targeted to Kamchatka and Sakhalin.

Romeo-20—Of the North Pacific routes from Alaska to Japan, the one closest to Soviet airspace at Kamchatka and the Kuril Islands.

Sai—A small village on the Shimo Kita peninsula, on the Tsugaru Strait, where debris from KAL 007 was found by the villagers on September 16, 1983. That prompted the JMSA to initiate a large-scale search operation for KAL 007 four hundred miles south of Moneron, where it had allegedly fallen.

Sakhalin Island—A Soviet island on the east coast of Siberia. Its southern half was under Japanese rule until the end of World War II.

Sakhalin time—The official time on Sakhalin Island, eleven hours ahead of GMT. Curiously, because of historical reasons, Sakhalin time is two hours ahead of Japan time, although both are in the same time zone. That explains why Sakhalin does not change to daylight saving time: its standard time is already two hours earlier than astronomical time.

Saturation diving—The pressure underwater increases by one atmosphere (one kilogram) every ten meters down. At one hundred meters it is thus ten atmospheres or ten kilograms per square centimeter. At these pressures, the nitrogen the diver breathes dissolves in the blood and can cause catastrophic disability when the diver comes back to the surface without having accomplished step-by-step decompression. To eliminate this severe drawback to operational diving, divers are first put in a closed compartment that is compressed to the same pressure the divers are expected to encounter on the bottom. From that compartment on the mother vessel, they go back and forth to the bottom, where they perform their work for several hours in a row, in a special diving bell that keeps them under the same pressure during their transit. The Soviet divers stayed in saturation at a pressure of eighteen atmospheres (eighteen kilograms per square centimeter) for one month at a time.

Sea of Japan—A body of water that separates Japan on the east from Korea, China, and Russia on the west. North of La Pérouse Strait it is usually referred to as the Tatar Gulf.

Sea of Okhotsk—A body of water bounded by Sakhalin Island, Siberia, the Kamchatka Peninsula, the Kuril Islands, and Hokkaido.

Smirnykh—A main fighter base on the middle of the island of Sakhalin, north of Sokol. It was the headquarters of the fighter division and the base of a fighter regiment equipped with MiG-23s.

Sokol—A main fighter base on south Sakhalin. Base of a fighter regiment, equipped since August 1, 1983, with MiG-31s.

Sound waves—Any sound perceived by the ear is a sound wave. High-energy sound waves are powerful, high-frequency sound waves, called ultrasonic waves. Not to be confused with *supersonic,* which refers to something faster than the sound waves.

Soya Strait—A narrow stretch of water between the Japanese island of Hokkaido and Sakhalin. Also called La Pérouse Strait from its French discoverer.

Squawk—To squawk is to activate a discrete code on the transponder that will allow an observing radar to identify the aircraft carrying the transponder.

Suchogruz—Call sign of an airborne command post from Vanino, in Siberia.

Tanker—Call sign of an airborne command post from Vanino, in Siberia.

Tarasov—The pilot of fighter 121, believed to be a MiG-31.

Target drones—Lightly built flying contraptions towed by aircraft and used by another aircraft as a target for cannon or machine-gun practice.

Tatar Gulf—A body of water between Sakhalin and Siberia. Its southern limit is La Pérouse Strait and the Sea of Japan.

Tatar Strait—Another name for the Tatar Gulf.

Terpeniya—A cape at the extreme end of a long and slender peninsula on the east coast of mid-Sakhalin, site of a main radar observation post, Oblozhka.

Too Nippo—An important provincial newspaper printed at Aomori on northern Honshu.

Transponder—An electronic device that sends an identification signal when "interrogated" by a surveillance radar. A kind of civilian IFF (identification friend or foe).

Tsuboi, Dr. K.—Chief of the Iwatsu Electric Company Laboratory in Japan and an expert with the Tokyo police for voice identification.

Tsugaru Strait—A narrow stretch of water between the Japanese islands of Honshu and Hokkaido.

Tsushima Shio—A powerful and permanent warm current on the east side of the Sea of Japan that carries tropical waters from the China Sea in the south to the Tatar Strait in the north.

TU-16—A Soviet airplane used as a transport, bomber, and reconnaissance aircraft, easily identifiable by its long and slender fuselage.

Tyuleniy—A tiny island south of Cape Terpeniya. In an interview, Osipovich said he pursued an intruder in that area. No other Soviet pilot we know of flew in that area.

UTC—Coordinated Universal time. A working average between Universal time as given by the earth's rotation, which is slightly irregular, and the atomic Universal time given by some two hundred atomic clocks in the world and reserved for scientific uses. It is also expressed as GMT (Greenwich mean time) and Z time.

Vanino—A town and major Soviet Air Force base in mainland Siberia.

VHF (very high frequency)—A type of radio communication more reliable than HF but shorter range, limited by the curvature of the earth. They propagate only in line of sight.

VOR (VHF omnirange)—A radio beacon for aircraft that uses VHF.

VOR/DME—A VOR to which is associated a DME (distance-measuring equipment).

VORTAC—Same as VOR/DME but where the DME is military.

Wakkanai—The northernmost town of Japan and the closest to Sakhalin. It was at the forefront of worldwide news during several months of the naval search off Sakhalin and the search for debris on the Hokkaido beaches on the Sea of Okhotsk.

Waypoint—A reporting point on an airway.

Yomiuri Shimbun—A major Japanese newspaper with a circulation of 7 million.

Yuzhno-Sakhalinsk—The administrative capital of Sakhalin; also an airfield there used by military as well as civilian aircraft.

Zeleny—An island in the Kurils that two squadrons of armed fighters from the carriers USS *Midway* and *Enterprise* overflew on April 4, 1983.

INTRODUCTION

1. As an inspector, I took part in the investigation of this crash. It taught me several things that were directly relevant in the KAL 007 case: (a) An aircraft hitting the water never explodes; it just splashes. (b) When an airliner crashes on the water, a huge amount of floating debris is immediately seen on the surface, including any survivors and many floating bodies. (c) This floating debris moves away from the crash site with the speed and in the direction of the surface current. (d) The testimony of professional fishermen who have witnessed this crash tends to be precise and reliable.

CHAPTER 1: The Flight From New York

1. These are the famous Northern Territories, the four Kuril Islands nearest Japan, which were taken over by the Soviet Union at the end of World War II. Japan has continued to demand their return.

2. The capital of Sakhalin. There is a civilian airport here that can accommodate a Boeing 747.

CHAPTER 2: The Landing at Sakhalin

1. David Pearson, *KAL 007: The Cover-Up* (Summit Books: New York, 1987), 102.

CHAPTER 3: The Investigation Begins

1. The September 1, 1983, *Hokkaido Shimbun* story also mentions a communiqué from Korean Air Lines headquarters in Tokyo, dated September 1, 11:00 A.M., which reads, "The plane was apparently forced to land at Sakhalin at approximately 4:00 in the morning." The fact that Korean Air Lines gives 4:00 in the morning as the hour the plane landed on Sakhalin is significant. This is the time determined from the radar observations at Wakkanai. It refers specifically to the interception at 03:53 by fighter C, whose track, together with that of the plane it was "escorting," disappeared from the screen around 04:01.

2. Note the reference to confirmation of these radio transmissions by an American satellite. U.S. ferret subsatellite 1982 41 C, in polar orbit, was in a position to monitor electronic events over Sakhalin at this time.

3. Before KAL 007's communications with Tokyo Control were interrupted at the time of the airliner's 03:27 (18:27 GMT) transmission, Tokyo Control may in fact have had reason to worry about KAL 007's position. JDA's highly

automated Air Defense "Badge" System may have registered KAL 007's failure to show up on the JDA radar at Nemuro when expected. JDA may have asked Narita control to verify KAL 007's position. No such Narita request to KAL 007 was made at that time. However, KAL 007 had given an ETA of 03:26 at waypoint NOKKA, and Narita might have decided to wait for the airliner to report its position then.

4. It should be pointed out that fighter A, which crossed the path of the Korean plane at 03:25 hours, was 6,500 feet below the airliner, whereas this plane, at the exact same time, is flying above it. The reference is, presumably, to two different interceptors and two different intruders.

5. At the same moment the "Korean plane" was observed 47° N and 142° E over the town of Kholmsk. This was another intruder.

6. See preceding footnote number 3.

7. In order to conform their version of events with the American version, the Japanese appear to have dropped their earlier statement of the firing sequence occurring "just before 03:25."

8. 1551Z = 1551 GMT = 1551 UTC.

9. We know that KAL 007 was within VFR radio range of Narita at 19:12 GMT off the west coast of Honshu south of the Tsugaru Strait. Time and distance factors indicate that KAL 007's speeds indicated by its position reports must have been approximately correct (although its stated course was, obviously, not).

10. On the Kirkpatrick map the track of the "Korean plane" continues across Sakhalin, and beyond it north of Moneron Island. Both in heading and geographical position it is similar to the track of fighter C, but because the times are different it cannot have been its target.

11. In chapter 16 I show that this sequence probably involved two interceptors and two targets.

CHAPTER 4: The Admiral's Frustration
1. Selvkhine, radar specialist aboard the *Baikal*, was quoted by *Izvestiya* as saying that the Soviets employed more than 130 vessels in this part of the search.

2. The recovery of the life raft was never officially announced, and the

American Navy never released any information about it. The JMSA found out about it when they intercepted the radio communications between the American planes and their base and reported it in their operations log. That was my source for the information. A similar raft was found among the debris turned over to the Japanese by the Soviets on September 26, 1983. This raft, too, did not come from the Korean Air Lines Boeing 747. The water was not too cold for a person to spend time in it and survive. The crew of a U.S. helicopter that crashed were left in the water for a couple of hours—despite Soviet offers to pick them up—and seem to have suffered no harm. The right clothing would, of course, have been critical.

3. Debris number 34 is a shell of white plastic, measuring 1.6 by 3.3 feet, and equipped with several straps, together with their buckles and reinforcements. Two circular channels on the right and left appear to have contained explosive charges, which have been fired.

4. Photograph taken by the Kyodo Press Agency on September 14 at Abashiri, on the northern coast of Hokkaido. Examination reveals, on a rib next to the left hand of the policeman who is holding it, the serial number C-87839, lightly engraved by hand the way certain aeronautical parts are engraved so as not to affect their mechanical properties. The number can be read from the exterior. Near the policeman's other hand is a second mark (4.0Y), which appears to have been stamped mechanically.

5. Debris N3 was found on September 10, 1983, at ten-thirty in the morning, by the patrol ship *Rishiri* of the JMSA at 46° 42'09" N, 141° 19'15" E, approximately twenty-nine miles from Moneron and seven miles north of the *Chidori Maru*'s position at the time of the sighting ten days earlier. The debris is marked N3 on both surfaces, and the serial number 7111032 appears on one of the surfaces. I later saw photographs of the piece and discussed it with JMSA officers. It was covered with a layer of fresh soot and appeared to be a sandwich of aluminum sheet wrapped around a honeycomb core with some polystyrene foam added to increase stiffness. The honeycomb core and polystyrene reinforcement bonded together with adhesive are typical of high-tech construction methods.

6. Ambassador Pavlov gave the following locations for the discovery:
47°10' N, 140°15' E
46°15' N, 140°15' E
47°10' N, 141°35' E
46°35' N, 141°25' E
The first two fragments were aligned in a north-south direction, clearly

indicating they had drifted with the current flowing from the south. They were found much too far west of Moneron to have fallen near the area of the *Chidori Maru* sighting. The third fragment could have fallen there, and the north-flowing current may have pushed it along to the spot where it was eventually picked up. Except for the fact that after nine days in the water, it would most likely have drifted far beyond the place where it was found. The fourth fragment was picked up at the exact coordinates of the *Chidori Maru* sighting and right under the nose of the destroyer USS *Elliot,* which was at the same location at the same time. The fact that it was found here nine days after the crash indicates that this was not the impact area for Flight 007.

7. *Los Angeles Times,* September 22, 1983.

CHAPTER 5: The Cemetery of Tsugaru
1. The following debris were found by the JMSA floating in the Sea of Okhotsk:

On September 10, 1983, at 16:30, the patrol ship *Yubari* found a piece of aluminum, measuring 20 by 12 by 0.5 inches, with a honeycomb core. On one side was marked LOT 495-ALIZING-12-3. This is not a Boeing marking. The fragment did not come from KAL 007.

On September 11, 1983, at 10:00 hours, the patrol ship *Daio* picked up, 10 NM out at sea, a gray fiberglass honeycomb core that measured 12 by 12 by 16 inches, with traces of fire on it and the word CONDUCT printed in black. The fragment was similar to the piece I had found on the beach of Okushiri, four hundred miles to the south.

The police found the following fragments along Japanese beaches near Mombetsu:

- A fragment made of composite material marked on one side BRUNSWICK, N.J. UNION MADE IN U.S.A. PVC10-MIL PIPEWRAPI, and LR.4. B30 on the other side. The MIL on the fragment shows it was intended for military use.
- A fragment of composite material marked L778 COVE LIGHT. This piece was part of a light fixture over a workstation on a military aircraft.
- A fragment of light metal with the following markings: BMS4-13 TYPE. BATCH NORTHROP. Northrop manufactures airplanes exclusively for the military.

2. Titanium 88.96%, aluminum 5.70%, molybdenum 4.12%, silicon 0.73%, tin 0.39%, vanadium 0.11%.

CHAPTER 6: The Meeting in Tokyo
1. At the time I did not realize that the 03:25 incident was more complex than the JDA statement at first sight implied. See chapter 16.

CHAPTER 7: KAL 007 Does Not Answer

1. John Keppel asked Boeing to inspect the debris I had found. Boeing replied that we would have to ask the NTSB (National Transportation Safety Board) to make a formal request to them. The NTSB referred us to the ICAO. The ICAO failed to answer Keppel's letter asking it to inspect the debris.

2. Mr. Kensuke Nakazawa, from Japan, Mr. Hyun Mo Hong from the Republic of Korea, Mr. William Henry Stevens from the U.S.A., and Mr. Peter G. Bates, second secretary and vice-consul at the Canadian embassy on behalf of the Canadian families.

3. Showa Aircraft's findings included the following points: (1) the debris from Sai and Okushiri (No. 10) did not come from the DART target drones used by the JASDF; (2) the debris from Sai and Okushiri (No. 10) were not made by a Japanese manufacturer because the step-by-step bonding method hasn't been used in Japan for years. Both of these findings have been confirmed by the discovery of Korean markings (hangul) on debris No. 14 from Okushiri.

The findings of Mr. Yazaki at Nippon Freuhauf included the following points: (1) debris No. 10 from Sai and Okushiri appear to be aeronautical materials. They are too light for maritime or land use; (2) debris No. 10 from Okushiri, which has two bolt holes and a layer of red paint applied directly without a primer, shows all the characteristics of a panel used for the manufacture of a transport container for valuable goods shipped by air, such as electronic instruments, computers, etc.; (3) the debris from Sai, which has a layer of primer, could be from an inside wall panel for a passenger compartment that was manufactured in Korea and installed by Korean Air Lines when they modified the airplane in 1978.

It should also be noted that the individual cells in the honeycomb used in DART drones have cuts in them that make them sink faster when in water. There are no such cuts in the cells in the honeycomb used in the debris.

4. A distance from the ground equal to one and a half times the wingspan. In the case of Ron's plane, a mere 150 feet.

CHAPTER 8: The Search for the Crash Site

1. The Bureau of Weapons is a term that has been dropped but existed in 1983.

2. I also learned that the stylized design that I thought was a film camera was, in fact, a motion-picture camera and three characters in hangul (used to symbolize Korean sounds) representing the letters *U, N,* and *IA,* which my Korean informant was unable to decipher.

CHAPTER 9: The Witnesses Speak Out

1. See chapter 6.

2. Illesh was wrong here. The conclusive voice-print and spectrographic analysis was conducted only in Japan, by Dr. Tsuboi of the Iwatsu Laboratory.

3. *Izvestiya's* handling of the map, like its correct quoting of revealing statements by witnesses contradicting the official line that was the main thrust of its KAL 007 series, is an example of the Russians' consistently ambiguous handling of the case. How much of the contradictory detail was put in purposely in defiance of the authorities, and how much was put in by the authorities, is not easy to determine and may vary from instance to instance.

4. *Izvestiya,* February 4, 1991.

5. *Izvestiya,* January 26, 1991.

6. The Japanese newspaper *Too Nippo* had published the news of a Soviet recovery of wreckage as early as September 18, 1983. See chapter 10.

7. *Izvestiya,* January 22, 1991.

8. *Izvestiya,* October 19, 1991, p. 12.

9. Capt. Boris Kosik, *Izvestiya,* October 29, 1991.

10. One wreck (maybe several) was found by the Soviet Navy and another one (in fact several) by the civilian divers.

11. *Izvestiya,* May 28, 1991.

12. Larry Ryckman AP dispatch printed on September 1, 1993, in the *Gazette,* Montreal.

13. The implication is, of course, that the civilian debris on the surface north of Moneron on September 1, 1983, was dropped there by aircraft or helicopter. There appears to have been sunken as well as floating evidence planted north of Moneron. In the German edition of Illesh's book there is an underwater photograph taken by the Soviets in 1983 of a KAL 007 life jacket. One lobe is somewhat raised from the sea floor and, from this fact and from its shape, clearly contains some air. Since the life jacket did not float, the

other lobe must have been weighted in one way or another. It is hard to conceive how this could have come about other than intentionally. Planted evidence in aircraft disasters is not unheard of. Re the PA 103 case, see Donald Goddard with Lister K. Coleman, *Trail of the Octopus* (London and New York: Signet, Penguin Books, 1994).

14. JMSA situation maps for September 1.

15. *Yomiuri Shimbun,* October 15, 1991.

16. Pavlov's "west of Moneron" could have been a reference to the crash site 16 NM northwest of Moneron later searched intensively by the United States.

17. Captain Anisimov added that the characteristics of the radar echo from the aircraft he tracked made him think it was a large plane. He was using a marine radar unit designed to detect ships on the surface of the sea. On this type of radar, a large airplane or a group of smaller aircraft would give an identical echo, that of a large target. Marine radar does not have the same sensitivity as aerial surveillance radars, which work at different frequencies. Another characteristic of marine radar systems is that their beam is directed toward the horizon, and therefore, they can only detect objects on or very near the surface of the water.

18. The 06:24 Sakhalin time mentioned by Ogarkov as that of the shootdown of an intruder aircraft is consistent with the details of what seems to have been Osipovich's second mission. Osipovich told *Izvestiya* he took off from Sokol Airbase a minute or two after 06:00 Sakhalin time on a mission on which he shot down an intruder aircraft.

The difference between Sakhalin and Japan time is two hours and not three hours as has sometimes been alleged. For example, James Oberg in *Air Force Magazine* and the 1993 ICAO KAL 007 investigation report both stated that 06:00 Sakhalin time was 18:00 UTC (03:00 Japan time), which is not so. I will discuss the matter of Sakhalin time and its implications at length later in the text of this book.

CHAPTER 10: The Soviet Underwater Search (1)
1. Illesh, *Izvestiya,* January 26, 1991.

2. *Izvestiya,* January 31, 1991.

3. Report on the Moscow Meeting for Families of the Victims of the Destruction of Korean Airlines Flight 007, March 11, 1993 (Canadian government document).

4. *Izvestiya,* January 28, 1991.

5. Ibid.

6. *Izvestiya,* January 31, 1991. A Boeing 747 is a huge plane with large and extremely strong components. It is constructed so sturdily that even the most violent shock wouldn't reduce it to the dimensions mentioned by the Russian observers. There are four enormous engines and five landing gear units (four main and one forward in the nose), each of which is several yards in length. Not to mention the immense wings with their extremely strong spars. Nor is there a "pivot support structure" or any titanium pivots on a Boeing 747.

7. On page 42 I mentioned that the piece of floating debris bearing the JMSA tag number 31 appears to be part of the flap from the wing of an F-111 or an EF-111. Since it was found in international waters north of Moneron, it cannot (given the nature of the currents) have come from the crash in Soviet territorial waters near Nevelsk. It thus appears that two EF-111s may have been shot down.

8. This is approximately 3 NM south-southeast of the spot where the *Chidori Maru* No. 58 saw a plane explode above the water at 03:30 on September 1. See Figure 13, page 136.

9. The second wreck is directly in line with the *Chidori Maru*'s observation, though somewhat farther away than the five thousand feet I had figured. The direction of the explosion was initially given by the *Chidori Maru*'s captain in relation to a land feature on Sakhalin (a lighthouse), so it is precise and can be relied on. As for the distance, my calculations were based on the fishermen's appreciation of the duration (in seconds) of the explosion and of the time it took for the smell of kerosene to reach their nostrils. These are subjective impressions with room for some adjustment. On the other hand, the location of the crash site discovered by Captain Bilyuk, slightly north of the point where the wreckage rests on the bottom, is exactly as expected, since he arrived on the site several hours after that aircraft went down, and by that time the debris had drifted slightly north with the Tsushima Shio. The distance from Captain Bilyuk's crash site to the location of the second wreck of September 16 (the ten-meter piece of wing) is a mere 1.5 NM. Since he found it about four hours after the crash, that indicates a moderate northward current with a velocity of 0.4 knots. This second wreck of September 16 thus corresponds to the explosion witnessed by the *Chidori Maru* and also to the crash site discovered by the *Uvarovsk* of Captain Bilyuk. Both constitute a single event.

10. *Izvestiya,* February 5, 1991.

11. Originally "secret," declassified and released in 1993. The entire U.S. search effort was classified "secret" virtually from the outset. I do not know of any precedent for this in a search for a civilian airliner.

12. *Izvestiya,* May 28, 1991.

CHAPTER 11: The Soviet Undersea Search (2)

1. *Izvestiya,* January 29, 1991.

2. *Izvestiya,* February 1, 1991.

3. *Izvestiya,* February 1, 1991.

4. *Izvestiya,* February 1, 1991.

5. *Izvestiya,* February 5, 1991. On September 25, 1983, foreign observers and representatives from the international press were, indeed, invited on board the USS *Callaghan.* They returned to port on September 27 and were replaced by an observer from the ICAO, Mr. Widdal, and an observer from the French government, Mr. Subrenat, who sailed on board the USS *Sterett.*

6. That the U.S. "intensive search area" included the crash site of a U.S. aircraft is also shown by the radar data given by NSA to Task Force 71's commanders before they left Washington. See chapter 12.

7. *Izvestiya,* January 28, 1991.

8. Confirmation of this is given by the U.S. Navy's after-action report. It indicates that the best suited among its three search vessels was the USCG *Munro* (a Coast Guard cutter on a visit to Japan at the time) because it was the largest vessel and could operate more easily in rough water than the *Narragansett* or the *Conserver.* The *Conserver,* an ocean-going tug, was not well suited to this phase of the search. The aft part of the ship sat too low, and it took on water too easily in rough weather, which endangered both men and materials. The small Soviet trawlers would have been even more vulnerable than the large American tugs.

9. *Izvestiya,* January 31, 1991.

10. *Izvestiya,* January 29, 1991.

11. Ibid.

12. Original text—Illesh may have deleted these sentences because of the "nowhere else," a reference to other crash sites.

13. *Izvestiya,* January 31, 1991.

14. *Izvestiya,* January 29, 1991.

15. *Izvestiya,* January 31, 1991.

16. *Izvestiya,* January 29, 1991.

17. This confirms that it was a fairly large aircraft with a good portion of the fuselage still intact.

18. KAL 007 left New York on August 31. It is highly unlikely that any of the passengers would have been wearing gloves at the end of August and kept them on in the airplane. And civilian pilots never wear gloves in the air-conditioned cockpit of an airliner because it would interfere with their work. Military pilots, on the other hand, do wear gloves. For safety reasons they are part of their regulation equipment.

19. *Izvestiya,* January 29, 1991.

20. *Izvestiya,* January 31, 1991.

21. Vadim, in the original text.

22. *Izvestiya,* January 31, 1991.

23. Illesh was not always well informed, as is illustrated by the matter of the KAL 007 logo. John Keppel, who lunched with him in New York, says Illesh drew (on a napkin) a bad map of the Sea of Okhotsk and the Kurils and did not know what KAL 015 was. Shalnev, who was also present, had to tell him. I do not, however, believe that most of Illesh's behavior should be ascribed to failure to understand. His insistence on the official one-intruder, one-shootdown thesis coupled with his printing of witness statements contradicting it is very like the ambiguous behavior of the Soviet and Russian governments in the KAL 007 case throughout. In a sense, Illesh was thus merely, for whatever reason, carrying out government policy. He may not have always been a reporter. A person who visited him at *Izvestiya* tells me

that he had a nameplate on his desk reading "Colonel Illesh"—although that may have been a jocular reference to his authority by other members of the *Izvestiya* staff.

24. On September 26, the Soviets turned over a life raft to the JMSA. This cannot be the same life raft the divers are describing here, for when that one was discovered, the divers were still resting in their dormitory. A third life raft was filmed by a television crew from Hiroshima in Nevelsk, on Sakhalin Island, in July 1991. And a fourth one, as we have seen, was spotted by an Orion P-3C on September 2.

25. *Izvestiya,* January 31, 1991.

26. *Izvestiya,* May 25, 1991. In 1983 the United States was still nominally claiming a three-mile limit to territorial waters, while a twelve-mile limit was much more widely observed. Kurkov's statement in this regard may refer to the fifth wreck. The sonar ordeal of the *Mirchink* divers sounds like the fourth wreck.

27. *Izvestiya,* January 31, 1991.

28. Ibid.

29. *Izvestiya,* January 26, 1991.

30. *Izvestiya,* May 28, 1991.

31. The divers interviewed were part of the second Murmansk team, which didn't arrive on Sakhalin until October 1. They joined the *Mikhail Mirchinko* on October 5 and entered the compression chamber on October 26 to relieve the first team of divers.

32. *Izvestiya,* May 28, 1991.

33. Personal letter to John Keppel, who had asked him about the crash and sent him the analysis of the titanium alloy.

34. *Izvestiya,* February 5, 1991.

35. *Izvestiya,* February 1, 1991.

36. *Izvestiya,* January 31, 1991.

37. Ibid.

38. JMSA Operations log of September 5, 1983.

39. In fact, no debris from the Korean airliner was found by JMSA floating in the search area due north from where the Korean fishermen were operating. The debris found on the beaches of Sakhalin and Hokkaido arrived there after (1) passing through the channel between the island of Rebun and the coast of Hokkaido and (2) passing to the east of Moneron Island and were not intercepted by the Korean fishermen.

Two of the four locations at which Ambassador Pavlov said the Soviets found KAL 007 debris were north of Moneron. It may be worthwhile to note that at least some of the debris to which Pavlov referred, e.g., documents, were not turned over to the Japanese by the Soviets.

40. *Izvestiya,* January 29, 1991.

41. Illesh in *Izvestiya,* January 29, 1991.

42. Zahkarchenko in *Izvestiya,* January 31, 1991.

43. *Izvestiya,* May 27, 1991.

CHAPTER 12: The U.S. Search Operations
1. Twelve-mile limit. In 1983 the U.S. still claimed the three-mile limit.

2. Initially classified "secret." Declassified and released ten years later.

3. That this radar track was given NAVSEA by NSA implies that it was based on interception of Soviet radar tracking data. If NSA intercepted this track, it stands to reason that it intercepted all the other Soviet radar tracks as well.

4. This remark applies only from September 26 to November 6. Before that, from September 10 to September 26 the *Mikhail Mirchinko* was within the territorial waters of Sakhalin, far from the area indicated here. Also, on the morning of September 26, the *Mikhail Mirchinko* was in the U.S. Navy high-probability area.

5. The U.S. interest in this crash site (that of the fourth wreck) is understandable. The aircraft on the bottom there gives every indication of being an RC-135, a signals-intelligence platform full of sensitive electronic equipment. That the United States gave preference to the crash site 16 NM northwest of Moneron makes one wonder what sort of aircraft crashed there. It could

have been an E-2 (Navy AWACs). Soviet photographs of debris suggest that one was shot down at this time. If the crash in the U.S. high-probability area was, indeed, an E-2, it may have come from a U.S. base in Japan, possibly by way of the Sea of Japan (rather, that is, than by way of the Sea of Okhotsk and Sakhalin Island). In which case it could have been shot down over international waters.

The highly useful U.S. Coast Guard cutter *Munro* was in Japan on a good-will visit at the time of the disaster.

CHAPTER 13: The Departure from Anchorage

1. See chapter 7.

2. Chun is the family name, Byung-In is the personal name, usually written with two capital initials because it is a composite of two names.

3. Pearson, *KAL 007*, 120. This information should not be taken lightly since it was also broadcast by NHK, the Japanese-government television network, in its first news bulletin at 7:00 A.M. on September 1. Generally, NHK has good information sources, and the network was twenty minutes ahead of Korean Air Lines Vice President, Charley Cho in stating it.

4. Johnson, *Shootdown*, 101.

5. Since KAL 007 had deviated from its route, this NEEVA does not indicate the NEEVA waypoint along airway route Romeo-20 but rather the point abeam NEEVA at which KAL 007 incorrectly announced it was at NEEVA.

6. British space expert Anthony Kendon said that a Vandenberg AFB ferret (electronic intelligence) subsatellite, 1982 41C in polar orbit, was in approximately the position claimed by Soviet air marshal Kirsanov, from which it would have come into line-of-sight range of KAL 007 on a subsequent pass at Sakhalin. See Pearson, *KAL 007*, 290.

7. The written question in its entirety and the government's response were published in the French Republic's *Gazette* for April 17, 1989, under number 9126 and dated February 6, 1989.

8. The interview was conducted in Murmansk aboard the specialized vessel *Sprut* (Octopus) by *Izvestiya* journalists.

9. I obtained a Japanese copy (translated from the Russian) of the interview from Mr. Ryuji Osaki, who went to Moscow from May 10 to 20, 1991, and

obtained it from *Izvestiya* journalist Illesh in exchange for documents per-taining to the voice analysis of KAL 007's communications, which I gave to Illesh through Ryuji Osaki while he was in Moscow, and other considera-tions. I subsequently translated the text of the interview from Japanese to English.

10. The passenger's name, however, could have been legible on the board-ing pass. If so, TBS or, more probably, Japanese intelligence would probably have preserved it with the idea that it might reveal the name of one of the U.S. military casualties.

11. If, as I suggest in chapter 17, a U.S. military aircraft was directing or pre-tending to be KAL 007, flying to the north of the route the Korean airliner itself actually followed, it could have been the one that crashed at Pereputye. Or one crashing elsewhere on Sakhalin whose debris was dumped in the hole there. The map of the DFDR (Digital Flight Data Recorder) recording that Yeltsin gave the U.S. next of kin and the Korean government in November 1992 shows a course starting at Anchorage, crossing Kamchatka, and ending on Sakhalin, which could have been that of a dummy KAL 007. A KCIA officer would have been useful aboard it. In chapter 14, I mention that abeam waypoint NABIE, KAL 007 appears to have been in radio contact with a Korean-speaking aircraft (not KAL 015) far enough to the north to have been out of range of the en route VHF antenna on St. Paul Island.

CHAPTER 14: The Flight

1. It is, of course, conceivable that KAL 007's extra weight consisted of some-thing other than fuel. Whatever it may have been, it was something that Captain Chun chose not to mention in the pages he submitted at Anchorage.

2. A VOR (VHF omni range) is a radio beacon transmitting on VHF (very high frequency) that aircraft use for their navigation. A VOR signal travels along the line of sight, and its range depends on the altitude of the aircraft and then eight of the VOR antenna.

3. Later on, in its 1993 investigation report, the analysis of what was falsely presented as KAL 007's black box indicated that the plane had followed a constant magnetic heading of 245 degrees. If that had been the case, given magnetic variation and the wind conditions at the time, KAL 007 would have passed directly over Bethel. Accordingly, the black box showing a 245-degree heading could not have been aboard the aircraft shown by the King Salmon radar to have passed Bethel 12 NM north.

4. Anchorage ARTCC Sector 10/11—127.8 MHz and 128.2 MHz, 13:45 to 17:47 UTC.

5. Had KAL 007's interlocutor been out of range of the Anchorage VHF en route antenna on St. Paul Island to the south, it would at the same time have been out of range of KAL 007.

6. Written for the KAL 007 investigation project of the Fund for Constitutional Government.

7. The Regional Operations Control Center at Elmendorf Air Force Base was nearby and frequently communicated with the FAA Center at Anchorage. Pearson, *KAL 007*, 350.

8. Porter's interpretation was later disputed in the Federal District Court of the District of Columbia by an FBI expert, who said the recording was unintelligible and that it was beyond the capability of the equipment to record it intelligibly. This is all very well—except that the key words *warn him* (never used lightly by a controller) are audible to an untrained ear without benefit of electronic enhancement.

9. Pearson, *KAL 007*, 350.

10. The requirements for a KAL 007-simulating aircraft, if there was one, would have been the communications capabilities of an RC-135 and the speed of a Boeing 747. An RC-10 might be a candidate.

11. The two airliners now appeared to be close enough together in time so that if they had been on the same flight level, the controller would have questioned whether they had adequate separation. As it was, the question did not arise. Although initially assigned the same flight level as KAL 007 at Anchorage, KAL 015 had requested and been given a higher level.

12. *Pravda*, September 10; *Izvestiya*, September 10 and 11.

13. *Pravda*, September 30, 1983.

CHAPTER 15: Kamchatka

1. Pearson, *KAL 007*, 62.

2. ICAO report of June 1993, 47.

3. The Soviets mentioned this to Hersh during his trip to the U.S.S.R. (Personal communication to John Keppel).

4. *Izvestiya,* May 29, 1991.

5. An NSA man in 1984 sent to tell a former RC-135 linguist to stop talking to the press told the latter that it was true that one of the aircraft southeast of Karaginski Island mentioned by Ogarkov did in fact dive down below the level of Soviet radar coverage. (Personal communication, Tom Bernard to John Keppel.)

6. Approximately 60 NM within Russian territory.

7. Quoted by Illesh in *Izvestiya,* May 29, 1991.

8. Ogarkov said the speed of the southwest-bound aircraft he discussed was that of an RC-135, which is a much slower 430 knots. The southwest-bound aircraft the admiral and Kretinin described was also implied to be flying at the speed of an RC-135 or KC-135. But their accounts differ in details that seem to relate to different aircraft.

9. Approaching and above both Kamchatka and Sakhalin radar tracking accompanies the DFDR track, though some 30 km to its south. That could represent a second aircraft or, perhaps, be an artifact of the aircraft's own radar-spoofing capability. These tracks pass somewhat closer to the Commandoro Islands than the Russian radar tracks in the page 48 and 50 maps in the 1993 ICAO report.

CHAPTER 16: The Air Battle of Sakhalin
1. Hersh, *Target Is Destroyed,* 223.

2. See meteorological information contained in the ICAO report of 1983 and particularly the Soviet meteorological information pertinent for Kamchatka.

3. Information Paper No. 2 contains the Russian-language texts. Information Paper No. 1 contains the ICAO's English translations.

4. Information Paper No. 1, 183.

5. Ibid., 50.

6. *Izvestiya,* May 29, 1991.

7. The alert was initiated at Sokol shortly after 04:30 local time, when Osipovich had just gotten dressed.

8. Because the parking area was empty and aircraft had been shot down that night, does it mean that Soviet fighters had also been shot down?

9. Illesh, *Mystery of the Black Boxes,* 61.

10. In this interview Osipovich said that the call sign of his interceptor was 804. Illesh in an editorial comment gratuitously contradicted him and said his call sign was 805. It wasn't, however. Dr. Tsuboi of the Iwatsu Laboratory has compared an identifiable Osipovich statement on the Kirkpatrick tape with a self-identified statement by the 805 pilot. Neither the voice-print nor the transmitter profile are the same. The same point emerges from examination of the Russian transcripts.

11. A squadron is generally twelve aircraft. This gives an idea of the scale of the incursion.

12. Related by Lt. Col. A. Dokuchayev in *Krasnaya Zvezda,* March 13, 1991.

13. Hersh, *Target Is Destroyed,* 17-18.

14. In the Russian transcripts a MiG-31 is referred to as an "Article 37"—or has been falsified to read "SU-15."

15. "Without identification signal" presumably means that the aircraft's transponder was turned off.

16. The Air Force base near Petropavlovsk.

17. ICAO 1993 report of June 1993, Information Paper No. 1, 139. Noglikov is a Soviet air base south of Petropavlovsk.

18. Ibid., 141.

19. Ibid., 142.

20. It is not known with certainty whether the two MiG-23s landed for refueling at Khomutovo, near Yuzhno-Sakhalinsk, in the meantime. According to Col. Ivan K., it appears that they did. At any rate, if they were already low on fuel, it does not seem likely that they could have resumed the pursuit without refueling first.

21. The intruder had already been identified by the two MiG-23s as an RC-135. There should have been no need for further identification by Osipovich, unless it was another intruder.

22. In other words, the two MiG-23s were behind Osipovich. They could have lost so much ground to Osipovich only because they had landed for refueling. If they had resumed their pursuit in flight, without landing, they would have found themselves in a good position, just behind the intruder and in front of Osipovich. There would have been no need to send Osipovich. If we suppose that both Osipovich and the two MiG-23s were after the same intruder, we also have to suppose that Osipovich's takeoff and the two MiG-23s' resuming of their pursuit had been ordered at the same time. If this had been the case, it would have been a lot quicker for a fighter already in the air and already in the general area of the intruder to reach the target than for a fighter on the ground, who had to takeoff, climb, and approach the target. All this suggests that the two MiG-23s did land for refueling.

23. As we have seen, they may actually have landed for refueling before the shooting.

24. Osipovich's MiG-31 had four missiles. He fired two at each of two targets, one in the first hour, one in the second. Once more we see the Soviets putting the events of three hours into two.

25. Hersh, *Target Is Destroyed*, 223.

26. ICAO report of June 1993, Information Paper No. 1, 101.

27. Ibid., 83. Strangely enough, Novoseletski gave the order directly to Burevestnik Fighter Regiment Commander Gerasimenko rather than through Kornukov.

28. Ibid., 102.

29. Ibid., 149.

30. Ibid., 173–74.

31. In the sequences that follow on several different tapes, the interceptor involved switches back and forth between Osipovich and 805. Probably two shootdown sequences are involved, with both the Russians and the ICAO seeking to obscure the distinction between Osipovich and 805, just as they sought to obscure the difference between the first and the second hour.

32. ICAO report of June 1993, Information Paper No. 1, 85.

33. ICAO Air Navigation Commission Report, February 23, 1983.

34. Exactly 8.3 statute miles per minute.

35. ICAO Air Navigation Commission Report, February 23, 1983; and ICAO report of June 1993, page 16, paragraph 1.10.3.10.

36. So should the time and distance factors of KAL 007's flight. If the Korean airliner had left Kamchatka at 17:08 GMT, it would have arrived at the point where the Japanese claim to have spotted it at 18:20 GMT rather than 18:12. Moreover, the plane would have been observed flying at a speed of 496 knots rather than 430 knots, the speed of the aircraft tracked by the Japanese.

On the other hand, if the plane located by the Japanese at 18:12 GMT and flying at 430 knots had left Kamchatka at 17:08, it would not have reached the point where the Japanese picked it up on their radar screens until 18:26, not 18:12. Or alternately, it would have left Kamchatka at 16:54.

37. Lieutenant Tarasov was the pilot of fighter 121, probably a MiG-31, from Sokol.

38. A MiG-23 from Smirnykh, pilot Litvinov.

39. "Interception radar" is the ICAO's translation. The Russian text says "RSP," which means "radar-controlled-approach radar." The text makes it clear that both the target and the interceptor were getting so close to Sokol that the controller's radar would lose them. Hence it was decided to issue the order to fire through the radar-controlled-approach radar, which covered nearby aircraft better.

40. Commander of the First (Smirnykh) Fighter Regiment.

41. ICAO report of June 1993, Information Paper No. 1, 191.

42. Marshal Ogarkov in his Moscow press conference of September 9, 1983.

43. The identification of Gerasimenko as commander of the Burevestnik Fighter Regiment is the ICAO's. In this instance, however, it is clear that Gerasimenko is giving orders to Osipovich, who is stationed at Sokol, not at Burevestnik on Iturup in the Kurils. Gerasimenko is taking orders from Kornukov, who is commander at Sokol.

44. ICAO report of June 1993, Information Paper No. 1, 151.

45. Ibid., 126-27.

46. Ibid., 133.

47. The subsequent sequence in which (Information Paper No. 1, 127) Kornukov asks Gerasimenko whether the target has its lights on and orders that Osipovich follow warning procedures appears to be a graft from the second hour. I believe the ICAO was given the Russian tapes, and even if it has given back the "originals," it presumably copied them. If so, electronic analysis would presumably reveal the places where splicing has been done—splice lines, discontinuities in background noise, etc.

48. ICAO report of June 1993, Information Paper No. 1, 193.

49. Information given the Japanese Diet (parliament) by Prime Minister Nakasone on July 10, 1985.

50. *Japan Times,* July 10, 1985.

51. The civilian airport of Yuzhno-Sakhalinsk, the capital city of Sakhalin Island, also used by the military.

52. The KGB is a civilian organization.

53. ICAO report of June 1993, Information Paper No. 1, 100.

54. Ibid., 15.

55. Ibid., 92.

56. See Figure 17, page 213.

57. Although there is evidence that at least one ground station (Trikotazh) was recorded on the Kirkpatrick tape, the overwhelming majority of ground station transmissions have been removed from the tape.

58. We have seen that Kozlov, the controller at Deputat, the combat control center of the fighter regiment at Sokol, was taking his orders from General Kornukov, the regimental commander. Kornukov was also acting as the Sokol base commander, presumably the basis for a recent promotion to

general. He was issuing his orders to 805 through Kozlov. Although Osipovich was also stationed at Sokol, he received his orders from Kornukov, not through Kozlov (Deputat), but through Gerasimenko. Gerasimenko is another regimental commander (the ICAO says of the Burevestnik Fighter Regiment), the call sign of whose controllers we do not know. The text of the transcripts makes it clear that in this instance both Gerasimenko and Osipovich were operating at or from Sokol.

59. At the end of his second mission Osipovich was out of missiles and virtually out of fuel. It is thus likely that he did not in fact land between the two interception sequences.

60. *Izvestiya,* January 23, 1991.

61. Illesh's excerpt contains some minor differences from the Kirkpatrick tape. It has, moreover, been stripped of the latter's misleading GMT times.

62. *Izvestiya,* ibid.

63. Osipovich's interview was continued in the January 25, 1991, issue of *Izvestiya.*

64. ICAO report of June 1993, 39, paragraph 1.16.1.8.

65. At this time 805 was trying to get into position to fire at its target. It is noteworthy that Osipovich told *Izvestiya* he had never heard of Deputat, 805's controller. Evidently he was on a different frequency. So the uproar he heard had to do with other events.

66. See footnote 58.

67. ICAO report of June 1993, Information Paper No. 1, 152–53.

68. Ibid., 72. Note that for ten years, the ICAO and the Kirkpatrick tape had this "Target destroyed" time twenty-one seconds later at 18:26:22 GMT. The time given now accords with the alleged KAL 007 tape also handed over to the ICAO by the Russians for the 1993 report.

69. "Article 37" appears to be a reference to a MiG-31.

70. ICAO report of June 1993, Information Paper No. 1, 153.

71. We hear of flight-control officer Oguslaev and Emir here for the first time.

Oguslaev appears to hold the fighter controller's job at a combat control center similar to Kozlov's at Deputat. Emir is probably the code name of a third combat control center. All three here appear to be reporting to Kornukov directly or through Solodkov, the duty officer at Kornukov's command post. Deputat is handling 805. We know that Osipovich is taking orders from Kornukov through Gerasimenko, evidently his regimental commander. Either Emir or Oguslaev was in all likelihood part of the operational chain of command between Gerasimenko and Osipovich (his deputy). The separate mentions of Oguslaev and Emir are the clue, probably intentional on the part of Russian intelligence, that we are dealing with three shootdowns, not just one by 805, which in the official story is supposed to be the only interceptor firing, just as KAL 007 is supposed to be the only target.

72. Hersh, *Target Is Destroyed*, 61.

73. ICAO report of June 1993, Information Paper No. 1, 77.

74. Ibid., 101, 146, 94, 206, 97.

75. Illesh, *Mystery of the Black Boxes*, 61.

76. The time Shultz mentioned may, however, have been chosen as a way of implying that the crash had been that of the plane 805 had shot down allegedly at 18:26 GMT.

77. ICAO report of June 1993, Information Paper No. 1, 203.

78. Ibid., 203, 96.

79. Ibid., 207. "Pencils" are air-to-air missiles obviously smaller than the R-98s.

80. Ibid., 93.

81. Ibid., 93.

82. Hersh, *The Target is Destroyed*, 68 and 220.

CHAPTER 17: Escape from Sakhalin and Destruction off Honshu
1. It is worth noting that Seymour Hersh, who apparently had good contacts among U.S. intelligence services, gives the time of KAL 007's exit from Kamchatka airspace in *The Target Is Destroyed* as 01:58 (16:58 GMT). It is, however, likely that the 16:58 GMT exit was that of another airplane.

2. Although much of the transmission is heavily distorted, Dr. Tsuboi says that in all likelihood it was all transmitted by KAL 007 but contains more than one voice with no carrier-wave shutdown between the different voices. That was probably the result of the partly intentional, partly unintentional nature of the transmission. As to the speaker of the last phrase, "must have been a bloodbath . . . real bad," John Keppel gave Charles Herrmann, a plaintiff's counsel in the civil KAL 007 suit against Korean Air Lines, who represented many of the airliner's crew, a section of the Narita tape containing the 18:27 transmission. Attorney Herrmann later told Keppel that he had played it for Kim Ok-hee, Captain Chun's widow, who said that the "bloodbath" phrase was in her husband's voice.

3. NOHO is a waypoint on the route to Seoul between NOKKA and NIIGATA.

4. Recorded on the Narita tape made public in 1985 by Prime Minister Nakasone.

5. In all likelihood, the fighters did not assemble directly at Chitose air base but had flown in after having taken off from their respective home bases an hour earlier, at around 04:00 Japan time. That is to say, before landing they would have accomplished their missions.

6. Less than two weeks later, on September 13, 1983, two pairs of Japanese fighters had been sent to intercept Soviet airplanes in international airspace over waypoint KADPO.

7. See chapter 7.

8. Could the Soviet sea and air operations have offered a disguised way of locating KAL 007's real crash site?

9. See chapter 5.

10. Letter of Lieutenant Commander Toner in *Armed Forces Journal International,* January 1990, also Prouty conversation with John Keppel.

11. In *The Target Is Destroyed,* page 58, Hersh discussed project CLEF, a formerly secret U.S. unit within the Japanese radar and SIGINT installation at Wakkanai. In 1983, Misawa was the largest U.S. signals intelligence station outside the United States.

12. The evidence presented in the 1993 ICAO report on these points is based

on data from the DFDR given the ICAO in that year by the Russians. It is untrustworthy since multiple evidence makes it clear that the DFDR in question must have been aboard an aircraft other than KAL 007. See Chapter 18. But reliable expert testimony may be available to a public investigation. Individuals from both Boeing and the National Transportation Safety Board are said to have reviewed the evidence on these points. They should be identified and questioned under oath.

CHAPTER 18: The Case for Truth

1. Hersh, op. cit., 74.

2. *Scientific American,* August 1988.

3. *Washington Times,* January 11, 1991.

4. The simulation explains why the ICAO's black boxes stopped functioning in midflight without a different cause. However realistic the simulators, they stopped short of crashing a real aircraft.

5. "Descending to one zero thousand" is unmistakably different acoustically from "Blood bath, really bad." It is, however, closer to the "one zero one zero delta" that Matsumi Suzuki, an independent Japanese acoustic expert, told the *Los Angeles Times*'s Sam Jameson he heard as the last phrase of the transmission when he examined that part of the tape in September 1983 for the Japanese Broadcasting Company (NHK) (*Los Angeles Times,* September 17, 1983). That "one zero one zero delta" did not persist as the last phrase may be related to the fact that "one zero one zero" is a U.S. intelligence code name of long standing for certain types of overhead reconnaissance. It was the name of the program under which Gary Powers flew his U-2 in 1960 and, according to James Bamford in *The Puzzle Palace,* has more recently been used for the KH-11 "Keyhole" close-look satellite. "Blood bath, really bad" was a rather extraordinary choice as a substitute and almost surely existed on the tape close by. Perhaps the Americans wanted "one zero one zero delta" taken out, and the Japanese, whose tape it was, complied but left something almost equally bad in its place.

6. The aircraft carrying the DFDR is presumably the same as that whose course was charted on the map made public by Yeltsin in October 1992. That map shows it taking off from Anchorage at 12:58 GMT (not 13:00 GMT, which we know was KAL 007's takeoff time). The DFDR aircraft may well have taken off from Elmendorf Air Force Base, which is close to Anchorage International Airport.

7. Some compensation from Korean Air Lines has been or will be received. However, any suits against the party primarily responsible for the deaths of those aboard the airliner, namely the United States, were dismissed by the courts. In the key case in the U.S., that in the District Court in Washington, D.C., Judge Robinson made it clear he would hear no evidence concerning the U.S. military.

Appendix: The Black Boxes

1. The aircraft that crashed north of Nevelsk may well have been the one at crash point 1 (see chapter 10). In that case, it would have been an EF-111, which may have accompanied a larger aircraft, the one carrying the DFDR, which crashed on land in the middle of Sakhalin.

2. Some of the plaintiffs' lawyers in the U.S. civil cases tried to use this part of the CVR transcript to show that the passengers were awake at the time of the disaster and thus suffered pain and anguish.

3. 1993 ICAO report, 6.

4. ICAO report of June 1993, Information Paper No. 1, 1.

5. Also referred to as the ambient microphone.

INDEX

Abashiri (on north coast of Hokkaido), 161
account of events in alleged KAL 007 shootdown.
    See KAL 007
After Action Report of U.S. Navy Task Force, 143-148
afterburners, aircraft, 193, 218
Agafonov, Sergei (*Izvestiya* representative in Tokyo),
    70, 109, 110
Agence France Presse, 70
air battle of Sakhalin, 189-191
    first hour, 189-211
    second hour, 211-229
Air Traffic Control (ATC), 3, 81, 231, 235, 237-238
    Japanese. See Tokyo Control
    U.S. See Anchorage Center
Airbus (airliner), 242, 246
Akita (town on west coast of Honshu), 94-99, 104
alert:
    airborne (U.S.), 214
    code Zero Zero (Soviet), 196, 197
    DEFCON THREE (Japanese), 214, 239
    Level One (Soviet), 197-198
Aleschenko, Zhan (chief mate of *Mikhail Mirchinko*),
    121-122, 140
Alexeiev, Vladimir (Captain of *Zabaikalaye*), 115
All Nippon Airways, 65
Allardyce, Robert W., 156, 167, 171-172
Anchorage:
    Center (Anchorage Control), 169, 171
    Elmendorf Air Force Base at. See Elmendorf
    International Airport, 152, 153, 158, 159, 165,
        166, 167, 264
    KAL 007 take-off at and departure from.
        See KAL 007
    Radio (HF station), 81, 84, 86, 174
Andropov (Chairman of Soviet Politburo), 205
Anisimov, Capt. (KGB patrol boat commander),
    113-114, 116-117, 145, 210, 215
antiradar aircraft. See EF-111
Antonov, Nikolai Sergeivich (Capt., Soviet
    fishing fleet), 120
Aomori (town on northern Honshu), 49, 50,
    53-55, 57, 123
article 37 (code name for MiG-31), 220
articles, absence of in Russian grammar, 111
Asahi Shimbun (Tokyo), 21, 22, 25, 26, 27,
    63, 68, 70, 78
Asahi Television, 109, 243
Association of the Families of the KAL 007
    Victims, Japanese, 13, 67, 70-71
    Fact Finding Committee (Research Committee,
        Technical Research Committee, Inquiry
        Group), of, 70
    press conference at, 67-68, 70-75, 109
Astakhov, Lt., 197
Atsugi (U.S. Air Force base, Japan), 89, 243
Autrand, Ron (French pilot lost over Pacific), 81-84
Aviation Magazine International (French), 110
AWACs, battlefield surveillance aircraft:
    Soviet, see also "Tanker." 190, 202, 215, 217, 223
    U.S.A.F., 41, 125, 195
    U.S. Navy (E-2), 256

B-52 (U.S. long range bomber), 214

back channel communications. See communications
Badge system, 236 See Japanese Air Self-Defense
    Agency (JASDF)
Badger, USS (frigate), 125, 138, 140, 144, 148, 239
battle, air, of Sakhalin. See Sakhalin
beaches, Japanese, searches for debris on, 53-62,
    94-106
beeper, black box. See pinger
Belov, Lt. (Soviet KGB officer at Pereputye), 161
Big Pine (U.S. tracking station in Australia), 253
Bilyuk, Capt. (commander of *Uvarovsk*), 10, 113-116,
    124, 137-138, 143, 145, 228
black boxes. See recorders
"blood bath, really bad" (phrase in KAL 007 18:27
    GMT transmission), 263, 316 (Note 5)
boarding pass, Pan Am, 161
bodies,
    of child, 46
    of KAL 007 victims, 37, 249
        falsely alleged to have been burned, 258
    of U.S. military dead, 41, 264-265
Bodies that Disappeared (book by Iwao Koyama), 37
Boeing:
    ambiguity in Soviet use of word, 111
    company, 297 (Note 1, Ch. 7), 315-316 (Note 12)
bomb:
    threat at Hokkaido Broadcasting Company, 65
    conceivable destruction of KAL 007 by, 247-248
Borisov, Capt. (flight controller at Deputat), 220
"bottle" from Sado Island, 57
Bradley, Bill, 258
Brockman, Orville (FAA representative in Tokyo), 7
Bureau of Weapons, U.S. Navy (BUWEPS), 98
Burevestnik Fighter Regiment, 204, 206
Burevestnik (Soviet airbase on Iturup Island),
    200, 223
Burminski, Col. (deputy commander, fighter
    division), 198

Callaghan, USS, 148
cannon bursts, 23, 73, 210-211, 214, 216-217
Capt. M (JASDF officer), 69
cargo flight, 152, 153
Casey, William, 251, 253
Central Intelligence Agency (CIA):
    in-house rules of self-protection, 257
    August 31/September 1, 1983 role, 253
Challenger (shuttle STS-8), 253
Chase, Edward T. (Senior Editor, Scribner's),
    xxiv-xxvi
Chidori Maru No. 58 (Japanese fishing vessel)
    observes an aircraft explode at 18:30 GMT,
    27-29, 39, 40
Chitose (Japanese civilian and military airfield on
    southern Hokkaido), 50, 63, 65-66, 214, 239,
    244, 247
Cho, Charley (Vice President Korean Air Lines), 4-5, 9
    receipt of "down on Sakhalin" report, 4-5
    flight to Japan to arrange passengers' release
        from Soviets, 5, 9
Chokai (JMSA patrol boat), 41
Chun Byung-in (pilot-in-command KAL 007):
    relationship to Park Young-man, 153

Soviet account of, 117, 184, 219, 255, 256
time of:
    alleged, 22 (U.S.), 18 (Japan), 117 (USSR),
        271 (ICAO)
    actual, 238, 249
    U.S. account of, 18-20
"down on Sakhalin," false story of, 4-7, 9, 264
    initially based on misreading of radar data,
        264
    reasons for CIA release of, 6, 253
effects of off-course flight, 248, 266
flight performance of, affected by weight, 158,
    165
Flight Plan, Operational, of, 32, 153-156
    marginal notations on, 158-159
Flight Release Sheet, of, 156-157
fuel aboard, 153-158, 166
localizer, black box. See pinger
navigation of by inertial navigation system, 67,
    166-167, 183, 262
next-of-kin of dead on. See next-of-kin.
overdue at Kimpo Airport, Seoul, 3-7, 9-12
passengers on, 159-160
passage and position reports abeam:
    BETHEL, 166-167, 229 (Fig. 20)
    NABIE, 167-173, 174, 175, 176, 177, 178, 229
        (Fig. 20), 234-237
    NEEVA, 158, 174-178, 184, 229 (Fig. 20)
    NIIGATA, 78, 85, 90, 91, 93, 234-240, 248
    NIPPI, 158-159, 174, 177, 229 (Fig. 20)
    NOKKA, 209, 229 (Fig. 20), 235
passage and position reports, time and distance
    factors in, 177, 234
pilot-in-command of. See Chun Byung-in
radio, failure to identify self on way south, 85-86
radio, simulated failure of, 85
radio transmissions after alleged shootdown at
    Sakhalin, xix, 85-91, 235-236, 238, 238, 249
radio transmissions in Korean, 86-88, 169-171
radios capabilities and procedures, 264, 276-277
receipt of clandestine transmission, 80
recorders (black boxes). See recorders
registration number of (HL-7442), 46-47, 247
simulations of KAL 007's flight. See simulations
Soviet documents allegedly concerning, 259-261,
    278-280
speed assigned to, 32
substitution of flight crew at Anchorage, 153
transponder code, deceptive use of, by 89-90,
    237-239
Weight and Balance Manifest, 153, 155-156
weight on take-off at Anchorage, 153-157, 158
Korean Air Lines Flight No. 015 (KAL 015, KE 015):
    relay of alleged KAL 007 position reports, 87,
        153, 168-169, 172, 174-175
    incorrect statement by co-pilot, 169
    late radio communications with KAL 007 and
        KAL 050, 86-91, 236
    pilot-in-command of. See Park Young-man
    substitution of flight crew at Anchorage, 153
Korean Air Lines Flight No. 050, 187, 241
    radio communications with KAL 007 and KAL
        015, 87-91, 237-238
Korean Air Lines Flight No. 902 (1978), 9
Korean Central Intelligence Agency (KCIA), 163
Kornukov, General (commander of Sokol airbase and

Second Fighter Regiment), 197, 201-202, 205-207,
    211, 219, 220, 224
Kosik, Capt. (Soviet Navy), 111
Kostenko, Maj. (operations duty officer, at Smirnykh),
    197
Kostroma (town on east coast of Sakhalin), 220
Kov, Vladimir (Soviet diver), 130, 132-133, 141
Koyama, Iwao (NHK representative at Wakkanai),
    37-38, 40, 51, 119
Kozlov, Capt. (flight controller at Deputat), 191
Krasnaya Zvezda (*Red Star,* Moscow), 195, 200, 210
Kretinin, Alexei (witness of Kamchatka), 181, 184-185
Kozmin. See *Georgi Kozmin*
Kronotsky Peninsula (on Kamchatka), 182-184
Kronotsky Reserve (on Kamchatka), 181, 185
Kuril Islands, 6, 20, 30, 45, 48, 173, 183, 194, 200,
    204, 252
Kuril Trench, 247
Kutepov, Capt. (flight controller, at Smirnykh), 197
Kyodo (Japanese press agency), 70

Lambert, Yves (ICAO Secretary General in 1983),
La Pérouse Strait (also Soya Strait, between Sakhalin
    and Hokkaido), 173, 226, 227, 229
lateral escalation, doctrine of, 251
Levin, Carl, 258
life rafts, 41, 61, 126, 132, 138, 143, 265
"little girl from Pereputye," photograph of, 162-163
Litvinov, Lt. (pilot of fighter 163), 206, 211, 217
Lobko, Misha (French investigative reporter), 114,
    141, 161-163, 197, 225
localizer, black box. See pinger
Lockerbie (in Scotland), 39, 248
Lockheed "Skunk Works," 138
log of naval search, JMSA, 41-42, 46 (Fig. 8).
        See also JMSA, maps
Loginov, Ensign (at Plantatsia airfield), 202
logo. See Korean Air Lines.

Mainichi Shimbun (Tokyo), 6, 20-21, 23, 33, 231
Makarov (Soviet Lt. Gen. of Aviation), 278
Makarov (town on east coast of Sakhalin), 203, 205
Mano Bay (on south coast of Sado Island), 103
Masuo (director of Japanese inquiry group), 13, 75
Matsumoto, Kenji (*Asahi Shimbun* reporter), 68-70
MAYDAY (distress message), 79, 81, 90, 125
McDonald, Larry, 7
media, cautious behavior by, 50, 254, 255, 259
memorial stele at Wakkanai, 266
        epitaph on, 266
Midway, USS (aircraft carrier), 194-195
MiG-21 (obsolescent Soviet fighter), 223
MiG 23 (Soviet fighter), 20, 192, 193, 195, 196,
        198-200, 206, 207, 208, 210, 225
    early pair, 199-200
    163 (Litvinov), 206, 211-213, 215, 220, 222
MiG 31 (high-tech, two-place Soviet fighter), 194,
        195, 196, 198, 201
    interceptor 121 (Tarasov), 206, 211, 213, 215,
        222, 225
    interceptor 731 and wingman (from Postovaya),
        210, 222, 223, 224
    804 (Osipovich). See Osipovich.
    805, 211, 215, 217, 220, 221, 222, 224
Migal (Chief of Rescue Services, on Sakhalin), 203
Migalk (nickname of Soviet fighter pilot), 218-219

143, 238
satellites:
elliptical orbit, in, 253
"Ferret D," (1982 41C), 202, 293 (Ch. 3, Note 2),
305 (Note 6)
Tracking Data and Relay, Number One
(TDRS-1), 253
Sea of Japan, 35, 49, 52, 74, 89, 94, 106, 138, 189, 211,
227, 229, 248. See Tatar Gulf
Sea of Okhotsk, See Okhotsk
search area off Sakhalin,
delineation by JMSA, 39, 145
depth of water in, 12, 137
search, underwater off Sakhalin:
by *Izvestiya* and Japanese media, 147
Also see Navy, U.S. and Soviet, and JMSA
Search and Rescue Coordination Center, JMSA, 3
Second Fighter Regiment Soviet (based at Sokol), 197
"second hour" of overflights. See Kamchatka
and Sakhalin
secrecy, excessive use of, xx, 252
Seoul, 3-7, 9, 78, 93, 101, 156, 157-158, 161-163, 242
serial numbers on debris. See debris
Seya, Hideyuki (Japanese Senator), 13, 70, 110
Shakerst (Soviet airbase, on Sakhalin), 214
Shalnev, Alexander (Izvestiya representative in
New York), 110, 114, 258
Shaydurov, Capt. Ivan Varfolomeievich
(in charge of group of trawlers), 129
Shultz, George, 11, 17-19, 251, 254
announcement of KAL 007 disaster by, 17, 251
version of events, 18-20
Sidorov, Adm. (commander of Soviet Pacific Fleet),
119-120, 123-124, 127-129, 137, 139-140, 197
signals, voiceless, carrier wave, 239, 241, 249
simulations of KAL 007's flight:
after the event (DFDR given ICAO), 261-263
climb performance compared to
KAL 007's, 276
constant magnetic heading of 245 degrees,
261, 262, 279, 280
landing sequence, 275
radio capabilities and usage compared to
KAL 007's, 277
take-off sequence compared to KAL 007's, 275
after the event and simultaneous compared,
260-261, 278-280
simultaneous (DFDR data disclosed by Yeltsin,
October 1992), 234, 261-262, 269
constant magnetic heading of 249 degrees,
260, 261, 278
reasons for use of constant magnetic
heading, 261
slowdown, sudden. See evasive action
Smirnykh, Soviet airbase of (on Sakhalin), 191-194,
196-202, 204-207, 210-211, 217
smoke marker, 97-98, 114, 144
Sokol, soviet airbase of (on Sakhalin), 191-192, 194,
196-198, 200-205, 207, 210-211, 214, 220,
223-225
Solodkov, Capt. (duty officer, Sokol Air Base
Command Post), 198, 202, 220
sonobuoys, 148
sonar, 120, 134, 143
side-looking, 128, 147
Sovetskaya Gavan (Soviet naval base on Siberian

mainland), 121, 127, 201, 210, 223
Soya Strait. See La Pérouse Strait
space, United States capabilities in, 253
spectrographic analysis, 172, 174, 217, 255
splice lines. See deletions from communications
tapes
SR-71 "Blackbird" (U.S. intelligence aircraft),
43, 44, 65-66, 138
Strogov, Gen. (deputy commander, Soviet Far East
Air Force), 211, 224
SU-15 (Soviet fighter), 20, 22, 23, 195, 196, 199
submarines, missile-firing, Soviet, 252
Sugimoto, Shigeki (Japan Air Lines engineer),
13, 70, 75
sunrise. See time
supersonic aircraft, non-Soviet, 182, 183, 187, 189,
212. See also SR-71
survivors, evidence regarding possible military, 113,
141, 264-266
Suzuki, Matsumi (Japanese acoustics expert),
316 (Note 5)

Tahiti, 81-84, 86
tail, aircraft:
engine in, 218
fragmentation of vertical fin in KAL 007, 139,
246, 247, 248-249
separation from aircraft in Japanese short-range,
747, 248
survival in accidents, 267
location of black boxes in, 139
See also explosive pressure in aircraft tail
Takemoto, Shôzo (director of Japanese investigative
group), 10-13, 265-266
"Tanker" (call sign of Soviet AWACs, from Vanino),
202, 218, 223
tanker aircraft. See KC-135
tapes, Air Traffic Control, 84
Kirkpatrick. See Kirkpatrick
Narita, time signal on, 84
Tarasov, Lt. (pilot of fighter 121), 206, 225
target drones, 50, 69, 77-78
"Target is Destroyed, The:"
Seymour Hersh book, 189
phrase apparently inserted into 805 shootdown
sequence, 221
Task Force 71 (TF-71), 131-201. See Navy, U.S.
Tatar Gulf (also Tatar Strait, northern end, See of
Japan), 31-32, 35, 38, 47-48, 52, 131, 201, 223
Tatewaki, Toshio (kelp gatherer at Sai), 47-49, 53
Technical Research Committee of the Association of
the Families of KAL 007 Incident Victims
(Japan), also Research Committee, inquiry
group. See Association
Terpeniya, Cape (on east coast of Sakhalin), 138, 191,
201-202, 205, 212, 219
territorial waters, Soviet, 37-40, 50-51, 120, 123, 134,
143-144, 148, 195, 265
throttle quadrant, 43
Tikhomirov, Lt. Gen. (head of 1983 Soviet expert
group), 269
time:
falsification of, 182-183, 191, 225
Moscow military, 182-183
Sakhalin, 191-192
of sunrise: